Force and Legitimacy
in World Politics

Edited by David Armstrong
Theo Farrell and Bice Maiguashca

CAMBRIDGE
UNIVERSITY PRESS

CAMBRIDGE
UNIVERSITY PRESS

University Printing House, Cambridge CB2 8BS, United Kingdom

One Liberty Plaza, 20th Floor, New York, NY 10006, USA

477 Williamstown Road, Port Melbourne, VIC 3207, Australia

314-321, 3rd Floor, Plot 3, Splendor Forum, Jasola District Centre, New Delhi - 110025, India

79 Anson Road, #06-04/06, Singapore 079906

Cambridge University Press is part of the University of Cambridge.

It furthers the University's mission by disseminating knowledge in the pursuit of education, learning and research at the highest international levels of excellence.

www.cambridge.org
Information on this title: www.cambridge.org/9780521691642

First published 2005

A catalogue record for this publication is available from the British Library

ISBN 978-0-521-69164-2 Paperback

Force and Legitimacy in World Politics

CONTENTS

Review of International Studies (2005), 31, 1–2

NOTES ON CONTRIBUTORS

David Armstrong is Professor of International Relations at the University of Exeter.

Jeremy Black is Professor of History at the University of Exeter.

Michael Byers holds the Canada Research Chair in Global Politics and International Law in the Department of Political Science at the University of British Columbia.

Richard Falk is Albert G. Milbank Professor Emeritus of International Law and Practice at Princeton University and since 2002, Visiting Professor of Global Studies, University of California at Santa Barbara.

Theo Farrell is Reader in War in the Modern World at King's College, London.

Martha Finnemore is Professor of Political Science and International Affairs at the George Washington University.

Sir Lawrence Freedman is Professor of War Studies at King's College, University of London.

Christine Gray is Reader in International Law at St John's College, Cambridge.

Ted Hopf is Associate Professor of Political Science at Ohio State University.

Andrew Hurrell is Director of the Centre for International Studies at Oxford University and Fellow of Nuffield College, Oxford.

Helen M. Kinsella is Assistant Professor in the Department of Political Science, University of Wisconsin-Madison.

Bice Maiguashca is Lecturer in International Relations at the University of Exeter.

John Mueller is Professor of Political Science and Woody Hayes Chair of National Security Studies at the Mershon Center, Ohio State University.

Nicholas Rengger is Professor of Political Theory and International Relations, St Andrews University.

2

Christian Reus-Smit is Professor of International Relations in the Research School of Pacific and Asian Studies at the Australian National University.

Michael Sherry is the Richard W. Leopold Professor of History at Northwestern University.

Force and Legitimacy in World Politics

Introduction

DAVID ARMSTRONG AND THEO FARRELL

This volume was produced in the context of the crisis of legitimacy that occasioned the 2003 Iraq War. As is well known, a bitter feud broke out in the United Nations Security Council (UNSC) over the legality of using force against Iraq. The US government justified going to war in the context of a new doctrine of preventive use of force for self-defence – a doctrine that was soon named after President George W. Bush.[1] The British government anchored its case for war in two previous UNSC resolutions; res. 678 which originally authorised use of force against Iraq in the 1990–91 Gulf War, and res. 687 which suspended res. 678 on a number of conditions including the disarming of Iraq's weapons of mass destruction (WMD) stockpiles, facilities and programmes.[2] Both the US and British positions were underpinned by intelligence, subsequently proved to be flawed, that Iraq had failed to get rid of its WMD.[3] Opponents of the war disputed this intelligence and, moreover, argued that the Bush Doctrine was plain illegal and ridiculed the British idea of resurrecting twelve-year-old UNSC resolutions.[4]

War is invariably accompanied by debate, if not controversy, over the legitimacy of using force. Whilst formal declarations of war have gone out of fashion, governments (both democratic and dictatorial alike) still justify their military action to home and foreign audiences – even if this requires fabricating manifestly false reasons to legitimate using force.[5] Alongside this longstanding state practice of justifying use of force is the increasing codification of legal rules on the use of force. Indeed, major wars periodically generate crises of confidence in international society about the legitimacy of military force as an instrument of world politics.[6] Thus the

---

[1] *The National Security Strategy of the United States of America* (Washington, DC: 2002), p. 15, at ⟨http://www.whitehouse.gov/nsc/nss.html⟩. The genesis of this doctrine and, in particular, the fact that it was produced with Iraq in mind, is discussed in Bob Woodward, *Plan of Attack* (New York: Simon and Schuster, 2004), pp. 132–8.

[2] 10 Downing Street, 'Legal Basis for Use of Force Against Iraq', ⟨http://www.pm.gov.uk/output/Page3287.asp⟩. The Attorney General's secret memorandum to the Prime Minister, which was subsequently released following much public pressure, indicates that he was of the view that the legal case for war was 'unclear' and that the 'safest legal course' would be to secure a new UNSC resolution explicitly authorising use of force against Iraq. See Attorney General note to the Prime Minister, 'Iraq Resolution 1441', 25 April 2005, available at ⟨http://www.number-10.gov.uk/output/page7443.asp⟩.

[3] Lawrence Freedman, 'War in Iraq: Selling the Threat', *Survival*, 46 (2004), pp. 7–50; Christoph Bluth, 'The British Road to War: Blair, Bush and the Decision to Invade Iraq', *International Affairs*, 80 (2004), pp. 871–92.

[4] A comprehensive archive of critiques is available at ⟨http://www.lawyersagainstthewar.org/⟩.

[5] Brian Hallett, *The Lost Art of Declaring War* (Champaign, IL: University of Illinois Press, 1998).

[6] The classic study on this is Paul Fussell, *The Great War and Modern Memory* (Oxford: Oxford University Press, 1975). See also John Mueller, *The Remnants of War* (Ithaca, NY: Cornell University Press, 2004), chs. 3–4.

world wars of the twentieth century spurred the development of legal restraints both on the resort to force in the United Nations (UN) Charter prohibitions against use of force, and the use of force in the 1949 Geneva Conventions on the treatment of prisoners and protection of civilians in war.[7]

From this perspective, we can readily see that underlining debate about the specifics of the legality of the 2003 Iraq War are broader issues regarding the principles and practices for legitimating use of force in contemporary world politics.[8] In general terms, these principles define who may employ force, how and when. Legitimating practices enable these principles to be enacted, through interpretation and application in particular cases, as well as revised in line with changing geostrategic and sociopolitical circumstances. But questions remain about the substance of principles legitimating use of force, their relationship to international law, and the role of the UNSC and of great powers in using force to restore international peace and security. More broadly, one may inquire into the temporal and spatial dimensions of legitimacy and force. How have legitimating principles and practices interacted and changed over time, and to what extent are they universal or regional (at any moment in time)? To address these various questions, we invited contributions from leading scholars on legitimacy and force working from a number of disciplinary perspectives (including international relations, political science, philosophy, history, and law).[9]

In this brief introduction, we do four things. First, we discuss the complex relationship between law, legitimacy and force, as it exists in both domestic and international orders. Second, and leading on from the above, we identify some of the questions raised in the volume and explored by our contributors. Third, we throw the subject into historical relief in order to problematise the notion of 'international legitimacy' in the use of force. Finally, we suggest a way of conceptualising legitimacy and force – in terms of 'sites' as well as 'sources' of legitimation.

Law, legitimacy and force

Even in domestic social orders, the relationship between law, legitimacy, and use of force is less straightforward than it might first appear. In national societies, the use of force is generally portrayed as a matter falling entirely within the remit of the country's legal system. Laws prohibit private violence, except in certain very limited circumstances, and they also set out the conditions under which state agencies may use force. The legal system, in the final analysis, is itself seen as a coercive order in which an individual's obligation to obey the law derives in large part from the fact that the state can compel him to obey.

---

[7] For recent introductory surveys see Christine Gray, 'The Use of Force and the International Legal Order' and Christopher Greenwood, 'The Law of War (International Humanitarian Law), both in Malcolm Evans (ed.), *International Law* (Oxford: Oxford University Press, 2003).

[8] The distinction between principles and practices of legitimacy in statecraft is developed and explored in Ian Clark, *Legitimacy in International Society* (Oxford: Oxford University Press, 2005).

[9] The exception here is Helen Kinsella's chapter, which was not commissioned but rather came through the normal refereeing process and, given the close thematic fit, was subsequently included in the volume with the author's consent.

In practice, however, this austere (indeed Austinian[10]) view of the relationship between law and force requires further consideration. If, for example, the only argument in favour of obeying the law is the threat of punishment by the superior power (that is, the state) does that not encourage a 'winner takes all' culture that justifies incessant challenges to those exercising state power? Are we obliged to obey laws that are clearly unjust? Does the concept of the rule of law have the same standing in all societies: in Hitler's Germany and Roosevelt's America, for example? These are all, of course, much debated and indeed controversial issues but one recurring theme in many of the contributions to this debate is that the law should not be seen as a self-contained normative system, capable of existing in splendid isolation from political and social factors. In particular, individuals do not obey the law simply because they are compelled to do so but because they are persuaded of its necessity, utility or moral value. In other words, they accept the *legitimacy* of the law and of the coercive apparatus of the state that underpins the law.[11] Indeed, many would argue that enduring stability in any social order is dependent primarily on the order's legitimacy rather than its legal system.[12]

The problem is that 'legitimacy' is a far more elusive concept than 'law'. Should we see it, for instance, as deriving from an objective condition of a particular order, such as some kind of social contract, or as an essentially subjective phenomenon, to be found in the perceptions and assumptions of the order's members? Does it denote primarily a set of *procedural* requirements (for instance, that accepted processes are followed in the actual operation of a politico-legal order) or does it consist of specific *substantive* norms (for instance, that civil liberties are protected) or does it depend on the capacity of a social order to achieve certain *outcomes* (such as economic progress, the advancement of social welfare, reduced crime rates)?[13] Or perhaps all three are necessary ingredients of a legitimate social order?

If the meaning of legitimacy, and its relation to law and force, are complex and controversial questions in domestic societies, they are far more so in the international context. This has particularly been the case since the end of the Cold War. The traditional basis of the international legal order has been respect for the sovereignty of states and the corollary of that principle: non-intervention in states' internal affairs. Both principles are enshrined in the UN Charter, which also restricts the lawful use of force to enforcement actions approved by the Security Council and self-defence measures to deal with an immediate threat pending Security Council action. Taken together, these principles constitute what Christian Reus-Smit in this volume calls the 'equalitarian regime'.

All of these central norms have come under challenge from two directions in recent years. First, faced with extreme violence and civil war in collapsing states like

---

[10] John Austin famously described 'law properly so-called' as the command of a sovereign backed by sanctions, thus excluding international law from 'true law'. John Austin, *The Province of Jurisprudence Determined*, ed. Wilfrid E. Rumble (Cambridge: Cambridge University Press, 1995).

[11] Ronald Dworkin, *Law's Empire* (Cambridge, MA: Harvard University Press, 1986), pp. 190–5; Thomas M. Franck, *The Power of Legitimacy among Nations* (Oxford: Oxford University Press, 1990).

[12] The key figure here was of course Max Weber. See his 'The Types of Legitimate Domination', in G. Roth and C. Wittich (eds.), *Economy and Society* (Berkeley, CA: California University Press, 1978).

[13] For the most recent and fullest discussion of these issues, see Ian Clark, *Legitimacy in International Society*. See also David Beetham, *The Legitimation of Power* (Houndmills: Macmillan, 1991.

Yugoslavia and Somalia, and severe human rights violations elsewhere, the international community has debated the possibility that the non-intervention norm
should be set aside in the case of dire humanitarian emergencies. In a few cases,
usually with considerable reluctance, it has gone beyond debate. Secondly, the huge
margin of military might over all conceivable rivals possessed by the United States
has left the world with the wholly unprecedented situation where one great power is
unaffected by the sort of balance of power considerations that, traditionally, have
formed the main constraint upon the most powerful states. The terrorist attack on the
United States in 2001 was soon followed by demonstrations of what this might mean
in practice, in the form of military action in Afghanistan and Iraq.[14]

Volume themes

The controversies surrounding these events provided the impetus behind this Special
Issue of the *Review of International Studies*. In particular, they raise seven important
questions:

1. If the international legal provisions relating to force in the UN Charter are
   inadequate to deal with contemporary problems, can the use of force be evaluated
   within a different, non-legal framework: one essentially comprising principles of
   international legitimacy? Richard Falk in this issue considers the tension between
   legality and legitimacy and argues that the discourse arising from this tension is a
   valuable means of framing the contemporary debate about the use of force.
   Michael Byers finds the legal rules on the use of force to be remarkably resilient
   in the face of the current challenge to them.
2. Does 'legitimacy' have a clear and uncontested meaning in world politics? Andrew
   Hurrell suggests that it is not only a multi-faceted term but that it interacts in
   complex ways with the changing security environment. In his view, however, a
   crucial element of legitimacy will always be the need to persuade others that a
   course of action, a rule, or a political order is right and appropriate, which points
   to the need to view the UNSC not as a constitutional 'source' of legitimacy but as
   'a deeply flawed and highly politicized body in which arguments can be presented
   and policies defended'.
3. If 'legitimacy' rather than 'legality' is to be the new criterion for the use of force,
   what fundamental norms should guide our evaluation of legitimacy? Nicholas
   Rengger discusses the revival of 'just war' principles in this regard, while Martha
   Finnemore examines the more recent debate about multilateralism as a possible
   basis for legitimacy.
4. To what specific activities do legitimacy norms apply? Traditional Just War
   doctrine distinguished between '*jus ad bellum*' (rightful causes of war) and '*jus in
   bello*' (moral conduct during war). Helen Kinsella here discusses the American
   administration's use of discourses of 'civilization' and 'barbarism' to explain
   differences in its own application of *jus in bello* to civilians and prisoners of war
   (the latter is also addressed by Michael Byers).

[14] Colin McInnes, 'A Different Kind of War? September 11 and the United States' Afghan War',
Review of International Studies, 29 (2003), pp. 165–84.

5. If the international community accepts a new principle of humanitarian intervention, what corresponding sets of duties does that imply for individual states? This is the question directly addressed by Christine Gray in her discussion of peacekeeping operations in Africa. In a similar vein, John Mueller speculates that an 'Iraq syndrome' might develop in the United States similar to the earlier 'Vietnam syndrome' that was thought to inhibit US military action for many years after that war. He argues that non-violent Western policies aimed at nurturing effective government might offer a better long term solution to the problem of failed or criminal states.

6. One of the most controversial aspects of the new legitimacy discourse concerns the degree to which it reflects essentially Western viewpoints. This has several dimensions. As Jeremy Black argues here, force itself – or technological changes that enhance military capability and increase the imbalance between states – may sometimes act as an independent variable that can influence norms relating to force and legitimacy: a phenomenon apparent through history but particularly relevant in the context of contemporary American policy. Moreover, as Christian Reus-Smit and Lawrence Freedman point out in their otherwise very different contributions, the debate about the legitimacy of force has interacted with another set of arguments to the effect that liberal democratic states form, in effect, an exclusive club of actors who are more pacific and moral than others. The implications of this are twofold: on the one hand, democratic governance and human rights have come to be seen as part of the new standard of international legitimacy; on the other, coalitions of democratic states, some argue, possess sufficient international legitimacy to justify the use of force in certain cases where full Security Council backing cannot be obtained.

7. Finally, we should not ignore the fact that, in many cases, states seek to legitimise their conduct, not by reference to some international standard but in terms of their own national culture, traditions and norms. The United States has often been analysed in such terms, as the notion of 'American exceptionalism' indicates: an idea that goes back even to colonial times and which became prominent from the late nineteenth century. Michael Sherry gives this perspective an original slant here by showing how American practice and rhetoric in relation to crime and punishment – with the United States now having six to twelve times the incarceration rates of Western Europe and Canada – has spilled over into America's international outlook. Another, highly original, slant on internal legitimation processes is offered by Ted Hopf, in considering Russian behaviour in Georgia in the 1990s. As Hopf points out, there were three distinct discursive communities in Russia during these years, with three different ways of conceptualising legitimate international conduct. The West, by failing to understand this, missed an opportunity to shape Russian policy through working with the more liberal factions to create a 'consensual set of standards of legitimate conduct'.

The problem with 'international legitimacy'

Grotius said that 'War is not one of the acts of life. On the contrary, it is a thing so horrible that nothing but the highest necessity or the deepest charity can make it right'.[15] Given that variants of 'necessity' and 'charity' (humanitarian motives) have been the most cited justifications for the use of force in recent years, this serves to show how enduring are not only the moral issues raised by war but the arguments used to rationalise wars. Indeed, 2,000 years before Grotius, the Roman Republic insisted that a college of priests (the *Fetiales*) should engage in lengthy deliberations over each possible declaration of war to determine whether it met clear criteria for it to be seen as a just war (*bellum justum*), after which point a majority of the Senate had to vote in favour of the war.[16] In the latter case, the legitimacy of particular wars was, therefore, entirely a matter for Romans to decide and, inevitably, as Rome's power and ambitions grew, so was its readiness to go to war less and less affected by 'just war' considerations and the procedural requirements for war to be declared became increasingly mere formalities. More recent discussions of international legitimacy have generally sought evidence of a wider consensus than that emanating from a single state. But earlier 'just war' doctrines, while not yet prepared to take the decision to use force away from the individual state, attempted to find criteria, such as the requirement that war be declared by a rightful authority or that the force used be proportionate to the objects of the war, that would, in effect, impose an externally determined set of standards, such as those of natural law, on war-making states.

The problem with all such standards is that they inevitably reflect some religious or political ideology and are, therefore, open to challenge from non-adherents of that ideology. The French revolutionaries, for example, challenged the prevailing eighteenth century concept of international legitimacy which upheld the divine right of kings and gave dynastic monarchs the sole right to commit their states to war. The new revolutionary doctrine that saw sovereignty as residing in the popular will was used to justify annexations of territories such as Avignon, which had been under Papal rule for many years, as well as the French wars to free territories from Habsburg or other external sovereignty. After the defeat of Napoleon, the Holy Alliance powers attempted to lay down a new, ultra-conservative principle of legitimacy, which justified interventions in states' internal affairs if there was a threat of revolution against the 'legitimate' (namely the dynastic) authority. A similar argument that tried to assert the principle of 'limited sovereignty' under specific circumstances was enunciated by the Soviet leader Leonid Brezhnev in 1968 when he justified the Soviet invasion of Czechoslovakia by asserting that sovereignty was not to be measured by some 'bourgeois yardstick' but only by the genuine standard of 'socialist self-determination'. If a state – such as Czechoslovakia – strayed away from the correct socialist path, its leadership was jeopardising this 'true sovereignty'. Moreover, by deviating from the 'common natural laws of socialist construction' it might deviate from socialism as such and so endanger the whole socialist camp which, therefore had the right, indeed duty, to intervene against such an eventuality.[17]

A further problem with attempts to place the use of force within some larger context of legitimating principles is that this opens the way for groups other than states to argue that their own use of force is legitimate. During the 1960s, the Third

[15] Hugo Grotius, *De Juri Belli et Pacis*, vol. 2, ed. William Whewell (Cambridge: Cambridge University Press, 1853), p. 442.
[16] Jacques Bex, *Essai sur L'Évolution du Droit des Gens* (Paris: Librairie des sciences politiques et socials, Paris, 1910), pp. 12–13.
[17] David Armstrong, *Revolution and World Order: The Revolutionary State in International Society* (Oxford: Clarendon Press, 1993), p. 151.

World majority in the United Nations argued (much as the French had done nearly two hundred years earlier) that national liberation wars fell outside the UN's restrictive conditions for the legal use of force because they were in pursuit of the higher principle of self determination. A far more controversial issue began to appear from the late 1960s when the United Nations found it almost impossible to arrive at a broadly agreed definition of 'terrorism' essentially because the General Assembly majority wished to exempt the Palestine liberation movement from any general condemnation of terrorism. Similarly, Islamist terrorists in the last decade have turned to the Islamic notion of 'just war' – the *jihad* – in their attempt to claim legitimacy for their acts of violence.

Sources of legitimacy, sites of legitimation

History underlines just how contested and contingent is the notion of legitimate use of force in world politics. It also invites us to consider where legitimacy comes from and how it is constructed.

One might adopt the method of international law scholars, who look for the 'sources' of international law. One obvious source is treaties, which concretely express what states understand to be law on specified matters. Treaties may take the form of contracts between two or more states on particular issues, or they may be designed to create new law for the whole international community. The other major source of international law is state custom. Neither treaty nor customary law are clear-cut, however.

The authoritative definition of custom is to be found in Article 38(1)(b) of the Statute of the International Court of Justice (ICJ): 'international custom, as evidence of a general practice accepted as law'. Most law scholars consider the definition of 'international custom' to be 'back to front'. It should read the 'general practice of states accepted by them as law provides evidence of customary law'.[18] Nonetheless, this definition has the virtue of distinguishing the two elements of customary law – state practice and *opinio juris* (that is, the belief that such practice embodies law).[19] Generally speaking, there must be consistency and general conformity in state practice for it to form the basis of a rule in customary law. Though, interestingly, in the *Nicaragua* case (1986), the ICJ stopped short of requiring 'absolutely rigorous conformity'. What matters is that most states – especially the most powerful states and those most closely concerned with the matter at hand – conform to the practice. States must also be engaging in such practice because they believe there to be a legal obligation to do so, as opposed to some other reason – courtesy, nicety, morality, or whatever. This is where *opinio juris* comes in. Often, in determining the existence of customary rules, the ICJ is willing to assume *opinio juris* on the basis of state practice. The problem is that it is tautological to see in state practice evidence of the legal

---

[18] Richard K. Gardiner, *International Law* (Harlow, UK: Person-Longman, 2003), p. 101. It may also be read: 'International custom as *evidenced by* a general practice accepted as law'. Rosalyn Higgins, *Problems and Prospects: International Law and How We Use It* (Oxford: Oxford University Press, 1994), p. 18.

[19] Thus Shaw refers to 'the actual practice of states' and Gardiner 'the general practice of states'. Malcolm Shaw, *International Law*, 4th edn. (Cambridge: Cambridge University Press, 1997), p. 58; Gardiner, *International Law*, p. 101.

obligation that is supposed to generate such practice in the first place.[20] In short, *opinio juris* is often grossly underspecified.While treaty law is generally more specific than customary law, here also there is room for disagreement among states as to what has been agreed in treaties. In part, this disagreement is rooted in different methods of treaty interpretation. Some states (such as France and Italy) favour an 'intention' approach, whereby the common will of the signatories is deduced from the preparatory discussions and documents. Other states (including the United Kingdom) favour a 'textual' approach, which seeks to identify an objective interpretation of the treaty based on a common sense reading of the document itself. Some international jurists and the United States favour a 'purposive' approach, by which treaties are interpreted in the context of their object and purpose. The 1969 Vienna Convention on Treaties prioritises the textual approach. *Travaux préparatories* are relegated to 'supplementary means of interpretation' that may only be used to confirm an interpretation derived from a literal reading of the text. Nevertheless, this difference of approach, combined with possible differences in interests, often leads to differences in opinion between states as to the content and application of treaties.[21]

Scratch below the surface then and it quickly becomes apparent how much room there is for state disagreement over the meaning, let alone the application, of international law. The problem is even more apparent when one considers the nature of legal obligation, which is fundamental to what constitutes law and how it works. Legal scholars have attributed state compliance with international law to consent, fear of sanctions, and notions of fairness. But these motivating factors do not create nor require a sense of legal obligation. Rather, obligation towards certain legal rights and duties is developed in an international political process involving instrumental, normative, and idiographic reasoning and action by states.[22] From this point of view, we may appreciate that international law does not provide clear rules to regulate state action so much as a framework and vocabulary for states to imagine, negotiate and realise social relations.[23]

An alternative way of thinking about international law might be as a *site of legitimation* for state action. Instead of seeing the UN Charter and humanitarian law as laying down the law on when and how states may use force, it might be more useful to view them as political spaces where states engage in normatively bounded deliberation about legitimate action.[24] These sites are normatively bounded in the sense that state reasoning, deliberation and action is constituted and constrained by pre-existing norms that shape social identities and situations. At the same time, states may exercise normative agency in altering norms in the process of interpreting and enacting them.[25] Viewed thus, the dispute in the UNSC over the use of force against

[20] Michael Byers, *Custom, Power and the Power of Rules* (Cambridge: Cambridge University Press, 1999), pp. 133–41.
[21] Shaw, *International Law*, pp. 655–60; Antonio Cassese, *International Law* (Oxford: Oxford University Press, 2001), pp. 133–4.
[22] Christian Reus-Smit, 'Politics and International Legal Obligation', *European Journal of International Relations*, 9 (2003), pp. 591–625.
[23] Antje Wiener, 'Contested Compliance: Interventions in the Normative Structure of World Politics', *European Journal of International Relations*, 10 (2004), pp. 189–234.
[24] This follows on from Ian Clark's suggestion that 'Legitimacy can be conceived as a political space, but not an unbounded or normatively autonomous one'. Clark, *Legitimacy in International Society*, p. 29.
[25] This dynamic is explored in Theo Farrell, 'World Culture and Military Power', *Security Studies*, 14 (forthcoming 2005).

Iraq is not simply a matter of the United States and Britain trying to circumvent article 2(4) of the UN Charter (which prohibits use of force), but rather these states, their supporters, and opponents, engaging in a process of argumentation about what action is appropriate in this case. To be sure, argumentation can take the form of strategic use of rhetoric to advance national self-interest, but it also involves truth-seeking deliberation, in this case, about the nature of the threat and the appropriate response.[26] Charter law provides the normative framework for such argumentation, bounding both rhetorical and truth-seeking action by states.

Law is not the only site of legitimation for state use of force. Other sites include various state moralities and ideologies. One such morality is the Western just war tradition, which has contributed to and is therefore similar to modern international law in some respects but elsewhere differs in substance. Thus both contain procedural norms defining rightful intention, authority, and conduct in the use of force but they differ, for example, in terms of what constitutes just cause (for example, in the just war tradition force may be used to punish whilst this is illegal in modern international law) and rightful authority (sovereigns in the just war tradition versus the UNSC in modern international law).[27] The just war tradition has been drawn on in recent attempts to revise the international legal rules on use of force, to permit such use for humanitarian purposes.[28] However, this falls foul of an even more profound difference between the two – one identified and explored by Nicholas Rengger in this volume. Namely, whereas modern international law is predicated on the enterprise of defining universal rules of state behaviour, the just war tradition is a casuistic one of practical moral reasoning about the use of force. In other words, the just war tradition provides a guide to thinking about moral action rather than a guide to moral action itself. This comes closer to the idea of morality, in this case the just war tradition, as a site rather than a source of legitimacy.

Ideology is another obvious source and site of legitimacy for use of force. 'Revolutionary ideologies' are commonly thought to be behind military action by revisionist states intended to alter the world order.[29] As noted earlier, this creates obvious opportunities for tension with legal restraints on the use of force. Indeed, Soviet socialist ideology did not recognise the legitimacy of Western derived principles of international law.[30] In contrast, liberalism is widely seen as providing a benign influence on world order, as it delegitimates use of force between democratic states.[31] But the liberal democratic peace, in so far as it exists, is an exclusive zone. Outside this zone of peace, liberalism works no such magic. More to the point, as Lawrence Freedman and Christian Reus-Smit discuss in this volume, liberalism may prompt use of force against states and other political communities perceived as

---

[26] Thomas Risse, ' "Let's Argue!" Communicative Action in World Politics', *International Organization*, 54 (2000), pp. 1–39.

[27] Michael Walzer, *Just and Unjust Wars* (New York: Basic Books, 1977); James Turner Johnson, *Morality and Contemporary Warfare* (New Haven, CT: Yale University Press, 1999).

[28] Report of the Secretary-General's High-Level Panel on Threats, Challenges and Change, *A More Secure World: Our Shared Responsibility* (New York: United Nations, 2004), para. 203, p. 66. See also Ian Holliday, 'When is a Cause Just?' *Review of International Studies*, 28 (2002), pp. 557–75.

[29] Stephen Walt, *Revolution and War* (Ithaca, NY: Cornell University Press, 1996).

[30] Iain Scobbie, 'Some Common Heresies about International Law: Sundry Theoretical Perspectives', in Evans (ed.), *International Law*, pp. 72–5.

[31] John M. Owen, 'How Liberalism Produces Democratic Peace', *International Security*, 19 (1994), pp. 87–125.

illiberal and dangerous towards it.[32] Indeed, such moral asymmetry has been advanced by some prominent international law scholars in the United States.[33] In the process, liberalism may also legitimate a project of imperial expansion.[34] Viewed as a site of legitimation, we can more readily appreciate how liberalism (and other state ideologies) provides the terms for social deliberation about the proper role of the state and what therefore constitutes proper and progressive states. The point is that such understandings are not fixed but are contingent on and evolve from the interplay of expectations and experiences. Thus, understandings of what it means to be a liberal state, and who are the foes of liberal states, will change over time and vary across the world.[35]

Conclusion

The 2003 Iraq War brought to the fore, in a very dramatic and public way, disagreements between and within states over the legitimate use of force in contemporary world politics. Obviously, such disagreements had boiled over before – most noticeably when the North Atlantic Treaty Organisation (NATO) decided to use force in March 1999 to stop ethnic cleansing by Yugoslav authorities in Kosovo. Forcible humanitarian intervention by NATO in this case was not authorised by the UNSC, principally because of blocking vetoes by Russia and China. But there was more than competing self-interests at play here. Rather the UNSC found itself locked in debate, as it would four years later over Iraq, about when was it right to use force. Most lawyers agreed that there was no legal basis for use of force for humanitarian purposes, but equally many accepted that it could be legitimate in Kosovo given the compelling moral basis for such action.[36] Against this, the Yugoslav state tried to project a competing morality, one of state security and sovereignty.[37] The Kosovo case illustrated, perhaps even more starkly than the Iraq case, the tension between law and legitimacy in the use of force. It also clearly demonstrated the tensions within international law – in this case between, on the one hand, the non-intervention and non-use of force norms, and on the other, norms of human rights. Arguably, Kosovo also revealed the crusading militancy of liberalism. Above all, it showed how law,

---

[32] Of course, this is not a new phenomenon. See, for example, Iain Hampsher-Monk, 'Edmund Burke's Changing Justification for Intervention', *The Historical Journal*, 48 (2005), pp. 65–100. For a contemporary example, see Lee Feinstein and Anne-Marie Slaughter, 'A Duty to Prevent', *Foreign Affairs*, 83 (2004).

[33] Thomas Franck, 'The Emerging Right to Democratic Government', *American Journal of International Law*, 46 (1992), pp. 46–91; Fernando R. Teson, 'The Kantian Theory of International Law', *Columbia Law Review*, 92 (1992), pp. 53–102; Anne-Marie Slaughter, 'International Law in a World of Liberal States', *European Journal of International Law*, 6 (1995), pp. 503–38.

[34] Tarak Barkawi and Mark Laffey, 'The Imperial Peace: Democracy, Force and Globalization', *European Journal of International Relations*, 5 (1999), pp. 403–34.

[35] Ido Oren, 'The Subjectivity of the Democratic Peace: Changing Perceptions of Imperial Germany', *International Security*, 20 (1995), pp. 147–84; Gerry Simpson, *Great Powers and Outlaw States: Unequal Sovereigns in the International Legal Order* (Cambridge: Cambridge University Press, 2004).

[36] See, for example, Bruno Simma, 'NATO, the UN and Use of Force: Legal Aspects', *European Journal of International Law*, 10 (1999), pp. 6–14; Alain Pellet, 'Brief Remarks on the Unilateral Use of Force', *European Journal of International Law*, 11 (2000), pp. 385–92. See also the special section on the Kosovo War in the *American Journal of International Law*, 93 (1999).

[37] Lawrence Freedman, 'Victors and Victims: Reflections on the Kosovo War', *Review of International Studies*, 26 (2000), pp. 335–58.

liberal ideology, and competing moralities provide sites for states and publics to deliberate about the legitimacy of using force in world politics.

Legitimacy and the use of force: can the circle be squared?

ANDREW HURRELL

It is no great surprise that in the contemporary world the use of deadly force by a political grouping or nation-state or on behalf of international society should raise troubling questions of legitimacy. The problem appears to be massively over-determined and the intellectual challenge is to bring some order to a confused and confusing debate; to distinguish between short-term problems and deep-rooted changes in both understandings of legitimacy and patterns in the use of force; and try and identify where there might be scope for narrowing the very deep disagreements that have come to surround this question. This article argues, first, that the legitimacy problems surrounding the use of force can only be understood by considering the way in which changing understandings of international legitimacy have interacted with developments in both the generation of insecurity and the management of insecurity; and, second, that although the ideology, strategy and policies of the Bush admin-istration have undoubtedly been central to recent debates, many of the most important aspects of the problem reflect broad and deep-seated developments within global politics. The article concentrates on questions of *international* rather than *domestic* legitimacy – although it needs to be recognised that sharply divergent national perspectives regarding the use of force are of course one aspect of the international problem.[1] The article addresses three questions:

1. What do we mean by legitimacy and how have both conceptions of legitimacy and practices of legitimacy politics evolved in ways relevant to the use of force?
2. How have changes in both the nature and management of international security complicated the legitimacy challenges facing international society?
3. Can the circle be squared? What might it mean to square the circle?

What do we mean by legitimacy and how have both conceptions of legitimacy and practices of legitimacy politics evolved in ways relevant to the use of force?

Legitimacy is sometimes understood in a sociological or psychological sense – the tendency of individuals or groups to accept and follow the rules of a political order.

---

[1] Thus the recent US emphasis on the use of military force needs to be seen in the context of a powerful and robust Jacksonian tradition within US foreign policy. See Walter Russell Mead, *Special Providence: American Foreign Policy and How it Changed the World* (New York: Alfred N. Knopf, 2001). See also Tony Judt's brave highlighting of those elements within US society that, in other places, we would not hesitate to label as militarist. See Tony Judt, 'The New World Order', *New York Review of Books*, 14 July 2005, pp. 14–18. It would be wrong, however, to focus too heavily on the US. For example, Putin has had no great difficulty in convincing many Russians that the brutal use of force in Chechnya is a perfectly legitimate means to restore 'order'.

However, the fact of actual acceptance or compliance is not enough and the study of legitimacy has for a long time focused on the beliefs of those who are complying and on the reasons why they come to accept a rule or a political order as appropriate and legitimate. Legitimacy therefore refers to a particular kind of rule-following or obedience, distinguishable from purely self-interested or instrumental behaviour on the one hand, and from straightforward imposed or coercive rule on the other.

It is true that legitimacy is often not easy to divorce from the calculation of interests. An international order that obtains in a given period may well be stable and considered legitimate to the degree that it reflects an agreed mutual satisfaction of interests. It has been common to argue that Great Power dominated systems have been legitimate to the extent that the major powers take account of the views and interests of weaker states and formulate their own policies in such a manner that others see themselves as having a stake in the system. But if acceptance can be understood solely in terms of interests and the instrumental calculation of interests, then it is unhelpful for the analyst to talk in terms of legitimacy, even if the actors themselves do so. Legitimacy implies a willingness to comply with rules or to accept a political order even if this goes against specific interests at specific times.[2] We may also need to invoke notions or principles of legitimacy precisely in order to understand how the idea of mutual satisfaction of interests is understood and interpreted by the parties involved.

Power is also central. It is, after all, the existence of an international order reflecting unequal power and involving the use of coercive force that creates the need for legitimation in the first place. On one side, the cultivation of legitimacy plays a vital role in the stabilisation of an order built around hierarchy, hegemony or empire. All major powers face the imperative of trying to turn a capacity for crude coercion into legitimate authority. As Martin Wight puts it: 'The fundamental problem of politics is the justification of power. ... Power is not self-justifying; it must be justified by reference to some source outside or beyond itself, and thus be transformed into "authority".'[3] On the other side, such power as the weak possess is often closely related to exploiting the arguments about legitimacy that have become embedded in international legal and political practice. There is undoubtedly a great deal of instrumentality in appeals to legitimacy, and nowhere more so than when weak states seek to strengthen legal and moral constraints against the use of force by the strong. Legitimacy can therefore be seen as a strategic move in a political game and needs to be understood as much a part of the messy world of politics as of the idealised world of legal or moral debate. The analyst needs to recognise the role of power and interest in the practice of legitimacy politics without falling into the trap of believing that understandings of power and interest can ever be fully grasped outside of the conceptions of legitimacy that predominate in a particular historical period or cultural context.

Legitimacy is not simply what people tend to accept in a sociological sense; it is what people accept because of some normative understanding or process of persuasion. Justification and reason-giving are fundamental. As the etymological origins of the concept suggest, this normative acceptance and the process of

---

[2] See Ian Hurd, 'Legitimacy and Authority in International Politics', *International Organization*, 53:2 (1999), pp. 379–408.
[3] Martin Wight, *International Theory: The Three Traditions*, eds. Gabriele Wight and Brian Porter (Leicester: Leicester University Press, 1991), p. 99.

justification are often based on law. In many situations legitimacy is often equated with lawfulness – lawfulness within the legal system itself, but also the lawfulness of a legally-structured constitutional order within which day to day politics takes place. But the problem of legitimacy arises precisely because of the unstable and problematic relationship between law and morality on the one side and law and power on the other. The law/morality relationship has been at the very heart of the great debates on legitimacy within both jurisprudence and political theory.[4] Can law and morality be separated, as one central strand of legal positivism has argued? Should a law be obeyed if it manifestly violates moral standards or stands in the way of morally-sanctioned action? As we shall see, these long-familiar arguments have been central to recent debates on the use of force. If we know what should be done – to protect our society against terrorism or to save distant strangers from murder and oppression – why should we allow a legalistic or formalist concern with rules and institutions to get in the way?

The relationship between law and the political order is equally central. Historically, it is often shared political norms and practices that underpin international order. Such norms are often in deep tension with the core principles of international law. The Cold War order, for example, was one in which the balance of power and shared understandings of spheres of influence played a central role and in ways that were very hard to reconcile with legal norms seeking to regulate the use of armed force. For those who stress the fragility of international society and the imperatives of national security, it is the demands of this political order that must be granted priority. This other long-familiar argument has also been central to recent debates surrounding the use of force. Why should we set such store by international institutions such as the United Nations when those institutions are clearly incapable of acting decisively and forcefully against challenges both to the security of individual states and to the broader security interests of international society as a whole?

Legitimacy is an extremely slippery concept. Not all 'legitimacy talk' should be accepted at its face value and the interpretative study of subjective and intersubjective beliefs about legitimacy needs to be set against more distanced accounts and explanations. Some have suggested that its very slipperiness means that the concept is best avoided or that it should be disaggregated into its component parts. However, as with sovereignty, the study of legitimacy takes us quickly into a site of contending claims that are so central to the analysis of political order that they cannot be easily ignored or avoided. Moreover, it is precisely the extent to which legitimacy represents an aggregate social quality (especially one attaching to a political order) that makes it valuable. Legitimacy and understandings of legitimacy are crucial if we are to understand the nature of state interests and how they change; the way in which the game of power politics is structured; and the character of the pervasive conflict over values that so disrupts efforts to capture shared interests and to secure the stable management of unequal power.

This is not the place to provide a detailed analysis of the concept of legitimacy;[5] nor of the role that it has played within international society.[6] My intention is rather

---

[4] For an excellent analysis of these classical debates, see David Dyzenhaus, *Legality and Legitimacy: Carl Schmitt, Hans Kelsen and Herman Heller in Weimar* (Oxford: Oxford University Press, 1999).

[5] See especially David Beetham, *The Legitimation of Power* (Basingstoke: Macmillan, 1991).

[6] See, in particular, Ian Clark, *Legitimacy in International Society* (Oxford: Oxford University Press, 2005); and Gelson Fonseca Jr., *A Legitimidade e Outras Questões Internacionais* (São Paulo: Paz e Terra, 1998).

to emphasise the many-sided character of legitimacy as it applies to the use of force and some of the principal ways in which conceptions of legitimacy have shifted and become more complex. Let me touch briefly on five dimensions of legitimacy.

The first dimension has to do with process and procedure. This is one aspect of what Fritz Scharpf labels 'input legitimacy'.[7] It involves the claim that an action or a rule is legitimate to the extent that it 'has come into being and operates in accordance with generally accepted principles of right process'.[8] Process-based conceptions of legitimacy mesh naturally with pluralist conceptions of international society. For the pluralist, international society aims at the creation of certain minimalist rules, understandings and institutions designed to limit the inevitable conflict that was to be expected within such a fragmented political system. These rules are to be built around the mutual recognition of states as independent and legally equal members of society, the unavoidable reliance on self-preservation and self-help, and the freedom of states to promote their own moral (or immoral) purposes subject to minimal external constraints. It is not difficult therefore to see why analysts of the pre-1914 European state system should so often view legitimacy in terms of shared procedural rules and practices – as with Bull's emphasis on the creation by common consent of rules and institutions by which clashes of interest and conflicting values can be mediated; or Kissinger's much-cited definition of legitimacy: '[I]t means no more than an international agreement about the nature of workable agreements and about the permissible aims and methods of foreign policy'.[9]

Whatever the exact character of legitimacy in the classical European state system, the crucial point here is to note the ways in which understandings of process legitimacy have evolved and expanded. In the first place, there have been fundamental changes in the character of international law – away from a system in which international law was made by the strong for the strong, and in which law was designed to fulfil a narrow set of specific purposes (its 'tool-kit function'); and towards a system in which norm creation becomes an increasingly complex and pluralist process, in which ideas of equality become more powerful and pervasive, and in which specific rules come to be understood and interpreted in the light of general legal principles and shared foundational values and as part of an increasingly integrated normative order. The degree to which the legal order has grown more complex and harder for even powerful states to control is one of the reasons why US frustration with international law has grown sharper, shifting the balance between law's power-cementing and legitimacy-creating advantages and its constraining and ensnaring costs. Of particular importance for the use of force has been the growth of those urging a form of international legal constitutionalism built around the UN Charter. As with all such constitutionalist designs, power, and especially coercive power, is to be thoroughly constrained by the exercise of constitutional authority. Proponents of this view tend naturally to stress the legal limits on the use of force, especially in relation to humanitarian intervention and self-defence, and to reject more open readings that would allow the use of force to promote broad policy goals

---

[7] Fritz Scharpf, *Governing Europe: Effective and Democratic?* (Oxford: Oxford University Press, 1999).
[8] Thomas M. Franck, *The Power of Legitimacy Among Nations* (Oxford: Oxford University Press, 1990), p. 19.
[9] Hedley Bull, *The Anarchical Society: A Study of Order in World Politics*, 3rd edn. (Basingstoke: Palgrave, 2002); Henry A. Kissinger, *A World Restored* (London: Weidenfeld and Nicolson, 1957), p. 1.

or allegedly shared moral values.[10] Viewing the UN Charter in constitutionalist or quasi-constitutionalist terms can be seen as part of a broader trend towards the judicialisation of international politics (as, for example, in relation to the EU or WTO) and, for its proponents, undoubtedly represents a powerful normative view of how the use of force should be managed.[11]

This leads to the second change in understandings of process legitimacy, namely the increasingly powerful demands that international institutions be subject to the same standards of legitimacy that are applied within liberal democratic states. The core intuition is indeed a powerful one: that the exercise of all power in political life should be subject to appropriate standards of democratic legitimacy; that the delegation of authority to international bodies has created increasingly serious 'democratic deficits' and 'crises of legitimacy'; and that these should be met by finding ways of implementing the values of participation, transparency, representation and accountability at the international level. How can anyone expect the UNSC to be viewed as legitimate given the dominance of the P5, the often murky back-room diplomacy that characterises the operation of the Security Council, and the non-representation or under-representation of important regions of the world? In a world where democratic values have gained such currency, how can the importance of representativeness not lead to legitimate demands for Security Council reform? [12]

Although there is very little agreement on what principles of democratic legitimacy might be applied within international institutions, the spread of such arguments has had three very important implications for the use of force. The first is to underpin a powerful challenge to the procedural legitimacy of established institutions and, in particular, the United Nations. If democratic legitimacy is to be central, then why should such great weight be placed on the legitimating role of institutions whose own democratic credentials are so plainly flawed. As Henry Nau puts it:

> Thus a decision by the United Nations as a whole, no less than one by the Security Council, may not reflect democratic law and certainly cannot be said to be the only legitimate way to decide on the use of force in world affairs. Legitimacy requires more than unanimity among the great powers or universal participation. It ultimately requires the consent of the governed, and many UN members do not operate on the basis of such consent.[13]

Second, and related, the democratic legitimacy of the individual state should outweigh the flawed workings of international institutions. Legitimacy should be based on domestic democratic consent and domestic constitutionalism, not on the

---

[10] For a clear example, see Bruno Simma (ed.), *The Charter of the United Nations: A Commentary*, 2nd edn. (Oxford: Oxford University Press, 2002). The emphasis on the need to 'constitutionalize international law' has also been visible amongst political theorists, again especially in Germany. Habermas, for example, has argued that 'The world organization . . . has a veritable constitution, which sets forth procedures according to which international breaches of rules can be determined and punished. There have been, since, no more just and unjust wars, only legal or illegal ones, justified or unjustified under international law.' 'America and the World: A Conversation with Jürgen Habermas', *Logos*, 3:2 (Summer 2004), p. 14.

[11] See John Ferejohn, 'Judicializing Politics, Politicizing Law', *Law and Contemporary Problems*, 41 (Summer 2002), pp. 41–63. The idea that the use of force should be tightly constrained by legal and constitutional structures is also central to many liberal theorists of global governance such as David Held.

[12] See David D. Caron, 'The Legitimacy of the Collective Authority of the Security Council', *American Journal of International Law*, 87:4 (1993), pp. 41–63.

[13] Henry R. Nau, 'The Truth about American Unilateralism', *The American Outlook* (Fall 2003).

agreement of others, nor on international law, nor on universal principles.[14] And third, if democratic legitimacy is so important, then the non-democratic character of many states should negate their own claims to strong and exclusive sovereignty. This is where democracy as a critical procedural value comes together with democracy and human rights as increasingly central constitutive norms of international society. Thus liberals attracted by the notion of the responsibility to protect have argued that sovereignty should be contingent upon the willingness and ability of a state to protect the core rights of its citizens, and that the violation of those rights creates a legitimate right of outside intervention for humanitarian purposes. The same logic appears in recent arguments about security – that 'sovereign status is contingent on the fulfilment of certain fundamental obligations, both to its own citizens and to the international community. When a regime fails to live up to these responsibilities or abuses its prerogatives, it risks forfeiting its sovereign privileges – including, in extreme cases, its immunity from armed intervention.'[15] The sovereignty of 'rogue regimes' that support terrorism or pursue weapons of mass destruction should therefore be viewed as conditional, and not absolute.

The deployment of these arguments by the US administration exemplifies the instrumental role of legitimacy in international politics. There are clearly many other ways of thinking about democratic legitimacy in international politics. For example, if one takes seriously the core democratic idea that coercive power should be made legitimate above all in the eyes of those who are directly subject to it, then democratic legitimation at the global level has far more radical and subversive implications than those envisaged by Nau, Bolton or Haas. But the crucial point here is simply to stress that the spread of arguments about democratic legitimation has immeasurably complicated understandings of what process legitimacy does, or should, consist of.

The second dimension of legitimacy has to do with substantive values. In order for an institution or political arrangement to be legitimate, its core principles need to be justifiable on the basis of shared goals and values. Central to this article is, of course, the extent to which increasingly tight constraints on the use of force have been central elements of the move towards a liberal solidarist conception of international law and society. Within the pre-1914 European state system, international law imposed few restrictions on the use of force and resort to war. War was, as Hall expressed it, 'a permitted mode of giving effect to decisions'; and conquest and subjugation were permitted modes of acquiring territory – mechanisms 'by which the successful deployment of armed force might serve not only to wrest the territory from the rightful sovereign but also to invest the conqueror with a superior title'.[16] There was no place for notions of self-determination, and the dominant powers determined the criteria by which non-European political communities could be admitted to

---

[14] See John R. Bolton, ' "Legitimacy" in International Affairs: The American Perspective in Theory and Operation', Remarks to the Federalist Society, November 2003, ⟨http://www.state.gov/t/us/rm26143.htm⟩, accessed 10 August 2005. Bolton's argument is strikingly inconsistent and he is happy to acknowledge the legitimacy-conferring role of international law and society whenever it suits his own understanding of US interests.

[15] Amongst the clearest statements of the conditional sovereignty idea is Richard N. Haas, 'Sovereignty: Existing Rights, Evolving Responsibilities', Speech at Georgetown University, 14 January 2003.

[16] R. Y. Jennings, *The Acquisition of Territory in International Law* (Manchester: Manchester University Press, 1963), pp. 3–4. See also Sharon Korman, *The Right of Conquest* (Oxford: Clarendon Press, 1996), ch. 4.

membership of international society, including the degree to which the laws of armed conflict were to apply to the non-European world.

The re-entry into the international legal order of rules governing the right to resort to force in the post-1919 and especially post-1945 period is well known. Equally well known are the ambiguities of the apparently clear-cut proscription of the aggressive use of force. These follow not only from the internal open-endedness of the concepts of aggression and self-defence but also from the increasingly complex relationship between *jus in bello* and *jus ad bellum*. But there are other aspects of the expanded normative ambition of international society that have also had very important implications for the use of force. The increasing value placed on the idea of national and political self-determination has played a major role in justifying and legitimising the many occasions in which force and violence have been used in anti-colonial and nationalist struggles – and indeed in many cases of contemporary terrorism, including Chechnya, Sri Lanka, and Palestine. And, as noted above, the increasingly powerful political and legal role of human rights and democracy has been central to the 1990s debates surrounding humanitarian intervention, as well as to the arguments of those who believe that non-democratic states possess only conditional sovereignty and that the use of force to promote regime change can be permissible.

If one of the central features of a liberal solidarist conception of international society is its increased normative ambition (including the ambition of constraining the aggressive use of force, of taming and harnessing the power of the strong), another concerns the justification and evaluation of norms. Alongside the old idea that actors create and uphold law because it provides them with functional benefits, the post-1945 period has seen the emergence of a range of internationally agreed core principles – respect for fundamental human rights, prohibition of aggression, self-determination – which are held to provide the basis for evaluating specific rules. This may be viewed in terms of the surreptitious return of natural law ideas or of a philosophically-anchorless, but nevertheless reasonably solid pragmatic consensus. Partly as a consequence we have also seen the emergence of powerful arguments that international law should escape from the limits (and genuine inadequacies) of a view of international legitimacy based on state consent and, instead, seek to build legitimacy around a shared conception of substantive justice. The most elaborate and persuasive account of this position has been developed by Allen Buchanan, for whom legitimacy is built around a Natural Duty of Justice defined as 'the limited moral obligation to contribute to ensuring that all persons have access to just institutions, where this means primarily institutions that protect human rights'.[17]

The important point to highlight is that, when it comes to the use of force, two of the most important sets of changes in the international legal and normative order point in diametrically opposite directions. For the liberal constitutionalist, legitimacy is dependent on the extent to which the use of coercive power is constrained by constitutionalist procedures, especially as embodied in the UN Charter. For the cosmopolitan moralist, rules relating to the use of force should be interpreted in the light of the substantive moral values on which the legitimacy of international law and of international society must ultimately depend.

---

[17] Allen Buchanan, *Justice, Legitimacy, and Self-Determination: Moral Foundations of International Law* (Oxford: Oxford University Press, 2004), p. 86.

A third component of legitimacy concerns specialised and specialist knowledge. Institutions and the norms and rules that they embody are legitimate to the degree that those centrally involved possess specialist knowledge or relevant expertise. Arguments of this kind have often been central to debates surrounding the legitimacy of multilateralism in relation to the global economy or the environment. Such claims are of less direct relevance to the use of force, but emerge in a number of places. Thus claims about the legitimacy of the preventive use of force are held to depend on access to secret knowledge and intelligence that only governments and intelligence agencies possess. Arguments justifying the use of force against rogue regimes have rested heavily on claims to privileged or specialist knowledge – about what their capabilities or potential capabilities might be and about their actual or future intentions. As with claims to legitimacy based on technocratic knowledge (for example in the cases of the IMF or the WTO), such arguments have suffered heavily in the face of both intelligence failures, manifestly insufficient knowledge of the countries under analysis, and the political manipulation of such intelligence. However, particularly in relation to the problem of pre-emptive or preventive use of force, there is a structural problem that cannot be easily evaded: the knowledge needed to legitimise the decision to use force cannot be easily or unproblematically made available to public scrutiny.

The fourth dimension of legitimacy has to do with effectiveness, one crucial aspect of what Scharpf labels 'output legitimacy'. In many areas of global governance, especially to do with the global economy, it is routinely argued that the delegation of authority to international organisations, to regulatory networks, or to private systems of governance is legitimate to the extent to which such delegation provides effective solutions to shared problems. A similar case is made in relation to security organisations. Thus those who reject calls for a reform and expansion of the permanent membership of the Council often rest their arguments on the importance of effectiveness. Yes, reform might promote representation; but at what cost? If a Council of 25 or 26 is even less able to act effectively than the current arrangement, then how has this increased the legitimacy of the organisation? Does not such reform carry with it the risk of repeating the very mistakes of the League that the founding fathers of the UN were so anxious to avoid?

Legitimising hierarchy in the name of effectiveness has a long history. A traditional defence of the role of Great Powers within international society was that: 'The desire for some minimum order is so powerful and universal that there is a certain disposition to accept an order that embodies the values of existing great powers as preferable to a breakdown of order'.[18] Even as international society moved into the age of sovereign equality and as the number of international institutions expanded, the importance of order via hierarchy persisted, as did its justification on grounds of effectiveness. This trend was visible in the permanent membership of the Security Council and the veto, in the voting structure of the World Bank and IMF, and in the informal norms by which negotiations in the WTO are conducted. One of the most important functions of informal groupings within formal institutions is to provide a way of combining effectiveness and legitimacy.[19]

---

[18] Hedley Bull, 'The Great Irresponsibles? The United States, the Soviet Union and World Order', *International Journal*, XXV (1979–80), p. 439.

[19] See Jochen Prantl, 'Informal Groups of States and the UN Security Council', *International Organization*, 59:3 (2005), especially pp. 582–5.

But the issue of effectiveness raises other more fundamental questions. If it is effectiveness that really matters, why bother with institutions that are both ineffective and unrepresentative? It is this line of argument that is central to those who are tempted by the possibilities of empire and hegemony – the idea of an American Empire as the only possible provider of global security and other international public goods; as the only state with the capacity to undertake the interventionist and state-building tasks that the changing character of security have rendered so vital; and as the essential power-political pivot for the expansion of global liberalism.

But even if we continue to think that institutions and international law matter, we need to think about the relationship between the legal and political order. A long tradition of thought has doubted whether coercive power can ever be wholly tied down within a legal constitutional order. Realists, for example, have long argued that some agent has to possess the effective power to safeguard international order when it comes under challenge and when institutions are unable to act. The *locus classicus* of such arguments is, of course, Carl Schmitt: his critique of both domestic and international legal constitutionalism; and his argument that the essence of sovereignty is the capacity to decide on the exceptional situation when effective action is unavoidable.[20] Albeit in more moderate and restrained tones, one strand of international legal thinking has continued to stress the custodial role of major powers in general, and of the United States in particular, in upholding the international legal order and in linking it to a politically prior security order.

> As the strongest power in the world community, the US is called upon to play an additional and unique role: that of the ultimate custodian of the fundamental goals of the multilateral institutions that it has helped to establish, when these institutions prove unable to act. And they often prove unable to act because one of the sad facts of international life is that multilateral institutions have certain inherent defects that arise from the very nature of international politics. . . . As currently structured, the institutions often prove unable to act, whether because of a veto right or a requirement of consensus. But a change of procedure will not resolve the problem, for the obstacles to action are reflections of the international political process itself. So the alternatives for a state that is able to act unilaterally are to do nothing, because unilateral action would be 'against the law', to act alone, if necessary, to preserve the system.[21]

It is not difficult to see why such arguments create problems of legitimacy, especially when the self-appointed custodial role involves the use of force.

The fifth component of legitimacy has to do with giving reasons and with persuasion. In many ways this is the most important element because it is here that the first four are brought together into an effective process of legitimation. Even in the case of effectiveness, legitimacy has to rely on more than 'brute facts on the ground' and depends on a reasoned and accepted argument that an order or institution is legitimate because it is able to provide effective security. Martin Shapiro has noted the tremendous significance of the apparently simple idea of giving

---

[20] Carl Schmitt, *The Concept of the Political*, trans. George Schab (New Brunswick: Rutgers University Press, 1976).
[21] W. Michael Reisman, 'The United States and International Institutions', *Survival*, 41:4 (1999–2000), pp. 71–2.

reasons.[22] Political, legal or moral debate necessarily involve providing reasons, and criticising, debating, accepting or discarding them. Legitimacy is about providing persuasive reasons as to why a course of action, a rule, or a political order is right and appropriate. Three issues are of particular and persistent importance: audience, institutions, and language.

The first issue concerns the audience. The politics of legitimacy are played out to an increasing range of audiences, domestic, international and transnational through an increasingly complex set of media. One of the great political challenges of legitimacy politics is to speak to these multiple audiences and to manage their divergent demands. Or take the example of regionalism. It is often argued that, in the global politics of legitimacy, endorsement of the use of force by a regional body is the next best thing to endorsement by the United Nations. And yet, in regions dominated by a hegemonic power (such as the Americas or the CIS), it is far from clear that the regional audience will see such legitimation in the same way. Asking which audience matters and why is therefore central to the analysis of legitimacy. How far, for example, is the Kissingerian insight still valid, namely that it is the acceptability of a policy to other major powers that is politically crucial rather than consensus within some broader, and perhaps illusory, international community?

The second issue concerns the institutionalised setting within which attempts at persuasion and justification take place. In an age of global communication, appeals and arguments can be made outside of any institutional structure. And yet attempts to legitimise policies are difficult to carry through in a sustained fashion if there are no institutions or institutionalised practices in which rules and norms can become embedded. The importance of the UN and, in particular, of the Security Council, is not best understood in strict legal constitutionalist terms as the authoritative body that can rule on the legality or illegality of a particular use of force. It should rather be viewed as a deeply flawed and heavily politicised body in which arguments can be presented and policies defended because other, better, forums simply do not exist. For example, it has become very common to argue that a community of liberal democratic states should be the body that legitimises the use of force in cases of humanitarian intervention or expanded self-defence. But this community has either no institutional embodiment or deeply imperfect ones (as in the claim that NATO as a military alliance should play such a role).

The third issue concerns language. In order to persuade and to justify, there has to be a shared language through which such claims can be articulated, addressed and received. Diplomacy is an important element of procedural legitimacy to the extent that it provides shared conventions for communication (linguistic and procedural) and an institutional framework to allow political negotiation and communication to take place in strained and often very difficult circumstances. One of the reasons why law has played such an important role in legitimacy comes not from the capacity of

---

[22] Martin Shapiro, 'The Giving Reason Requirement', in Martin Shapiro and Alec Stone Sweet, *On Law, Politics and Judicialization* (Oxford: Oxford University Press, 2002), pp. 228–57. See also Jens Steffek, 'The Legitimation of International Governance: A Discourse Approach', *European Journal of International Relations*, 9:2 (2003), especially pp. 260–5. As Steffek makes clear, the importance of argument, persuasion and communication explains why the figure of Habermas is so central to the understanding of legitimacy.

a legal system (even a well-functioning domestic legal system) to deliver an unambiguous answer as to what the law is – whether, for example, the war in Iraq was legal or illegal. It comes rather from the existence within law of well-established patterns of argumentation about the use of force, about the rules that have governed and might govern the use of force, about the ways in which political interests can be expressed in a common language of claim and counter-claim. Moral argument, too, takes place within an inherited tradition of ideas that may well have emerged from within the European and indeed Christian world but which have become deeply embedded in the institutions and practices of international society. This is particularly true of war. The continual involvement of individuals and societies in war and conflict, the moral and political necessity of trying to make sense of what war involves, and the limited range of plausible arguments have led over time to the creation of intelligible patterns, traditions and ideologies. These form the core of legal debates over the use of force and also of moral debates, including understandings of what might constitute a just war. As Michael Walzer puts it: 'Reiterated over time, our arguments and judgements shape what I want to call *the moral reality of war* – that is, all those experiences of which moral language is descriptive or within which it is necessarily employed'.[23]

Although we can appeal to diplomacy, to international law, to a shared moral understanding of war, it is the difficulties of communication and of rational persuasion that need to be stressed. The politics of legitimacy is also about asking difficult questions about who is included or excluded from these allegedly shared languages and where the gaps and breakdowns occur. Language cannot be understood as a straightforward or easy facilitator of communication and agreed collective action. Rather it is central to the immensely difficult task of imposing some minimum rationality on the chaos and contingency of political life and to understanding the perverse internal logics of power and the destructive role of rhetoric in political affairs. The problem is that all too often:

Words carry us forward towards ideological confrontations from which there is no retreat. This is the root of the tragedy of politics. Slogans, clichés, rhetorical abstractions, false antitheses come to possess the mind. . . . Political conduct is no longer spontaneous or responsive to reality. It freezes around a core of dead rhetoric. Instead of making politics dubious and provisional in the manner of Montaigne (who knew that principles are endurable only when they are tentative), language encloses politicians in the blindness of certainty or the illusion of justice. The life of the mind is narrowed or arrested by the weight of its eloquence. Instead of becoming masters of language, we become its servants.[24]

It is precisely this enclosure in the blindness of certainty and the illusion of justice that stands in the way of the debate and dialogue on which legitimacy must depend and that, all too often, persuades the true believer that rational persuasion is unnecessary. How can anyone except the irrational fanatic not see that my use of force is perfectly justified?

---

[23] Michael Walzer, *Just and Unjust Wars: A Moral Argument with Historical Illustrations* (New York: Basic Books, 1977), p. 15.
[24] George Steiner, *The Death of Tragedy* (London: Faber and Faber, 1961), pp. 56–7.

How have changes in both the nature and management of international security complicated the legitimacy challenges facing international society?

The period since the end of the Cold War has seen an enormous literature on the changing character of security and the changing dynamics of the global security landscape: the fading into the background of the old agenda of major power rivalry and conflict; the emergence of a wide range of new security challenges connected with civil wars, domestic social conflict, ethnic strife, refugee crises, and humanitarian disasters; intensified concern over weapons of mass destruction and over the adequacy of existing multilateral constraints on nuclear proliferation; and, of course, the way in which new weapons technologies and the infrastructure of globalisation have interacted with both new and ongoing forms of non-state terrorism. In many cases the new security threats derive not from state strength, military power, and geopolitical ambition; but rather from state weakness and the absence of political legitimacy; from the failure of states to provide minimal conditions of public order within their borders; from the way in which domestic instability and internal violence can spill into the international arena; and from the incapacity of weak states to form viable building blocks of a stable regional order and to contribute towards the resolution of broader common purposes. The declining capacity of the state to enforce legitimate order has led in many parts of the world to the privatisation of violence as diverse social groups are increasingly able to mobilise armed force; and to the privatisation of security as social groups seek to protect themselves, whether through the growth of vigilantism, the formation of paramilitary groups, or the purchase of security within an expanding commercial marketplace.

There are five implications of these changes that are central to debates about legitimacy and the use of force. First, and most obviously, the management of such insecurity is highly likely to require deep intrusion and often persistent and continuing intervention. In common with many other aspects of contemporary global governance, security is clearly a 'beyond the border' issue. Given the embeddedness of norms relating to non-intervention and to self-determination, it is hardly surprising that the inevitability of deep intrusion has created problems of legitimacy. Second, the character of new security challenges, especially in relation to terrorism and weapons of mass destruction, have led to calls for a rethinking of the categories of pre-emptive and preventive self-defence. The US attempt to enunciate such a doctrine has been the focus of a great deal of criticism, and for good reason. As with unsanctioned humanitarian intervention, the dangers of predation and abuse appear to many states and commentators to be unacceptably high; and the idea that a state can unilaterally decide to use force against a long-term and remote threat represents a fundamental challenge to accepted legal understandings. However, the need to engage in such rethinking has been acknowledged in the security strategies of other states and in the UN High Level Report. The problem is therefore a real one even if the US 'solution' is rejected.

Third, new security challenges have led to a blurring of the legal categories around which the use of force has been legally and morally structured, especially between waging war on the one hand and pursuing criminals on the other. Again, the particular policies adopted by the United States, especially in relation to the treatment of detainees, have been the subject of much well deserved criticism. But it is important to note that the structural characteristics of the struggle against terrorism make increased tensions amongst different bodies of law inevitable. And these are tensions that the current international legal order is singularly ill-equipped to deal with. Fourth, the broadening in the security agenda has increased the problem of selectivity. Already by the late 1990s the legitimacy of UN involvement in peace and security was threatened by charges that collective security had become selective security and reflected the values and political interests of the dominant Western states.

The fifth factor is the most important and has to do with the essential contestability of security. Whose security is to be protected and promoted? Against what kinds of threats? Through the use of what sorts of instruments? Some seek to answer this question in objective and material terms. Thus liberals have consistently argued that the rich and industrialised world should be concerned with the insecurity of the South because of intensified interdependence. The insecurity of the weak 'matters' to those living both in neighbouring states and in more distant regions because of the direct spillovers and material externalities that war and conflict generate. The new security agenda is important to international security because of the way in which drugs, social upheaval, political violence, refugee crises, and the growth of terrorism directly affects outsiders. Globalisation, mass communications, and the liberalisation of economic exchanges are problematic for this new security agenda because of the way in which they facilitate illicit flows of all sorts. More recently, realists who were once so critical of what they saw as global social policy have become far more concerned with the consequences of state failure, partly because of arguments that the number of 'failed states' has risen, but above all because of the negative material spillover effects.[25]

Others seek to answer these questions in moral terms. For advocates of human security, morality dictates that security is fundamentally about the promotion of human security in the face of all kinds of existential threats. Human security should include safety from hunger and disease as well as from all forms of violence. For nationalists and communitarians, the answer is equally simple. There is in reality no such thing as international security. The only security that matters is the security of our own state or community. Limited costs may be incurred to safeguard the security of other groups or to promote a more benign international environment. But such efforts must be subject to a test of national interest, not merely because of the legitimate political imperatives faced by the leaders of states but also because of a particular view of what morality requires.[26]

A great deal of the divisiveness over when it is legitimate to use force in the interest of security follows naturally from the essentially contested character of the concept of security and from the intensely and unavoidably political character of contemporary processes of securitisation. There is nothing self-evident about the statement that the greatest threat to peace and security comes from international terrorism. Indeed, from a variety of legitimate moral and analytical perspectives such a statement is manifestly wrong.

One side of the problem, then, concerns the nature of the security agenda and the changing character of security challenges. The other side concerns the management

---

[25] See Stephen Krasner, 'Sharing Sovereignty: New Institutions for Collapsed and Failing States', *International Security*, 29:2 (2004), pp. 85–120.
[26] See, for example, Jack Goldsmith, 'Liberal Democracy and Cosmopolitan Duty', *Stanford Law Review*, 55 (2002–2003), pp. 1667–97.

of insecurity and, in particular, the abiding difficulties of increasing the collective element in security management. Particularly for the strong legalist, overcoming the legitimacy problems surrounding the use of force necessarily involves increasing the collective element in security management. This does not necessarily mean a fully functioning system of collective security in which every state accepts that the security of one is the concern of all and agrees to join in a collective response to threats to international peace and security.[27] But it does involve the weaker idea of collective security: the idea of a system that commits states to develop and enforce generally accepted rules, norms and principles in the area of international peace and security and to do so through action that has been authorised by international institutions.

The collective element of security management expanded significantly in the 1990s and it is the very notion of possible progress that has done much to underpin the current belief that self-help and the unilateral use of force are illegitimate and can, at least in principle, be superseded by something better. Equally, for all the failures associated with the UN, its defenders argue powerfully, and correctly, that interest and institutional engagement can coincide even for the strong: partly because of the burden-sharing opportunities created by effective multilateralism; partly because multilateralism has the immensely difficult task of state- and nation-building; but most especially, because of the unique role of the UN as the source of collective legitimation for the use of force and the forum within which the norms surrounding the use of force are maintained, developed and interpreted.[28]

However, the structural obstacles to both collective security and more limited collective action remain severe and it is an illusion of the critics of the US unilateralism that there is an easy multilateral alternative waiting around the corner (especially given the degree to which the legitimacy of the top-down, prescriptive multilateralism of the 1990s was already coming under strain well before the first Bush administration came into office). The three core dilemmas are well known: (1) the dilemma of common interest: the prioritisation of national interests and the problems of free-riding and buck-passing; (2) the dilemma of preponderance: the dependence under any likely system of collective security on the resources of a small group of major powers (and, in the military realm, increasingly on a single power);[29] and (3) the dilemma of constraint versus expansion: the extent to which collective security does have an expansionary logic, not as Schmitt argued in terms of necessarily eroding the laws of war, but in terms of growing demand that individuals be punished and societies remade and democratised. The changing character of

[27] It is noteworthy that the UN High Level Panel spoke explicitly of the need for a collective security system, despite all of the problems associated with the concept and despite failing to address those problems. See especially Part IID: Elements of a Credible Collective Security System, in *A More Secure World: Our Shared Responsibility*, Report of the Secretary-General's High Level Panel on Threats, Challenges and Change (New York: United Nations, December 2004).

[28] The classic statement is Inis Claude, 'Collective Legitimation as a Political Function of the United Nations', *International Organization*, 20:3 (1966), pp. 367–79; see, more recently, Mats Berdal, 'The UN Security Council: Ineffective but Indispensable', *Survival*, 45:2 (2003), pp. 7–30.

[29] The United States and the United Kingdom sought legal justification for the use of force against Iraq in March 2003 on the basis that previous UNSC resolutions provided 'continuing authority'. Whilst there are very good legal reasons to counter such a claim, the political point remains valid. If international society is capable only of such actions in the field of international security built around the authorisation of individual states or groups of states to act on its behalf, what sense does it make to deny those states the autonomy to carry through the agreed goals? See Adam Roberts, 'Legal Controversies in the War on Terror', keynote address, US Pacific Command, International Military Operations and Law Conference, Singapore 21–24 March 2005, pp. 4–5.

security challenges, particularly in terms of their non-state, intrastate and transnational character, therefore raise politically difficult questions of selectivity, of moral contestability, and of unavoidably deep intrusion into the organisation of domestic society. And, however important the role of the UN, there are today, as there were during the Cold War, many aspects of international security in which its role will remain marginal and where the management of security will continue to depend on the harsher power-political mechanisms of the traditional pluralist international society.

Can the circle be squared?

It is common to distinguish between a normative meaning of legitimacy (a political order is legitimate to the extent that it meets certain criteria) and a descriptive meaning (the willingness of individuals to accept and follow the rules of a particular order). In truth, this distinction is problematic. As Steffek notes: 'For both Weber and Habermas, legitimacy is the conceptual place where facts and norms merge, where the de facto validity (*Geltung*) of a social order springs from a shared conviction about the normative validity of values (*Gültigkeit*)'.[30] Moreover, legitimacy is a political concept and like all political concepts it is quite literally meaningless outside of a particular historical context and outside of a particular set of linguistic conventions and justificatory structures. To paraphrase Ronald Dworkin, legitimacy has no DNA.[31]

Nevertheless, one approach to squaring the circle is to come at the problem from the normative side. There are, for example, powerful legal and moral arguments for seeking to reinstate the centrality of procedural legitimacy and for rejecting the view that international legitimacy should be based around the effective implementation of a set of allegedly shared substantive moral values. Although the positivist attempt to separate law and morality has always faced many powerful objections, the core intuition is a powerful one: that, in an international society characterised by deep and fundamental value conflict and by the constant difficulty of managing unequal power, a viable and stable international legal order must be built around shared processes and procedures, accepted understandings of legal sources, and a commitment to diplomatic negotiation and dialogue. The alternative is both normatively unacceptable and politically unviable, namely to open the door to a situation in which it is the strength of a single state or group of states that decides what shall count as law. Equally, a global moral community in which claims about justice can secure both authority and be genuinely accessible to a broad swathe of humanity will be one that is built around some minimal notion of just process, that prioritises institutions that embed procedural fairness, and that cultivates the shared political culture and the habits of argumentation and deliberation on which such institutions necessarily depend. Even if there is consensus on the content of moral rules, politics and, in particular, institutional politics cannot be avoided. As Dallmayr argues:

---

[30] Steffek, 'Legitimation of International Governance', p. 263.
[31] Ronald Dworkin, 'Hart's Postscript and the Character of Political Philosophy', *Oxford Journal of Legal Studies*, 24:1 (2004), pp. 1–37.

The notion of *praxis*, however, brings to the fore a domain usually shunned or sidelined by universalist morality: the domain of politics. ... Even assuming widespread acceptance of universal norms, we know at least since Aristotle that rules do not translate directly into *praxis* but require careful interpretation and application. At this point eminently political questions arise: who has the right of interpretation? And, in the case of conflict: who is entitled to rule between different interpretations? This right or competence cannot simply be left to 'universal' theorists or intellectuals – in the absence of an explicitly *political* delegation or empowerment. These considerations indicate that it is insufficient – on moral and practical grounds – to throw a mantle of universal rules over humankind without paying simultaneous attention to public debate and the role of political will formation.[32]

However, if legitimacy is principally about the beliefs and related behaviour of political actors, then it is not clear what status such abstract arguments should have. At a second level, therefore, we might consider proposals within the political world designed to mitigate the legitimacy challenges posed by the use of force. It has, for example, become common to argue that international society requires new rules. Terrorism requires that international society rethink rules relating to self-defence and new understandings of the legal and legitimate definition of prevention and pre-emption. The degree to which international society is affected morally and practically by humanitarian catastrophe means that we need new rules on humanitarian intervention. Clearer rules may serve a useful purpose. But it is a myth that, for example, a new rule on humanitarian intervention would obviate the need for institutions and for institutional debate. Even if the rule is agreed and even if the background criteria for evaluation are agreed, all rules have to be interpreted and applied to the circumstances of a particular case. It is therefore impossible to avoid the fundamental political issue: what is the body that has the authority to interpret and to apply the rule?

In related vein, the Report of the UN High Level Panel on Threats, Challenges and Change, issued in December 2004, identified five 'basic criteria for legitimacy' that the Security Council should consider before authorising the use of force: seriousness of the threat, proper purpose, last resort, proportionate means, and the balance of consequences. In this case the proposed criteria are related to the body authorised to interpret and apply them. The problem, however, concerns the structural obstacles that work against effective collective action noted above. The Security Council already has considerable freedom to interpret the mean of 'threats to international peace and security' and there is nothing that stands in the way of authorising more expansive notions of preventive or pre-emptive self-defence. The Panel therefore evaded the crucial issue: what status are these 'criteria for legitimacy' supposed to have in precisely those difficult cases when the Council is unable to act?[33]

If we move beyond such proposals, understanding how the circle might be squared will involve assessing the underlying political dynamics that explain why legitimacy in relation to the use of force has become so problematic. There are clearly good reasons why so much of the debate since 2001 has focused around the problems engendered by the ideology, strategies and actions of the Bush administration: the centrality of military force in US foreign policy; the enunciation of a doctrine

[32] Fred Dallmayr, 'Cosmopolitanism, Moral and Political', *Political Theory*, 31:3 (June 2003), p. 434.
[33] *A More Secure World*, paras. 204–9. See also Roberts, 'Legal Controversies in the War on Terror', pp. 9–10.

involving both expanded pre-emption and prevention that clearly represents a far-reaching change in established legal understandings of the justifiable use of force; the determination to take emerging notions of qualified or conditional sovereignty but to give them a much harder edge, for example, by arguing that certain sorts of states have lost the sovereign right to possess certain sorts of weapons, or that conditional or qualified sovereignty legitimises intervention to change a political regime; and the decision to move away from a predominantly multilateral approach to non-proliferation in which legitimacy depended on mutual obligation and a careful balance of rights and obligations, and to replace it by a doctrine of counter-proliferation in which the unilateral use of force is to play a central role.[34]

Clearly any hegemonic state is likely to lean on the international legal order to secure its purposes and to escape from its constraints whenever it can do so at acceptable cost. This structural problem has been enormously aggravated by the character of the policies adopted by this particular hegemon: an emphasis on its own unalienable right to security even at the cost of the insecurity of others; an emphasis on upholding a traditional rigid conception of its own sovereignty whilst at the same time arguing that the sovereignty of others should be conditional; a strident moralism which has brought back the language of the holy war (or rather reciprocated the arguments of its enemies who want nothing more than conflicts to be interpreted in these terms); and a profoundly revisionist attitude to the structure of international society.

But the politics of legitimacy have not been static. The US has found itself in exactly the dilemma identified many years ago by Raymond Aron. 'Either a great power will not tolerate equals, and then must proceed to the last degree of empire, or else it consents to stand first among sovereign units, and must win acceptance for such pre-eminence.'[35] Thus the early reliance on the potential of shock and awe and on a power-based view of the stability of unipolarity has given way to a greater recognition of the importance of legitimacy. Thus even neoconservative commentators have come to lay far greater emphasis on the need for engaging in the politics of legitimacy: principally in terms of shared values (democracy and freedom); and effectiveness (for example the argument that only US power can tackle common challenges such as terrorism and WMD and its broader position as the 'indispensable nation').[36]

However, even if the US were to move further down the road of cultivating legitimacy, there is no reason why this should necessarily involve a wholehearted embrace of international law and institutions. Two obvious policy alternatives exist, both of which have a long history in both international practice and in US diplomacy. The first is to re-engage with institutions but at the same time to reshape those institutions in ways that more closely reflect current US interests. In John Ikenberry's terms this would involve not a return to the constitutionalist order that the US did so much to shape in the post-1945 period, but rather a recasting of that

[34] For an excellent analysis of the impact of this change on international legitimacy, see William Walker, *Weapons of Mass Destruction and International Order*, Adelphi Paper 370 (London: IISS, 2004).
[35] Raymond Aron, *Peace and War: A Theory of International Relations* (London: Weidenfeld and Nicolson, 1966), p. 70.
[36] For a neoconservative view of legitimacy in this context, see Robert Kagan, 'America's Crisis of Legitimacy', *Foreign Affairs*, 83:2 (2004), pp. 65–88.

order with a much harder hegemonic edge.[37] The second would be to return to an older notion of a legitimate order – not based on universal institutions, but on power and hierarchy and involving the themes of decentralisation and devolution and the cultivation of closer relations with second-tier and regional powers.

It is important, then, to think through some of the alternative ways in which a legitimate order might be re-established within which the specific challenges posed by the use of force would be mitigated. The other still more pressing need is to see legitimacy other than from the perspective of the dominant state. In much academic analysis, legitimacy is often reduced to a strategy for the powerful and is seen as a tool or an instrument of US policy. Whether an order is legitimate depends on the beliefs, understandings and calculations of other states and on how far acceptance is the result of internalised belief rather than temporary acquiescence or purchased silence. How far this is the case is something that can only be determined by empirical research.

However, the thrust of this article has been to argue that the problems of legitimacy in relation to the use of force are deeper than those emanating from the character of a particular US administration. In terms of procedural legitimacy, the spread of democratic ideas and the political mobilisation of previously subordinated states, societies and groups make it difficult to believe that narrow, top-down, or exclusive notions of procedural legitimacy are likely to prove viable. There is no obvious sign of agreement on what alternative models of procedural legitimacy should look like – witness the impasse on Security Council reform. But political contestation on this issue is unlikely to disappear. In terms of substantive values, the changing character of global governance, not least in the area of international peace and security, necessitate international norms, rules and institutional practices that go beyond a thin pluralist conception characterised by notions of 'live and let live' and that affect very deeply how societies are to be organised domestically. In terms of effectiveness, however much the United Nations remains an important body, the limits of effective multilateralism mean that questions of effectiveness will continue to shape debates on legitimacy – both as to how institutions can be made more effective and what should happen if they fail to become so. And finally, despite the emergence of ever more sophisticated means of communication, finding a stable language for the negotiation of legitimacy across the proliferation of new audiences remains perhaps the most serious challenge. The problematic character of legitimacy in relation to the use of force does not therefore depend on a belief in the eternal logic of politics and insecurity as preached by classical realists, nor on the structural determinism of the neo-realists. Rather it results from the very difficult combination of recurring political dilemmas and powerful processes of historical change that are unlikely to be quickly, or easily, reversed.

---

[37] G. John Ikenberry, *After Victory: Institutions, Strategic Restraint and the Rebuilding of Order after Major War* (Princeton, NJ: Princeton University Press, 2001).

Legality and legitimacy: the quest for principled flexibility and restraint

RICHARD FALK

Points of departure

What follows is an attempt to acknowledge the complexity and relevance of debates about the relation between legality and legitimacy as it bears on political behaviour. The opening section is intended to orient these international policy debates in wider traditions of political theory, particularly as they bear on the nature of sovereignty and the state. On this basis, the two prominent, recent instances of controversial recourse to war (Kosovo and Iraq) are considered from the perspective of legality and legitimacy, first as a matter of juridical evaluation and then from the perspective of international reputation. The focus throughout reflects a concern with the qualities of American global leadership since September 11th, and how this leadership should or should not be guided by canons of legality.

Throughout the period between the end of World War II and the present there have been periodic challenges directed at the core commitment of the United Nations Charter that prohibits unconditionally recourse to force other than in instances of self-defence strictly construed.[1] These challenges have commanded major attention in the last several years in the settings of two sets of global circumstances: alleged humanitarian emergencies, and expanding claims of defensive necessity. In the first instance, the legal debate tends to be focused on the propriety of 'humanitarian intervention', while in the second instance, the emphasis has been upon American claims and security policy since 9/11 that are associated with recourse to 'preemptive war', or what is better known as anticipatory self-defence.

These developments have important policy and jurisprudential implications, and have been sharply contested in practice and doctrine. One important mode of legal reasoning that has emerged in both settings to defend or critique the contested use of force has rested on a distinction drawn between 'legality' and 'legitimacy'. Much of the serious discussion, at least in the United States, has been so far devoted to the application of these ideas to the Kosovo War of 1999 and the Iraq War of 2003. In the article that follows these two controversial wars are considered from the perspective of legality and legitimacy. The domestic law historical background of this distinction is also superficially considered, as well as the jurisprudential implications of blurring the edges of legality by invoking guidelines of legitimacy. Finally, attention is given to whether the distinction performs a constructive role under

---

[1] Thomas M. Franck, 'Who Killed Article 2(4)? Or: Changing Norms Governing the Use of Force by States', *American Journal of International Law*, 64:109 (1970); Louis Henkin, 'The Reports of the Death of Article 2(4) Are Greatly Exaggerated', *American Journal of International Law*, 65:544 (1971).

present conditions of world order, and what might be done to reconstitute the domain of legality so as to minimise pressures to rely for justification on legitimacy, which simultaneously offer a juridical argument in support of a given course of action while violating the law.

In some senses, recourse to legitimacy as a supplement to legality is a discourse that parallels the revival of the Just War doctrine, especially in thinking about the propriety of 'war' as a response to the 9/11 attacks.[2] Indeed, supplying content and criteria for legitimating war resembles the process of validating war by reference to the Just War doctrine. In this regard, invoking legitimacy as the basis for validating international uses of force both acknowledges the authority of law as serving normal needs of global society, and its dysfunctionality when extended to govern *selected* exceptional situations. But which circumstances, and by whom identified? And by whom appraised? Is not, in the end, the danger of relying on legitimacy to overcome the inadequacies of legality a means to assert the primacy of politics and the subordination of law.[3]

But why not, then, merely acknowledge that the law is violated for certain ethical and political reasons, and generalise such a framework? It is possible that *principled* violations of the Charter norm on force would serve an equivalent purpose to that of complementing legality with legitimacy. Yet to engage in behaviour that is admittedly 'illegal' seems to diminish respect for law more than to contend that incompleteness or new circumstances produce *reasonable* exceptions to law that should be con-strained by principled considerations and treated as temporary. In this usage of 'legitimacy' it might be better to think of the exception as *quasi-legal* rather than in the seminal usage of Carl Schmitt as *political*.

The distinction between legality and legitimacy originated and developed in the context of state/society relation, highlighting the significance of specific historical and structural circumstances of public order. The prominent assessment of this relation-ship between legality and legitimacy in late Weimar Germany sparked a complex and remarkably durable jurisprudential controversy about how to conceive of legality in circumstances where a political order is assaulted by an ultra-authoritarian move-ment such as the Nazis.[4] When dealing with the limits of legality within a state that possesses a functioning government, the issues are fundamentally different. The main issue is whether the forms of legality provide the ultimate answer to the question of legitimacy, providing the citizens with final authority by way of legislative represen-tation, or whether this legality should be tempered by societal norms interpreted by courts or subjected to emergency decrees issued by the source of 'sovereign' authority, the head of state. In the historical context of Germany, the influence of legal positivism is often blamed for facilitating the rise of Nazism, encouraging the passivity and obedience of the German citizenry and the willingness of the bureauc-racy to preside over the destruction of democratic constitutionalism. But it seems doubtful that any view of law could have effectively obstructed the Nazi political

---

[2] Jean Bethke Elstein, *Just War Against Terror* (New York: Basic Books, 2003); Michael Walzer, *Arguing About War* (New Haven, CT: Yale University Press); Richard Falk, *The Great Terror War* (Northampton, MA: Interlink Press, 2003).

[3] The locus classicus for such discussions is Carl Schmitt, *Legality and Legitimacy*, trans. John P. McCormick and ed. Jeffrey Seitzer (Durham, NC: Duke University Press).

[4] For a fascinating account see David Dyzenhaus, *Legality and Legitimacy: Carl Schmitt, Hans Kelsen and Hermann Heller in Weimar* (Oxford, UK: Oxford University Press, 1997).

onslaught associated with the rise of Hitler to absolute power, given the climate of popular opinion in crisis-ridden Germany. The legal arena in Germany, as well as theories about law, was certainly a site of struggle, but it was the inevitable prevalence of 'the political' in periods of crisis rather than the choice of legal theory that determined the fate of Germany. Perhaps Germany was more susceptible to this dynamic of subservience to secular authority, given its political culture, including the deep influence of Lutherism, the late consolidation of state power, and its long experience of autocratic rule.

If we turn from domestic public order to world public order we discern dramatic differences. There are no governmental institutions beyond the state that can claim 'sovereignty', in the sense of autonomous and ultimate authority to pronounce the law. The United Nations is best conceived as 'a club of states', and is organised in such a way as to acknowledge geopolitical realities expressed formally by granting permanent membership in the Security Council and veto power to the five states that dominated world politics in 1945 when the UN was established. The International Court of Justice (ICJ), the judicial arm of the UN, has no general authority to decide disputes among states unless asked to do so, or even to review contested decisions of the Security Council, possessing only a residual authority to issue 'advisory opinions' if so requested by an organ of the organisation. No tradition of deference has emerged within the UN system to overcome the autonomy of leading states in relation to uses of force, although the effort to oppose 'aggression' has activated the UN from time to time.[5] Some legal scholars concluded that the legal prohibition embodied in the Charter had been seriously eroded or compromised by inconsistent patterns of practice, some reasonable, others not.[6] At the same time, the ICJ interpreted legality with respect to uses of force as specified by international law and the UN Charter as fully operative, and did not acknowledge any weakening of Charter norms as a result of the practice of states.[7] Additionally, there is widespread opposition to recent moves by the United States to view war as ultimately a discretionary instrument of foreign policy, as well as to the sort of unilateralism associated with the presidency of George W. Bush. Again, Kosovo and Iraq provide litmus tests for this push and pull.

Legality clarifies the core obligations relating to force, while legitimacy tries to identify *and delimit* a zone of exception that takes account of supposedly special circumstances. It is so far a problematic and controversial means of achieving flexibility because the delimitation proposed lacks endorsement by the United Nations or acceptance by the governments of leading states. The legality/legitimacy discourse is largely an expression of concern in civil society about contested uses of international force, especially involving the United States. There is some inter-national effort to move toward a more authoritative intergovernmental status for the distinction, given its use with approval in the Report of the Independent International Commission on Kosovo, and considering the call by the UN Secretary

---

[5] Instances where the UNSC has applied Charter norms to oppose aggression in an effective manner include the Korean War (1950–52), The Suez Operation (1956); and the First Gulf War (1991).

[6] Anthony Clark and Robert J. Beck, *International Law and the Use of Force* (London: Routledge, 1993); A. Mark Weisbrud, *Use of Force: The Practice of States Since World War II* (University Park, PA: Pennsylvania State University Press, 1997).

[7] Case Concerning Military and Paramilitary Activities In and Against Nicaragua (Nicaragua v. United States) 1986 International Court of Justice Reports 14.

General for a resolution by the Security Council clarifying the Charter approach to uses of force under varying conditions. The official UN approach has been to insist that the Charter concept of legality is itself flexible enough to incorporate the *substance* of the Bush Doctrine on pre-emptive war, but not the *process* of unilateral invocation. *In Larger Freedom*, the Secretary General's comprehensive report to the Security Council on UN reform, drawing on recommendations made by an expert panel, insists that while pre-emptive war or anticipatory self-defence might be justifiable to address an emerging threat, that determination must be entrusted *without exception* to the Security Council.[8] Put this way makes it evident that the essential objection to American diplomacy since 9/11 is its unilateralism, but indirectly as well, as evident in the Iraq debate prior to the war, to the application of the doctrine in particular circumstances. Put differently, the United States tried hard to obtain approval for its claim to wage war against Iraq from the Security Council, but it refused, and then the United States acted in concert with its partners.

Force beyond legality: the Kosovo debate

The debate occasioned by the Kosovo War of 1999 now seems overshadowed by the response to the 9/11 attacks, but the issues raised then with respect to the appropriateness of 'humanitarian intervention' have a persisting relevance to the role of international law and the UNSC in setting *and suspending* limits on acceptable behaviour by sovereign states in relation to international uses of force. At bottom the concern is with the method and style of embedding elements of morality, politics, and reasonableness in the interpretation of legal standards, whether this 'loosening' of law is generally better done by stretching the meaning of the standards, that is, *internal* to the domain of 'legality,' or by acknowledging that it better preserves the core constraints of law (here the basic prohibition on non-defensive force) to acknowledge the limits of law by creating an *external* domain of exception, labelled 'legitimacy'.[9] Another way of expressing the inquiry is to consider under what conditions political and moral pressures for adjustment with respect to legal restraints should be dealt with by techniques of flexible interpretation and when these pressures should be handled by explicitly admitting that a gap exists between legality and legitimacy. If interpretative flexibility rejects textual guidance of carefully drafted treaty language, it undermines confidence in law as truly separate from politics and morality. It is this jurisprudential urge to sustain the authority of law as law that provides the inner strength of positivist orientations. However, if interpretative rigidity makes law incapable of adapting legal guidelines to changing circumstances in situations of widely perceived crisis, then law tends to be cast aside as 'irrelevant' by power-wielders and politically minded jurists or is upheld and regarded as 'oppressive'. This tension between the benefits of certainty and the need for flexibility is what inspires the quest for a golden mean of interpretation that necessarily relies,

---

[8] 'In Larger Freedom: Towards Development, Security and Human Rights for All', Report of the Secretary-General, A/59/2005, 21 March 2005, para. 122–6.

[9] The issue is much discussed recently in political and legal theory in relation to the statist thinking of Carl Schmitt and now Geogio Agamben. See particularly Agamben, *State of Exception* (Chicago, IL: University of Chicago Press, 2005).

however phrased, on the power to create exceptions. The goldenness of the process depends on explaining the exception as reasonable rather than arbitrary, and placing limitations based on principled criteria.[10] It contrasts with the Schmitt view that law should give way to politics whenever there is present a clash, and that any stricter legalism such as is espoused by democratic liberalism, involves a dangerous weakening of the state as a political actor that must protect society against its internal and external 'enemies'.

Drastic responses to this unavoidable dilemma arise whenever the moral and political imperatives of policy appear to exceed the limits of legality. Such responses rose to the surface in the course of the Kosovo debate. An influential response to the implications of the Kosovo War was developed by Michael Glennon who proposed viewing the entire legal framework of constraint embodied in the United Nations Charter as having been sufficiently superseded by the present global setting to lose its restraining force, thereby allowing behaviour to be authoritatively shaped by discretionary initiatives ('coalitions of the willing') until a new legal regime responsive to current realities of power and values can be established by the consent of major states.[11] A different accommodation to these same realities of power was proposed by Thomas Franck who advocated a forthright repudiation of the legal constraint to explain the action taken in the circumstances of Kosovo.[12]

The now infamous John Bolton, in contrast, acted as if the efforts of jurists to find a legal rationale for or against intervening in Kosovo were a waste of time, insisting instead that the United States should refrain from intervening in Kosovo *solely* because it had insufficient national interests at stake to warrant the risks and costs. If the assessment is based on such an extra-legal calculation of interests, international law becomes almost totally irrelevant, except possibly for a dominant state such as the United States, which may or may not be concerned with its profile and reputation as a law-abiding global leader. Such a concern can work in both directions, either conveying a willingness to play the geopolitical game within the rule-governed framework of international law and the UN, or demonstrating its contempt for existing norms and institutions while claiming a freedom of manoeuvre with respect to such a framework for the sake of the greater public good.[13] The extreme version of this kind of politicised approach is to claim an exemption from legal constraint for itself while acting as an enforcer of the very same constraints with respect to those other states seen as challenging the established order of world politics. Such a posture has been adopted by the Bush administration with respect to the accountability of political leaders for crimes under international law, insisting on an exemption for itself, while having the temerity to assist in the Iraqi preparation of the prosecution of Saddam Hussein and close associates as war criminals.

The specific circumstances prompting the Kosovo War have been frequently recounted. The historical context and short-term memory were definitely important.

[10] See *Kosovo Report* (Independent International Commission on Kosovo) (Oxford: Oxford University Press, 2000), esp. pp. 192–5 [hereinafter cited as Kosovo Report].
[11] Michael J. Glennon, *Limits of Law; Prerogatives of Power; Interventionism after Kosovo* (New York: Palgrave, 2001).
[12] Thomas M. Franck, 'Break It, Don't Fake It', *Foreign Affairs*, 78 (1999), pp. 116–22.
[13] Richard Perle, 'Thank God for the Death of the UN: Its Abject Failure Gave Us only Anarchy', *Guardian*, 20 March 2003.

Serb brutality in Bosnia, climaxing in the massacre of some 7,000 Muslim males within the UN 'safe haven' of Srebrenica in 1995 while UN peacekeepers looked on as spectators, was certainly a factor encouraging effective international action in the face of an imminent threat of another phase of ethnic cleansing in Kosovo. Possibly as well, although more conjectural, an interest in confirming the vitality of the NATO alliance as it neared its 50th anniversary, despite the ending of the Cold War and the collapse of the Soviet Union, was also an encouragement for timely and effective intervention under NATO auspices. Beyond this, the growing perception of a developing humanitarian emergency in Kosovo, associated with atrocities allegedly perpetrated by the Serbs against Kosovar civilians combined with a stream of refugees, solidified public opinion in Europe and stiffened the will of European governments to take some protective action before the process of ethnic cleansing was underway in full force, even without a mandate from the Security Council.[14] In effect, a humanitarian emergency highlighted by media attention was present in Kosovo posing a moral challenge. This challenge was reinforced by such political considerations as demonstrating NATO effectiveness, establishing an American military presence in the Balkans, and showing that the United States remained involved in Europe despite the ending of the Cold War.

Such a convergence of moral and political factors was not able to control fully the mechanisms of decision within the UN Security Council. Russia, traditionally aligned with Serbia, and China, uncomfortable about encroaching on sovereign rights, let it be known that any effort to obtain a mandate for military intervention within the Security Council would fail because of their veto. But without the approval of the Security Council even a humanitarian intervention would violate the Charter prohibition on recourse to non-defensive force. The US-led pro-intervention countries were faced with a difficult choice: either abandon the Kosovar people to an oppressive regime imposed by Belgrade and apparently bent on ethnic cleansing to create a demographic balance more favourable to minority Serb domination, or act in violation of the core obligation of the UN Charter to obtain advance approval for any use of international force that cannot be explained as self-defence against a prior armed attack. As we know, NATO chose to act, relying on the regional nature of the initiative, and the support of all neighbours except Greece, and seems to have rescued the Kosovar Albanian population, which comprised 90 per cent of the totality. The intervention was effective, although criticised for its reliance on high-altitude bombing, its failure to do more to protect the Serb minority in the aftermath of the war, and its insufficient reconstructive effort. At the same time, the Security Council rejected a proposed resolution of censure relating to the intervention, and took on the task of working with the NATO occupying forces entrusted with peacekeeping operations, which could be viewed as a retrospective validation of the intervention by the UN, or at the very least, a refusal to censure the violation of the Charter. Of course, the refusal can itself be discounted as an expression of *political* realities associated with the strength of the United States and its European partners in the Security Council, rather than as a belated acknowledgement of either the *legality* or *legitimacy* of the intervention.

---

[14] The incident in the Kosovo village of Recak on 15 January 1999 was particularly influential, where Yugoslav military forces killed some 45 Kosovars, allegedly civilians, although Serbs claim that the casualties were the result of a skirmish with the KLA, and were paramilitary combat officers. See Kosovo Report, pp. 81, 83.

It was against this background that the Independent Commission on Kosovo believed that the best way to handle the mixture of contradictory legal, political, and moral pressures was to rely on a distinction between legality and legitimacy. In effect, the NATO intervention was viewed as *illegal* because of its irreconcilability with the UN Charter prohibition on non-defensive force, yet *legitimate* because of its effective response to an imminent humanitarian catastrophe. The need to rely on this extra-legal justification was acknowledged in the Report as unfortunate, disclosing a deficiency in the legal regime governing the use of force, which suggested the importance of legal reform. Such reform is difficult within the UN setting because it is cumbersome to amend the Charter, but more fundamentally, because some major states distrust or oppose humanitarian rationales for intervention, and would surely withhold their consent from an expanded notion of permissible force even if under UN authority.[15] For these reasons, the recommendation to overcome the gap between legality and legitimacy seems unlikely to materialise in the near future.

The Kosovo Commission additionally recommended a framework of principles that would, in effect, provide a quasi-legal framework to guide and assess legitimacy claims and undertakings. What was proposed consisted of a set of principles, which themselves depended on considerable interpretative discretion if applied to actual situations. The Kosovo Report puts forward three threshold principles and eight contextual principles that try to provide guidance as to *when* an intervention would be legitimate, and *how* such an intervention should be carried out to maintain its legitimate character.[16] The overall purpose of these principles is to depict conditions of what might be described as 'humanitarian necessity', that is, only by acting promptly and proportionately can an acutely vulnerable people or minority be protected against massive suffering. The principles make clear that the case for necessity must be strong, that diplomatic alternatives have been exhausted in good faith, and recourse to war is a last resort and undertaken in a manner that minimises destructive effects for the civilian population being protected. In the Kosovo setting, these criteria were only partially met, and so the Kosovo War did not rank as high as it might have on the legitimacy scoreboard. There were doubts about whether the diplomatic efforts preceding the war were serious efforts to find a solution, there were some suspicions that the KLA had provoked the Yugoslav military forces in Kosovo so as to generate incidents that could be then reported to the world media as 'atrocities', and there was much criticism of the failure of the international community to extend support to the non-violent resistance efforts led by Ibrahim Rugova during the 1990s.[17]

A somewhat different approach to the Kosovo challenge was proposed by the International Commission on Intervention and State Sovereignty.[18] It tried to

---

[15] There were also independent sceptics. Noam Chomsky, *The New Military Humanism: Lessons from Kosovo* (Monroe, ME: Common Courage Press, 1999). For a wider, deeper scepticism about claims of humanitarian intervention, see Anne Orfeld, *Reading Humanitarian Intervention: Human Rights and the Use of Force in International Law* (Cambridge: Cambridge University Press, 2003); as well, the domestic jurisdiction provision of the UN Charter, Article 2(7), can be understood as a deliberate legal obstacle to preclude the UN from endorsing humanitarian intervention.

[16] Kosovo Report, pp. 193–5; also Appendix A.

[17] On Rugova see Kosovo Report, pp. 43–65.

[18] 'The Responsibility to Protect', Report of the International Commission on Intervention and State Sovereignty, 2001.

circumvent the rough edges of political disagreement by abandoning the anti-sovereignty language of humanitarian intervention, substituting the phrasing 'the responsibility to protect'. The outcome of both frameworks is similarly shaped by the formulation of a framework of principles for military intervention designed to get the job done, but minimise the use of force.[19] The frameworks are complementary in content and intention, with *The Responsibility to Protect* seemingly more directly incorporating the sort of language of guidance that is associated with the Just War doctrine, and also more intent on changing Security Council practice. Its emphasis on what it calls 'Right Authority' is designed to encourage the Security Council to reconsider its role under the Charter in light of the development of international human rights since the founding of the UN. The Security Council is encouraged strongly to discharge its responsibilities, but if it fails to do so, then action may be taken by a descending hierarchy of empowered actors: the General Assembly, regional and sub-regional actors, and finally, 'concerned states'. In the light of the actuality of an impending humanitarian catastrophe, the main point is that external actors have an obligation to act in a timely and effective fashion. To bolster the capability of the Security Council to discharge this function and in direct response to the Kosovo prospect of vetoes, the Report recommends that the five permanent members should agree not use their veto if there exists otherwise majority support for taking protective action. Kofi Annan in his report on UN Reform, titled *In Larger Freedom,* appears to endorse the approach advocated by *The Responsibility to Protect.* The Secretary General asks rhetorically, 'As to genocide, ethnic cleansing, and other such crimes against humanity, are they not also threats to international peace and security, against which humanity should be able to look to the Security Council for protection?' He adds, 'The task is not to find alternatives to the Security Council as a source of authority but to make it work better'. And then listing some criteria resembling those proposed by the two commissions, Kofi Annan concludes, '*I therefore recommend that the Security Council adopt a resolution setting out these principles and expressing its intention to be guided by them when deciding whether to authorise or mandate the use of force'.*[20]

Both reports, as well as the Secretary General, offer constructive responses to the challenge, but it is unlikely, due to the underlying political differences that pertain to this subject-matter, that anything formal will be agreed upon for some years. The impacts of 9/11 make such a prospect even more remote in one sense, but less important from another angle, given the likely continued decline in the willingness of major states, especially the United States, to use its power directly for the sake of overcoming a humanitarian catastrophe. The more immediate policy issue is whether the report of the Kosovo Commission or that of the Intervention and State Sovereignty Commission is more deserving of support. In my view the Kosovo Commission is to be preferred because it directly confronts the dilemma that arises at the outer limits of law when moral and political factors strongly favour moving beyond those limits. It also does not pretend that 'intervention' is not 'intervention-ary'. But as earlier argued, both reports are constructive, move in generally the same direction, and should be reflected upon in addressing future contexts of humanitarian

---

[19] Report, Note 18, pp. xii–xiii, and Appendix B.
[20] Emphasis in the original; all references in this paragraph are to *In Larger Freedom,* cited n. 8, A/59/2005, paras. 122–6.

emergency in which interventionary responses are under consideration. The simmering genocidal circumstance in the Darfur region of Sudan is precisely such a context, but characterised by an absence of a sufficient political will on the part of major states to discharge 'the responsibility to protect'.[21]

Legality, legitimacy and the Iraq War

The main justifications for the Iraq War offered by the US Government prior to its onset were related to the threats posed by Iraq's possession of weapons of mass destruction (WMD), and secondarily, Iraq's failure to comply with a series of UN resolutions. This set of circumstances supposedly, according to official representations on behalf of American policy, validated a use of force despite the absence of explicit authorisation. And this absence was itself contested by Administration supporters who read into Security Resolution 1441 an implicit authorisation to use necessary force to achieve Iraqi compliance with earlier UN directives.[22] Unlike Kosovo where the factual grounds for claims of humanitarian necessity seemed widely accepted, the claims of defensive necessity relating to Iraq could not be convincingly made, and thus the claims of self-defence or implementation of UNSC resolutions were neither formally persuasive in the Security Council, nor accepted by public opinion either in the region of Iraq or in Europe, the locus of America's traditional allies. Opposition to the Iraq War was more intense elsewhere in the world, being most unified in Islamic countries that viewed the conflict through the lens of 'a clash of civilizations', neither more nor less. This scepticism has been generally viewed as vindicated by the failure to discover WMD, the main *pre-invasion* pretext for recourse to a pre-emptive war, the growing evidence that the US Government was resolved to invade and occupy Iraq quite apart from whether or not Baghdad complied with UN authority, the indications that oppressive circumstances in Iraq, while persisting, were not approaching an emergency phase (and had been far worse in prior years), and the absence of any clear evidence that the American occupation has been accepted by the majority of the Iraqi people as a welcomed liberation. In effect, there seemed insufficient grounds to validate the Iraq War because of its legality, and no persuasive reason to affirm its legitimacy.[23] In other words, the recommended approach to the Kosovo War, even if accepted, does not provide a justification for the Iraq War, but on the contrary suggests the conclusion that it was both illegal and illegitimate.

[21] See Report of the International Commission of Inquiry on Darfur to the United Nations Secretary General (Pursuant to UNSC Res. 1564, 18 Sept 2004), Geneva, 25 January 2005; Scott Straus, 'Darfur and the Genocide Debate', *Foreign Affairs*, 84:1 (2005), pp. 123–33.

[22] For definitive statements of US Government official arguments along these lines, see William H. Taft IV and Todd F. Buchwald, 'Preemption, Iraq, and International Law'; John Yoo, 'International Law and the War in Iraq'; and Ruth Wedgewood, 'The Fall of Saddam Hussein: Security Council Mandates and Preemptive Self-Defense', in *Future Implications of the Iraq Conflict*, selections from the *American Journal of International Law*, September 2003.

[23] For comprehensive assessments along these lines, see C/G. Weeramantry, *Armageddon or Brave New World? Reflections on the Hostilities in Iraq*, 2nd edn. (Ratmalana, Sri Lanka: Weeramantry International Centre, 2005); Domenic McGoldrick, *From 9–11 to the Iraq War 2003* (Oxford, UK: Hart Publishing, 2004), esp. pp. 24–86; see also R. Falk and David Krieger (eds.), *The Iraq Crisis and International Law* (Santa Barbara, CA: Nuclear Age Peace Foundation, January 2003).

Shortly before the start of the Iraq War, Anne-Marie Slaughter did attempt a variation explicitly modelled on the approach taken by the Kosovo Commission. Pointing out that the states favouring a use of force in Kosovo 'sidestepped the United Nations completely and sought authorisation for the use of force within NATO itself', she noted that '[t]he airwaves and newspaper opinion columns were filled with dire predictions that this move would fatally damage the United Nations as arbitrator of the use of force', but that after the generally successful outcome of the Kosovo War the Kosovo Commission found that 'although formally illegal . . . the intervention was nonetheless legitimate in the eyes of the international community.'[24] Writing days before the invasion, Slaughter saw a similar possibility for the American recourse to the war against Iraq but this could be established, if at all, only after the fact of an invasion. Slaughter somewhat surprisingly argued that '. . . the Bush administration has started on a course that could be called "illegal but legitimate", a course that could end up, paradoxically, winning United Nations approval for a military campaign in Iraq – though only after an invasion'. This rather ingenious argument reasoned that the American recourse to the UN in search of approval was itself an implicit, although a conditional, endorsement of UN authority showing that the United States Government would not act 'without any reference to the United Nations at all'. Slaughter sees this twilight zone of 'compliance/violation' as part of 'an unruly process of pushing and shoving toward a redefined role for the United Nations'. In the end, despite the US failure to receive authorisation from the Security Council to initiate a war against Iraq '. . . the lesson that the United Nations and all of us should draw from the crisis' is this: 'Overall, everyone involved is still playing by the rules. But depending on what we find in Iraq, the rules may have to evolve, so that what is legitimate is also legal.' If playing by the rules means only that dubious claims to use force will first be vetted at the Security Council, and if not approved, will then be exercised, it limits the role of the UN to that of a debating society, where if the state seeking to engage in controversial behaviour cannot make its case persuasively, it will proceed to act in any event. Slaughter's *approach* is untenable as it so seriously blurs the distinction between compliance and violation, disabling a critique from the perspective of either legality or legitimacy *in advance* of a challenged use of force. Reverting to the Kosovo precedent, it would seem that the case for legitimacy, in the face of illegality, was based on circumstances that *preceded* recourse to war. In my view, a retrospective construction of legitimacy as proposed by Slaughter provides an unacceptable validation of the primacy of geopolitics in relation to global governance.

Writing a year later, Slaughter applied the proposed approach, contending that her earlier analysis was based on the invasion of Iraq being '*potentially* legitimate in the eyes of the international community' if certain conditions were satisfied: finding WMD; a welcoming reception by the Iraqi people; and an acceptance of UN supervision of the occupation and political reconstruction of Iraq by the United States, United Kingdom, and their array of lesser allies. Her entirely convincing conclusion in 2004 was that none of these conditions had been met, and thus the use of force against Iraq was illegal and illegitimate. She suggests that Kosovo shows that '[i]t is sometimes necessary to break the law to change it', and that the international community should respond by adapting the law to these changed circumstances

[24] Slaughter, 'Good Reasons for Going Around the UN', New York Times, 18 March 2003.

associated with discharging the responsibility to protect. But she argues *after* the fact that '[t]he lesson of the invasion of Iraq is quite different', vindicating the opposition within the UN to the use of force by those governments that asked the United States to defer recourse to war until more evidence existed of an WMD presence in Iraq or more time for the UN inspection to produce an assessment of the Iraqi threat. Slaughter shares the view of the Bush administration that pre-emptive uses of force need to be made permissible in specified circumstances in view of the altered security threats posed after 9/11: 'The world faces very different threats than it did in 1945'. Yet for Slaughter this widening of the right of self-defence does not validate the abandonment of the core legal constraints of the Charter. In her words, 'the most important lesson of the invasion of Iraq is that the safeguards built into the requirement of the *multilateral* authorisation of the use of force by UN members are both justified and necessary. If nations seeking to use force cannot mount strong enough evidence of a security threat to convince a majority of the Security Council and to avoid a veto (provided that the veto is not clearly motivated by countervailing political interests), the world should wait and try another way before sending in the troops.'[25] I think Slaughter 'before' and 'after' discloses the difficulties of making a clear analysis of legality in circumstances of pre-emptive claims if the distinction between legality and legitimately is employed too loosely. In my view, the proposed American war against Iraq was definitively illegitimate as well as illegal *before* any use of force against Iraq was undertaken, and could not have been rendered retroactively legitimate regardless of whether WMD were found, the public welcomed the intervention, and the UN took over the post-conflict occupation and reconstruction.[26] For Slaughter, in contrast, it would seem that a *potential* demonstration of legitimacy was a sufficient sign of adherence to the rules of world order even if such a claim should subsequently be shown as lacking a factual foundation. In my view, the claim to use force is only potentially legitimate if there can be made a *prior* demonstration of defensive necessity based on the imminence, plausibility, and severity of a security threat, with these conditions *normally* to be determined by a *multilateral* process, preferably by the Security Council. This is the approach now advocated by Kofi Annan, and the basis of the finding that the Kosovo War was illegal, yet legitimate.[27]

Slaughter seems to endorse a superficially similar approach, but more closely considered, her views contain some significant variations. For Slaughter, if approval by the Security Council is thwarted by an actual or anticipated veto that is politically motivated, then recourse to force would be justified, even without UN approval. But she never clarifies how to identify a political motivation for an exercise of a veto. To this day, the US Government regards the French opposition to its effort to obtain a mandate for the invasion of Iraq as politically motivated. So long as the power of exception is a matter of decision by a hegemonic government, the limitations associated with the constraining guidelines are not likely to inhibit discretionary wars.

Beyond this, the possibility of retrospective legitimation opens wide the door to abuse of the legality/legitimacy approach. Perhaps, a middle ground exists that rests

---

[25] All quotes in this paragraph are from Slaughter, 'The Use of Force in Iraq: Illegal and Illegitimate', *ASIL Proceedings 2004*, pp. 262–3.

[26] Richard Falk, 'The Iraq War and the Future of International Law', in n. 25, pp. 263–6.

[27] See text at n. 8; also Kofi Annan, Address by the Secretary General. Kofi Annan, UN Doc. SG/SM/8891, 23 September 2003.

on the provisional legitimacy of recourse to war, that is, where there is probable cause to suppose that the threshold criteria of legitimacy will be satisfied. In the instance of Iraq that would have meant untainted evidence of a massive WMD programme, strategic objectives that include support for global terror and future war plans, and an alienated population that would welcome intervention (as the majority of the Kosovar citizenry clearly did). In my view, there was no way for the US Government to uphold the burden of persuasion prior to the invasion, and thus, unlike Slaughter, I would maintain that the position taken by the Bush administration was illegal and illegitimate from the outset, and not susceptible to being legitimated after the fact. At most, the degree of illegitimacy could have been considerably mitigated if large stockpiles of WMD had been discovered together with plans for future wars and if the Iraqi people had overwhelmingly welcomed the foreign forces as liberators. Then, and only then, could one credibly dismiss the resisting elements in Iraq, as was done by Donald Rumsfeld, as 'dead enders'.

A second legitimacy debate in public policy circles

It is important to distinguish 'legitimacy' as used to denote the status of the United States as global hegemon, and legitimacy as a benchmark of judgment with respect to a particular use of force that falls outside the orbit of legality. The two views of legitimacy may or may not be linked, depending upon whether hegemonic legitimacy is associated, or not, with a reputation for generally adhering to international law. In the aftermath of the Iraq War, there has emerged a debate in the mainstream on the nature of hegemonic legitimacy, and whether or not it presupposes law abidingness. This debate can be most usefully framed by presenting the views of a prominent neoconservative commentator on foreign affairs, Robert Kagan, and that of an equally prominent geopolitical realist, Robert W. Tucker (in collaboration with David Hendrickson).

The more intellectual neoconservatives acknowledge that the invasion of Iraq without a mandate from the Security Council cost the United States heavily in terms of perceived legitimacy, especially among European democratic states. This viewpoint has been most clearly expressed by Robert Kagan.[28] What is most interesting about Kagan's argument is that he delinks this loss of legitimacy from legality, and connects it to what he calls 'the unipolar predicament' of having capabilities and vulnerabilities, but not the leadership to command adherence to defining policies. In Kagan's view it was this failure, abetted by clumsy diplomacy, which was exhibited by the split with traditional European allies in relation to the Iraq War. His point here is that the loss of legitimacy by the United States is not a consequence of Washington's refusal to have its policy shaped by reference to international law, a general posture of lawfulness, and deference to the United Nations. Kagan insists that this refusal has long characterised US foreign policy, but that previously it did not produce political difficulties because America's traditional European allies were supportive.

It is Kagan's view that '[c]ontrary to much mythologising on both sides of the Atlantic these days, the foundations of US legitimacy during the Cold War had little

[28] 'Robert Kagan, America's Crisis of Legitimacy', *Foreign Affairs*, 83:2 (2004), pp. 65–87.

to do with the fact that the United States had helped to create the UN or faithfully abided by the precepts of international law laid out in the organization's charter'. In the same vein, '[i]t was not international law and institutions but the circumstances of the Cold War, and Washington's special role in it, that conferred legitimacy on the United States, at least within the West'.[29] What led to this European acceptance of the legitimacy of American leadership were three pillars: the Soviet Union posed a strategic threat to Europe that could only be addressed by means of a European acceptance of American leadership; the Soviet Union was also a common ideological enemy enabling America to be the acknowledged leader of 'the free world'; and thirdly, the structure of bipolarity meant that American power was kept in check by Soviet power, and this reassured Europeans that the United States would not be too reckless in pursuing its foreign policy (unlike the current circumstance of unchecked power in the relations between Europe and the United States).

The changed circumstances and their consequences for American hegemonic legitimacy came to a crisis in the run-up to the Iraq War. Europe perceived no strategic threat arising from Iraq's behaviour, and was deeply put off by the American insistence that such a strategic threat existed. At the same time, according to Kagan, the Europeans were disturbed by their inability to mount an effective opposition, or to induce the United States to act only to the extent of UN authorisation. Europeans perceived that their legimacy was 'an asset they have in abundance ... they see it as a comparative advantage – the great equaliser in an otherwise lopsided relationship.'[30] Kagan indicts the Europeans for their hypocrisy. He argues that Europe's central contention that the United States was dependent on Security Council approval before it acted against Iraq was inconsistent with European support for evading the Security Council in order to proceed with the humanitarian intervention in Kosovo back in 1999. Kagan's central thesis is as follows: 'There are indeed sound reasons for the United States to seek European approval. But they are unrelated to international law, the authority of the Security Council, and the as-yet fabric of the international order. Europe matters to the United States because it and the United States form the heart of the liberal, democratic world.'[31] From this perspective the prescription is simple: 'The United States, in short, must pursue legitimacy in the manner truest to its nature: by promoting the principles of liberal democracy not only as a means to greater security but as an end in itself.'[32] The question of whether or not the rift between two competing visions of world order can be healed, the one predominant in Europe and the other in the United States, depends in the last analysis in how they perceive the basic threat to world order: is it an exaggerated perception of the threat by the United States or an insufficient appreciation of it by Europe? Kagan regard this divergence as a 'tragedy', and sides in the end with the American view, saying of the Europeans '[i]n their effort to constrain the superpower, they might lose sight of the mounting dangers in the world, which are far greater than those posed by the United States'.[33] There are from this perspective three main conclusions implied by Kagan's analysis: first of all, departures from legality are not of significant relevance to an assessment

[29] Ibid., at p. 67.
[30] Ibid., at p. 72.
[31] Ibid., at p. 84.
[32] Ibid., at p. 85.
[33] Ibid., at p. 87.

of legitimacy; secondly, legitimacy matters far more than legality in evaluating criticisms of foreign policy; and thirdly, the American threat assessment, even if producing certain dysfunctional policies, is generally accurate, and should be regarded by European governments as a legitimate approach to world order in the period since 9/11. At the same time, Kagan acknowledges that it is not so regarded, and that part of the fault lies with the 'maladroit' diplomacy of the Bush administration. In effect, Kagan would presumably like to see the Europeans respect the American view on the common threats posed to the established order of global security arising from the new terrorism and would encourage Washington to be more consultative and collegial in relation to European sensibilities when shaping its future foreign policy.

At issue, is whether the disagreements that surfaced during the pre-war debate on Iraq were primarily matters of diplomatic style or exhibited deep substantive differences. There is no doubt that the abrasive Bush approach, especially considering the earlier record of unilateralism and repudiation of lawmaking treaties, contributed to the image of the United States as a global leader of severely diminished legitimacy. But there were also significant substantive differences on the nature of terrorist threat, and widely divergent interpretations as to whether the regime of Saddam Hussein should be regarded as part of the threat, and these differences could not have been removed by smoother diplomacy. In that sense, the Iraq War challenged the legitimacy of American global leadership in much more serious ways than were associated with objections to the Kosovo War of 1999 or the Afghanistan War.

Returning to the legality/legitimacy connection, Robert W. Tucker and David C. Hendrickson, with firm realist credentials, challenged the Kagan approach, mainly on the level of conceptualisation.[34] It was the Tucker/Henrickson view, expressed in an article published in *Foreign Affairs*, that the American fall from legitimacy was directly linked to its refusal to guide and justify its foreign policy by reference to international law. In their view, '[l]egitimacy arises from the conviction that state action proceeds within the ambit of law, in two senses: first, that action issues from rightful authority, that is, from the political institution authorised to take it; and second, that it does not violate a legal or moral norm'.[35] They acknowledge that legitimacy is elusive as it is at least possible that illegal or unlawful action may on occasion be deemed legitimate, but despite this, their view is that 'illegitimacy [is] a condition devoutly to be avoided'.

The main burden of Tucker/Hendrickson's analysis is take explicit issue with Kagan's view of how the United States sustained its legitimacy in the period of the Cold War. They argue that American legitimacy emerged out of four related features of its foreign policy – 'its commitment to international law, its acceptance of consensual decision-making, its reputation for moderation, and its identification with the preservation of peace'.[36] In contrast, they view each of these 'pillars' of legitimacy to be severely weakened by the style and substance of American foreign policy during the Bush presidency. Tucker and Hendrickson acknowledge that there had been previous American initiatives that had challenged these principles, but that the overall posture of the country was one that maintained the link between legality and

---

[34] 'The Sources of American Legitimacy', *Foreign Affairs*, 83:6 (2004), pp. 18–32.
[35] Ibid., at p. 18.
[36] Ibid., at p. 24.

legitimacy, and that this was widely understood by our main allies in the world. In their view, American problems can be structurally understood in relation to its inability to handle 'the unipolar moment' that emerged after the collapse of the Soviet Union. They also show the implausibility of initiating the Iraq War by invoking the so-called Bush Doctrine claiming a right to wage pre-emptive wars. The absence of the imminence of any threat, made all too clear by the failure to find WMD in Iraq, deprived the American policy of any plausible basis to argue either legality or legitimacy. But even more damaging from the Tucker/Hendrickson perspective was the evident indifference to legality: 'In truth, the Bush administration did not care a fig for whether the war was lawful'.[37] And further along this line was their conclusion that the US Government was now exhibiting 'a fundamentally contemptuous attitude toward principles that had previously sustained US legiti-macy'.[38]

Tucker/Hendrickson do not adopt an unconditional attitude toward legality, acknowledging that considerations of prudence and morality may justify unlawful conduct in exceptional circumstances. But in their view the Iraq War was not such an instance. Such illegal uses of force are 'in fact unnecessary for US security and actually imperil it'. They argue that 'containment and deterrence' had provided 'a perfectly workable method of dealing with Saddam Hussein', while the occupation of Iraq has made 'Americans much more insecure'.[39] They are also critical of the Kosovo War, contending that the factual basis for claiming that an imminent humanitarian catastrophe justified the NATO intervention did not exist, but was fabricated on the basis of exaggerated accounts of Serb atrocities and disregard of KLA provocations.[40] In other words, maintaining legitimacy depends, according to Tucker/Hendrickson, on limiting departures from legality to situations of compelling necessity. The road back to legitimacy for the United States is a difficult one given current perceptions, but it is a vital part of restoring American security, as well as being of intrinsic benefit. Their closing words: '. . . the importance of legitimacy goes beyond its unquestionable utility . . . a good in itself. For its own sake, and for the sake of a peaceful international order, the nation must find its way back to that conviction again.'[41]

Continuing the debate in the pages of *Foreign Affairs*, Kagan argues mainly that Tucker and Henrickson are now arguing a position that is inconsistent with their past acceptance of departures from legality, and are allowing their dissatisfaction with Bush's foreign policy to colour their discussion of principle.[42] I think Kagan scores points here, but he fails to address the most fundamental issue, which is, under conditions of unipolarity, international law assumes a more important role than within global settings where countervailing centres of state power exist: providing the only available source of constraining discipline for the United States. This structural factor has been rendered more important by the sort of blunt approach that the Bush administration brings to diplomacy, virtually inviting other states to withhold

---

[37] Ibid., at p. 26.
[38] Ibid., at p. 23.
[39] Ibid., at p. 29.
[40] Ibid., at pp. 30–1.
[41] Ibid., at p. 32.
[42] Robert Kagan, 'A Matter of Record: Security, Not Law, Established American Legitimacy', *Foreign Affairs*, 84:1 (2005), pp. 170–3.

support for American leadership on grounds of both legality and legitimacy. Kagan fails to deal with the bearing of extremist ideology in a context of unipolarity as aggravating the legitimacy crisis, and therefore understates the relevance of legality.

Kagan shares with Tucker/Hendrickson a deep concern about the loss of American legitimacy in world affairs, but insists that sustaining, losing, and regaining legitimacy has never been closely tied to a record of compliance with international law. In the end, Kagan thinks that more skilful diplomacy is all that is needed to restore American legitimacy, as Washington is essentially correct about the nature of the post-9/11 world and what to do about it. It is my judgment that elevating style above substance will work to repair some of the damage, but that American legitimacy cannot be recovered until there is a strong sense that US foreign policy is basically, although not invariably, constrained by international law and the United Nations Charter.

The flexibility of lawyers versus the flexibility of law

It is one thing to advocate a general adherence to legal guidelines, but it is quite another to translate this advocacy into agreed lines of behaviour. There are always lawyers available to support the preferred policy options of political leaders either motivated by careerist or nationalist goals. Never has this subordination of lawyers to the political mood been more obvious than during the Bush administration.[43] There were always government lawyers available in Washington to justify casting aside the Geneva Conventions or to validate pre-emptive/preventive uses of force. It is this availability that led the philosopher Immanuel Kant long ago to call international lawyers 'miserable consolers'.[44]

There is little doubt that it is difficult to attain the perspective of a detached and informed observer in the United States, given the traumatising effects of the 9/11 attacks, although with the passage of time that difficulty seems to have diminished. (See McDougal on the evaluative objectivity essential for judgments about legality). The proper assessment of legality needs to be outside the orbit of official rationalisations, but should not subscribe to legalistic understandings of law that are rigidly disconnected from context or changing circumstances. As legal expectations are always subject to interpretation, and are presumed to be consistent with prevailing ethical values and underlying security needs, there is room for considerable interpretative latitude without ever reaching the precarious domain of 'illegal, but legitimate'.[45]

---

[43] See Mark Danner, *Torture and Truth;* also Lisa Hajjar, 'What's the Matter with Yoo?' and R. Falk, 'Law, Lawyers, Liars and the Limits of Professionalism', papers presented at the 2005 Law & Society Annual Meeting, 2–5 June 2005, Las Vegas, Nevada.

[44] 'Perpetual Peace', in *Kant On History*, ed. Lewis White Beck (Indianapolis, IN: Bobbs-Merrill, 1963), pp. 85–135, 99. See also the Busiris scene in Jean Giradoux, *Tiger at the Gates* (New York: Oxford University Press, 1955), pp. 43–47.

[45] This issue has been decisively elaborated by Harold Lasswell and Myres S. McDougal in their influential article, 'The Identification and Appraisal of Diverse Systems of Public Order', reprinted in McDougal, *Studies in World Public Order* (New Haven, CT: Yale University Press, 1960), pp. 3–41; for the wider issues associated with interpretative discretion see Myres S. McDougal, Harold D. Lasswell, and James C. Miller, *The Interpretation of Agreements and World Public Order* (New Haven, CT: Yale University Press, 1967).

In the setting of the main controversies of recent years, there is no evidence that torture provides the best source of information in the course of interrogating prisoners, and there is massive evidence that revelations of torture as official policy have damaged American security and contributed heavily to the decline in American legitimacy in both senses discussed above, that is, reputation for law abidingness, reputation as hegemonic leader. The pictures of abuse of detainees at Abu Ghraib and elsewhere in similar detention facilities suggest a pattern of sadistic behaviour by guards condoned, if not induced and abetted, at the highest levels of the US Government. The portrayal of detention at Guantanamo contributes further to a portrait of depravity in dealing with the religious and human sensibilities of individuals under the total control of their captors and minders, most of whom lack any possible useful knowledge and many of whom are innocent. A picture of gratuitous abuse emerges, connected to no reasonable public purpose, and the result is damage to American legitimacy in both its wider and narrow senses. In other words, it is not only the Iraq War that provides the most notorious instance of illegal and illegitimate, but the general pattern of practices associated with the conduct of the War Against Global Terror.

Legality and legitimacy: the dilemma reconsidered

The ongoing preoccupation in political theory generated by Carl Schmitt's conceptualisations of legality and legitimacy have seldom explicitly influenced the application of such terminology to the *international* behaviour and status of a sovereign state. The Schmitt perspective, arising in the context of emergent Nazi dictatorial rule, was supportive of the view that 'legitimacy' was essentially an expression of political will that was inherently rooted in sovereignty, and took precedence over deference to 'legality' in the internal and international operations of government. The sovereign should not be constrained by illusions about the primacy of law, which for Schmitt was the fatal flaw of liberal democracy. This way of deploying legality and legitimacy forms the background of discussion, but the foreground is associated with foreign policy debates about controversial uses of international force, or recourse to war.

These debates have been principally concerned about the propriety of the wars in Kosovo in 1999 and in Iraq since 2003. The earlier presentation of these debates was intended to convey the confused, even contradictory, history of legitimacy in both international relations and international law. In these intellectual settings legitimacy functions both as a statist benchmark of reputation and propriety, and as linked to legality. With respect to reputation, there is disagreement as to whether the reputation of a state, particularly a hegemonic actor, is or is not dependent on a record of compliance with international law, whether legitimacy is essentially concerned with diplomatic decorum as to a responsible and effective use of hegemonic power or is rooted, above all, in substantive behaviour that exhibits respect for the core principles of international law.[46] For the Kosovo Commission

---

[46] See generally Thomas M. Franck, *The Power of Legitimacy Among Nations* (New York: Oxford University Press, 1990).

invoking legitimacy was a means of endorsing an intervention on moral and political grounds that could not meet tests of legality. At the same time, it was hoped that the constraints of legality would be soon loosened to incorporate the Kosovo precedent, thereby obviating future pressures to depart from these constraints. From these perspectives, reliance on legitimacy is a signal of the need and desirability of law reform.

In contrast, although invoking the approach of the Kosovo Commission, Anne-Marie Slaughter, writing in the tradition of international liberalism, supposes that if a state seeks legality, and is denied, as the United States was when it sought approval from the United Nations of its plan to wage war against Iraq, it could still *subsequently* be regarded as having acted legitimately if certain specified conditions were satisfied in the course of the war. Slaughter's eventual denial of legitimacy was not based on the illegality of recourse to a non-defensive war against Iraq, but on the failure of the Bush administration to demonstrate the accuracy of its own rationale for the war.

The recommended approach taken here is based on approval of the Kosovo Commission approach to the legality/legitimacy divide, but not to Slaughter's effort to allow legitimacy to be demonstrated after the fact. The positive role played by legitimacy is to impart a measure of flexibility with respect to the application of legal constraints on the use of international force in two, and only two, sets of circumstances: conditions of humanitarian necessity (Kosovo; Darfur, Sudan) and circumstances of defensive necessity (1967 War in the Middle East; Afghanistan War of 2002). As pointed out above, it is supportive of these views that the moral and political rationales for war in these two sets of circumstances have been endorsed by the UN Secretary General and expert bodies as *already embodied* in the UN Charter if correctly understood. In other words, the gap between legality and legitimacy is not a matter of substantive standard, but interpretative clarity. Whether this is the proper approach to a concern about the limits of legality itself deserves further debate. By incorporating through interpretation changing circumstances, flexibility is achieved, but the clarity of an inhibiting text is definitely weakened. A motive for inflexibility in formulating constraints on the use of international force is to minimise the ambit of discretion available to governments, and thereby contribute to the basic undertaking of the United Nations 'to save succeeding generations from the scourge of war'.

There are no enduring solutions for these issues of war and peace that will recur in varying settings as history continues to unfold. It does seem that debating legality and legitimacy is one means to encourage deliberative reflection about controversial recourse to war to resolve international conflict. This reflection is needed in these contexts of decision to address the tension between a desired clarity in standards of constraint and a needed relief from such clarity in situations where moral and political imperatives push up against these constraints. The legality/legitimacy debate at its best, as in Kosovo, did perform this function. Since the September 11th attacks there have been renewed, and more radical pressures directed at the framework of constraint understood as legality, but there has also been unprecedented resistance to these pressures by states and civil society actors in relation to the Iraq War, including an international consensus that this particular war was both illegal and illegitimate. Whether this discourse based on legality/legitimacy will help frame future foreign policy debates is itself uncertain at this juncture.

Not yet havoc: geopolitical change and the international rules on military force

MICHAEL BYERS*

> 'Cry havoc and let slip the dogs of war'
>
> William Shakespeare, *Julius Caesar*, Act III, Scene I

Introduction

This article considers the relationship between geopolitical change and the evolving international rules on military force. Its focus is the impact of the United States' rise to hegemonic status on the rules governing recourse to force (the *jus ad bellum*) and the conduct of hostilities (the *jus in bello*, otherwise known as 'international humanitarian law').[1] For reasons of space and clarity of analysis, the article does not focus on the different, more traditional IR questions of whether and why the behaviour of the United States might be constrained by these rules.

Two specific sets of rules are examined: the right of self-defence and the rules governing the treatment of detainees. The article concludes that geopolitical change frequently leads to normative change, though on some issues – such as pre-emptive self-defence – even a hegemonic state cannot change international law on its own. The challenge facing the international community is to maintain rules on military action that are reasonable, effective and widely accepted – including by the most powerful state, at least most of the time.

Self-defence

The right of self-defence in contemporary international law dates back to 1837, when the British were crushing a rebellion in Upper Canada (now Ontario). The United States, while unwilling to antagonise a superpower by supporting the rebels directly, did not prevent a private militia from being formed in up-state New York. The 'volunteers' used a steamboat, the *Caroline*, to transport arms and men to the rebel headquarters on Navy Island, on the Canadian side of the Niagara River. The British

* I am grateful for helpful comments from Katharina Coleman, Richard Price and Adriana Sinclair. Parts of this article draw on Michael Byers, *War Law* (London: Atlantic Books, 2005).
[1] In this article, the term 'hegemony' is used to describe, not only coercive power, but also the softer, less deliberate and hierarchical forms of influence exercised by a leading state. See Michael Byers and Georg Nolte (eds.), *United States Hegemony and the Foundations of International Law*, vol. 1 (Cambridge: Cambridge University Press, 2003), pp. 450–1 and 492–3.

responded with a night raid, capturing the vessel as it was docked at Fort Schlosser, New York. They set the boat on fire and sent it over Niagara Falls. Two men were killed as they fled the steamer and two prisoners were taken back to Canada but later released.

The incident caused disquiet in Washington, DC. British forces, having torched the White House and Capitol Building in 1814, were again intervening on US territory. Some careful diplomacy followed, with US Secretary of State Daniel Webster conceding that the use of force in self-defence could be justified when 'the necessity of that self-defence is instant, overwhelming, leaving no choice of means, and no moment of deliberation', and provided that nothing 'unreasonable or excessive' was done.[2] The British accepted Webster's criteria. Over time, as other countries expressed the same view of the law in other disputes, the *Caroline* criteria – often referred to simply as 'necessity and proportionality' – were transformed into the parameters of a new right of self-defence in customary international law.

In 1945, the drafters of the UN Charter included self-defence as an exception to their new, general prohibition on the use of military force. In addition to the existing customary criteria, three further restrictions were introduced: (1) a state could act in self-defence only if subject to an 'armed attack'; (2) acts of self-defence had to be reported immediately to the Security Council; and (3) the right to respond would terminate as soon as the Council took action.[3]

Despite this careful attempt at definition, the precise limits of self-defence still depend greatly on customary international law, in part because the UN Charter refers explicitly to the 'inherent' character of the right. And so, while the right of self-defence is codified in an almost universally ratified treaty, its parameters have evolved gradually – or at least become more easily discernible – as the result of the behaviour of states since 1945. For example, it is unclear, on a straightforward reading of the Charter, whether armed attacks against a country's citizens *outside* its territory are sufficient to trigger the right to self-defence. The story of how this particular ambiguity was resolved provides an example of how the international rules on military force traditionally evolved – at least before the emergence of a single superpower.

Self-defence and the protection of nationals abroad

In June 1976, an Air France flight from Tel Aviv to Paris was hijacked and diverted to Entebbe, Uganda. The hijackers threatened to kill the passengers and crew unless 153 pro-Palestinian terrorists were released from jails in France, Israel, Kenya, Switzerland and West Germany. On the third day of the hijacking, 47 non-Jewish passengers were released. On the fourth day another 100 were let go. The Ugandan government, led by Idi Amin, took no apparent steps to secure the release of the remaining, mostly Israeli hostages.

On 3 July 1976, shortly before the deadline set by the hijackers, Israeli commandos mounted an audacious rescue operation. Without notifying the Ugandan

---

[2] See R. Y. Jennings, 'The *Caroline* and McLeod Cases', *American Journal of International Law*, 32 (1938), p. 82.

[3] Article 51, UN Charter, available at: ⟨http://www.un.org/aboutun/charter/index.html⟩.

government, they landed at Entebbe airport, killed the hijackers, saved the lives of all but three of the hostages and flew them back to Israel. Only one Israeli soldier died in the raid, but a number of Ugandan soldiers were killed and several Ugandan military aircraft destroyed. Israel claimed that the right of self-defence allowed force to be used to protect nationals abroad – when the country in which they had fallen into danger was unable or unwilling to do so. Up to this point, similar claims had never been widely accepted as legal under international law.[4]

Two draft resolutions were introduced in the UN Security Council. The first, prepared by Britain and the United States, condemned the hijackers rather than Israel and called on states to prevent and punish all such terrorist attacks. This resolution was put to a vote but failed to obtain the necessary support of nine or more Council members. The second draft resolution, submitted by Benin, Libya and Tanzania, condemned Israel for its violation of Ugandan sovereignty and territorial integrity and demanded that it pay compensation for all damage caused. This second resolution was never put to a vote. The response of countries outside the Security Council was even more muted, signalling widespread, tacit acceptance of the Israeli claim. Today, the Entebbe incident is regarded as having contributed decisively to a limited extension of the right of self-defence to include the protection of nationals abroad. When civil strife elsewhere threatens a country's citizens, whether in Haiti, Liberia or Sierra Leone, sending soldiers to rescue them has become so commonplace that the issue of legality is rarely raised.

Traditionally, when international rules on military force evolved, they did so as the result of an individual country or group of countries advancing a novel claim, often in conjunction with military action, and most other countries endorsing the claim, either by concluding a treaty to that effect or by evincing their support through acts, statements or even inaction and silence (acquiescence) formative of customary international law. This process of change was equally available to all states, though powerful states have always had certain advantages when shaping international law.[5] Moreover, as the following example begins to indicate, the end of the Cold War and the emergence of the United States as a single superpower have heightened that country's influence over international law-making.

Self-defence and reprisals

If the right of self-defence extends to the protection of nationals abroad, what then of situations where an armed attack has occurred but the immediate threat has passed? In other words, is self-defence limited to warding off attacks-in-progress or does the right extend to action taken in response to a recent attack? If so, what, if any, line is to be drawn between defensive and punitive armed responses?

Reprisals became illegal under international law in 1945, when Security Council authorisation and the right of self-defence were the only two exceptions provided to the UN Charter's general prohibition on the use of force. In response, some countries

---

[4] See Michael Akehurst, 'The Use of Force to Protect Nationals Abroad', *International Relations*, 5:3 (1977).
[5] See Michael Byers, *Custom, Power and the Power of Rules: International Relations and Customary International Law* (Cambridge: Cambridge University Press, 1999).

have sought to extend the right of self-defence to include acts designed more to punish than repel.

In 1964, eight British warplanes attacked the Harib Fortress in Yemen. The British government sought to justify the action as self-defence, following incursions by Yemenese aircraft into the Federation of South Arabia the previous day. The Security Council responded by adopting a resolution that deplored 'all attacks and incidents which have occurred in the area' and, more importantly, singled out 'reprisals as incompatible with the purposes and principles of the United Nations'.[6] Remarkably, Britain (along with the United States) abstained on the resolution – though it did so while continuing to insist, in the face of widespread criticism of its apparently punitive action, that it had engaged in nothing more than self-defence.[7] In the context of the Cold War, countries uniformly opposed changing international law to permit reprisals, or at least acts formally identified as such, while most but not all countries opposed a concomitant extension of the right of self-defence.

In April 1993, an attempt to assassinate former US President George H.W. Bush was thwarted when a sophisticated car bomb was discovered in Kuwait. Two months later, the United States fired 23 cruise missiles at the Iraqi military intelligence headquarters in Baghdad. Madeline Albright, the US permanent representative to the United Nations at the time, presented evidence of the Iraqi government's involvement in the assassination attempt to the UN Security Council. She asserted that the attempt to kill the former president was 'a direct attack on the United States, an attack that required a direct United States response'. Moreover, Albright claimed, the response was permitted under the right of self-defence in the UN Charter.[8]

The armed response took place two months after the assassination attempt had been foiled and the threat to the former president eliminated. Rather than being necessary for self-defence, it was aimed at the dual goals of punishing Iraq and deterring future plots – and was therefore a reprisal in all but name. Yet the members of the Security Council responded favourably to the US action and its claim of self-defence. Japan said that the use of force was an 'unavoidable situation'. Germany described the strike as a 'justified response'. Reaction outside the Security Council was less favourable. Iran and Libya condemned the strike as an act of aggression, while the Arab League expressed 'extreme regret' and said that force should only have been used if authorised by the Security Council. But most countries expressed no view on the legality of the US action.

The widespread acquiescence, and the change it represented from 1945 and 1964, was most likely linked to the geopolitical changes that had occurred a few years earlier. The United States was now a single superpower and its opponent, Saddam Hussein's Iraq, was no longer supported by any significant state. Still, the United States probably failed in this instance to modify the right of self-defence to allow purely punitive and deterrent action. Some rules, including those (like the right of self-defence) which protect fundamental aspects of state sovereignty, are highly resistant to change and take numerous interactions to alter; other, less deeply

---

[6] SC Res. 188 (1964), UN Doc. S/5650, available at: ⟨http://www.un.org/documkents/sc/res/1964/scres64.htm⟩.

[7] *Repertoire of the Practice of the Security Council*, 1964–65, ch. XI, p. 195, available at ⟨http://www.un.org/Depts/dpa/repertoire/⟩.

[8] See Dino Kritsiotis, 'The Legality of the 1993 Missile Strike on Iraq and the Right of Self-Defence in International Law', *International and Comparative Law Quarterly*, 45 (1996), p. 163.

embedded rules, are more easily changed. Yet the US response – coupled with its newly augmented influence – will have rendered the law less clear and therefore more susceptible to modification in future. This modification has not yet happened, but if and when it does, the consequences for the UN system could be quite serious.

Often, determining whether an action falls within the parameters of self-defence will turn on the facts of the specific situation. In the case of the foiled 1993 assassination attempt, Washington explained that it had taken two months to gather conclusive evidence of Iraqi involvement in the plot and, once it was certain that Baghdad was responsible, wasted no time in acting. But once an armed attack has come and gone and there is no continuing or immediate threat, there is nothing to stop the attacked country from asking the UN Security Council to respond instead. In most domestic legal systems, the right of self-defence ends the moment an attack has ceased and there is time to call the police.

During the Cold War, one could have argued for an extension of the right of self-defence to the period following an attack on the basis that an attacked country had little reason to believe that the Security Council would respond to its pleas. The argument does not carry the same weight in the post-Cold War period. Following the 1990 Iraqi invasion of Kuwait, and on several occasions since then, the Security Council has demonstrated a new-found willingness to respond to breaches of the peace. In this changed context, attempts to extend the right of self-defence to the period following an attack could have a perverse and possibly cascading series of consequences. By allowing countries to bypass the Council, any extension of the right would render that body less effective and less authoritative, which in turn could be used to justify a further extension of the right, and so on. This problem does not present itself solely with regard to punitive actions: a similar outcome is already discernible following a successful attempt to extend the right of self-defence to include, not only responses against attacks by states, but also responses against states that willingly support or harbour terrorists – when it is the terrorists rather than the state who have mounted the attack.

Self-defence against terrorism

On 11 September 2001, nineteen Al'Qaeda operatives seized four passenger jets, crashing two of them into the World Trade Center and another into the Pentagon; the fourth plane was brought down in a Pennsylvanian field after the passengers revolted against the hijackers. Nearly 3,000 people were killed in the attacks. Almost immediately, the US government declared that it would respond militarily on the basis of self-defence. But as a legal justification for the use of force in Afghanistan – the country harbouring and indirectly supporting the Al'Qaeda leadership – the right of self-defence was not as readily available then as it is today.

Even when countries were directly implicated in terrorism, acts of self-defence directed against them did not attract much international support – prior to 2001. In April 1986, a terrorist bomb exploded in a West Berlin nightclub crowded with US servicemen. Two soldiers and a Turkish woman were killed and 230 people were wounded, including 50 US military personnel. Two weeks later, the United States responded by bombing a number of targets in Tripoli. Thirty-six people were killed, including an adopted daughter of Libyan leader Muammar Gadaffi.

Washington claimed the strike on Libya was legally justified as an act of self-defence. As then-Secretary of State George P. Shultz said:

[T]he Charter's restrictions on the use or threat of force in international relations include a specific exception for the right of self-defence. It is absurd to argue that international law prohibits us from capturing terrorists in international waters or airspace; from attacking them on the soil of other nations, even for the purpose of rescuing hostages; or from using force against states that support, train, and harbour terrorists or guerrillas.[9]

Yet the claim was widely rejected, with many governments also expressing doubt as to whether the strike – with its two week delay and use of heavy munitions – met the 'necessity and proportionality' criteria for self-defence. The most significant evidence of the lack of support was the refusal of France and Spain – both NATO allies of the United States – to allow their airspace to be used by the bombers that conducted the raid. As a result, the pilots, who began their mission at a US airbase in Britain, had to fly westward around the Iberian Peninsula. The widespread negative reactions from other countries meant that the legal claim and associated military action did not succeed in changing international law.

Around the same time, the additional question arose as to whether the right of self-defence extended to situations where military responses took place on the territory of countries not directly implicated in terrorist acts. In 1985, Israel claimed to be acting in self-defence when it attacked the headquarters of the Palestine Liberation Organisation in Tunisia. The UN Security Council condemned the action, with the United States, unusually, abstaining rather than voting against (and thus vetoing) the resolution.[10] A number of governments expressed concern that the territorial integrity of a sovereign state had been violated in an attempt to target, not the state itself, but alleged terrorists present there.

In 1986, the International Court of Justice ruled in a case, brought against the United States, in which Nicaragua argued that it was the victim of an illegal military intervention.[11] Washington had justified its actions as collective self-defence, on the basis that Nicaragua's support for rebel groups in surrounding countries amounted to armed attacks on those countries, to whose assistance the United States could then come. The Court held that 'assistance to rebels in the form of the provision of weapons or logistical or other support' did not amount to an armed attack triggering the right of self-defence. It also decided that collective self-defence may only be exercised if the country under attack requests assistance, and this Nicaragua's neighbours had not done. Although the decision in the *Nicaragua Case* concerned support for rebels rather than terrorists, it did confirm that countries which merely harboured or provided indirect support for terrorists were not open to attack on that basis.

---

[9] 'Address by Secretary of State George P. Shultz, Low-Intensity Warfare Conference, National Defense University, Washington, DC, 15 January 1986', reproduced in *International Legal Materials*, 25 (1986), p. 204.

[10] SC Res. 573 (1985), available at: ⟨http://www.un.org/Docs/scres/1985/scres85.htm⟩.

[11] See *Military and Paramilitary Activities in and against Nicaragua (Nicaragua v. United States of America)*, judgment on the merits, 27 June 1986, available at: ⟨http://www.icj-cij.org/icjwww/icases/inus/inusframe.htm⟩.

The legal situation concerning self-defence and terrorism began to change in 1998 after two bombs exploded outside the US embassies in Nairobi, Kenya and Dar es Salaam, Tanzania. Twelve Americans and almost 300 Kenyans and Tanzanians were killed; thousands more were injured. United States intelligence sources indicated that Osama bin Laden and his Al'Qaeda organisation were responsible for the attacks. Two weeks later, the United States fired 79 cruise missiles at six terrorist training camps around Khowst, Afghanistan and at a pharmaceutical plant on the outskirts of Khartoum, Sudan. At the time, the Central Intelligence Agency was convinced that the plant was producing precursors to chemical weapons; it subsequently emerged that the intelligence was flawed.

As Israel had done in 1985, the United States sought to justify its actions on the basis of self-defence. As then National Security Adviser Sandy Berger said: 'I think it is appropriate, under Article 51 of the UN Charter, for protecting the self-defence of the United States . . . for us to try and disrupt and destroy those kinds of military terrorist targets.'[12] In addition to making the claim, the US government deployed its considerable influence in support of the legal argument. President Bill Clinton telephoned Tony Blair, Jacques Chirac and German Chancellor Helmut Kohl shortly before the cruise missile strikes and asked for their support. Without having time to consult their lawyers, all three leaders agreed – and subsequently made concurring public statements immediately following the US action. As a result of the timely expressions of support, other countries were more restrained in their response than they might have been. And this muted response probably contributed, again, to obfuscating the limits of self-defence, making the rule more susceptible to change in a subsequent situation.

That situation soon arose as a result of the terrorist attacks of 11 September 2001. At the time, there were several legal justifications available to the United States for the use of force in Afghanistan. Washington could have argued that it was acting at the invitation of the Northern Alliance, it could have sought explicit authorisation for military action from the UN Security Council, or it could (perhaps) have claimed a right of humanitarian intervention – since millions of Afghan lives were at risk from famine during the winter of 2001–2002.[13] Yet it chose to focus on a single justification: a right of self-defence against terrorism.

In focusing on self-defence against terrorism, the United States found itself in something of a legal dilemma. In order to build and maintain a coalition of countries willing to use force against terrorism, the response to the 11 September 2001 attacks had to comply with the *Caroline* criteria of necessity and proportionality.[14] The military action thus had to be focused on those individuals believed responsible for the 3,000 deaths. But if the United States had singled out Bin Laden and Al'Qaeda as its targets, it would have run up against the widely held view that terrorist attacks, in and of themselves, do not justify military responses within the territory of sovereign countries. Even today, most countries are wary of a rule that could expose them to attack whenever terrorists were thought to operate from within their borders.

---

[12] Secretary of State Madeline Albright and National Security Adviser Samuel Berger, 'News Briefing', FDCH Political Transcripts, Thursday, 20 August 1998.
[13] See Michael Byers, 'Terrorism, the Use of Force and International Law after 11 September', *International & Comparative Law Quarterly*, 51 (2002), p. 401; reprinted in *International Relations*, 16 (2002), p. 155.
[14] See discussion: *supra*, p. 52.

Consider, for instance, the position of Germany after 11 September 2001: although the City of Hamburg unwittingly harboured several of the terrorists, few people would maintain that this fact alone could have justified a US attack.

The dilemma was overcome when the United States implicated the Taliban. By giving refuge to Bin Laden and Al'Qaeda and refusing to hand them over, the Taliban was alleged to have deliberately facilitated and endorsed their actions. The United States even gave the Taliban a deadline for surrendering Bin Laden, a move that served to ensure their complicity. Moreover, the Taliban's continued control over Afghanistan was portrayed as a threat, in and of itself, of even more terrorism.[15]

In this way, the United States framed its claim in a manner that encompassed action against the state of Afghanistan, without asserting the right to use force against terrorists regardless of their location. Although still contentious, this claim was much less of a stretch from pre-existing international law than a claimed right to attack terrorists who simply happened to be within another country. Subsequent statements by the Taliban that endorsed the terrorist acts further raised the level of their alleged responsibility. For these reasons, the claim to be acting in self-defence in Afghanistan – and the modification of customary international law that claim entailed – had a much better chance of securing the expressed or tacit support of other countries.

The United States also deployed its considerable influence to secure widespread support in advance of military action. The collective self-defence provisions of the 1949 North Atlantic Treaty and the 1947 Inter-American Treaty of Reciprocal Assistance were engaged, and both NATO and the Organization of American States formally deemed the events of 11 September 2001 an 'armed attack' – legally relevant language under the self-defence provision of the UN Charter. Similarly, UN Security Council resolutions adopted on 12 and 28 September 2001 were carefully worded to affirm the right of self-defence in customary international law, within the context of the terrorist attacks on New York and Washington, DC.[16]

As a result of the strategic approach adopted by the United States, its newfound influence as the single superpower and the resulting widespread support for its legal argument and action against Afghanistan, the right of self-defence now includes military responses against countries that willingly harbour or support terrorist groups, provided that the terrorists have already struck the responding state. The long-term consequences of this development may be significant. Few countries would have objected if the United States had relied on arguments of invitation, Security Council authorisation or even humanitarian intervention, but acting alone might have been made more difficult for Washington in future. Having seized the opportunity to establish self-defence as a basis for military action against terrorists and governments that willingly support them, the United States, and other countries, will be able to invoke it again in circumstances which are less grave, or where the responsibility of the targeted state is less clear. And, as with the possible extension of self-defence to include punitive actions, the newly elongated right will diminish the

[15] See John Negroponte, 'Letter dated 7 October 2001 from the Permanent Representative of the United States of America to the United Nations addressed to the President of the Security Council', UN Doc. S/2001/946, 7 October 2001, available at ⟨http://www.un.int/usa/s-2001/6946.htm⟩.

[16] SC Res. 1368, UN Doc SC/7143; SC Res. 1373, UN Doc SC/7158; both available at ⟨http://www.un.org/Docs/scres/2001/sc2001.htm⟩.

relevance and authority of the United Nations on matters concerning the use of military force.

The extension of the right of self-defence to include military action against states that willingly harbour or support terrorists was the result of a deliberate effort to change the rules on military action. The single superpower is able to exercise considerable influence on international law-making, at least when it consciously and strategically seeks to do so. Yet it still needs to persuade other countries. The following example, of an equally deliberate effort to secure an extended right of pre-emptive self-defence, demonstrates the limits that exist upon the United States' ability to influence law-making.

Pre-emptive self-defence

On 7 June 1981, nine Israeli air force pilots conducted a bold and dangerous raid deep into hostile territory. Hugging the ground to avoid detection, they flew more than 600 miles before dropping their bombs on a nuclear reactor under construction at Osirak, near Baghdad. The reactor was badly damaged, Iraq's nuclear programme was seriously impaired, and none of the attacking planes were lost. Israel claimed that it had engaged in pre-emptive self-defence on the basis that a nuclear-armed Iraq would constitute an unacceptable threat, especially given Saddam Hussein's overt hostility towards the Jewish state. The UN Security Council immediately and unanimously condemned the action as illegal.[17] The condemnation was all the stronger because the United States joined in the vote rather than abstaining. In the British House of Commons, then-Prime Minister Margaret Thatcher said that an 'armed attack in such circumstances cannot be justified; it represents a grave breach of international law'.[18] Other governments were equally critical.

More than customary international law was at issue, since the UN Charter sets out its general prohibition on the use of force before recognising the right of self-defence 'if an armed attack occurs'. Interpreting the self-defence provision of the Charter requires that we look to the customary international law rules of treaty interpretation, which are codified in the 1969 Vienna Convention on the Law of Treaties and stipulate that treaties must be interpreted in accordance with the 'ordinary meaning of the terms'.[19] When this approach is applied, any pre-existing right of pre-emptive self-defence is apparently superseded by the 'if an armed attack occurs' language – particularly since self-defence is codified as an exception to the prohibition on the use of force and, as an exception, should be construed narrowly.

However, the UN Charter also refers to the 'inherent' character of the right of self-defence. This reference complicates the analysis by implicitly incorporating the pre-existing customary international law of self-defence into the treaty. Consequently, it is sometimes argued that pre-emptive action is justified if there is a 'necessity of self-defence, instant, overwhelming, leaving no choice of means, and no

---

[17] SC Res. 487 (1981), available at ⟨http://www.un.org/Docs/scres/1981/scres81.htm⟩.

[18] 'Israel blasts Iraq's reactor and creates a global shock wave', *Time Magazine* (US edition), 22 June 1981, p. 24.

[19] Article 31, *Vienna Convention on the Law of Treaties*, available at ⟨http://www.un.org/law/ilc/texts/treatfra.htm⟩.

moment of deliberation' – the *Caroline* criteria in their original, full expression. Until the adoption of the UN Charter in 1945, these criteria were widely accepted as delimiting a narrow right of pre-emptive self-defence in customary international law. Today, even a narrow right of pre-emption can only exist if the language of the Charter is ignored, re-read, or viewed as having been modified by subsequent state practice. Yet during the latter half of the twentieth century, most of the state practice cut the other way.

Since 1945, most governments have refrained from claiming pre-emptive self-defence.[20] The United States, concerned about establishing a precedent that other countries might employ, implausibly justified its 1962 blockade of Cuba as 'regional peacekeeping'. Israel, concerned not to be seen as an aggressor state, justified the strikes that initiated the 1967 Six-Day War on the basis that Egypt's blocking of the Straits of Tiran constituted a prior act of aggression. And in 1988, the United States argued that the shooting down of an Iranian civilian Airbus by the USS *Vincennes*, although mistaken, had been in response to an ongoing attack by Iranian military helicopters and patrol boats. Even the most hawkish leaders baulked at a right of pre-emptive action during the Cold War, at a time when both the world's principal disputants possessed armadas of nuclear missile submarines designed to survive first strikes and ensure 'mutually assured destruction'. The unanimous vote in the Security Council to condemn the 1981 Osirak bombing was but the clearest indication of this thinking. That said, during the Cold War there was widespread acceptance, in one very particular context, of what could be considered a narrow right of pre-emption: namely, the right to launch missiles as soon as it became clear that enemy missiles were incoming, without having to wait for them to strike.

Today, as seen from the White House, the situation looks quite different. Relations with Russia have improved, no other potential enemy has submarine-based nuclear missiles (though China may eventually acquire some), and the first phase of a missile defence system has been initiated. When President George W. Bush announced an expansive new policy of pre-emptive military action on 1 June 2002, he clearly did not feel deterred by the prospect of Armageddon.

During a commencement speech at West Point, President Bush addressed the threat of weapons of mass destruction (WMD) in association with international terrorism. He advocated a degree of pre-emption that extended towards the preventive or even precautionary use of force: 'We must take the battle to the enemy, disrupt his plans, and confront the worst threats before they emerge'. Even if the threats are not imminent, 'if we wait for threats to fully materialise, we will have waited too long'.[21] The new policy – now widely referred to as the 'Bush Doctrine' – made no attempt to satisfy the *Caroline* criteria. There was no suggestion of waiting for a 'necessity of self-defence' that was 'instant, overwhelming, leaving no choice of means, and no moment of deliberation'. As a policy statement, the Bush Doctrine was a radical departure from the US position during the Cold War.

The staff lawyers and diplomats in the US State Department were undoubtedly aware that the President's words at West Point had little chance of achieving the

---

[20] See Michael Byers, 'Preemptive Self-defense: Hegemony, Equality and Strategies of Legal Change', *Journal of Political Philosophy*, 11 (2003), p. 171.

[21] Remarks by President George W. Bush at 2002 Graduation Exercise of the United States Military Academy West Point, New York, available at ⟨http://www.whitehouse.gov/news/releases/2002/06/20020601-3.htm⟩.

widespread international support required to change customary international law. Relatively few countries possess enough of a military deterrence to be able to contemplate a world without the combined protections of the UN Charter and the *Caroline* criteria. Accordingly, the Bush Doctrine was reformulated to make it more acceptable to other countries, and thereby more effective in promoting legal change. The National Security Strategy of the United States, released on 20 September 2002, explicitly adopted – and then sought to extend – the criteria for self-defence articulated by Daniel Webster following the *Caroline* incident:

> For centuries, international law recognised that nations need not suffer an attack before they can lawfully take action to defend themselves against forces that present an imminent danger of attack. Legal scholars and international jurists often conditioned the legitimacy of preemption on the existence of an imminent threat – most often a visible mobilisation of armies, navies, and air forces preparing to attack.
>   We must adapt the concept of imminent threat to the capabilities and objectives of today's adversaries.[22]

In other words, the National Security Strategy took George W. Bush's newly articulated policy of prevention or precaution and recast it within the widely accepted, pre-existing framework of pre-emptive self-defence. It did so, first, by omitting any mention of the UN Charter, thus implicitly asserting that the pre-1945 customary right of self-defence remained the applicable law. By glossing over the problematic relationship between the *Caroline* criteria and the Charter, the document strategically sought to establish a new baseline for the legal discussion. Only then did it go further, asserting that the criterion of imminence now extends beyond threats which are 'instant, overwhelming, leaving no choice of means, and no moment of deliberation', to include more distant and uncertain challenges.

The claim was made within a context that at least suggested the need for legal change. Few would contest that terrorism and WMD are serious problems. But more significantly, other governments were not actually asked to agree to a change in the rule. Instead, all the National Security Strategy proposed was an adaptation of how the (supposed) existing rule is applied in practice. The claim was designed to appear patently reasonable and, as such, deserving of widespread support and acquiescence. Such support and acquiescence, once combined with military action justified on the basis of the claim, would then generate new customary international law.

Yet the reformulated doctrine of pre-emptive self-defence is not as innocuous as it first appears. By adopting the pre-1945 criterion of imminence and stretching it to encompass new facts, the approach advocated in the National Security Strategy could introduce considerably more ambiguity into the law. This ambiguity could, in turn, allow power and influence to play a greater role in the law's application. In future, whether the criterion of imminence is fulfilled would depend in large part on the factual circumstances – as assessed by individual states and groups of states. And the ability of the powerful to influence these assessments could be considerable, given the various forms of political, economic and military pressure that can be brought to bear in international affairs. In addition, powerful countries sometimes have special knowledge based on secret intelligence, or at least claim such knowledge in an

---

[22] National Security Strategy of the United States, 20 September 2002, p. 19, available at ⟨http://www.whitehouse/gov/nsc/nss.html⟩.

attempt to augment their influence, as occurred before the 2003 Iraq War. As a result, the criterion of imminence would more likely be regarded as fulfilled when the United States wished to act militarily, than when other countries wished to do the same. The law on self-defence would remain generally applicable – available as a diplomatic tool to be deployed against weak states – while the most powerful of countries would gain greater freedom to act as it chose.

Fortunately, the US government does not have a monopoly on good international lawyers. A few regional powers, such as India, Israel, and Russia, responded favourably to the claim set out in the National Security Strategy, as did Australian Prime Minister John Howard, who suggested that the UN Charter be amended to allow for a right of unilateral pre-emptive action. But Howard's comments sparked angry protests from other Southeast Asian states – protests that contribute to reinforcing the pre-existing customary international law. Other countries, including France, Germany and Mexico, expressed concern in more moderate terms while Japan voiced support for a right of pre-emptive self-defence but was careful to confine its claim to the *Caroline* criteria. More recently, it has been revealed that the British Attorney General, Lord Goldsmith, deemed the Bush Doctrine illegal in a highly confidential legal opinion that was provided to Prime Minister Tony Blair on 7 March 2003.[23]

This at-best mixed reaction would, in itself, have prevented any change in the customary international law of self-defence. And as the Iraq crisis escalated, it also contributed to bringing the United States to the UN Security Council where, on 8 November 2002, Resolution 1441 was adopted unanimously.[24] Although the resolution did not expressly authorise the use of force against Iraq, it did provide some support for an argument that a previous authorisation, accorded in 1990, had been revived as a result of Iraq's 'material breaches' of the 1991 cease-fire resolution and, later, Resolution 1441. The Bush administration relied on both this argument and the pre-emptive self-defence claim to justify the 2003 Iraq War, while its two principal allies, Britain and Australia, relied solely on the Security Council resolutions. The advancement of two distinct arguments, with the latter receiving broader support, reduced any effect that the claim to an extended right of pre-emption might have had on customary international law.

Opposition to the Bush Doctrine has continued to grow, and not just among governments. In December 2004, the UN Secretary General's High Level Panel on Threats, Challenges and Change, a group of 16 former prime ministers, foreign ministers and ambassadors (including Brent Scowcroft, who served as National Security Adviser to President George H.W. Bush), presented its highly authoritative response to the US President's claim:

The short answer is that if there are good arguments for preventive military action, with good evidence to support them, they should be put to the Security Council, which can authorise such action if it chooses to. If it does not so choose, there will be, by definition, time to pursue other strategies, including persuasion, negotiation, deterrence and containment – and to visit again the military option.

For those impatient with such a response, the answer must be that, in a world full of perceived potential threats, the risk to the global order and the norm of non-intervention on which it continues to be based is simply too great for the legality of unilateral

---

[23] Available at ⟨http://news.bbc.co.uk/1/shared/bsp/hi/pdfs/28_04_05_attorney_general.pdf⟩.
[24] SC Res. 1441 (2002), available at: ⟨http://www.un.org/Docs/scres/2002/sc2002.htm⟩.

preventive action, as distinct from collectively endorsed action, to be accepted. Allowing one to so act is to allow all.[25]

The Bush Doctrine of pre-emptive self-defence represents a failure of US policy with regard to international law-making, resulting from a refusal to pay greater heed to the law-making interests of other countries and frame the claim accordingly. Nevertheless, the claim has resulted in a degree of legal change, or at least legal clarification. Today, much more than just five years ago, it is difficult to find an international lawyer who argues that there is *no* right of pre-emptive self-defence whatsoever. The academic debates over the meaning of 'if an armed attack occurs' that raged during the latter half of the twentieth century, have been replaced by a general acceptance that a narrow right of pre-emptive self-defence exists, as it did before 1945, in 'cases in which the necessity of that self-defence is instant, overwhelming, leaving no choice of means, and no moment of deliberation'. The power and influence of the United States is such that, even when it fails in a law-making effort, it still leaves a mark on international rules.

A similar pattern, of an unsuccessful effort at major legal change resulting in smaller but still significant normative alterations, can be seen in US efforts to justify violations of international humanitarian law with regard to the treatment of detainees.

Treatment of detainees

The treatment of detainees during and after armed conflict is governed by rules of customary international law that have been codified in the four Geneva Conventions of 1949 and a number of other treaties. According to this body of law – the *jus in bello* or international humanitarian law – soldiers are legitimate targets during armed conflict. Killing members of the enemy's armed forces is one of the goals of military action.

Civilians, in contrast, must not intentionally be killed. However, civilians can be protected in time of armed conflict only if a distinction is maintained between combatants and non-combatants. This differentiation is achieved by offering combatants the protection of prisoner of war status if captured, as long as they are in a chain of command, wearing a fixed distinctive emblem (usually a shoulder patch), carrying their arms openly and acting in accordance with international humanitarian law. Prisoners of war must be treated humanely. They cannot be killed, tortured, used as human shields, held hostage, or used to clear landmines.

The incentive of prisoner of war status is not always effective, especially in conflicts involving irregular forces in poorer countries, and some experts argue that the distinctive emblem requirement is inconsistent with modern forms of war. Apart from their turbans, the armed forces of the Taliban government did not wear anything approaching uniforms during the 2001 Afghanistan War, though they were in a chain of command, carried their arms openly and, for the most part, abided by international humanitarian law.

---

[25] 'A More Secure World: Our Shared Responsibility – Report of the Secretary General's High Level Panel on Threats, Challenges and Change', p. 63, available at ⟨http://www.un.org/secureworld⟩.

The distinction between combatants and non-combatants is also threatened by the practice of US special forces, which constitute an increasingly important part of the US military yet have – with the apparent support of Secretary of Defense Donald Rumsfeld – taken to wearing civilian clothing. The practice has been challenged. When the New Zealand government sent a contingent of commandos to fight in Afghanistan, it refused to allow the soldiers to wear civilian clothes, a decision that created some friction with the United States. The decision was correct: if special forces – indeed, any soldiers – are captured operating out of uniform, they are not entitled to the protections owed prisoners of war regardless of the country for which they fight.

Rumsfeld's disdain for international humanitarian law became public in January 2002 when suspected Taliban and Al'Qaeda members were transported to the US naval base at Guantanamo Bay, Cuba. Ignoring public criticism from a number of European leaders, the UN High Commissioner for Human Rights and even the normally neutral and very discrete International Committee of the Red Cross, the Defense Secretary insisted the detainees could not be prisoners of war and refused to convene the tribunals required under Article 5 of the Third Geneva Convention to determine their status. Rumsfeld also ignored advice from the Pentagon's own lawyers, the 'judge advocates', and based his decision on an analysis of international humanitarian law by then White House Counsel (now Attorney General) Alberto Gonzales, a former corporate lawyer. Four years after the war in Afghanistan, some 550 suspects remain at Guantanamo Bay despite having never been charged or granted access to counsel.

In November 2002, the English Court of Appeal described the position of the Guantanamo Bay detainees as 'legally objectionable'; it was as if they were in a 'legal black hole'.[26] The situation has improved marginally since then. In June 2004, the US Supreme Court finally addressed the matter. On behalf of a 6-3 majority of judges, Justice John Paul Stevens wrote:

Executive imprisonment has been considered oppressive and lawless since John, at Runnymede, pledged that no free man should be imprisoned, dispossessed, outlawed, or exiled save by judgment of his peers or by the law of the land. The judges of England developed the writ of habeas corpus largely to preserve these immunities from executive restraint.[27]

Justice Stevens went on to hold that anyone detained by the US government outside the United States has the right to have the legal basis for his detention reviewed by a US federal court. Just one week later, the Pentagon announced that it would in fact convene the status determination tribunals required by Article 5 of the Third Geneva Convention.

Other violations of international humanitarian law have been committed against detainees in Afghanistan, Iraq, and elsewhere. In November 2001, a prisoner revolt at Mazar-i-Sharif in Afghanistan was put down with air-to-surface missiles and B-52 launched bombs. More than 175 detainees were killed; 50 died with their hands tied

---

[26] *Abbasi & Anor., R (on the application of)* v. *Secretary of State for Foreign & Commonwealth Affairs & Secretary of State for the Home Department*, Court of Appeal of England and Wales (Civil Division), 6 November 2002, available at ⟨http://www.bailii.org.cgi-bin/markup.cgi?doc=/ew/cases/ EWCA/Civ/2002/1598.html⟩.

[27] *Rasul* v. *Bush*, 321 F.3d 1134, reversed and remanded, 8 June 2004, available at ⟨http:// supct.law.cornell.edu/supct/html/03-334.ZO.html⟩.

behind their backs. In December 2002, the *Washington Post* reported on the use of 'stress and duress' techniques during interrogations at Bagram Air Base, also in Afghanistan.[28] In March 2003, the *New York Times* reported that, while in custody over a three month period, a suspected member of Al'Qaeda was 'fed very little, while being subjected to sleep and light deprivation, prolonged isolation and room temperatures that varied from 100 degrees to 10 degrees.'[29] Also in March 2003, the *New York Times* reported that a death certificate, signed by a US military pathologist, stated the cause of death of a 22 year-old Afghan detainee at Bagram Air Base in December 2002 as 'blunt force injuries to lower extremities complicating coronary artery disease.'[30] The form gave the pathologist four choices for 'mode of death': 'natural, accident, suicide, homicide'. She marked the box for homicide.

In July 2003, UN Secretary General Kofi Annan reported to the Security Council that his Special Representative for Iraq, the late Sergio Vieira de Mello, had expressed concern to the United States and Britain about their treatment of thousands of detained Iraqis. One week later, Amnesty International claimed that US forces in Iraq were resorting to 'prolonged sleep deprivation, prolonged restraint in painful positions – sometimes combined with exposure to loud music, prolonged hooding and exposure to bright lights'.[31]

Regrettably, the reports failed to attract widespread media attention until March 2004, when it became known that the *New Yorker* was about to publish photographs of prisoner abuse at Abu Ghraib Prison near Baghdad, together with a damning report by investigative journalist Seymour Hersh. At this point, CBS television decided to air photographs it had been suppressing for several weeks, reportedly at the behest of the Bush administration. The photographs showed detainees stripped naked, ridiculed, piled on top of each other, being raped, forced to masturbate, bitten by dogs, and terrorised with the threat of electrocution. The actions were blatant violations of international humanitarian law.

Given the proximity to the 2003 Iraq War, it is likely that some of the detainees at Abu Ghraib were prisoners of war. If so, the captors who abused them violated the Third Geneva Convention, Article 13 of which provides that POWs 'must at all times be protected, particularly against acts of violence or intimidation and against insults and public curiosity.'[32] To reinforce the point, Article 14 stipulates that prisoners of war 'are entitled in all circumstances to respect for their persons and their honour'.

Any of the captives at Abu Ghraib who were not prisoners of war were probably still protected by Common Article 3 of the Geneva Conventions. This provision requires that, even in armed conflicts not of an international character (as, arguably, the situation in Iraq had become), persons taking no part in the hostilities are protected absolutely from 'violence to life and person, in particular murder of all

---

[28] Dana Priest and Barton Gellman, 'US Decries Abuse but Defends Interrogations; 'Stress and Duress' Tactics Used on Terrorism Suspects Held in Secret Overseas Facilities', *Washington Post*, 26 Dec. 2002, A1.

[29] Don Van Natta Jr.,' Questioning Terror Suspects In a Dark and Surreal World', *New York Times*, 9 March 2003, p. 1.

[30] Carlotta Gall, 'US Military Investigating Death of Afghan in Custody', *New York Times*, 4 March 2003, A14.

[31] Amnesty International, 'The Threat of a Bad Example – Undermining International Standards as "War on Terror" Detentions Continue', AI Index: AMR 51/114/2003, 19 August 2003, available at ⟨http://web.amnesty.org/library/Index/ENGAMR511142003⟩.

[32] *Third Geneva Convention relative to the Treatment of Prisoners of War*, available at ⟨http://www.icrc.org/Web/Eng/siteeng0.nsf/html/genevaconventions⟩.

kinds, mutilation, cruel treatment and torture' as well as 'outrages upon personal dignity, in particular, humiliating and degrading treatment'.

Regardless of the status of the detainees, some of the outrages committed against them were violations of their right not be tortured. This fundamental rule of customary international law was codified prominently in the 1984 Convention against Torture, a treaty ratified by the United States. Article 1 of the Convention defines torture as:

[A]ny act by which severe pain or suffering, whether physical or mental, is intentionally inflicted on a person for such purposes as obtaining from him or a third person information or a confession, punishing him for an act he or a third person has committed or is suspected of having committed, or intimidating or coercing him or a third person, or for any reason based on discrimination of any kind, when such pain or suffering is inflicted by or at the instigation of or with the consent or acquiescence of a public official or other person acting in an official capacity.[33]

A confidential memorandum, prepared for Secretary of Defense Rumsfeld by a group of Bush administration lawyers in March 2003 and obtained by the *Washington Post* in June 2004, argued that the President was not bound by the provisions of the Third Geneva Convention or the Convention against Torture, at least insofar as these international rules have been implemented in US domestic law.[34] The analysis was based on an earlier Department of Justice memorandum that made a series of dubious assumptions – including that none of the detainees were prisoners of war and that customary international law and US federal law are hermetically sealed from each other – that together transformed legal analysis into an exercise in politically motivated justification. The memorandum was written by John Yoo, a political appointee who has since returned to his regular position as a law professor at the University of California, Berkeley. The *New York Times* reported that the then State Department Legal Adviser, William Taft IV, dissented from the group's analysis and its conclusions, 'warning that such a position would weaken the protections of the Geneva Conventions for American Troops'.[35]

The abuse of detainees engages the responsibility not only of individual soldiers. Under a principle of international criminal law known as 'command responsibility', individuals higher in the chain of command – including defense secretaries and presidents who serve as commanders-in-chief – may also commit war crimes if they know, or have reason to know, that their subordinates are committing or about to commit crimes and fail to take all feasible steps to prevent or stop them. The existence of memoranda seeking to justify war crimes, originating from the central legal offices of the White House, Pentagon and Department of Justice, certainly suggests that in this instance there was knowledge well up the chain of command.

Additional violations of international humanitarian law were committed when the International Committee of the Red Cross was denied access to some parts of Abu Ghraib Prison, and to some detainees, as reportedly occurred early in 2004. Under the 1949 Geneva Conventions and the 1977 Additional Protocols, the ICRC is

---

[33] *Convention against Torture and Other Cruel, Inhuman or Degrading Treatment or Punishment*, available at ⟨http://www.ohchr.org/english/law/cat.htm⟩.

[34] Dana Priest and R. Jeffrey Smith, 'Memo Offered Justification for Use of Torture; Justice Dept. Gave Advice in 2002', *Washington Post*, 8 June 2004, A1.

[35] Neil A. Lewis and Eric Schmitt, 'Lawyers Decided Bans on Torture Didn't Bind Bush', *New York Times*, 8 June 2004, A1.

mandated to visit and register prisoners of war. This right of access is essential because it promotes the good treatment of prisoners of war and ensures they do not disappear. Although the ICRC traditionally does not publicly denounce governments that fail to uphold international humanitarian law – in order to preserve its neutrality, thereby ensuring future access to prisoners and civilians in need – it has, on several occasions since 2001, openly expressed concern about the actions of the United States.

Many of the ICRC's concerns persist today with regard to persons detained by the United States or its allies in a variety of known and unknown locations, including at a US airbase on the British-owned Indian Ocean island of Diego Garcia. The ICRC has not been provided access to these individuals – itself a violation – and there is no way of knowing whether they are being tortured, otherwise mistreated, or killed.

In the same context, a second confidential memorandum obtained by the *Washington Post* in October 2004 was reportedly used to justify a related war crime: the transfer of detainees out of occupied Iraq for interrogation elsewhere.[36] Article 49 of the Fourth Geneva Convention protects civilians during an occupation by unambiguously prohibiting 'individual or mass forcible transfers, as well as deportation of protected persons from occupied territory . . . regardless of their motive.' Indeed, one of the principal purposes of the Fourth Geneva Convention is to prevent persons from being moved out of an occupied territory and thus out of the oversight of the ICRC. The memorandum, which strains legal credulity, was written by Jack Goldsmith, who served as a political appointee in the Pentagon and Department of Justice and is now a professor of law at Harvard University.

Finally, even alleged terrorists are protected by a ban on extra-judicial killing found in customary international law and numerous human rights treaties. When it comes to extra-judicial killings, George W. Bush's State of the Union address in January 2003 included a seemingly indicative admission: 'All told, more than 3,000 suspected terrorists have been arrested in many countries. Many others have met a different fate. Let's put it this way – they are no longer a problem to the United States and our friends and allies.'[37] Previous administrations at least paid lip service to the existence of normative constraints by concealing and denying their covert operations.

The existence of all this law-breaking is all the more troubling because of its possible effects on international humanitarian law. The problem is not so much that other countries will take up the dubious justifications advanced by US government lawyers and use them to support their own mistreatment of detainees, though there are certain arguments – such as an argument that a new category of 'unlawful combatants' should be read into the Third Geneva Convention alongside prisoners of war and civilians – that have resonated with some decision-makers and commentators. The problem, rather, is that the United States has abdicated its position as the leading champion of strong protections for combatants and civilians during and after armed conflict. Instead of serving as a positive role model for other countries, the United States undermines the rules by demonstrating contempt for them. The long-term effects of this negative signalling should not be underestimated. Even in better times, protections for individual human beings rarely counted among the

---

[36] Dana Priest, 'Memo Lets CIA Take Detainees Out of Iraq; Practice Is Called Serious Breach of Geneva Conventions', *Washington Post*, 24 October 2004, A1.

[37] President George W. Bush, State of the Union, 28 January 2003, available at: ⟨http://www.whitehouse.gov/news/releases/2003/01/20030128-19.html⟩.

principal interests of states. In a world in turmoil after 11 September 2001 and America's subsequent over-reaction, secondary interests are more easily sacrificed, particularly when no country has, as yet, assumed the positive leadership role left vacant by the United States.

Analysis

Hegemonic powers have always shaped the international legal system to their advantage. In the sixteenth century, Spain redefined basic concepts of justice and universality to justify the conquest of indigenous Americans. In the eighteenth century, France developed the modern concepts of borders and the 'balance of power' to suit its continental strengths. In the nineteenth century, Britain introduced new rules on piracy, neutrality and colonialism, again to suit its interests as the leading country of the age.[38]

In the early twenty-first century, when there is little prospect of a conventional war being fought on US territory, there are those who argue that the interests of the United States would be advanced by eliminating the legal restrictions on the use of force.[39] At the same time, however, the United States regularly depends on allies who value and abide by international law. On other occasions, the United States finds it useful to deploy legal arguments when seeking to persuade others not to use force themselves. This combined desire for flexibility, constraint and general compliance would seem to be one of the factors behind the law-making and law-changing efforts of the United States, as seen in several of the examples above. Even when the US government wishes to act inconsistently with international law, it usually seeks to justify its behaviour in legal terms. Moreover, its lawyers regularly and actively seek to change the law, by renouncing existing treaties or negotiating new ones, or by provoking and steering changing patterns of behaviour with a view to modifying customary rules and widely accepted treaty interpretations. They do not generally seek an absence of legal constraints.

The administration of George W. Bush has been particularly well placed to modify international law, having inherited a country with almost unprecedented military, economic and political power. The events of 11 September 2001 strengthened its position yet further, generating global concern about terrorism, widespread sympathy for the United States, and concern about what might happen to those that stood in its way. The President's advisers have taken full advantage of the situation, applying pressure in pursuit of goals that, under normal circumstances, would have been more difficult to achieve. Among these goals has been greater flexibility to use force outside the UN Charter, and more leeway in the treatment of detainees.

To the degree the Bush administration succeeds in its law-changing efforts – and it has not yet succeeded with regard to pre-emptive self-defence and the treatment of detainees – its successes will have deleterious effects. Whenever it creates greater

[38] See generally, Wilhelm G. Grewe, *The Epochs of International Law* translated and revised by Michael Byers, (Berlin: Walter De Gruyter, 2000).
[39] See John R. Bolton, 'Is There Really "Law" in International Affairs?' *Transnational Law & Contemporary Problems*, 10 (2000), p. 1; Michael J. Glennon, *Limits of Law, Prerogatives of Power: Interventionism After Kosovo* (New York: Palgrave Macmillan, 2001).

flexibility to use force, it contributes to marginalising the United Nations in the field of international peace and security, thus rendering it more difficult for governments to draw upon this important source of legitimacy for the use of military force. Whenever it seeks more leeway in the treatment of detainees, it squanders moral authority and the capability to influence and persuade. All this in turn diminishes the potential for cooperative, multilateral responses to threats and breaches of the peace – responses that would share the military and financial burdens of intervention among larger numbers of countries, and reduce the resentments that armed interventions so easily feed.

Yet the international rules on military force have proven quite resilient in the face of US efforts. This is probably due to several factors, including a widespread realisation that the changes sought would result in less rather than more international peace and security. Governments everywhere are now aware that, while terrorism can cause great destruction and upheaval, efforts to stamp it out can serve as a smokescreen for the pursuit of less worthy goals, or at least have serious unanticipated consequences. Even some of the United States' closest allies, while providing strong support for the American people, have begun providing cooperation on specific issues only after careful consideration of their best interests, which prominently include the maintenance of a just, strong, equal and effective system of international law.

A second factor explaining the resilience is that rules, by their very nature, are more resistant to change than many of the other components of the international system. Indeed, a norm or standard can hardly be considered a rule if it is subject to alteration at the whim of those whom it supposedly constrains. And some rules of international law are more resistant to change, more deeply embedded in the international system, than others.[40] In the case of customary international law, this resistance to change develops through the gradual accretion of state practice and *opinio juris* (a subjective belief in the existence of obligation). In the case of treaties, resistance develops through the widespread ratification of the treaty in question, which renders renegotiation difficult, or through the inclusion of a super-majority requirement or veto in the treaty's amendment provisions. Not surprisingly, some of the international legal system's most resistant rules protect foundational aspects of state sovereignty, such as the right of non-intervention, or core aspects of human dignity such as the prohibition on torture. It could take decades before the full impact of the United States' post-Cold War rise to hegemonic status, together with the paradigm-shifting events of 11 September 2001, is manifested in the rules governing recourse to military force, the conduct of hostilities, and the treatment of detainees.

A third factor in the resilience of the rules on military force could be the growing complexity of the international legal system and the multiplicity and diversity of actors involved in it. During the 1990s, academic commentators ascribed considerable significance to the decline of the sovereign state and the rise of inter-governmental organisations, transnational corporations and NGOs. It is indisputable that non-state actors such as the International Committee of the Red Cross and Amnesty International play an important role in the maintenance, development and change of international rules. The contemporary international legal

[40] See generally, Michael Byers, *Custom, Power and the Power of Rules* (Cambridge: Cambridge University Press, 1999).

system involves a matrix of diverse law-making interests and influences that make it qualitatively different from previous configurations of that system, and more difficult for hegemonic influence to be exercised.[41]

At the same time, the impact of a larger and more varied group of actors may be less significant with regard to rules, such as those on military force, that operate in areas where the monopoly of state power remains relatively unchallenged. The need for analytical caution is particularly evident when one considers the scale of US military predominance: troops deployed in over 140 countries and a defence budget that comprises 47 per cent of global military expenditures.[42] One of the more startling consequences of 11 September 2001 has been the return of the state as the dominant force in international affairs, with security as its central obsession.

Finally, it is not clear that one should wish to deny the United States significant influence on the making and changing of the international rules governing military force. Although the United States has an interest in maintaining a system of widely agreed rules, both to facilitate cooperation and to constrain others, it is also powerful enough to walk away from these rules, or at least to frequently violate them – if it felt its particular circumstances and interests were not adequately taken into account. The international community thus finds itself in a peculiar position: unable to impose new rules on the single superpower, able to impede its law-changing efforts, and fully aware that too much intransigence could carry a heavy price. It is therefore important that we pay attention to US perspectives and interests concerning the use of military force, while standing firm in defence of existing rules if and when the United States unreasonably violates or otherwise seeks to undermine them. The prevention of havoc involves an ongoing effort to keep the rules in place *and* to keep the powerful within the rules. That effort may have been a struggle of late, but the dogs of war remain closely leashed.

---

[41] See Grewe, *Epochs of International Law*, Epilogue.
[42] See *SIPR Yearbook 2005* (Stockholm: Stockholm Institute for Peace Research, 2005), summary at: ⟨http://yearbook2005.sipri.org/pressrl/SIPRIYB2005PRfinal.pdf⟩.

Liberal hierarchy and the licence to use force

CHRISTIAN REUS-SMIT*

Introduction

Determining when states can use force legitimately is the central normative problematic in world politics. Domestically, constraining the state's use of force with social and legal norms that confine state-sanctioned violence to a limited and clearly defined set of purposes and circumstances is essential to the maintenance of civil society and the protection of basic human rights. Internationally, circumscribing the conditions under which states may use force legitimately is critical to the maintenance of peace and stability in international society. And the degree to which legitimate force may be used internationally to constrain illegitimate force domestically lies at the heart of the problematic relationship between order and justice in world politics.

Ever so gradually, through the trials of war and colonialism, a set of principles have evolved internationally to govern when states may use force legitimately. First, recognised sovereign states are held to be legal equals, even if differences in capabilities are profound and certain institutional accommodations have been made to placate great powers. Second, sovereign equality gives all states a basket of governance rights internationally – enshrined in the general principle (if not in practice) of 'one state, one vote' – and rights of autonomy domestically, most notably the paired rights of self-determination and non-intervention. Third, to uphold these sovereign rights, the international use of force has been severely circumscribed. States may only use force in their relations with one another if (1) they are acting in self-defence, or (2) they are acting collectively to uphold international peace and security. Finally, in situations other than self-defence, decisions to use force must be made multilaterally through the Security Council of the United Nations.

Together, these principles constitute what I shall call the 'equalitarian regime', a regime codified in international law and practice in the period between the signing of the United Nations' Charter and the near complete dissolution of the European empires by the early 1970s. It is a regime riddled with contradictions. Legal equality sits uncomfortably with material inequality. The great powers have special rights in international institutions, most notably the veto power of the Permanent Five in the Security Council and weighted voting rights in international financial institutions. The rights of self-determination and non-intervention have been regularly compromised by great powers and corporate actors, while at the same time protecting autocrats from external interference. The concept of 'international peace and security' is one of protean flexibility, and the Security Council is at best a qualified multilateral forum.

* I would like to thank Alex Bellamy, Peter Lawler, Richard Price, Heather Rae, and the editors for their feedback on the arguments advanced in this article.

Notwithstanding these contradictions, the equalitarian regime's contribution to reducing interstate warfare represents one of the most significant (if qualified) achievements of the amorphous 'international community'. Since 1945 the number of recognised sovereign states has quadrupled, and with this the number of potential disputes over territory, identity, and resources. Yet as international society has expanded the number of traditional interstate wars has declined.

Despite this contribution, the equalitarian regime is now under challenge, and some of its most articulate challengers are prominent liberal scholars of political philosophy and international relations.[1] Informed by a mixture of Kantian liberalism and democratic peace theory, cosmopolitan sensibilities and activism, neoliberal institutionalism and new liberal legal theory, and post-September 11th security anxieties, these scholars question the equalitarian regime's version of international liberalism, advancing a markedly different formulation. They advocate the formal rehierarchisation of international society, whereby democratic states would gain special governance rights – particularly with regard to the legitimate use of force – and other states would have their categorical rights to self-determination and non-intervention qualified. With this move, an increasingly prominent strand of international liberalism risks converging, in unintended yet disturbing ways, with strands of neo-conservative thought and with the central policy prescriptions of the Bush Doctrine.

This article explores and critiques this liberal argument for the rehierarchisation of international society and its attendant prescriptions for the legitimate use of force.[2] After explaining the philosophical foundations of the equalitarian regime and its tortuous construction over the past century, I detail a range of factors that have, over the past decade, gnawed away at the regime's foundations. The article then turns to the exposition and critique of the new liberal argument. My critique has three nested layers. I begin by outlining a series of practical concerns about operationalising the new liberal argument. These practical concerns are reinforced by a series of prudential objections, objections that stress the harmful consequences for international order of replacing the equalitarian regime with a new hierarchy. Granting democracies special rights, especially in decisions to use force, can only exacerbate already widespread feelings about the inequities of the present international order, reduce the sense of investment of many states in the institutional architecture and rules of international society, and, as a consequence, heighten rather than diminish conflict and discord. The final layer of my critique turns liberalism itself against the case for renewed hierarchy. Above all else, liberalism, in both its domestic and international manifestations, has sought to separate political rights from the distribution of material power. Absolutism conjoined political right and material power in the figure of the sovereign, and the nineteenth century standard of civilisation conjoined such rights and power in the European states that placed themselves at the pinnacle of the civilisational hierarchy. Wittingly or not,

---

[1] See, for instance, Francis Fukuyama, *The End of History and the Last Man* (New York: The Free Press, 1992); John Rawls, *The Law of Peoples* (Cambridge, MA: Harvard University Press, 1999); David Held, *Democracy and the Global* Order (Stanford, CA: Stanford University Press, 1995), pp. 273–4; and Allen Buchanan and Robert O. Keohane, 'The Preventive Use of Force: A Cosmopolitan Institutional Proposal', *Ethics and International Affairs*, 18:1 (2004), pp. 1–22.

[2] For a different but complementary analysis of hierarchy in contemporary international society, see Tim Dunne, 'Society and Hierarchy in International Relations', *International Relations*, 17:3 (2003), pp. 303–20.

proponents of liberal hierarchy contradict the foundational tenets of liberalism by promoting a reconjoining of right and might.

The equalitarian regime

The equalitarian regime is a relatively new innovation in international relations. Before the Napoleonic Wars, the idea that all sovereigns were legally or socially equal was a radical proposition, one explicitly rejected at great moments of system building, such as the Peace of Westphalia.[3] Even when it took root among European states in the nineteenth century, it was drastically compromised by political and legal hierarchy that was integral to Europe's colonial rule of much of Asia, Africa, and the Americas.[4] The principle was only firmly enshrined with the signing of the United Nations Charter, Article 2 of which specifies that the 'Organization is based on the principle of the sovereign equality of all of its members'.[5] And even then it only became a general organising principle for the international system as a whole when decolonisation replaced the formal hierarchies of empire with the first global system of sovereign states.[6]

With the codification of sovereign equality, recognised states gained a basket of rights and entitlements. Some of these were governance rights, or rights of legal standing and participation in international society, including everything from the right to exchange ambassadors, membership of the United Nations, and an equal vote in international fora (notwithstanding several significant exceptions). Others were rights of domestic autonomy, principally the rights of self-determination and non-intervention. The UN Charter is categorical in asserting the 'territorial integrity' and 'political independence' of all states, and pledges that nothing 'shall authorise the United Nations to intervene in matters which are essentially within the domestic jurisdiction of any State . . .'.[7] The right to self-determination was also acknowledged in the Charter, but it was not until after the 1960 Declaration on the Granting of Independence to Colonial Countries and Peoples that its legal status was secured. The legal centrality of both the right to self-determination and the right to non-intervention was confirmed and reiterated in 1970 by the Declaration on Principles of International Law Concerning Friendly Relations and Cooperation Among States in Accordance with the Charter of the United Nations. 'The equal rights and self-determination of peoples' were upheld as 'a significant contribution to contemporary international law', and states were said to have 'The duty not to intervene in matters within the domestic jurisdiction of any State . . .'.[8]

---

[3] On the general question of when sovereign equality took root, see Martin Wight, *Systems of States* (Leicester: Leicester University Press, 1977), p. 136, and on sovereign equality at Westphalia see Francois de Callieres, *The Art of Diplomacy* (New York: Holmes and Meier, 1983), pp. 125–6.

[4] On the formal hierarchy of European imperialism, see Gerrit Gong, *The 'Standard of Civilization' in International Society* (Oxford: Clarendon Press, 1984).

[5] Charter of the United Nations, Article 2.1.

[6] The account presented here is broadly consistent with that presented by Gerry Simpson in his excellent study *Great Powers and Outlaw States: Unequal Sovereigns in the International Legal Order* (Cambridge: Cambridge University Press, 2004).

[7] Charter of the United Nations, Article 2.4, 2.7.

[8] Declaration on Principles of International Law Concerning Friendly Relations and Cooperation Among Sates in Accordance with the Charter of the United Nations, 1970, Preamble.

To prevent the scourge of war and protect the sovereign rights of all states, the legitimate use of force internationally has been confined to two specific occasions, the first being self-defence, the second collective actions to uphold international peace and security. Prior to the Second World War legal efforts to reduce interstate conflict had focused on banning 'war'. In the Kellogg-Briand Pact of 1928, the parties 'condemned "war" for the "solution of international controversies" and renounced war as an instrument of national policy'.[9] States soon found a way around this ban by becoming pedantic legalists. As both the Japanese and Chinese demonstrated in the Manchurian conflict of 1931, it was possible to remain within the bounds of the law by simply fighting without declaring war. The United Nations Charter adopted the more robust formulation of proscribing the 'threat or use of force against the territorial integrity or political independence of any State' (Article 2), irrespective of whether the protagonists have declared war officially. The exceptions to this proscription are the 'inherent right of individual or collective self-defence' (Article 51), and collective measures 'to maintain or restore international peace and security' (Article 42).

The final component of the equalitarian regime is the principle of multilateralism – the idea that decisions to use force collectively to uphold international peace and security can only be made by the Security Council of the United Nations. Although greatly complicated by the growth of international humanitarian law, and the clear obligations legal instruments such as the 1948 Genocide Convention place on states to act decisively, the baseline principle since the Second World War has been that a Security Council mandate is required to establish the legal legitimacy of collective deployments of force. If the UN Charter sets out the legal rules governing the legitimate use of force, the Security Council is the institutional mechanism designed to ensure that these rules are applied fairly and forcefully. Of course the principle of multilateralism is imperfectly expressed in the Security Council. On the one hand, a majority of Council members are elected by the General Assembly for two-year terms, giving even the smallest and weakest states an opportunity to participate, at least theoretically. On the other hand, the Council is dominated by the Permanent Five, all of whom enjoy the notorious power of veto. Notwithstanding these qualifications, however, the role of the Security Council in ordaining collective deployments of force with legitimacy is clearly evident in the differing public assessments of the first Gulf War and the on-going 'War in Iraq'. The former received unqualified Council endorsement, and is now seen as a classic example of a legally legitimate peace enforcement action; the latter, in contrast, failed to gain Council support, and the war has since been dogged by a persistent aura of illegitimacy, undermining the 'coalition of the willing's' capacity to socialise the substantial human and financial costs of the occupation.[10]

As noted above, the equalitarian regime is riddled with contradictions. Yet its contribution to reducing the incidence of interstate warfare should not be under-stated. In the life of the regime, the membership of the United Nations has grown from 51 to 191, and in the same period wars between states have declined. Data on the incidence of war is notoriously inconsistent – some scholars count any conflict

---

[9] Dino Kritsiotis, 'When States Use Armed Force', in Christian Reus-Smit (ed.), *The Politics of International Law* (Cambridge: Cambridge University Press, 2004), pp. 52–3.

[10] Christian Reus-Smit, *American Power and World Order* (Cambridge: Polity Press, 2004), ch. 6.

involving a state, others focus on conflicts between states that caused more than 1,000 deaths, and others include only conflicts that involved a great power.[11] Two things are clear, though: since 1945 the incidence of interstate conflicts has declined in absolute terms, even if marginally; and the ratio of recognised states to conflicts has dropped, dramatically.[12] This achievement has gone singularly unremarked, eclipsed by a decade of euphoria about the 'democratic peace'. It is closely linked, however, with parallel developments in the international system, especially the survival of militarily, economically, and institutionally weak states in the developing world, a phenomenon Robert Jackson links persuasively to the protections afforded by juridical sovereignty.[13]

A critic might respond that the relative decline in interstate war is more appropriately attributed to four decades of bipolarity, nuclear deterrence, the transformation of the great powers into trading states, or the spread of democracy. But the norms underlying the equalitarian regime have been a constant, system-wide factor, at least since the 1960s. These other factors were either distinctive to the Cold War, or relevant only to particular zones of international society. Bipolarity may have constrained war across the system, but it is now sixteen years since the fall of the Berlin Wall, and scholars are divided about whether the present amalgam of unipolarity and multipolarity is conducive or unconducive to international peace and stability. Nuclear deterrence may limit great-power war, but its capacity to impede conflict beyond the core of the system was always dependent upon the tight links that bipolarity forged between the superpowers and their 'Third World' spheres of influence. Some of the great powers may have transmuted into trading states, but the procrustean state is hardly extinct. And even the most ardent exponents of the democratic peace admit that it does not constrain violence between democratic and non-democratic states. None of this is to suggest that factors such as these have been irrelevant to the relative decline in interstate conflict, only that the equalitarian regime has been a necessary, if insufficient, condition for this system-wide phenomenon.

Despite its contribution, several factors have recently gnawed away at the foundations of the equalitarian regime. A critical factor has been the liberal triumphalism that has swept the 'West' since the end of the Cold War, a triumphalism that attributes to 'liberal democracies' an inherent peacefulness in their relations with one another, a greater 'moral reliability' than other states in their international relations, and an unmatched record of achievement in the protection of their citizens' civil and political rights. This ideological revolution has been reinforced by a series of empirical phenomena: principally, the plethora of humanitarian crises that punctuated the 1990s, and the unedifying responses of regional and global institutions; the related rise of the discourse and practice of humanitarian inter-vention, and associated notions of 'qualified', 'compromised', or 'associated' sovereignty; the attacks of September 11, and the heightened attention given to the

[11] See, for example, the Correlates of War project at ⟨http://www.correlatesofwar.org/⟩, Paul Huth and Todd Allee, *The Democratic Peace and Territorial Conflict in the Twentieth Century* (Cambridge: Cambridge University Press, 2003); and Evan Luard, *War in International Society* (I. B. Tauris, 1986).
[12] See John Mueller's article in this Special Issue.
[13] Robert Jackson, *Quasi-States: Sovereignty, International Relations, and the Third World* (Cambridge: Cambridge University Press, 1990).

relationship between terrorism, rogue states, and weapons of mass destruction; the removal of Cold War constraints on what Louis Hartz once called America's 'liberal absolutism', and the quasi-religious manifestation of this in the Bush Doctrine; and, finally, the growing consensus among American policymakers and commentators that the prevailing legal and institutional architecture of international society is ill-suited to the prosecution of a revisionist foreign policy agenda, whether liberal or neo-conservative.

Liberals for hierarchy

The liberal foundations of the equalitarian regime have often been alluded to. The regime transposes onto the international stage core liberal ideas of the legal equality of the individual before the law, the individual's rights to liberty and self-determination, and the inviolability of the individual's physical person. The state becomes the individual 'writ large', bearing the right of sovereignty (qua individual liberty) within a putative international society. Defenders of this 'international' variant of liberalism beyond the state – of whom Michael Walzer is the most renowned – claim that granting states rights akin to individuals is justified not only because it contributes to international order, but because legal sovereignty, and its attendant rights of non-intervention and self-determination, provides peoples with a protective shield that allows them to develop a common life, free from external interference, in which the liberty of individuals can flourish.[14] The liberty of the state is thus essential to the liberty of the individual.

Since the end of the Cold War, a growing number of prominent liberal scholars have questioned this form of international liberalism, advancing instead a 'cosmopolitan' variant that contests core elements of the equalitarian regime. Prominent among these have been Francis Fukuyama, John Rawls, David Held, and, most recently, Allen Buchanan and Robert Keohane. The writings of these scholars differ in crucial ways, as do their individual political orientations. Yet each advances, in one form or another, four ideas that go to the heart of the equalitarian regime: (1) that 'liberal democracies' are distinguished by a set of empirical characteristics, principal among which are their passivity toward one another, their constitutional commitment to the protection of civil and political rights, and their 'comparative moral reliability'; (2) that these characteristics make liberal democracies the most advanced historical form of polity; (3) that because of their distinctive qualities and historical standing, liberal democracies ought to have special rights in international society, both in international decision-making and with regard to domestic autonomy; and (4) that granting such rights would necessarily reintroduce a form of legal hierarchy into international society. This section elaborates these ideas through an exposition of Francis Fukuyama's and Buchanan and Keohane's writings. Fukuyama provided the first post-Cold War articulation of the liberal hierarchy thesis, while Buchanan and Keohane advance its most sophisticated and thought-provoking statement.

---

[14] See Michael Walzer's classic work *Just and Unjust Wars* (Harmondsworth: Penguin, 1977).

Fukuyama

The principal elements of Francis Fukuyama's 'end of history' thesis are well known, and warrant merely summarising here. Fukuyama argued that history should not be seen simply as 'the occurrence of events', but rather it should be understood, following Hegel then Marx, as 'a single, coherent, evolutionary process', in which humanity moves toward 'a form of society that satisfied its deepest and most fundamental longings'.[15] For Fukuyama, these 'most fundamental longings' were liberty and equality, or as he came to formulate it in *The End of History and the Last Man*, 'the struggle for recognition'. Of the great ideologies of political and social organisation, which Fukuyama defined as hereditary monarchy, fascism, communism, and liberal democracy, only the latter could satisfy this struggle, while at the same time meeting history's simultaneous march toward economic capitalism. 'That is, while earlier forms of government were characterised by grave defects and irrationalities that led to their eventual collapse, liberal democracy was arguably free from such fundamental internal contradictions'.[16] For Fukuyama, the collapse of Soviet communism thus meant more than the decline of yet another great power, or even the failure of a grand social and political experiment. Its collapse marked the last in a series of great victories that liberal democracy had won over autocratic and authoritarian alternatives, and now liberal democracy stood unchallenged. Because liberal democracy does not contradict humanity's 'most fundamental longings', Fukuyama argued that this victory should rightly be seen as the end of history, that moment when 'there would be no further progress in the development of underlying principles and institutions, because all of the really big questions had been settled'.[17]

None of this meant, however, that international relations would be free of conflict or division, at least in the short- to medium-term. The end of the Cold War signalled the ideological victory of liberal democracy, and the number of 'really-existing' democracies multiplied throughout the 1990s. But Fukuyama was at pains to stress that for the foreseeable future international relations would be divided into two worlds: an expanding post-historical world of liberal democracies, and a contracting historical world of autocracies. The post-historical world would still be organised into sovereign states, but aggressive nationalism would decline, traditional interstate warfare would all but disappear, and economic interaction would take centre-stage, ultimately eroding many traditional features of categorical sovereignty. In contrast, the historical world would remain a realm of power politics, one 'riven with a variety of religious, national, and ideological conflicts depending on the stage of development of the particular countries concerned . . .'.[18] While these worlds would, to a large extent, 'maintain parallel but separate existences', Fukuyama identified three likely points of collision: the politics of oil, immigration, the proliferation of weapons of mass destruction. The ideological divide between the post-historical and historical worlds means that their relations will inevitably be characterised 'by mutual distrust and fear, and despite growing economic interdependence, force will continue to be the *ultima ratio* in their mutual relations'.[19]

[15] Francis Fukuyama, *The End of History and the Last Man* (New York: The Free Press, 1992), p. xii.
[16] Ibid., p. xi.
[17] Ibid., p. xii.
[18] Ibid., p. 276.
[19] Ibid., p. 279.

78   *Christian Reus-Smit*

How then is international society to be governed? It is here that Fukuyama takes the crucial step from describing the ethical (and hence historical) superiority of liberal democracy to advocating the rehierarchisation of international society to reflect this superiority. If it is true that liberal democracies seldom if ever fight each other, and if liberal democracy satisfies, like no other political system, the human desire for recognition, then democracies have strong interests in preserving and expanding the international sphere of democracy. Liberals have long embraced these goals, and have invested heavily in international institutions, such as the League of Nations and the United Nations, to deliver the requisite collective security and humanitarian progress. Yet Fukuyama argues that these institutional experiments have been based on a fundamentally flawed form of Kantianism. Advocates of the equalitarian regime have mistakenly thought that liberal institutions could function effectively with mixed membership, with equal participation of liberal democracies and autocracies. But, as Fukuyama points out, Kant's 'Second Definitive Article' in *Perpetual Peace* holds that the law of nations ought to be based on a federation of free states. Only within such a federation would liberal principles of right prevail and war be constrained by the reluctance of self-governing peoples to accept its costs. 'The United Nations', Fukuyama contends, 'did not live up to these conditions from the beginning. The Charter of the United Nations dropped any reference to a league of "free nations", in favour of the weaker principle of the "sovereign equality of all its members" . . . With no pre-existing consensus on just principles of political order or the nature of rights, it is not surprising', he concludes, 'that the United Nations has not been able to accomplish anything of real importance since its founding, in the critical area of collective security'.[20]

For Fukuyama, the only way to correct this institutional failure is to move toward a genuine 'pacific union', 'a league of truly free states brought together by their common commitment to liberal principles'.[21] This would mean abandoning the long-standing goal of a universal conference of states, a goal first articulated at the Hague Conferences of 1899 and 1907, and given its most concrete expression in the contemporary United Nations. Liberal democracies would need to recognise that effective international governance – the sort that can provide genuine collective security and economic well-being for the post-historical world, and effectively promote the democratisation and pacification of the historical world – would have to be bounded, that its membership could not, and should not, extend to non-democracies. 'Such a league', Fukuyama claims, 'should be much more capable of forceful action to protect its collective security from threats arising from the non-democratic part of the world. The states making it up would be able to live according to the rules of international law in their mutual dealings'.[22] Fukuyama's message here is simple: there is a fundamental incompatibility between the international liberalism of the equalitarian regime and the pursuit of real and effective liberal international governance. All states are not equal, and only those with liberal attributes domestically are capable of bearing the rights and obligations of liberal governance internationally.

[20] Ibid., pp. 280–2.
[21] Ibid., p. 283.
[22] Ibid.

Buchanan and Keohane

In the past five years Robert Keohane's work has taken a distinctive and little-remarked normative turn. In his 2000 Presidential address to the American Political Science Association, he argued that 'Political science as a profession should accept the challenge of discovering how well-structured institutions could enable the *world* to have a "new birth of freedom" '.[23] To meet this challenge, political science – and International Relations in particular – would need to engage in both empirical and normative enquiry, in explorations of the 'real' and the 'ideal'. Since making this appeal, Keohane's work has sought to bring the empirical and the normative into dialogue. For our purposes, the most important product of this work is his 2004 article with the moral philosopher Allen Buchanan, 'The Preventive Use of Force: A Cosmopolitan Institutional Proposal'.[24] This piece fuses elements of Buchanan's quite radical cosmopolitanism[25] with Keohane's long-standing, more pluralist emphasis on the importance of rational institutional design for furthering the human good.

Buchanan and Keohane's purpose is twofold: to demonstrate that a compelling normative argument can be made in favour of the preventive use of force to combat actions with severe humanitarian consequences, and to outline a set of institutional mechanisms that can minimise unjustified interventions. Their concern is not with the 'pre-emptive' use of force, which involves countering immanent threats, but with the more controversial 'preventive' use, which they define as 'the initiation of military action in anticipation of harmful actions that are neither presently occurring nor immanent'.[26]

Their cosmopolitan normative argument begins with the assumption that 'it can be morally permissible to use force to stop *presently occurring* massive violations of basic human rights',[27] of which the clearest examples are the Cambodian and Rwandan genocides. If this is true, they contend, then there is 'at least a prima facie case for the moral permissibility of using force to *prevent* massive violations of basic human rights'.[28] It is important to note here that Buchanan and Keohane extend the category of 'massive violations of basic human rights' beyond extreme acts of tyrannical abuse or neglect, such as enslavement, massacre or starvation, to encompass the use, by state or non-state actors, of weapons of mass destruction. If basic human rights are understood to include the right to physical security and subsistence, as well as the rights against torture, discrimination, slavery and servitude, then the use of nuclear, chemical or biological weapons would constitute just as much a violation of these rights as extreme acts of tyranny. Buchanan and Keohane are at pains to stress that their 'prima facie justification for the preventive use of force does

[23] Robert O. Keohane, 'Governance in a Partially Globalized World', *American Political Science Review*, 95:1 (March 2001), p. 1.
[24] Allen Buchanan and Robert O. Keohane, 'The Preventive Use of Force: A Cosmopolitan Institutional Proposal', *Ethics and International Affairs*, 18:1 (2004), pp. 1–22. See also J. L. Holzgrefe and Robert O. Keohane (eds), *Humanitarian Intervention: Ethical, Legal, and Political Dilemmas* (Cambridge: Cambridge University Press, 2003).
[25] See Allen Buchanan, *Justice, Legitimacy, and Self-Determination: Moral Foundations for International Law* (Oxford: Oxford University Press, 2004).
[26] Buchanan and Keohane, 'The Preventive Use of Force', p. 1.
[27] Ibid., p. 4.
[28] Ibid., p. 5.

not apply to all cases where harm may be prevented but only to situations in which there is a significant risk of sudden and very serious harms on a massive scale'.[29] In particular, it does not apply to cases in which violence is increasing incrementally, as they believe '[a]ction to respond to aggression or acts of ethnic violence can feasibly be taken in such contexts with far less uncertainty regarding the need to act after the first human rights violations have already occurred'.[30]

For our purposes, the most important component of Buchanan and Keohane's argument is the institutional mechanisms they propose to prevent abuse of the cosmopolitan justification for the preventive use of force, abuse readily apparent in present justifications for the invasion of Iraq. Since states cannot be trusted to restrain naked self-interest or to consider the interests of others when deciding to use force, institutional processes are needed to hold them accountable. 'Accountability', Buchanan and Keohane argue, 'operates both *ex ante* and *ex post*. Those states that propose to use force preventively must, under cosmopolitan principles, consult with other states and make their intentions known to international society more generally before using force. Having used force, they must provide information, answer questions, and subject themselves to sanctions according to rules that have been established in advance.'[31] A defensible accountability system, they go on to suggest, would need to have three 'components': clear standards of accountability, setting out when and how preventive force may be used; the provision of comprehensive information by those proposing the use of force about the risks of massive human rights violations and the likely consequences of military action; and an effective system of sanctions to punish those who violate the defined standards of accountability and/or manipulate information to justify self-interested interventions.[32]

Buchanan and Keohane conclude by considering three institutional models that might embody these components of an accountability system, and it is here that they advocate giving democracies special rights in decisions to use force. After rejecting as politically impractical an institutional model centred on a reformed Security Council without the veto, they recommend a combination of their second and third models: new accountability mechanisms through the existing Security Council, combined with a special role for a newly constituted 'democratic coalition'. Under this hybrid model, 'the Security Council would have to approve military action by the procedures currently in the Charter. The Council would appoint an impartial body to determine whether the intervener's *ex ante* justification for preventive action is confirmed *ex post*'.[33] The Council would also be charged with formulating and applying 'suitable penalties to be applied in the case of a negative *ex post* evaluation'.[34] These procedures, Buchanan and Keohane contend, would deter powerful states from engaging in morally dubious interventions, as the process of *ex post* evaluation and the threat of sanctions would raise the potential costs of nakedly self-interested preventive wars. They would not, however, prevent Council processes from becoming deadlocked by arbitrary and self-interested uses of the veto.

---

[29] Ibid.
[30] Ibid.
[31] Ibid., p. 11. It is worth noting here that both the Kosovo intervention and the 'war in Iraq' would fail both the *ex ante* and *ex post* tests of accountability suggested here.
[32] Ibid., pp. 11–12.
[33] Ibid., p. 17.
[34] Ibid.

To correct this problem Buchanan and Keohane give a special 'supporting' role to a coalition of democratic states (their third institutional model). They define democratic states as 'those with constitutional, representative governments, competition for elected positions through reasonably fair elections, and entrenched basic civil and political rights'.[35] A coalition of such states would begin, they imagine, with a core group of states with uncontroversial democratic credentials, and these founding members would 'admit additional countries through a transparent process of utilising publicly stated criteria for membership'.[36] Buchanan and Keohane's reason for establishing such a democratic coalition, and for giving it special rights in decisions to use force, is that democratic states meet their 'standard for comparative moral reliability'.[37] They believe that 'when democracies violate cosmopolitan principles, they are more likely to be criticised by their citizens for doing so, and will be more likely to rectify their behavior in response'.[38] Given this 'comparative moral reliability', Buchanan and Keohane recommend that if a state, or group of states, was unable to gain Security Council authorisation for the preventive use of force, it could appeal to the democratic coalition. Applying its own *ex ante* and *ex post* accountability procedures, the coalition would then evaluate the case for preventive war and judge subsequent applications. Buchanan and Keohane stress that the democratic coalition would not replace the Security Council, as it would only come into operation in the case of a Council deadlock. If anything, they conclude, the existence of the coalition would make the Security Council more effective, as Council members would have a strong incentive to act more effectively and responsibly, heading off reference of an issue to the democratic coalition.

Problems of practice, prudence, and principle

At first glance, there seems much to recommend these arguments for replacing the equalitarian regime with a new hierarchy that grants liberal democracies privileged rights of international governance, particularly with regard to the use of force. To begin with, they resonate with an idea that has gained heightened currency since the early 1990s, the idea that sovereignty can, and should, be compromised, to further certain cosmopolitan/humanitarian ends. If it is legitimate to derogate a state's domestic sovereignty when it fails to meet certain minimum standards of liberal (let alone humane) governance, surely it is legitimate to derogate its international sovereign rights under the equalitarian regime for the same violations? Second, liberal arguments for renewed hierarchy appear plausible, even attractive, because many of the ideas on which they are predicated have now attained the status of truisms, particularly within the United States. And if these ideas are true, then it is but a short logical step to accept the liberal case for hierarchy. If it is indeed the case that democracies are pacific toward one another, that they are institutionally committed to the preservation of their peoples' civil and political rights, and that they are comparatively morally reliable, then surely this entitles them to distinct, more

[35] Ibid., p. 18.
[36] Ibid., p. 19.
[37] Ibid.
[38] Ibid.

powerful, rights in an evolving liberal international order? Finally, the arguments proffered by Fukuyama and Buchanan and Keohane are rhetorically powerful, especially when stated in the negative, as their less scholarly proponents frequently present them. Why should states that disrespect their peoples' civil and political rights enjoy the same international rights, especially when it comes to decisions concerning the protection of those rights? Why should Sudan have the same right to membership of the Security Council as Australia; why should Burma have the same right to join the Human Rights Commission as Canada?

These reasons go a long way to explaining why liberal arguments for renewed hierarchy are gaining widespread credence. They obscure, however, the very substantial problems with these arguments and the practices they might engender. These problems fall into three broad categories: problems of practice, prudence, and principle.

Practice

Any attempt to give democracies special governance rights in international society faces three practical questions: What constitutes a democratic state, with qualities deserving special international rights? What constitutes a 'democratic coalition of states' or a 'pacific union', with the collective right to make privileged decisions on the use of force? And could a democratic coalition of states be established that commanded legitimacy within international society?

Before one can grant special rights to democracies, one has to specify clearly what constitutes a democratic state. Advocates of liberal hierarchy write as though this is unproblematic. Their strategy is usually to propose a set of institutional criteria, with a democratic state being one that meets these formal characteristics. Fukuyama writes that a 'country is democratic if it grants its people the right to choose their own government through periodic, secret ballot, multi-party elections, on the basis of universal and equal adult suffrage'.[39] Buchanan and Keohane define democratic states as 'those with constitutional, representative governments, competition for elected positions through reasonably fair elections, and entrenched civil and political rights'.[40] While this appears straightforward, in adopting this institutional strategy, Fukuyama and Buchanan and Keohane make a common mistake, 'that of identifying democracy with a particular institution or set of institutional arrangements, rather than with the principles they embody or are designed to realize'.[41] The assumption is that the preferred institutions necessarily instantiate these principles, with the two standing in a symbiotic relationship. The problem is, of course, that states commonly exhibit these institutional arrangements but violate the underlying principles. David Beetham identifies two of these principles as especially important: that a society's system for making collectively binding decisions be subject to control by all of society's members; and that all who are subject to the authority of that system of collective decision-making are considered equals.[42] Most 'really-existing'

---

[39] Fukuyama, *The End of History*, p. 43.
[40] Buchanan and Keohane, 'The Preventive Use of Force', p. 18.
[41] David Beetham, *Democracy and Human Rights* (Cambridge: Polity Press, 1999), p. 3.
[42] Ibid., p. 5.

democracies uphold these principles rhetorically, but fail to meet them empirically. Gerrymanders, democratic seizure by powerful lobby groups, politicised media, lack of control of the executive by the legislature, discrimination of minorities by majorities, first-past-the-post voting systems, and more, have hollowed out many states' formal democratic institutions, creating widespread political alienation and disaffection.

Advocates of liberal hierarchy may well acknowledge this gap between institutions and principles, but reply that what ultimately matters is that states have the institutional characteristics, however flawed. This is unpersuasive, though. Key constitutive ideas of the liberal hierarchy thesis collapse if the institutional arrangements of democratic states fail to realise Beetham's two principles. The idea of the democratic peace, and the notion that democratic states are comparatively morally reliable, both depend upon a society's system for making collectively binding decisions being subject to control by all of society's members. If this system is not subject to such control, then Kant's principal reason for believing that republics are more peaceful than monarchies drops out.[43] And it was Buchanan and Keohane who argued that democracies were comparatively morally reliable because when they 'violate cosmopolitan principles, they are more likely to be criticised by their citizens for doing so, and will be more likely to rectify their behaviour in response'.[44] Liberal hierarchy arguments thus depend, in a deep and fundamental sense, on democratic institutions expressing democratic principles, something rarely seen in practice. One could try to salvage the argument by holding that only democratic states whose institutions actually instantiate democratic principles should be entitled to special rights. This is close to the position advanced by Rawls, who parts company with Fukuyama and Buchanan and Keohane to argue that only 'well-ordered constitutional democracies' should be part of a 'society of liberal peoples'. Such democracies have more than a set of standard institutional characteristics – they are 'deliberative' in the true sense of the word, with 'the knowledge and desire on the part of the citizens generally to follow public reason and to realise its ideas in their political conduct'.[45] The problem is, though, that the task of identifying democratic states deserving of special rights would be practically impossible, and the club of appropriately qualified states would be small indeed.

The practical problem of defining what constitutes a democratic state is so substantial that it makes the question of what would constitute a 'democratic coalition of states' or a 'pacific union' almost moot. If this initial problem of definition could be overcome, however, the issue of a coalition or union would throw up problems of its own. Would such a coalition comprise all democratic states or just a fraction? Would it be constituted through authoritative international institutional processes, or would it be created by democratic states themselves, or a sub-group thereof? Fukuyama and Buchanan and Keohane clearly favour the latter. For Fukuyama, this is matter of post-historical liberal democracies recognising that the rules and methods that ought to govern their mutual relations are not those best

---

[43] Kant wrote in his First Definitive Article that if 'the consent of the citizenry is required in order to determine whether or not there will be war, it is natural that they consider all its calamities before committing themselves to so risky a game'. Immanuel Kant, *Perpetual Peace and Other Essays* (Indianapolis, IN: Hackett Publishing Company, 1983), p. 113.

[44] Buchanan and Keohane, 'The Preventive Use of Force', p. 19.

[45] John Rawls, *The Law of Peoples* (Cambridge, MA: Harvard University Press, 1999), pp. 138–9.

suited to navigating their interactions with the post-historical world. A pacific union would form, therefore, as 'truly free states' recognise their 'common commitment to liberal principles', as they formulate 'binding legal agreements' to manage their interrelations, and as they recognise that 'the post-historical half [of the world] must make use of realist methods when dealing with the part still in history'.[46] For Buchanan and Keohane, a 'democratic coalition of states' would form around an 'initial core' of 'self-designated states whose credentials as stable democracies are unassailable. They would then develop membership criteria that would determine which other states would be eligible'. They imagine that the 'democratic coalition would be based on agreements among its members – not necessarily through a formal treaty. Over time', they suggest, 'its practices could become part of customary international law'.[47] Under this model, the instigation of the coalition is voluntarist, and the only authoritative institutional processes are internal to the coalition itself, formulated and employed by the founding membership to admit newcomers.

By favouring a voluntarist means of constituting a democratic coalition or pacific union, Fukuyama and Buchanan and Keohane dodge one set of potentially insurmountable problems, those associated with establishing a coalition or union through authoritative international institutional processes, such as those of the present United Nations. They immediately encounter, however, another set of equally challenging problems. Foremost among these is the question of when a democratic coalition or pacific union can be said to exist, ready to make decisions about the use of force. What if the United States, Britain and Australia declared themselves the initial core of a democratic coalition, and proceeded to formulate transparent rules for the admission of other democracies? Would they constitute, at this moment of inception, a coalition for the purposes of decision-making? If not, then at what point, as the coalition's membership expanded, would it constitute a legitimate decision-making forum? Is 20 per cent, 50 per cent, 80 per cent, or 100 per cent of the world's qualifying democracies required? From a liberal perspective, only one answer seems compelling. A coalition could only reach decision-making maturity when all of the world's qualifying democracies are granted the right to participate in decisions to licence the use of force, whether or not they choose to exercise that right. It is an axiomatic liberal principle that all citizens capable of fully developed moral agency should have a right to vote. Advocates of liberal hierarchy have drawn a line between democracies and non-democracies, with only the former possessing the requisite moral agency. But it is decidedly unclear how, given the logic of their arguments, they could justify enfranchising some democracies and not others. And if this is the case, then the fate of our nascent democratic coalition would hinge on the United States, Britain, and Australia convincing a broad spectrum of democracies to join, democracies with markedly different (even incompatible) conceptions of international responsibility. One would have to rate this prospect remote indeed.

The final practical problem facing liberal hierarchy arguments is how to establish within international society a *legitimate* democratic coalition or pacific union, as opposed to an illegitimate one. Legitimacy is a vital ingredient of effective social power. The more legitimacy an actor commands, and the more legitimate its actions

---

[46] Fukuyama, *The End of History*, p. 279.
[47] Buchanan and Keohane, 'The Preventive Use of Force', p. 19.

are deemed, the more it can conscript voluntary compliance and assistance, and the more it can minimise opposition. For a democratic coalition to function effectively, it would need to command broad-based international legitimacy, otherwise its decisions would attract widespread opposition and resistance from the still sizeable population of non-democratic states, states who are themselves unlikely to provoke attack, but with whom a democratic coalition would need quiet, if not happy, non-involvement or compliance. Curiously, this need for international legitimacy has been all but ignored by advocates of liberal hierarchy. They strongly imply, of course, that a democratic coalition or pacific union would be legitimate, but they attribute this legitimacy to the superior political and moral qualities of the member democracies, and to the hypothesised goods that such a grouping could provide to international society. This is not, however, a coherent account of legitimacy. By definition, legitimacy is a social phenomenon, it depends on the judgment of others. An individual or collective actor is only legitimate if other actors in its social domain define it as such. Theorists, such as Fukuyama and Buchanan and Keohane, might decide that a democratic coalition is legitimate *a priori*, but if international society determines otherwise, then their judgment is moot. Similarly, a putative coalition might define itself as legitimate, but this would be a vain hope if no one else agreed.

The challenge then is for a democratic coalition or pacific union to establish its legitimacy in the eyes of international society generally. Here we confront one of the central contradictions in liberal hierarchy arguments. As noted above, in proposing a voluntarist approach to the constitution of a coalition or union, Fukuyama and Buchanan and Keohane avoid the complications associated with authoritative international institutional processes. In doing so, however, they risk creating substantial problems of international legitimation. If a select group of democratic states can themselves found a coalition or union, and then define the rules dictating which states may subsequently join, they will, in the process, create two categories of 'others': non-member democracies, and non-democracies. Both of these groups would lose rights they currently enjoy under the equalitarian regime: the first until they joined the club, the second until they underwent democratic transitions. And both would lose these rights through a process in which they had no say. Why these groups should ordain the new democratic coalition or pacific union with legitimacy is decidedly unclear, and if they see it as illegitimate, the likelihood of non-compliance and resistance would be high. Advocates of liberal hierarchy seem to think that a democratic coalition would be sufficiently magnetic that opposition would be quickly displaced by a rush to join. In Buchanan and Keohane's words, 'members would receive valuable recognition as democratic states that are regarded as sufficiently trustworthy to participate in important decisions regarding the use of force. More importantly, they would gain decision-making authority, both with respect to legitimising the preventive use of force and for determining which other states should be allowed to join.'[48] But even if some democracies were susceptible to such magnetism, others would not be, and this would leave the coalition with less than universal democratic membership, which, as we have seen, would undermine its claim to special decision-making authority. And even if some autocracies were prepared to embark on democratic transitions to gain entry, many would not, including some of the most

---

[48] Ibid., p. 20.

powerful, such as China. It is hard to imagine, therefore, how a democratic coalition could be established without an attendant legitimation crisis.

Prudence

Let us assume, for the sake of argument, that these practical problems did not exist or could be satisfactorily resolved. Would the case for liberal hierarchy then be more compelling? A principal reason for replacing the present equalitarian regime with a more hierarchical social order is that this would enhance international order. For advocates of liberal hierarchy, international order means two things: it means a level of peace and stability such that economic interaction becomes the core of international relations, and it means the realisation of certain cosmopolitan ends, particularly the maximum protection of individuals' civil and political rights. For Fukuyama, this is a matter of securing a pacific union from the deleterious impacts of the historical world, while at the same time expanding that union through the spread of democracy globally. For Buchanan and Keohane, it is a matter of establishing a revised framework of global governance that can better deliver peace and civility to the international system as a whole. In part, therefore, the veracity of liberal hierarchy arguments hinges on the likelihood that granting democratic states special decision-making rights would deliver net improvements in international order, especially in the critical areas of peace and the protection of basic rights. There are good reasons to believe, however, that attempts to institute a new hierarchy would be deleterious to international order instead of beneficial.

The crux of the problem lies in the resolution advocates of liberal hierarchy imply to the classic problem of the relationship between order and justice in international relations. Nothing here suggests that they consider such a resolution easy, only that they present a new hierarchy as a missing link, a move that can reconcile seemingly incompatible ends. Their chain of reasoning is most clearly articulated by Buchanan and Keohane. If democratic states were granted special rights to use force – rights exercised within an appropriate framework of accountability – a number of consequences would follow: the zone of peace between democracies would be reinforced by enmeshing such states in a denser web of rights and obligations; the comparatively morally reliable members of international society would be empowered to respond preventively to major threats to international human rights, either in the form of the use of weapons of mass destruction or massacre, enslavement and starvation; and the existence of a specially enfranchised democratic coalition would have a powerful socialising impact on the remainder of international society, encouraging movement toward a global democratic order. Instituting a new hierarchy would thus enable the realisation of both dimensions of its advocates' conception of international order: the simultaneous pursuit of peace and the protection of basic human rights, a classic liberal vision.

While this resolution of the relationship between order and justice will be attractive to all those who favour democracy over autocracy, and who rightly lament the agonising trade-offs between peace and civility, it nevertheless confronts a number of substantial problems. So serious are these problems, that prudence would counsel against any move to a hierarchy privileging democratic states.

The first problem is that two ideas that liberal hierarchy advocates take as axiomatic are in fact questionable, at best. The first is the democratic peace, the idea that liberal democracies do not fight each other. Some have suggested that this is as close to a law of international politics as one gets, but in reality the jury is still out. Democratic peace theory has been challenged on multiple grounds, from the inconsistency of its key definitions, such as democracy and war, to the statistical insignificance of its empirical findings. Democratic peace theorists have responded vigorously to each of these challenges, but the best one can say is that the debate is stalemated: there appears to be something unique and interesting about relations between democracies, but precisely what this is, and why it is, remains uncertain and unproven.[49] The second idea is Buchanan and Keohane's proposition that democracies are comparatively morally reliable. How one would demonstrate this is less than clear. If the measure is how states have responded to major humanitarian crises, such the massacre, enslavement, or starvation of a people, the record of the world's leading democracies is not especially edifying. Their failure of will in Somalia, prevarication over Bosnia, inaction in Rwanda, belated burst of humanitarian commitment over Kosovo, and characteristic words without action in the Sudan, all suggest moral unreliability, not reliability. Even when compared with the record of autocracies the situation is far from clear. It was Tanzania that deposed Idi Amin in Uganda and Vietnam that halted Pol Pot's genocide in Cambodia. Self-interest was a crucial motivation in both of these cases, but it was also a decisive motivation behind the world's leading democracies sitting on their hands.[50]

The second problem is that lessons learned from past instances of self-ordained privilege in international society are not encouraging. The closest analogue is the successful move by European states during the nineteenth century to codify a 'standard of civilization' in international law, a standard that gave these states privileged rights in international society, rights to grant or decline sovereign recognition to other polities, and rights to intervene in those judged unworthy of such recognition.[51] Informing this standard were deep-seated assumptions of racial superiority, assumptions absent from present liberal hierarchy arguments. Nevertheless, the parallels (and the lessons) are clear. The 'standard', and the practices it licensed, fuelled grievances that fractured the international system for the best part of a century, and the effects can still be felt today. No account of the rise of Japanese imperialism in the first half of the twentieth century, or of China's nationalist and

[49] For these debates on the democratic peace, see Michael Brown, Sean M. Lynn-Jones, and Steven E. Miller (eds.), *Debating the Democratic Peace* (Cambridge, MA: MIT Press, 1996); Zeev Maoz, 'The Controversy over the Democratic Peace: Rearguard Action or Cracks in the Wall?', *International Security*, 22:1 (1997), pp. 162–98; and, more recently, Andreas Hasenclever and Wolfgang Wagner (eds.), 'The Dynamics of the Democratic Peace', *International Politics*, Special Issue, 41:4 (December 2004).

[50] Other measures also point to the moral unreliability of the world's democracies. For example, Alexander Downes has shown that democracies are no less likely to brutalise non-combatants in war than autocracies. See Alexander Downes, *Targetting Civilians in War* (Ph.D thesis, University of Chicago, 2004), and 'Civilian Victimization and International Wars Since 1945: Are Democracies Different Now?' (Unpublished Paper, 2005). For related arguments, see Theo Farrell, 'Strategic Culture and American Empire', *SAIS Review of International Affairs*, 25:2 (2005), and Jose Alvarez, 'Do Liberal States Behave Better? A Critique of Slaughter's Liberal Theory', *European Journal of International Law*, 12:2 (2001), pp. 183–246.

[51] Gong, *The 'Standard of Civilization' in International Society*; and Michael Adas, *Machines as the Measure of Men: Science, Technology, and Ideologies of Western Domination* (Ithaca, NY: Cornell University Press, 1989).

communist revolutions, would be complete without reference to the humiliation generated by the hierarchical practices propagated by the European powers, not the least being the unequal treaties and military interventions. The likelihood of a new liberal hierarchy generating similarly destabilising grievances is far from insignificant, in part because of the path-dependency that would connect the two exercises. With the memory of nineteenth century hierarchy still fresh, the prospect is slim of leading non-democracies such as China passively accepting a democratic coalition of the kind envisaged, especially when they are faced with the same kind of sheathed ultimatum – 'transform your domestic political system and gain a new slate of international rights, or refuse change and lose some of your core sovereign rights'.

If the lessons of history are unedifying, so too is the contemporary experience of institutionalised hierarchy. While the equalitarian regime constitutes the institutional bedrock of present international society, peaks of institutional hierarchy punctuate the horizon, and each of these peaks has become a focal point for disenchantment and contestation. The Permanent Five and their veto power in the Security Council is one such peak, an understandable gesture to the realities of post-1945 power, and for most of its history a near guarantee of institutional politicisation and paralysis. Weighted voting rights in the major international financial institutions are another peak, one that has persistently marred their reputations as institutions for the common good. And a peak looming high over the present international order is the regime of differential rights and obligations that nuclear and non-nuclear states enjoy under the Nuclear Non-Proliferation Treaty. In a bargain frayed to the point of breaking, nuclear states are constrained by little more than the now cynical promise to disarm, while non-nuclear states must succumb to an intrusive, though largely successful, regulatory regime. None of these peaks of institutional hierarchy have achieved anything like a governance equilibrium; in fact, if one were to identify the principal points of institutional contestation in the present international system, each would loom large.

If the propositions that democracies don't fight each other and that they are comparatively morally reliable are contentious ideas not truths, and if the historical record suggests that institutionalised hierarchy generates deep-seated grievances, with destabilising consequences for international order, one would have to approach the institution of a hierarchy privileging democratic states with great caution. Pluralist international society theorists have long argued that international society is a practical association, one in which states with different identities and interests participate nonetheless in the maintenance of rules and institutions that facilitate coexistence and cooperation. As noted earlier, over the past six decades this association has proven remarkably successful, with the number of recognised sovereign states quadrupling while the incidence of interstate warfare has declined. We should not forget, however, that society among sovereign states is as vulnerable as it is impressive. It rests ultimately upon a series of social understandings that have become enshrined as cardinal international norms. Principal among these are mutual recognition and the legal fiction of sovereign equality, the keystone of the equalitarian regime. Informed by a set of contentious ideas about the qualities of democracies, liberal hierarchy arguments propose overlaying the historical legacy of nineteenth and early twentieth century hierarchy, and contemporary instances of institutionalised privilege, with a systemic division between democracies and non-democracies. Furthermore, they recommend that this be instituted by democracies themselves, and not through any authoritative international institutional processes. This project cuts right to the heart of the social compact that presently undergirds international order, and whatever gains it might bring for international order, the potential costs are substantial. As we have seen, Buchanan and Keohane go to great lengths to specify the accountability procedures that would govern the work of a democratic coalition, but to other, excluded states, this would undoubtedly look like a self-ordained group of privileged states policing themselves.

Principle

To this point our discussion has focused on a series of practical and prudential problems with liberal hierarchy arguments. Granting democratic states special rights in decisions to use force would be near impossible to operationalise, at least in a manner deemed legitimate by wider international society, and instituting a privileged democratic coalition or pacific union would risk replicating past experiences of institutionalised hierarchy, with profoundly destabilising consequences for international order. A further criticism remains, however: a criticism from within liberalism itself.

The conventional path here would be to follow Michael Walzer who, as noted above, provides one of the most systematic liberal defences of the equalitarian regime. Walzer is a staunch defender of the equal, inviolable sovereignty of all states, but he justifies this through reference to the rights and liberties of individuals. 'The rights of the member states must be vindicated', he argues, 'for it is only by virtue of those rights that there is a society at all. If they cannot be upheld (at least sometimes), international society collapses into a state of war or it is transformed into a universal tyranny.'[52] The rights to which he refers are territorial integrity and political sovereignty, and 'they derive ultimately from the rights of individuals, and from them they take their force'.[53] For Walzer, individuals have inalienable rights to life and liberty, rights which are 'somehow entailed by our sense of what it means to be a human being'.[54] It is the state, protected and empowered by its international rights, that provides the necessary protection of its members rights and of the collective life they have created. This leads Walzer to defend strongly the paired rights of self-determination and non-intervention. Because individuals have inviolable rights to liberty (as well as life), they have a collective right to determine their own affairs. Following John Stuart Mill, Walzer argues that this right to self-determination must be respected even if a people does not enjoy free institutions, for '[T]he (internal) freedom of a political community can be won only by the members of that community'.[55] The principle of non-intervention is designed to protect this right to self-determination. It is 'the principle guaranteeing that their success will not be impeded or their failure prevented by the intrusions of an alien power'.[56]

---

[52] Walzer, *Just and Unjust Wars*, p. 59.
[53] Ibid., p. 53.
[54] Ibid., p. 54.
[55] Ibid., p. 88.
[56] Ibid.

The strengths of this argument have long been acknowledged, as have its weaknesses. There is, however, a second possible line of liberal critique. It is a fundamental principle of all liberal thought that political right must be separated from other forms of morally arbitrary social power. That is, rights of political decision, participation or representation ought to be held by all members of a political community equally, irrespective of their beliefs, social status, or material power. Absolutist sovereignty conjoined political right and social power in the figure of the sovereign, and liberalism's radicalism lay in its critique of this conjunction. One dimension of liberalism's contradictory political history has been the way in which disenfranchised groups – from the unpropertied classes and religious minorities, to women and indigenous peoples – have deployed this fundamental principle to leverage political rights within liberalising polities. And the separation of powers that defines the institutional architecture of the vast majority of these polities is an attempt, however flawed, to prevent political right being captured by particu-laristic interests. It is this fundamental principle of liberal thought that proponents of liberal hierarchy betray when they propose giving democratic states special rights in decisions to use force. The states that would form the core of a democratic coalition or pacific union are also the states that currently possess – and will continue to possess for the foreseeable future – the bulk of the world's wealth, technological capacity, and military might. It is also these states that occupy the existing peaks of institutionalised hierarchy in international society. Giving democratic states special rights, therefore, would be giving privileges to the powerful. One might respond that their social power already enables them to shape international order to their will. There is a fundamental difference, however, between the capacity to influence outcomes and the right to legislate them. The former leaves space for legally grounded political resistance, the latter forecloses such options, seriously disempowering materially weak actors.

This assignment of political right to already powerful social actors also betrays a cognate liberal principle: that the distribution of political rights must be contractually based. Within liberal thought there are three contending models of social contract. The Hobbesian model, which is proto-liberal at best, sees individuals fleeing the state of nature give up their natural rights to a sovereign, who then assumes absolute political right in return for order and security.[57] The Lockeian model has individuals contract with one another to create a single, collective body politic, transferring their natural rights to a 'commonwealth' in return for 'the mutual preservation of their lives, liberties, and estates . . .'.[58] The Rousseauian model imagines individuals contracting with each other to exchange their natural rights for political rights: 'Each person, in giving himself up to all, gives himself to no one, and as there are no associates over whom he does not acquire the same right as he concedes to them over himself, he gains the equivalent of all he loses and more to preserve what he has'.[59] None of these contractual models for allocating political right are evident in liberal hierarchy arguments, even the Hobbesian model in which individuals alienate their rights to an all powerful sovereign. One could argue that democratic states are contracting when they form a democratic coalition or pacific union, and this is

[57] Thomas Hobbes, *Leviathan* (London: William Collins, 1962), p. 176.
[58] John Locke, *Two Treatises of Government* (Cambridge: Cambridge University Press, 1988), p. 350.
[59] Jean Jacques Rousseau, 'On Social Contract or the Principles of Political Right', in Alan Ritter and Julia Conway Bonadella (eds.), *Rousseau's Political Writings* (New York: Norton, 1988), p. 89.

certainly what Rawls imagines in his version of the liberal hierarchy thesis.[60] But this would be a contract that not only granted democracies special political rights, it would be one that deprived other states of their existing rights.

Advocates of liberal hierarchy might reply that this criticism assumes that all existing states are qualified moral (and hence political) agents, which they would claim is manifestly false. Democracies represent the will of their peoples, autocracies do not. Why should latter enjoy the same political rights as the former, and why is it wrong for the former to aggregate special rights to themselves, with or without the latter's approval? This kind of argument is heard frequently, but it is based on two dubious assumptions. First, that because autocracies do not represent their peoples' will, the governments of democracies have a right to interpret that will and to act accordingly. And, second, that it would be the will of such peoples to see democratic states gain special international rights while the rights of their own states were compromised. Neither of these assumptions is sustainable. If an autocratic state were about to engage in genocide, it would be reasonable for democratic states (or any states, for that matter) to judge that the will of the threatened people favoured humanitarian intervention. But this is very different from democracies making judgments about how subject peoples would view the general allocation of political rights within international society. As for the second assumption, even if we assume that most subject peoples abhor the unrepresentative nature of their autocratic governments and would willingly take the road to democracy, it would be naïve to think that a systematic attempt to erode the international rights of those governments would be met with anything less than popular hostility. Rightly or wrongly, in all bar the most severe forms of tyranny, the qualifying of an autocratic state's international status is likely to be seen by its people as a qualifying of their international status.

Conclusion

The preceding discussion has explored and critiqued recent calls by prominent liberal scholars for the rehierarchisation of international society, for the granting of democratic states differential rights in decisions to deploy force internationally. The zone of peace existing between such states, their comparative moral reliability, and their entrenched commitment of their peoples' civil and political rights, are said to justify enfranchising a democratic coalition or pacific union with special governance rights, and simultaneously qualifying the existing sovereign rights of non-democracies. The import of these ideas is that they are no longer intellectual marginalia. Variants inform the numerous proposals currently circulating for reform of the international system, from the notion that universal membership of the United Nations should not be considered sacrosanct, to the proposition that 'rogue states' should forfeit their membership rights altogether. Furthermore, these ideas now resonate well beyond the liberal circles from which they emanate. In his outline of a conservative grand strategy, Henry Nau asks: 'By what right do nations that are not free decide on legitimacy in international affairs when they deny their own citizens that same right in domestic affairs'. 'Purposes', he goes on to argue, 'matter more

---

[60] Rawls, *The Law of Peoples*, pp. 32–5.

than participation, and liberty struggles in international organisations against despotic purposes. . . . Sometimes institutions simply empower non-democratic states to make law internationally when they break domestic law with impunity.'[61] For liberals like Buchanan and Keohane, the answer is to reconstitute the institutional architecture of international society, creating a specially empowered forum for democracies. For conservatives, the answer is Bush-style 'coalitions of the willing'.

For reasons outlined in previous sections, liberal hierarchy arguments ought to be treated with considerable scepticism. There are compelling reasons to believe that attempts to operationalise them would be fraught with difficulties, that they may do more harm to international order than good, and that they would violate long-standing liberal principles of governance. At the very minimum, advocates of liberal hierarchy need to answer the following critical questions: How could one ensure that a democratic coalition included only those states in which democratic institutions genuinely expressed democratic principles? How many of these states would need to be members before a democratic coalition constituted a mature decision-making body – 20 per cent, 60 per cent, 100 per cent? How could a democratic coalition be constructed without generating an attendant legitimation crisis? If the democratic peace and the comparative moral reliability of democracies are questionable ideas, why should we believe that a democratic coalition would be a more ethically or practically effective decision-making forum on humanitarian issues than existing fora? And if there is little reason to believe this, why should we take the decisively illiberal step of handing those with preponderant material might disproportionate political right? Unless these questions can be answered satisfactorily, replacing the equalitarian regime with a renewed form of hierarchy would be a gamble only for the foolhardy and brave-hearted.

---

[61] Henry Nau, 'A Conservative Grand Strategy for America', in Henry R. Nau and David Shambaugh (eds.), *Divided Diplomacy and the Next Administration: Conservative and Liberal Alternatives* (Washington, DC: The Elliott School of International Affairs, The George Washington University, 2004).

The age of liberal wars

LAWRENCE FREEDMAN

Three different types of arguments were used to justify the 2003 Iraq War. The first was based on the requirements of national security. Iraq was believed to be developing deadly weapons which it might use against neighbouring states or hand over to terrorist groups such as al-Qaeda. A second argument was based on international security. Iraq was supposed to comply with a series of UN Security Council Resolutions and was failing to do so, thereby undermining the credibility of the leading international institutions. The third argument was based on human security. The Iraqi people had suffered too long under a tyrannical regime and this was an opportunity to overthrow it and replace it with something much better.

It was also the case, of course, that these arguments were matched by opponents of the war. The national security argument against war not only questioned the existence of weapons of mass destruction (WMD), or their relevance if they did exist, but also argued that the occupation of a Muslim country would provoke support for and the ire of terrorist groups. The international security argument noted the divisions within the Security Council, and the consequent risk to the credibility of the institution should leading states go to war regardless of the majority view. The human security argument questioned whether people could be liberated by means that would in themselves be bound to cost many innocent lives.

These arguments were all in play prior to the war. Afterwards, as it became apparent that there were no WMD to be found, the pro-war case increasingly depended on the human security arguments. This argument could be challenged from all three perspectives. On its own terms the human security case, that the war would be a net gain for the Iraqi people in terms of democracy and human rights, had to be set against the chaos and violence of the aftermath and the apparent unpopularity of the coalition forces. The international security perspective, though sympathetic to the humanitarian claims, worried that uninvited meddling was bound to end in tears and pointed out how such claims could be used to justify all sorts of mischievous interventions. The only way to sort out the weak from the strong cases was to test it for international support, and this could only be achieved through the Security Council. The failure to get a second Security Council Resolution to support military action meant that the test had been failed and so the case must be weak. From the national security perspective, conservatives could argue that Western countries had no business getting involved in the affairs of other countries other than for defensive reasons. Even after the successful elections at the end of January 2005 this argument still enjoyed considerable credibility as the effort to transform Iraq into a liberal democracy faced stiff resistance from a combination of disaffected Sunnis, Ba'athists and Islamic militants.

My concern in this article is not with the particulars of the Iraqi case or the 'real reasons' why states go to war. I start with the assumption that the cases made for war are not simply surface froth, designed to beguile and bemuse public and wider international opinion. During the debates on Iraq, radicals who found it hard to argue against the idea of removing Saddam Hussein questioned the methods but also charged the coalition with hypocrisy. The invasion of Iraq, they charged, had nothing to do with security at any level, but was 'really about oil' or even about securing contracts for American firms such as Halliburton. This radical critique now looks even less compelling than it did before the war given its economic consequences, and the lack of evidence to support the original propositions on motives. There is a view that in the harsh world of international affairs the structure of the system obliges states, even against their better nature, invariably to give priority to the starkest calculations of interest and power. Certainly governments unable to provide convincing answers to questions of short-term outcomes and long-term benefit will be handicapped when making the case for a military intervention, but they will also wish to demonstrate that they are doing the right thing as well as the safe thing. Justifications for war habitually draw on normative arguments, on expectations about how governments should behave towards their own people, and on how human beings and states should behave towards each other.

From this starting assumption that legitimacy matters in foreign policymaking in Western countries I argue that, at least in Western countries and at least until recently, a vital source of legitimacy is evidence that any force is being used in pursuit of essentially liberal values. Whether or not they meant what they said, coalition leaders felt that they were on firm ground using humanitarian arguments to justify a substantial and potentially hazardous military operation in Iraq. At the very least they believed such arguments had some purchase with the bodies of opinion they were seeking to influence. This tendency in justification is not difficult to explain. Governments no longer enjoy such natural authority with their own publics that claims of raison d'etat can serve as a blanket explanation for the more doubtful aspects of foreign policy. This is in part a consequence of the international system no longer appearing so anarchic, as a remorseless competition between great powers. As a result established methods of evaluating power and interest are under challenge.

Legitimacy has an elusive quality, involving questions of ethics and analysis as well as legality. In terms of definition legitimacy refers to the ability of governments to gain acceptance for their laws. It is about those aspects of compliance with law and policy that turn on respect for authority rather than fear of power, and reflect internalised norms as much as calculated interests. Part of the difficulty with legitimacy is the interaction between these relatively hard coercive and soft consensual sources of support. Authority can represent the successful institutionalisation of power gained through armed force while public debate consists of a continuing attempt to reconcile the demands of doing what is right and what is self-interested.

The potential sources of legitimacy can be summarised by the concepts of national, international and human security. Their individual characters, distinctiveness and mutual interaction are bound to be fuzzy. Because they reflect alternative political priorities and competing analyses of the international environment they may all be supported to a degree within the society. They are not necessarily exclusive and can on occasion reinforce each other in combination. During the course of an intense and polarising debate, as over Iraq, the protagonists will try to show that their preferred course supports all three, even though in practice they may have to be weighed against each other. In each case their definition may be contested. Indeed I would describe them as normative streams, within which values and meaning change over time according to recent experience and current challenge, and in relation to broader cultural changes and debates about public morality. Understanding these normative streams is essential if sense is to be made of contemporary debates about the legitimate use of armed force.

In the next section I suggest that the normative streams associated with national and international security, at least as reflected in traditional international relations theory, take familiar forms while that within the area of human security has yet to be established, because they focus on the structures of power within states rather than between states. In recent years, out of the normative stream of human security the strongest theme to emerge, for purposes of international relations, is the need to protect the weak and the vulnerable, especially in the face of great violence. The wars that are conducted for this purpose I call liberal wars. While this is consistent with classic liberalism, I address in subsequent sections the objections that such an approach is now being encouraged by American neo-conservatives while resisted by many associated with European liberalism. Certainly mainstream politics during the Cold War gave priority to international security because of the dangers of pursuing egoistical national security policies regardless of the consequences. The neo-conservatives (and the label initially had an ironic quality) demonstrated a moral unease with a policy of détente, that sought to reduce the risk of further Soviet expansionism by tolerating repression in the territories already under Moscow's domination. The West was intimidated because it had allowed the Soviet Union to gain an advantage in the military balance. In Europe this line of argument was weaker, because the local stakes were higher and it was assumed that in an age of mutually assured destruction traditional notions of the balance of power had become meaningless. With the end of the Cold War, more traditional liberal concerns reasserted themselves and led to a number of examples of humanitarian intervention. The problem with the notion of liberal wars, I argue, lies less with the ends than the means. Wars are inherently illiberal in their effects and their consequences. Against this must be posed the illiberal consequences of inaction and the possibilities of mitigation, but this explains the discretionary aspect of humanitarian interventions. The concluding section considers whether events since September 2001 have transformed the debate. While noting that they have thrust the issue of war back into the realms of national and international security, it is argued that the philosophy behind the campaigns of al-Qaeda and associated groups is profoundly illiberal while mass casualty terrorism in itself is an affront to liberal values. At the same time, the stress on the liberal dimension to current struggles has important implications for Western conduct.

The human security agenda

Traditionally international relations theory has assumed that for states national security is the prime value because it deals with threats to their very existence. This renders them self-reliant and encourages a wary view of other states. If attacked (or sure that they are about to be attacked) states have a right to defend themselves. Giving priority to national security therefore encourages military provisions to ensure that direct aggression can be resisted. One risk is that the military provision will prove to be insufficiently substantial to act as a deterrent; another is that it will be excessive and so appear to threaten other states. These two types of risk have argued for a more enlightened form of self-interest which seeks to reduce exaggerated senses of threat and deal with disputes between states before they turn into violent conflict. A stable international order is the goal of international security. This value underpins foreign policies based on cooperation with other states, which could involve international institutions and law, but might also depend on more informal contacts and transactions. Simply put, a good solution to the problem of major war is to ensure that strong states get along. It may of course be the case that some disputes between states are too fundamental to be readily resolved and that perceptions of threat are accurate. In such cases attempting to get on well with a radical state may just mean a lowering of the guard. The values of national and international security are not necessarily opposed: it is possible to cooperate while keeping guard. The costs and benefits of the competing approaches have, however, been the stuff of much foreign policy debate, often presented as a contest between realists and idealists.

This contest, reflecting a dominant fear of major war, concerns the best way of securing the rights of states. From neither perspective do the rights of individuals or of groups count for much. From the national perspective these rights must be subservient to those of the state, especially at time of national emergency. From the international perspective it is essential that all states recognise each others' rights. Order depends on prohibiting aggression and, critically, upholding the principle of non-interference in internal affairs.

So far so familiar. Yet a national security agenda must be about more than external enemies. States are not only threatened from within but they often deem internal threats to be the most serious, whether in the form of insurrection, subversion, civil war or secessionism. The relationship between the requirements of internal order and those of external order is complex. States facing such problems regularly blame the meddling of outsiders, sometimes correctly. In principle international security requires that the temptation to meddle in the problems of others should be prohibited. Yet in practice the consequences of a state's internal problems can have repercussions beyond its borders, for example flows of refugees, or the methods of dealing with opponents become so obnoxious that they can no longer be spoken of as a purely internal matter. At this point the needs of international and human security can clash. Meanwhile, from the national perspective intervention in the name of justice risks creating security problems where none existed and, at the very least, putting one's own troops at risk in another's civil wars.

The debate between the demands of national and of international security has some continuity because these normative streams are not difficult to follow. This is not the case with questions of human security. These focus on the structures of power within states rather than those between states. Class, religion, ethnicity, language can serve as the basis of alternative power structures. Democracy may be advocated as a means of sorting out these alternatives, yet in Western societies at least the concept of human rights is taken to be antithetical to attempts to establish an internal political order based on the dominance of one section of society, even if the majority. This is a reflection of an attachment to classical liberalism with its commitment to free markets and human rights. Yet within the normative stream of human security, free markets are often blamed, for example by 'anti-globalisation' activists, for economic injustice. Human rights can be posed in terms of essential needs (food, shelter, basic amenities, and a degree of personal safety) rather than the political terms of freedom of expression, movement and ideas and a degree of self-determination. These are areas of considerable analytical and even ideological controversy. Accepting all these problems, the general impact of concerns about human security as a foreign policy issue has been to encourage attempts to rebalance political structures in other countries, in favour of the weak and the vulnerable, while encouraging, as an underlying theme, more open political systems, with improved governance, popular participation and respect for civil liberties.

This tendency has been at work since the end of the Cold War. Iraq was hardly unusual in this respect. Comparable arguments were an essential ingredient for the rationales of the 'humanitarian interventions' of the 1990s. During this decade the Clinton Administration was clearly attracted by the notion, adduced by some international relations theorists, that increased global democratisation would mean increased peace. The Bush Administration has committed itself, if anything with even greater vigour, to the same path. More seriously, a number of members of the non-governmental humanitarian community bought into these arguments in ways that they would have been loath to do during earlier decades. Even with Iraq, a number of commentators who were clearly unhappy about many aspects of this war were enthusiastic about the end of the Saddam regime. Buoyed by important elections in Afghanistan, Palestine, and Ukraine, as well as Iraq, all of which could be said to set these countries on a new course, President Bush made what could be described as a 'war on tyranny' the core theme of his second term. Such a 'war' does not necessarily require military operations. Bush has insisted armed force is not the only and not necessarily the best means to achieve democratic breakthroughs. Events in Georgia in 2003, Ukraine in 2004 and Lebanon in 2005 were eloquent testimonies to 'people power' when challenging corrupt elites who were trying to hold on to power. The very fact that a President, and particularly one from the Republican Party, has taken such an avowedly interventionist stance in itself indicates an important shift in American foreign policy. The support coming from a Labour Prime Minister in Britain suggests that this approach cuts across traditional political lines of left and right, and certainly the campaigns for and against the Iraq war produced some political coalitions that would have seemed curious in the past. Robert Cooper, now a major influence on European foreign policy, has spoken approvingly of the robust adoption of democratic norms as 'liberal imperialism'.

A challenge had been mounted to the consensus behind the old core principle that there should be no interference in the internal affairs of other states, and that, even if confined to non-military means, and violation of this principle was detrimental to international order. In the conditions of the Cold War this restraint had a national as well as an international security rationale. External intervention from one direction risked prompting an equal and opposing external reaction from another. The end of the Cold War, bringing with it a marked increase in comity, and even amity, among the great powers, has reduced this more prudential concern. A general Western confidence with regard to the universality of their political values, especially after their triumph in the confrontation with state socialism, has discouraged attempts to justify the privileged position of the state in all circumstances, especially in conditions of civil war, repression, or genocide, and encouraged account being taken of the fate of individuals or minority groups.

To what extent might this lead to the use of force? Scepticism about state power was at the heart of classical liberalism, which was anti-militarist. Military expenditure was considered to be as wasteful as military elites were reactionary. Liberalism challenged the mercantilist assumption that military power was essential to the growth and consolidation of economic power. With no territory left for conquering, the old empires dismantled, and great-power antagonism much reduced, classic liberalism therefore would expect the potential role of armed forces to have shrunk considerably. While the 'victory' in the Cold War, which was at root an ideological triumph, may have turned the erstwhile status quo Western powers into radicals, simply by living successfully according to their core values. Through this example, they undermine disagreeable regimes and encourage changes in inefficient economic practices, without any question of employing force.

Even classical liberals recognised that force might be required to protect the weak against the strong in circumstances where violence is already being used on a substantial scale. Such violence is not unknown within Western societies but it is most likely to be found in states marked by social cleavages, fragile economies and non-consensual political systems. The processes of decolonisation have resulted in the proliferation of states that either have fallen into this category in the past or might do so in the future. In this context the shift from a focus on preparations for great-power conflict to humanitarian intervention is a natural one. The states that prompt such intervention are unlikely to be liberal capitalist in character, but Western interventions, even when they are largely economic in character, tend to encourage a move in that direction.

Wars conducted in pursuit of a humanitarian agenda, and which are likely to lead to pressures for domestic political reform and reconstruction, I call liberal wars. The ideal type for a liberal war is that it is altruistic in inspiration and execution. Such a war would focus on the balance of power within a state rather than between states, and can be presented as rescuing whole populations, or particularly vulnerable sections, from tyrannical governments or social breakdown. It addresses and rectifies some abuse of human rights but does not act as the cause of abuse. It is liberating and empowering while involving as few casualties as possible.

Liberal wars are not pursued in the name of strategic imperatives but because values are being affronted. Interests might be involved at the margins, but these are unlikely to count as 'vital', except in the most enlightened terms. For this reason liberal wars have acquired a discretionary aspect, to be assessed on a case-by-case basis. On this basis they have been described as 'wars of choice' to be contrasted with those of the past, which were 'wars of necessity' or 'of survival'. These involved great-power competition and direct threats to security, often prompted by the rise of radical but strong states. Wars of choice, of course, appear as wars of necessity for the local belligerents, who may well consider their most vital interests to be at stake, including their right to persist with their illiberalism. Questions of choice arise only for those whose survival is not threatened. I shall return to this question of choice in the conclusion of this essay: for the moment suffice it to note that this issue took on a different complexion after the terrorist attacks of 11 September 2001.

Liberalism and neo-conservatism

Describing such interventions as liberal wars raises a number of objections. These objections tend in one direction to accusations of hypocrisy, of bad intentions masquerading as good, and in the other to accusations of naivety, of bad consequences flowing from good intentions. I do not intend to cover those objections which claim that the altruism is a guise, and that there are other, more traditionally 'imperialistic' motives behind these wars, including the desire to control oil supplies, or to make the world safe for multinational companies. The question of 'real' motives may be interesting, and a degree of cynicism may be warranted, but the validity of the rationales can and should be assessed on their own terms.

A more serious objection is that a 'liberal war' is a misnomer. It assumes a concept of liberalism that does not reflect its actual use in contemporary politics, particularly in the United States where the urge to war is associated with neo-conservatives and is largely opposed by liberals. Yet it has often been noted that many of the views now associated with neo-conservatism derive from the liberal President Woodrow Wilson who believed that American power could be used to promote justice and democracy abroad. Conservatives would tend towards a much more cautious approach, more in the sceptical mould of President John Quincy Adams. While it is the case that the meanings of conservatism and liberalism in the American context have changed, they also remain fluid, at least in the area of foreign policy. There are certainly many American conservatives who reject the interventionism of the neo-conservatives, while many American liberals are drawn towards it in principle even if they recoil from the way it has been implemented.

Furthermore, the origins of neo-conservatism in the United States are truly liberal. They lie in the response to a section of the Democratic – not Republican – Party to the foreign policy debates of the early 1970s. On the one hand the neo-conservatives opposed the McGovernite tendency in the Party which questioned the need for defence expenditure and doubted the role of force in international affairs. This they thought was naïve. In this they were exactly in the tradition of the liberal realists of the mid-century, who insisted on the need to fight for the good life when dealing with totalitarianism, whether Nazi or Communist. Where they diverged was in resisting the logic of containment, originally promoted by the liberal realists to demonstrate the recklessness of the right. This manifested itself in opposition to the foreign policy of détente as practiced by both the US and European governments during the Nixon/Ford periods. This they also thought to be naïve because it assumed that the Soviet Union could be a status quo, conservative power, prepared to follow the same norms as the United States, for example in honouring arms control treaties, or in accepting the logic of mutual assured destruction in the nuclear field. But the human security agenda was very strong as well – reflected in the support for the right of Jews to leave Russia for Israel – the 'refuseniks'. This led to the Jackson-Vanik amendment to the 1974 US trade bill that would only allow Most Favoured Nation status to be granted to the Soviet Union in return for concessions on emigration. Another example was the objection to President Ford's refusal to meet notable dissident Alexandr Solzhenitsyn. There was a continued undercurrent of opposition to accepting repressive rule in East Europe as a price worth paying for regional order and dismay at the ease with which deals were done with authoritarian governments, from China to Saudi Arabia.

The propensity to exaggerate threats to national security, and to insist on high levels of defence preparedness, may be an enduring characteristic of neo-conservatism, which gives it a natural point of contact with more traditional conservatism, but it flowed in the 1970s from a view that the rottenness of the Soviet system was apt to make its leaders lash out as much externally as internally. Traditional conservatives, such as Nixon and Kissinger, assumed that there was no necessary correlation between beastliness towards one's own population and a propensity to external aggression. Regimes anxious about their own survival tended to be cautious in their assessments of power balances.

In this both Kissinger and, for that matter, Soviet leader Leonid Brezhnev missed the full significance of the human rights provisions contained in 'Basket Three' of the 1975 'Final Act' of the Helsinki Conference on Security and Cooperation in Europe (CSCE), which they saw as a collection of platitudes of minor importance because they lacked legal force. Brezhnev saw the purpose of CSCE as confirming Soviet hegemony over Eastern Europe, without appreciating the extent to which this minor concession would undermine this hegemony by providing dissident elements with the basis upon which to make their voices heard and make common cause with Western opponents of the Soviet system. President Gerald Ford's maladroit attempts to defend a pragmatic and therefore weak approach to change in the Eastern bloc was one reason he was so badly skewered in the 1976 election. The cause of human rights was still clearly a liberal one in the US as Jimmy Carter became President. The neo-conservatives were happy with that but unhappy over Carter's caution on military matters and readiness to engage in arms control negotiations. His perceived softness on national security issues proved to be Carter's undoing, and it was on that basis that a number of neo-conservatives joined the Reagan Administration. Their views influenced its rhetoric, particularly with regard to the Soviet Union. It is fair to say, however, that in a clash between anti-communism and anti-repression, the former tended to win. This was evident in both Latin America and the Middle East. The first President Bush was a traditional conservative, concerned more with stability and order than with justice – hence his slow response to the stirrings in Eastern Europe that marked the end of the Cold War and his reluctance to continue with military operations to overthrow the regime of Saddam Hussein, although he had an opportunity to do so. During the 1990s it was President Clinton who embraced the humanitarian agenda, although, like Carter, he combined this with a cautious approach to armed force.

The second President Bush's theme of using power to end tyranny around the globe would traditionally, therefore, have been seen as a liberal theme. It is true that those who would describe themselves as liberals tend to be firm opponents of President Bush, but more because of the other themes in foreign policy, and the execution of specific initiatives, including the ineptitude in the diplomacy prior to the Iraq War, and the mismanagement of the occupation after it. As was evident from the circumlocutions adopted by Senator Kerry during his failed bid for the presidency, liberals were loath either to reject the Wilsonian tradition or to disavow the human security agenda.

Liberalism and European moderation

A further objection is that in Europe liberalism has been more associated with the international security than the human security agenda. Not surprisingly, in view of twentieth century history, European liberalism has been designed to solve the problem of war rather than the problem of injustice and has, in consequence, stressed the potential role of international organisations and law. The experience of the nineteenth century would, however, have led to a different conclusion, with liberalism less uneasy with the occasional interference in the internal affairs of others and always celebrating the erosion of authoritarian governments.

The point of the realist critique of liberal internationalism was that the maintenance of order, and the protection of the weak against the strong, could not be sensibly considered as a matter of the rule of law and the support for institutions, but also had to consider matters of power and interest. The realists, however, were vulnerable to the charge of being too cynical in assuming that power and interest were all that mattered. Contrary to the view that the domestic politics of the great powers were largely an irrelevance, and that the individual units related to each other on the basis of a straightforward calculus of relative strength, varied by means of alliances and the occasional war, the ideological battle was always central to prevailing concepts of international order. The system was sensitive not only to acts of external aggression but also internal subversion, and the boundary between the two was never as clear-cut as the classic 'realist' texts would have it. If threats to international order do not simply take the form of criminal, aggressor states who disregard the rules, but a challenge to the philosophical basis upon which power *within* individual states rests, then great powers cannot duck issues of ideological hegemony.

So the occasions when the rights and duties of the Great Powers were established, such as the Congress of Vienna in 1815, the League of Nations in 1919 and the United Nations in 1945, each followed the defeat of a threatening ideology – revolutionary republicanism, anti-democratic authoritarianism, racist nationalism. Each time the hope was that a new consensus could be based on a set of shared principles. They failed when new ideological fault lines opened up. In practice, therefore, the principle of non-interference in internal affairs was always conditional. Disinterest in each others' internal affairs was only possible for states when their respective ideologies did not threaten each other. The Napoleonic Wars left Europe dominated by essentially conservative states. They shared hostility towards any revolutionary ideology which might provide not only a motor for the accumulation of power and territory but also contest their very legitimacy. The radical ideologies of socialism and anarchism posed the most direct threat to internal order yet it was the rise of liberalism that was most influential. Liberalism if taken seriously is inherently disorderly. It promotes the right to liberty at the individual level and self-determination at the national, and also poses a free market challenge to mercantilism. Demands for self-determination were particularly subversive. A sense of nationhood could lead to new aggregations of states, as with Italy and Germany, as well fragmentation, as in the Ottoman and Austro-Hungarian Empires.

By the twentieth century, liberalism was the ascendant ideology, even amongst the status quo powers. It therefore became associated with the maintenance of a stable international order. The attempts to establish the rule of international law, and even move towards world government, assumed that the core principles of liberalism could provide the foundation. If there was mutual respect for individual and group rights there would be no basis for conflict. The problem for European liberalism therefore lay in the potential disconnect between the requirements of international security and human security. When political movements challenged basic rights, the issue for international order, as with domestic order, was to ensure that the community as a whole protected them. This required a theory of political obligation, always a difficult area for liberalism in that it qualified the basic freedom to ignore the problems of others. Once key states in the system were led by illiberal regimes, then prioritising international security meant overcoming distaste for these regimes in order to achieve war-avoiding accommodations.

During the Cold War there was an impasse between liberal democracy and state socialism. This meant that any attempt by either to roll back the boundaries of the other carried a risk of major, and possibly nuclear, war. Common prudence suggested caution, however distasteful the accommodation. This was confirmed in the détente of the 1970s, which began with the 'Ostpolitik' of the German social democrats in the late 1960s. This was a deliberate decision to ease tensions between East and West Germany, and by extension the two halves of Europe, by ignoring the aspirations of those in the satellite states of Eastern Europe. Although this was picked up and taken forward by the Nixon/Kissinger team, Europeans always had the greatest stake in its continuation, and they became alarmed when, under the early influence of the neo-conservatives, détente was subjected to a severe American challenge. It was easy enough to dismiss the paranoid tendency in neo-conservatism, which could be criticised for exaggerating the military prowess and inherent strength of the Warsaw Pact. The moral critique was much more difficult, reflected in the ambivalent attitudes shown towards President Carter's preoccupation with human rights and then the rise of Solidarity in Poland. Even during the 1980s, many European 'moderates' saw progress being made through détente and arms control, arranged at grand summits, rather than through the ideological subversion of communism, although that is how the Cold War in fact ended. They had assumed that communism would continue indefinitely.

Once communism collapsed, the focus of European foreign policy was, in the first instance, to work out how to put an institutional lock on the new European constellation. Enlargement of the European Community (as it was then) initially came up against the preference for 'deepening rather than widening'. It was the Clinton Administration more than the governments of what became the European Union that appreciated that the logic of the new situation was to support rather than resist the aspirations of the former Communist states to join the Western world, however destabilising that might appear (especially in Moscow). This is why the post-communist states have been more supportive of American foreign policy.

As a liberal hegemony was steadily being established in Europe the human security agenda moved into the rest of the world. If 'failed' and 'rogue' states were menaces to their own people and also their neighbours, sovereignty came to be seen to be increasingly conditional. The foreign policy debate in Europe as in the United States struggled with how to identify the point at which states were no longer allowed to mismanage their internal affairs without interference, when their behaviour becomes so offensive as to demand action. During the 1990s the trend was towards acceptance of the need to intervene and that this might require resolute and robust force. The consequences of passivity in Rwanda in 1994 and Srebrenica the next year weighed heavily on liberal consciences. The high point of this approach came in the 1999 operation in Kosovo. Here legitimacy won over legality (at least in so far as not requiring any Security Council vote, which Russia and China would have vetoed). European governments could take comfort in a sense that they were riding the tide of history. The international consensus was moving in this direction, reflected in the assertion of a 'responsibility to protect', in a report commissioned by the Canadian government and the increasing embrace of this norm by international organisations, most recently by the Secretary-General's High-Level Panel on Threats, Challenges and Change.

Unnatural wars

Before considering the impact of events since 11 September 2001 on such thinking, a further and potentially more substantial objection to the notion of a liberal war must be addressed. Wars are inherently illiberal in their effects and their consequences and so a liberal war constitutes an unnatural act. War appeals to the baser human instincts and requires the suppression of individuality in pursuit of the collective good. Large-scale violence, whatever the motives which prompt its use or the precision with which it is applied, is bound to put people and property at risk, threatening the most fundamental human right of all – the right to life. They are violent and unpredictable and can develop a ferocious dynamic which can lead to consequences which in their human cost appear to contradict the claims made on their behalf.

In principle this can be countered by fighting in the just war tradition, not only in terms of just cause but also with a methodology that distinguishes between combatants and non-combatants and achieves a degree of proportionality in the force used, sufficient to right the original wrong but not so much as to make matters worse. Wars fought with excessive force and indifference to all casualties, but particularly civilian, will be drained of legitimacy. One of the claims made for modern military technologies that it allows lethal firepower to be directed with extraordinary and discriminating precision, thereby mitigating this risk to legitimacy. If civilians suffer it will not be because they are deliberate targets but because of 'collateral damage', and so the suffering will be far less than in past wars.

Yet despite the possibilities of the new technologies, summed in the notion of the 'revolution in military affairs', it remains difficult in war to relate means to ends in a reliably proportionate manner. Military methods must be geared not only to the political stakes but also to the capacities and methods of the adversary. The political pressures may be towards minimum force but the military pressures may point in the opposite direction. While the stakes for the intervening powers may be limited those for the local parties are likely to be total. The intervention will be unlikely to have occurred were it not for illiberal actions against civilians. The strategies adopted to counter or deter external intervention will play on the determination of the intervener to keep the war limited by challenging attempts to separate the civilian from the military in targeting, and threaten considerable casualties all round over a prolonged period. If the costs of the commitment can be made to rise then a choice to enter can soon be overtaken by a determination to exit. Except that exit also carries a political cost: a reputation for reneging on commitments and vulnerability to pressure. Western governments soon become well aware of the reputational risks, as could be seen with NATO deciding that it had to continue with the Kosovo War or the US concluding that it had to accept an unexpectedly high level of casualties among its own troops in Iraq.

Lastly, there may be an underlying cultural arrogance, not only in the belief that such wars can be undertaken without causing major casualties but also that they might improve conditions in troubled parts of the world where conflicts have multiple and deep-seated causes. It is one thing to enter a broken country to relieve immediate suffering, but it is quite another to mend the country. If the suffering is not to return then it is not enough to deal with the immediate problem and then leave, but experience suggests that the effort required to turn a country round, especially if it remains internally divided, can be substantial and prolonged.

There are therefore both principled and prudential reasons to object to war as a means of achieving supposedly liberal goals. This leads to a view that it is best if the Western world leaves the weak and failed states of the world alone. The bombast of petty dictators, the sufferings they inflict and the fear they engender should all be deplored, but we need do no more because in the end they are irrelevant to our own prosperity and security. There are a number of problems with this alternative view. In a world of permeable borders and easy movement across continents, the conflicts of one region are soon imported by others. It is not so easy to avoid the impact of events elsewhere. Such a view also overstates the ease with which governments can note the pain of others and move on, especially once the international media have taken an interest. As things stand there are good reasons for the current levels of discomfort at the international responses to the plague of HIV/Aids or the terrible carnage of some of the civil wars in Africa.

It would of course be better to use non-military means to achieve the same goals. The most successful instruments of liberal (or potentially liberal) change in recent years have been popular movements. This was evident in the 1989 collapse of communism in central and eastern Europe, then in the later undermining of many post-Soviet regimes. Popular movements work best against regimes which are one step away from being completely ruthless and, crucially, cannot rely on the support of the police or army. Alternative forms of external pressure to armed force, and in particular economic sanctions, can have an influence over time, but, as the Iraqi case demonstrates, they raise their own problems. The net result of sanctions can be to strengthen a regime, by giving it greater control over residual trade flows, including smuggling, thereby allowing it to look after its own needs first and put those of the populace second, while blaming the international community for any hardships. Even when forceful methods are contemplated, it may still be the case that sometimes these problems appear too great to handle, even when states work in concert together or through the UN.

So the inherent illiberality of war may at times have to be set against the even more illiberal consequences of inaction. Sometimes the consequences of passivity may be too awful and the military options credible; at other times the case for intervention may be strong but the military options poor or the economic requirements too large. Political leaders in democratic societies dare not take on too many external problems. The needs of a particular country – for example Sierra Leone – might be addressed, but when the cases are multiplied and become so diverse and geographically spread, then it is not surprising that even the most committed governments from the more stable and prosperous states tend to pick and choose, dealing only with the problems with which they can cope. There are therefore a number of opportunities to engage in liberal wars, but only a few are likely to be taken up. This is why these wars have been presented as discretionary.

A liberal war on terror?

I have argued that liberal attitudes to war reflect the combined impact of the ideological currents at play at different stages in the history of the international system as well as the contemporary configurations of power. There is a traditional dislike of the primacy given to the rights of states in the international system. In the absence of a utopian world government, a moral foreign policy requires that at least stronger states think beyond their narrow self-interest and accept a responsibility to promote and enforce essential values, and, when necessary, protect the weak. Historically the focus was on defending weak states against larger, predatory, aggressive states. More recently there has been a shift towards what is happening within states, particularly those which are either being torn apart through civil war or whose ruling elites can only achieve security for themselves through the systematic oppression of their own people or the victimisation of vulnerable groups.

Defending weak states against aggressors meant upholding the rights of states to conduct their own affairs as they wish. The new focus poses the question of the extent to which the sovereignty of states can be compromised or qualified or just ignored because of the impact of their weakness on others, or because of their treatment of their own people. The need to prevent great human suffering must limit the rights of states to conduct their own affairs without external interference. Because there is a reluctance to jettison the old principle of non-interference, deemed essential for international security, much contemporary diplomatic discourse takes the form of establishing the conditions in which it is legitimate to set it aside. One relevant example might be Prime Minister Blair's speech in Chicago of April 1999, clearly delivered with the ongoing Kosovo war in mind, which was one of the first by a senior Western leader to address this problem directly, and set out a series of tests, which taken together were potentially restrictive, including the quality of the case, the exhaustion of diplomatic remedies and the feasibility of military remedies, the readiness to commit for the long-term and some conformity with national interests. Others have put a greater focus on process, for example only engaging in interventions sanctioned by the United Nations, or on consequences, ensuring that at the very least more harm is avoided than caused. Most recently, the Secretary-General's high-level panel came up with seriousness of threat, proper primary purpose, last resort, proportional means and a favourable balance of likely consequences. Going back to Caspar Weinberger, after the fiasco of the Beirut intervention of 1982–4, whose unhappy conclusion reflected a clash between initial, liberal humanitarian motives and grander strategic ambitions, American policymakers when considering any non-essential operation have paid particular attention to their ability to sustain public support. This has involved considerations of likely casualties, the ability to apply overwhelming force and appropriate command structures.

Few of these tests could be considered objective, in many cases because they involve anticipating the outcomes of inherently unpredictable events, and there is always the problem with such lists as to what should be done when most but not all of the tests can be passed. All assume military engagements out of choice rather than necessity, so they are particularly relevant to contingencies connected to human security. As my starting example of Iraq illustrates, however, in rationalising war political leaders will seek to address the international and national security dimensions as well as the human. Indeed, when the non-interference principle ruled supreme, the core rationales were normally national, and the evident humanitarian benefits were if anything played down, for example during the 1970s with India into Pakistan, Tanzania into Uganda and Vietnam into Cambodia.

An important feature of the 2000s is the insistence by the United States that the two major military interventions it has led, into Afghanistan and Iraq, have been wars of necessity as much as choice, with a primary purpose of national security although clear benefits for international and human security. The case for war was based on the need to prevent further, and even more devastating, terrorist attacks, following the outrage of September 2001. They came under the umbrella heading of a 'global war on terror' as declared by President Bush. Liberal critics have objected to casting this struggle as a war rather than as a multi-faceted problem with social, cultural, economic and political aspects, thereby encouraging a search for military solutions, which can make these other aspects worse, and a disregard of civil liberties.

But there have been evident tensions within liberal opinion. There are often links to situations which prompted past humanitarian interventions, such as Kosovo or East Timor, or might have done had not prudence dictated otherwise, such as Chechnya or Sudan, as well as to other long-standing struggles, such as those over Afghanistan, Kashmir or Palestine. But the stakes go well beyond ethnic cleansing or repression to the propagation of particular worldviews, and to direct threat to homelands as much as to innocents abroad. The ideological roots of the jihadist terrorism, of which al-Qaeda is the most notable exponent, are profoundly illiberal, in stressing theocracy and intolerance of diversity and dissent above democracy, as well as being socially homophobic and misogynist. The enemy is not a rogue regime or faction, which though nasty might be isolated, but rather a movement that seeks to draw upon a sense of grievance, humiliation and outrage throughout the Islamic world, connecting a range of conflicts in a global struggle. In many Western cities this ideological struggle is evident, as extreme Islamist groups are seen to challenge the prevailing secular, liberal consensus.

This ideological threat to liberal values is not at the same level as Nazism or Communism, because it is not backed by a powerful state, and within the normative streams that make up Islam it is controversial and contested. It appears dangerous because of the violence at its centre, often described in a somewhat apocalyptical and vengeful form. So while it has been observed correctly that it is odd to declare war against a particular tactic, often defined carelessly to include any irregular action against a repressive state, mass casualty terrorism has a particular quality, which can readily be framed as an issue of human security. As with the acts that prompt humanitarian intervention, the victims are most likely to be defenceless civilians. The moral objection lies in the use of violent means against non-combatants for political objectives. Over the past century we moved from a situation where 90 per cent of the casualties of war were combatants to one where 90 per cent were civilians. To stress the importance of protecting civilians, is to reinforce the trend in Western military thinking that emphasises capabilities to deal with enemy armed forces, and to stress the importance of restraint in situations where innocent civilians may get harmed.

There is an important difference between vicious domestic persecution or ethnic cleansing as measures used by the strong against the weak, and the desperate measures to which the weak may resort to find redress, which may tend towards the terroristic. So while the victims of ethnic cleansing and other human rights abuses have by definition already been marginalised, the victims of terrorism are more likely to be found in the cities of the strong. This is why terrorism is more likely to prompt a response by the strong, and why a war to ease humanitarian distress may well be against the established regime yet a war against terrorism may well be in its support. Hence concerns that authoritarian regimes will label all dissident groups as terroristic as a means of avoiding addressing legitimate grievances.

The greatest concern is that the readiness to inflict mass casualties will be facilitated by access to weapons that would hitherto have been only available to the more powerful states. We now call these capabilities weapons of mass destruction, but perhaps that is the wrong term. Our concern is weapons of civil destruction. The problem lies in the intent rather than the method. In sufficient quantities machetes and handguns can have the effects of large bombs while a few knives can turn airliners into lethal missiles, just as chemical and biological weapons can be used on quite small scales.

So although concerns about terrorism and weapons of civil destruction appear to put Western security interests to the fore, they link back to the concerns that might prompt liberal wars in two critical respects. First terrorism feeds off the conflicts of the troubled regions of the world. The more these can be calmed the less scope there will be for the terrorists to find sanctuary and recruits. Second, there is an underlying theme that attacks on those unable to defend themselves, whether in a Western skyscraper or an African village, must always be condemned and those who perpetrate such crimes against humanity must be restrained and if possible brought to justice. The ideological dimension adds a third linkage, because of the profound illiberalism of the jihadist movement.

The tense turn in international politics since 2001 does not therefore take Western considerations of the use of force away from liberal norms but adds a further dimension. It is important to be clear that this is not an argument for additional militancy in foreign policy. The stress on democracy and human rights that has now become a feature of the pronouncements of Western governments and international organisations will make itself felt in many ways. Change will often come about through popular movements or authoritarian governments attempting to adjust to the new normative environment. Nor should this be taken to suggest that because liberal values may be involved, all Western military actions are thereby vindicated. The advantage of stressing the importance of the liberal dimension is that it sets standards for Western governments, against which they should be judged when putting civilians at risk or in their treatment of prisoners. It reinforces the argument that the values at stake must be reflected in the conduct of wars and the struggle against terrorist groups. In addition, because interventions risk lives, cost money, and can last a long time they must always require special justification, and in practice will normally be viewed with reluctance rather than enthusiasm. My point is only that we may now be entering a stage where all wars in which the major Western powers get involved will take on aspects of liberal wars, designed to provide relief to the displaced and the dispossessed and prevent mass murder. In sum, the legitimate use of armed force will be in support of liberal values, and in particular against those preparing for, supporting or engaging in acts of civil destruction.

Force, legitimacy, success, and Iraq

JOHN MUELLER

Having apparently abandoned war as a device for settling their own quarrels, developed countries, in the wake of the Cold War, have had an opportunity to cooperate to deal with the two chief remaining sources of artificial or human-made death: civil war and vicious regimes. In addition, international law has evolved to allow them to do so, variously conferring legitimacy on most international policing measures even when they involve the use of military force and even when they violate the policed country's sovereignty.

Until 2003, these policing ventures had generally been successful, at least in their own terms. However, despite this general record of success, it seems unlikely that developed countries will be able to carry out such exercises with any sort of consistency or reliability. This is because they often have little interest in humanitarian problems in distant areas of the globe, because they sometimes subscribe to a misguided impression about ancient ethnic hatreds that provides them with a convenient excuse for neglect, because they have a low tolerance for casualties in such ventures, because they have an aversion to the costs and problems that attend long-term policing, because there seems to be little domestic political gain from success in policing ventures, and because they harbour something of a bias against undertakings that could be construed as aggression.

Moreover, the war upon Iraq being conducted by the United States and the United Kingdom will very likely substantially reinforce the developed world's already considerable reticence about such enterprises. Had the invasion been a success by quickly establishing an effective domestic government and by discovering banned and threatening weapons of mass destruction in Iraq and convincing links between the deposed Iraqi regime and international terrorism, the venture, despite the very considerable misgivings, even hostility, of most of the international community, would probably have been accepted as legitimate in time. By contrast, because of the essential failure of the mission in its primary goals and because of the unexpectedly massive human and economic costs of the occupation and state-building effort, the venture is unlikely to garner much in the way of international approval and, more importantly, will hardly enhance enthusiasm for similar ventures, even ones likely to be successful and far less costly,

However, there does seem to be another approach to the problems of civil war and of vicious regimes: establishing and nurturing competent and effective domestic governments, something that seems to be coming about more or less on its own. This less-noticed development could prove to be an effective, and long-term, solution to the problem.

The decline of international war

Throughout history international wars have often been immediately motivated by ideology, religion, pique, aggressive impulse, military rivalry, nationalism, revenge,

109

economic deprivation or exuberance, and the lust for battle. But such impelling motives and passions have generally been expressed in a quest to conquer and to possess territory: 'I came, I saw, I conquered', Julius Caesar pronounced self-importantly. That sort of impetus is, in various ways, very frequently found at the core of war. Thus, notes John Vasquez, territory is 'a general underlying cause of war', and he stresses that 'of all the possible issues states can fight over, the evidence overwhelmingly indicates that issues involving territory . . . are the main ones prone to collective violence'. And 'Few interstate wars are fought without any territorial issues being involved in one way or another'.[1]

Therefore, it would appear that a potential cure for international war would be to disallow territorial expansion by states.

The effort to do so was begun with determination in the wake of the First World War. For the most part, war ceased to be embraced as it often had been before 1914 – as supreme theatre, redemptive turmoil, a cleansing thunderstorm, or an uplifting affirmation of manhood. Now people who had often praised war and eagerly anticipated its terrible, determining convulsions found themselves appalled by it. Within half a decade, war opponents, once a derided minority, became a decided majority: everyone now seemed to be a peace advocate.[2]

The peacemakers of 1918, substantially convinced now that the institution of war must be controlled or eradicated, adapted several of the devices peace advocates had long been promoting, at least in part. A sort of world government, the League of Nations, was fabricated to speak for the world community and to apply moral and physical pressure on potential peace-breakers. Aggression – the expansion of international boundaries by military force – was ceremoniously outlawed, and in the League Covenant signatory states solemnly undertook for the first time in history 'to respect and preserve . . . the territorial integrity and existing political independence' of all League members.[3]

The Second World War, none too surprisingly, embellished this perspective. For somewhat differing reasons, the three countries that started the war had done so to conquer territory: Hitler sought living space to the east, Mussolini domination in Africa and the Balkans, the Japanese glorious empire in east and southeast Asia.

Accordingly, building on efforts conducted after the First World War, the peacemakers of 1945 declared international boundaries to be fixed, no matter how illogical or unjust some of them might seem to interested observers. And the peoples residing in the chunks of territory contained within them would be expected to establish governments which, no matter how disgusting or reprehensible, would then be dutifully admitted to a special club of 'sovereign' states known as the United

---

[1] John A. Vasquez, *The War Puzzle* (Cambridge, UK: Cambridge University Press, 1993), pp. 151, 293.

[2] On this process, see John Mueller, *Retreat from Doomsday: The Obsolescence of Major War* (New York: Basic Books, 1989); John Mueller, *Quiet Cataclysm: Reflections on the Recent Transformation of World Politics* (New York: HarperCollins, 1995), ch. 9. See also Robert Cooper, *The Breaking of Nations: Order and Chaos in the Twenty-first Century* (New York: Atlantic Monthly Press, 2003), pp. 101, 111, 151. A. A. Milne crisply characterised the change this way: 'In 1913, with a few exceptions we all thought war was a natural and fine thing to happen, so long as we were well prepared for it and had no doubt about coming out the victor. Now, with a few exceptions, we have lost our illusions, we are agreed that war is neither natural nor fine, and that the victor suffers from it equally with the vanquished'. *Peace with Honour* (New York: Dutton, 1935), pp. 9–10.

[3] Mark Zacher, 'The Territorial Integrity Norm: International Boundaries and the Use of Force', *International Organization*, 55 (Spring 2001), pp. 219–20.

Nations. Efforts to change international frontiers by force or the threat of force were sternly declared to be unacceptable.[4]

Rather amazingly, this process has, for various reasons and for the most part, worked. Despite the fact that many international frontiers were in dispute, despite the fact that there remained vast colonial empires in which certain countries possessed certain other countries or proto-countries, and despite the fact that some of the largest states quickly became increasingly enmeshed in a profound ideological and military rivalry known as the Cold War, the prohibition against territorial aggression has been astoundingly successful. In the decades since 1945, reversing the experience and patterns of all recorded history, there have been very few alterations of international boundaries through force.[5] Indeed, the only time one United Nations member tried to conquer another and to incorporate it into its own territory was when Iraq invaded Kuwait in 1990, an act that inspired almost total condemnation in the world and one that was reversed in 1991 by military force.[6]

It took 100 years to extinguish slavery as a major institution in human affairs: the first notable anti-slavery protests erupted in 1788 and the last substantial slave system, that of Brazil, was dismantled in 1888. An organised political movement agitating for the elimination of war really began, or at any rate took off, in 1889 with the publication in Europe of Bertha von Suttner's best-selling potboiler, *Die Waffen Nieder!* When the Cold War ended, one hundred years later, war – at least the kind of war von Suttner was concerned about – had slumped, if not into obsolescence, at least into considerable and most notable disuse. Shattering centuries of bloody practice, the developed countries of Europe and elsewhere had substantially abandoned it as a method for dealing with their disagreements. In the history of warfare, the most interesting statistic is zero (or near-zero): the number of wars between developed states since 1945. Moreover, as Figure 1 makes clear, international war of any sort had become quite rare by 1989.

Force, legitimacy, and intervention in the new world order

When the Cold War ended, the world entered what some were given to calling 'a new world order'. Developed countries came basically to see the world in much the same way, and there was little or no fear of war between them. Notable problems remained, of course. High among these, certainly, is managing the entry of Russia and China, the main losers of the Cold War, into the world community – a process that generally seems to be going reasonably well.

---

[4] On this process, see Zacher, 'Territorial Integrity Norm'. See also Mary Kaldor, *New and Old Wars: Organized Violence in a Global Era* (Cambridge, UK: Polity Press, 1999), p. 5; Christine Gray, *International Law and the Use of Force*, 2nd edn. (Oxford, UK: Oxford University Press, 2004), p. 59.

[5] For a detailed discussion and enumeration, see Zacher, 'Territorial Integrity Norm'. It should not be concluded that the international norm *caused* this process, however. The norm and its associated institutional structure stress peace, but they are not so much the cause of the desire for peace as its result. That is, the norm was specifically fabricated and developed because war-averse countries, noting that disputes over territory had been a major cause of international war in the past, were seeking to enforce and enshrine the norm. Its existence did not cause them to be war-averse, but rather the reverse.

[6] Gray, *International Law*, p. 252.

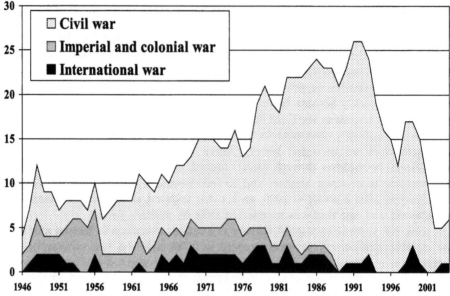

Figure 1. *Frequency of war, 1946–2004.*

Note: The data are for 'wars', violent armed conflicts which result in at least 1,000 battle deaths over the duration of the dispute for international wars, an average of at least 1,000 battle deaths per year for imperial and colonial wars, and at least 1,000 military and civilian battle-related deaths per year for civil wars.

Source: Kristian S. Gleditsch, 'A Revised List of Wars Between and Within Independent States, 1861–2002', *International Interactions*, 30 (2004), pp. 231–62, plus additional correspondence with Gleditsch.

Another central problem, more ambiguous and tentative, is the establishment of mechanisms for dealing with what remains of disorder in the new world order. Specifically, in their new era of essential consensus, the developed countries have been free to explore various devices for managing the world. Some of these devices are diplomatic, social, or economic, but the judicious application of military force is also potentially available.

It may therefore be time to go back to first principles. The problem with war, of course, is not the institution in the abstract – it does often settle differences – but rather in its consequences: the death and destruction that inevitably ensue. Although there remain places and issues over which international war could erupt, this once-perennial problem has been substantially brought under control. Nonetheless, two very notable sources of artificial or human-made death and destruction continue to exist.[7]

One of these is civil war. As Figure 1 makes clear, this is the chief remaining form of war. And many of these wars, some of them with considerable intervention from

---

[7] International terrorism is not included because it actually accounts (so far at least) for comparatively few deaths – apart from 2001, only a few hundred a year worldwide. Domestic terrorism can be costlier, but when it is sufficiently extensive, it is usually considered to constitute civil warfare or insurgency, not terrorism. For a discussion, see John Mueller, 'Simplicity and Spook: Terrorism and the Dynamics of Threat Exaggeration', *International Studies Perspectives*, 6 (May 2005), pp. 220–1.

outside governments, have been highly destructive. For example, in the late 1990s, a semi-internationalised civil war – or set of civil wars – in the Congo resulted in the deaths, by some estimates, of three million people, mostly from the starvation and disease it caused. If the death tally is accurate, that little-noticed war would be the most costly since World War II.

The second is government. In fact, over the course of the bloody twentieth century, far more people were killed by their own governments than were killed by all wars put together.[8] During the 1990s, for example, the government of Rwanda systematically tried to kill off a minority group resulting perhaps in upwards of half a million deaths; in North Korea at the same time, the regime so mismanaged and exacerbated famine conditions that hundreds of thousands of people died, with some careful estimates putting the number at over two million.[9]

In principle, the international community is ill-prepared to deal with civil conflict and with vicious or destructively incompetent domestic governments because it is chiefly set up to confront problems that transcend international borders, not ones that lurk within them. Effectively, the international community is supposed to stand aloof when governments devastate their own populations and when countries become enmeshed in catastrophic civil wars that governments either create or find themselves incapable of controlling.

However, having substantially abandoned war and armed conflict among themselves, the developed countries can, if they so desire, expand their efforts and collaborate on international police work to deal with civil war and with vicious domestic regimes. And, indeed, the Security Council of the United Nations does appear in recent years to have developed or evolved the legal ability to authorise military intervention to police civil wars or to oust a state government deemed too incompetent or too venal to be allowed to continue to exist.[10]

As it happens, the opportunities are considerable. Most civil warfare, though certainly not all, is readily policeable because it is chiefly perpetrated by poorly-coordinated, if often savage, thugs. Moreover, many of the most vicious governments that exist are substantially of the criminal variety, enjoy little popular support, and could readily be toppled by coordinated forces sent from outside.[11] This is because criminal or near-criminal forces tend to be cowardly and incompetent when confronted by effective disciplined forces. The intimidating, opportunistic thugs have been successful mainly because they are the biggest bullies on the block. However, like most bullies (and sadists and torturers), they tend not to be particularly interested in engaging a formidable opponent. Moreover, they substantially lack organisation, discipline, coherent tactics or strategy, deep motivation, broad popular support, ideological commitment, and, essentially, courage.

[8] Rudolph Rummel, *Death by Government* (New Brunswick, NJ: Transaction, 1994); Benjamin Valentino, *Final Solutions* (Ithaca, NY: Cornell University Press, 2003), ch. 1.

[9] Andrew S. Natsios, *The Great North Korean Famine* (Washington, DC: United States Institute of Peace Press, 2001), p. 215.

[10] Gray, *International Law*, pp. 250–1. On this issue, see also John Rawls, *The Law of Peoples* (Cambridge, MA: Harvard University Press, 1999), pp. 81, 93n; Kofi Annan, 'Two Concepts of Sovereignty', *Economist*, 16 September 1999; Lee Feinstein and Anne-Marie Slaughter, 'A Duty to Prevent', *Foreign Affairs* (January/February 2004), pp. 136–41; and, 'A More Secure World: Our Shared Responsibility', Report of the High-level Panel on Threats, Challenges and Change, United Nations, 2004, paragraph 203.

[11] John Mueller, *The Remnants of War* (Ithaca, NY: Cornell University Press, 2004), chs. 6–7.

Mostly success: policing by developed countries before 2003

In fact, since the Cold War, there have been a number of instances in which developed countries have applied, or credibly threatened to apply, military force in other countries to seek to correct conditions they consider sufficiently unsuitable: in Panama in 1989, in Kuwait and Iraq in 1991, in Somalia in 1992–93, in Haiti in 1994, in Bosnia in 1995, in Kosovo and East Timor in 1999, in Sierra Leone in 2000, in Afghanistan in 2001, and in Iraq in 2003. Except for the last, they were able to engage in these ventures at remarkably little cost to themselves, particularly in casualties.

Moreover, again until the 2003 war in Iraq, these armed interventions were eventually accepted as legitimate, and (perhaps) in effect legal. In large part this seems to have been because they were successful in their own terms. Many of them were conducted under the legal umbrella of Security Council authorisation, but some of them were not – most importantly, NATO's intervention in the civil war in Kosovo in 1999. Yet later in that year, UN Secretary General Kofi Annan extrapolated from the venture in Kosovo as well as from the UN-authorised peace mission to East Timor to argue for 'the need for timely intervention by the international community when death and suffering are being inflicted on large numbers of people, and when the state nominally in charge is unable or unwilling to stop it'.[12]

Impediments to international policing

However, despite the fact that these ventures have mostly been successful at least in their own terms, it seems unlikely that the developed states will be able systematically to create and support mechanisms for policing civil warfare and for dealing with vicious domestic regimes. There seem to be several reasons for this.

Lack of interest. The dynamic of the Cold War contest caused the two sides to believe that their interests were importantly engaged almost everywhere. A central tenet of Communist ideology was that violent revolutionary conflict was pretty much inevitable and that Communist states were duty-bound to help out wherever it cropped up. Meanwhile, the Western policy of containment was based on the notion that any gain anywhere for Communism would lead to further Western losses elsewhere and thus that just about all Communist thrusts must be actively opposed.

Once this elemental contest evaporated, however, most areas of the world became substantially less important to developed countries. In the 1960s, civil war in the Congo inspired dedicated meddling by both sides; in the 1990s no one wanted to become involved very much in the complicated and hugely destructive civil war that ravaged that country.

Thus, in the wake of the Cold War, two contradictory, even paradoxical, developments took place. On the one hand, East-West and major country cooperation became far easier to arrange than before. On the other, the major countries found few trouble spots worthy of their efforts.

---

[12] Annan, 'Two Concepts of Sovereignty'.

When active, militarised interest has been stirred, it is generally because developed countries have concluded that their own interests have become involved. Iraq and North Korea may sport regimes which are contemptible in the extreme and disasters to their own people, but the concern of the developed states has almost entirely been bound up with the fear that those countries might develop weapons which could threaten the outside world.[13] The United States was impelled into the Haitian morass substantially because of the politically embarrassing flow of refugees that was being created (partly by the economic sanctions it had imposed). The Australians sent policing forces to East Timor in large part because they want to live in a stable neighbourhood. In several cases – Panama, Haiti, Bosnia, Kosovo, East Timor, and Iraq – developed nations became enmeshed, or self-entrapped, in part by their own previous rhetoric. But, in the meantime, tolerance of ongoing human disasters within Zimbabwe, Zambia, Congo, Sudan, Burma, and North Korea (unless that country becomes threatening to outsiders) continues.

Increased fears of international terrorism could modify this conclusion in the future because, like threatening Communist revolutionaries, terrorists can be based just about anywhere. This is, of course, what impelled the United States into military action in Afghanistan in 2001; it had not previously shown all that much concern about the destruction that country's regime was visiting upon its own people.

It is doubtful, however, that the campaign against terrorism will lead to very many similar episodes. In the future, regimes which harbour terrorists are unlikely to be so open about it while, insofar as they need bases at all, international terrorists are likely to concentrate even less than they do now. Moreover, terrorism is much more like crime than it is like warfare in its essential dynamics. Military measures may sometimes be useful, but what is mostly required is police work: intelligence gathering, staking out suspects, gathering evidence, checking and rechecking, guarding potential targets, and so on. And, like all good police work, it should be carried out selectively and with discrimination since overreaction can be counterproductive, doing more to create terrorists and terrorism than to snuff them out.

The convenient ancient hatreds image. Second, leaders and publics in developed states have concluded that many civil wars are essentially inexplicable all-against-all conflicts, rooted in old hatreds that could hardly be ameliorated by well-meaning, but innocent and naive, outsiders. It follows therefore that intervention would at best be simply a short-term palliative and thus a pointless exertion.

This convenient excuse for inaction seems to have emerged in the early 1990s when civil war shockingly broke out in Yugoslavia, on a continent that had been free from civil war for over 40 years. The need for an explanation, preferably a simple one, was handily supplied by pundits like the fashionable travel writer and congenital pessimist, Robert Kaplan. In a book and, probably much more importantly, in a front page article in the Sunday *New York Times Book Review* in 1993, he portentously proclaimed the Balkans to be 'a region of pure memory' where 'each

---

[13] As Francis Fukuyama has put it of the Iraq War, if the Republicans 'had gone to Congress in the autumn of 2002 asking for war powers by saying that they wanted to expend several hundred billion dollars and several thousand American lives in order to bring democracy to ... Iraq, they would have been laughed out of court'. 'America's Parties and their Foreign Policy Masquerade', *Financial Times*, 8 March 2005, p. 21.

individual sensation and memory affects the grand movement of clashing peoples'. These processes of history and memory had been 'kept on hold' by Communism for 45 years 'thereby creating a kind of multiplier effect for violence'. With the demise of that suppressing force, he argued, ancient, seething national and ethnic hatreds were allowed spontaneously to explode into nationalist violence.[14]

This perspective informed some of the reluctance of the first Bush administration to become involved in Bosnia in the early 1990s and also, initially, in Somalia, and it was soon also embraced by the Clinton administration. As Brian Hall observes, 'Literary clichés do not die easily, especially when informed by superficialities'.[15] And they linger still.

Low tolerance for casualties. Third, the international community has had an extremely low tolerance for casualties in military missions that are essentially humanitarian – that is, for ventures in which clear national interests do not appear to be at stake.

This was suggested most clearly in the American and UN experience in Somalia in 1993 where the peacekeepers found their casualties to be insufficiently low given the value of the stakes. This experience led to what might be called the 'Somalia Syndrome' in the United States, and it can also be seen in the general reluctance to become involved in the fighting in Bosnia in the early 1990s despite years of the supposedly action-impelling 'CNN effect' and despite the fact that Yugoslavia is generally held to be closer to American and European interests than impoverished areas of Africa. No country was willing to send troops into combat conditions in Bosnia, though the war there did inspire an unusually large amount of public hand-wringing. Similarly, Belgium abruptly withdrew from Rwanda – and, to save face, urged others to do so as well – when ten of its policing troops were massacred and mutilated early in the genocide.[16] It seems clear that policing efforts in ventures considered humanitarian in nature will be politically tolerable only as long as the cost in lives for the policing forces remains extremely low – and perhaps not even then.[17]

[14] 'A Reader's Guide to the Balkans', *New York Times Book Review*, 18 April 1993. Later the perspective was elaborated into a cosmic worldview by Samuel Huntington under the snappy label, 'Clash of Civilizations'. *The Clash of Civilizations and the Remaking of the World Order* (New York: Touchstone, 1996). For a devastating early critique of the Kaplan argument, see Noel Malcolm, 'Seeing Ghosts', *National Interest*, Summer 1993, pp. 83–8. See also Mueller, *Remnants of War*, pp. 94–5, 145–6; V. P. Gagnon, *The Myth of Ethnic War* (Ithaca, NY: Cornell University Press, 2004).

[15] *The Impossible Country: A Journey Through the Last Days of Yugoslavia* (New York: Penguin, 1994), p. 68. On Bosnia and Somalia, see Jon Western, 'Sources of Humanitarian Intervention: Beliefs, Information, and Advocacy in the US Decisions on Somalia and Bosnia', *International Security*, 26 (Spring 2002), pp. 113, 119–21, 131–3.

[16] Alison Des Forges, *'Leave None to Tell the Story': Genocide in Rwanda* (New York: Human Rights Watch, 1999), pp. 618–20.

[17] It is sometimes argued that effective cheer-leading by leaders can induce a reluctant public to accept dangerous peacekeeping missions. However, President Bill Clinton tried that at the end of 1995 as he was about to send policing troops to Bosnia, and poll data demonstrate that (in part because he confronted vocal Republican opposition on the issue) he was never able to increase the numbers of Americans who saw wisdom or value in sending the troops there even though it was expected that there would be few casualties. See John Mueller, 'American Foreign Policy and Public Opinion in a New Era: Eleven Propositions', in Barbara Norrander and Clyde Wilcox (eds.), *Understanding Public Opinion* (Washington, DC: CQ Press, 2002), p. 167.

This reluctance should not be seen as some sort of new isolationist impulse. Americans were willing, at least at the outset, to send troops to die in Korea and Vietnam, but that was because they subscribed to the containment notion holding Communism to be a genuine threat to the United States that needed to be stopped wherever it was advancing. Polls from the time make it clear they had little interest in losing American lives simply to help out the South Koreans or South Vietnamese.[18] Thus, an unwillingness to send troops to die for purposes that are essentially humanitarian is hardly new. Nor is the sentiment confined to armed humanitarians: if Red Cross or other workers are killed in the line of duty, their organisations frequently withdraw no matter how much good they may be doing, essentially indicating that the saving of lives is not worth the deaths of even a few of their personnel.[19]

As suggested earlier, policing thug-dominated conflicts and toppling thuggish regimes is not likely to be terribly difficult or costly in most cases. In Yugoslavia, for example, it might have taken a fair number of troops, perhaps over a hundred thousand, but there would most likely have been very little real fighting and most of the troops would probably not have had to stay long. And in estimates that seem to be regarded as militarily sound, the local UN commander and other experts have suggested that 5,000 well-equipped and determined soldiers with a free hand to fight could probably have rapidly halted the genocide perpetrated by murderous, rampaging, government-authorised thugs in Rwanda.[20]

However, it would be impossible to guarantee that such operations could be carried off with extremely few – or no – casualties. Thugs may be cowardly, but a few might fight, especially if cornered, and some might lob shells or snipe at the policing forces. And even the most criminalised forces may contain among their membership a few dedicated, even fanatical, combatants who are willing to die for the cause.

Aversion to long-term policing. Fourth, even though they may be successful in the first instance, developed countries often have an aversion to long-term policing, and a realistic concern about the long, unpleasant aftermath often inspires a reluctance to

[18] See John Mueller, *War, Presidents and Public Opinion* (New York: Wiley, 1973), pp. 44, 48–9, 58, 100–1.
[19] On the other hand, there seems to be little political problem in keeping occupying forces in place, even in ventures deemed of little importance, as long as they are not being killed. After the Somalia fiasco of 1993, the Americans stayed on for several months and, since none were being killed, little attention was paid or concern voiced. Similarly, although there was little public or political support for sending US troops to Haiti in 1994, there was also almost no protest about keeping them there, since none were killed. At the end of 1995, Clinton told a sceptical American public that the policing troops being sent to Bosnia would only be there for a year. Although many Americans afterward came to see Clinton as a liar, this is not the instance of deception upon which they based that conclusion. In fact, there was little protest, or even much notice, that the troops were still there when the nation entered a new millennium. If they are not being killed, it scarcely matters whether the troops are in Macedonia or in Minnesota. For a broader discussion of American casualty tolerance in military ventures, see Mueller, 'American Foreign Policy and Public Opinion in a New Era', pp. 156–60.
[20] Des Forges, '*Leave None to Tell the Story*', pp. 22, 607–8. But on logistic and other potential difficulties, see Alan J. Kuperman, *The Limits of Humanitarian Intervention: Genocide in Rwanda* (Washington, DC: Brookings Institution Press, 2001).

intervene in the first place. The frustrating experience with nation-building in Haiti after 1994 certainly would enhance this perception. And it is most impressive that the interest of the developed world in Afghanistan dropped so greatly after it no longer served as a base for international terrorists.

A contrast of the edgy tedium of Cyprus and Northern Ireland with the dramatic catastrophe of Bosnia suggests that the patient police work carried out in Nicosia and Belfast probably saved thousands of lives over the years. But it tends to be a profoundly thankless job because the people whose lives have been saved don't know who they are, and they are often critical or even contemptuous of their unappreciated saviours. Such probable ingratitude further deflates the policing enthusiasm of the international community.

Lack of political gain from success. Fifth, leaders probably sense that there is not much to be gained politically from ventures that are taken to be humanitarian. If George H. W. Bush achieved little lasting electoral advantage from his dramatic victory in the Gulf War of 1991 where important interests were, or seemed to be, at stake, lesser accomplishments have been at least as unrewarding. Clinton found that the more purely humanitarian (and costless) intervention in Bosnia of 1995 scarcely helped in his re-election efforts a year later – by the time the election came around, people could scarcely remember the venture. Similarly, at the time of the Kosovo bombings of 1999, press accounts argued that the presidential ambitions and political future of Clinton's vice president, Al Gore, hung in the balance. From the standpoint of public opinion, the Kosovo venture seems to have been a success, but when he launched his campaign for the presidency a few months later, Gore scarcely thought it important or memorable enough to bring up.[21]

The bias against war and aggression. Finally, for effective international policing to become standard practice, it would be necessary for the international community explicitly, clearly, and systematically to abandon or reinterpret the concept of sovereignty, and there seems to be a notable reluctance to do so. That is, it seems unlikely that the biases against aggression and war and in favour of sovereignty so carefully and deeply cultivated in the developed world and elsewhere over the last century can be adequately overcome except in special cases. Moreover, some members with vetoes in the United Nations are wary of the precedent. Thus, Russia, with its civil war in Chechnya, and China, with secessionist movements in its west, were notably unenthusiastic about sanctifying the NATO venture to aid secessionists in Kosovo in 1999.

---

[21] On the other hand, this lack of attention also means that, if things go wrong – at least in low-valued ventures – troops can be readily removed with little concern about saving face or about longer political consequences. For example, the abrupt combat deaths of US soldiers in Somalia in 1993 enhanced demands for withdrawal, not calls to revenge the humiliation, and by the time the 1996 election rolled around, the public had substantially forgotten about the fiasco. Similarly, Ronald Reagan's withdrawal of American policing troops from Lebanon after a terrorist bomb had killed over 200 of them in 1983 scarcely dampened his re-election success a year later. However, the fact that failure does not necessarily bring politicians disaster hardly compensates for the fact that there is no political gain from success.

Mostly failure: the policing war in Iraq

These impediments to international policing are likely to be considerably enhanced by the experience of the Americans and the British in Iraq, the first real failure in the policing process.

The winner of the 2000 presidential election in the United States, George W. Bush, came into office suggesting that the United States ought to develop a 'humble' foreign policy, and, along with some of his foreign policy advisers, such as Condoleezza Rice, he reflected the Somalia Syndrome by expressing an aversion to 'nation-building'.[22] However, after international terrorists shockingly flew airliners into New York's World Trade Center and Washington's Pentagon on 11 September 2001, Bush instantly shucked off that perspective and proclaimed that he was taking on the distinctly unhumble responsibility to 'rid the world of evil'.[23]

The first stage of that campaign was to intervene very forcefully in an ongoing civil war in Afghanistan in an effort to attack a group of international terrorists based in that country. The American venture – essentially an act of naked aggression – enjoyed a considerable amount of international support. It also proved to be remarkably successful and was unexpectedly easy. In the wake of the war, a new, rather broadly based government was set up, and an expensive, trouble-plagued nation-building effort was begun that was far greater than anything ever contemplated for Somalia.

Encouraged by the easy success in Afghanistan, the Bush administration now set its sights on the Saddam Hussein regime in Iraq. It was reasonable to expect that a conventional military invasion by a disciplined foreign army could eliminate the regime, and it seemed entirely possible that Iraq's ill-led and demoralised army, which fought almost not at all when challenged in the 1991 Gulf War, would put up little armed resistance to such an attack.[24] There were efforts to tie Iraq to international terrorism, and fears that the dictatorial and unstable Saddam could develop weapons of mass destruction remained high, now embellished by the argument that he might palm them off for dedicated terrorists to explode in distant lands. These arguments enjoyed quite a bit of support with the American public and Congress, still reeling from the September 11th attacks. They generated much less backing abroad, however, and, although it tried, the American administration was never able to get a resolution of support from any international body. The leaders of most countries, including those bordering Iraq, never seemed to see that country as nearly as much of a threat as did the distant United States and its only notable ally on the issue, Tony Blair's United Kingdom.

Determined to see it out, Bush and Blair shrugged off international disapproval, fabricated a rather small and personalised 'coalition of the willing', and launched

---

[22] See, in particular, Rice's 'Promoting the National Interest', in the January/February 2000 issue of *Foreign Affairs*, in which she observes that 'the military is a special instrument. It is lethal, and is meant to be. It is not a civilian police force. It is not a political referee. And it is most certainly not designed to build a civilian society. . . . Using the American armed forces as the world's "911" will degrade capabilities, bog soldiers down in peacekeeping roles, and fuel concern among other great powers that the United States has decided to enforce notions of "limited sovereignty" worldwide in the name of humanitarianism' (pp. 53–4).

[23] Memorial Service speech at the National Cathedral, 14 September 2001.

[24] On the pathetic capacities of the Iraq army in 1991, see John Mueller, 'The Perfect Enemy: Assessing the Gulf War', *Security Studies*, 5 (Autumn 1995), pp. 77–117.

naked aggression against Iraq in which forces from the United States and Britain were joined by some from Australia. As expected, the Iraqi military disintegrated under the onslaught and seems to have lacked any semblance of a coherent strategy of resistance.

The invaders had quickly and easily toppled a regime held in wide contempt – though not much urgent fear – around the world. But to have the mission accepted as a success, the invaders would have had to establish quickly a stable, acceptable, effective, moderate government there, and it would have been highly desirable as well to uncover convincing links between the Iraqi regime and global terrorism while seizing sizeable caches of the much touted weapons of mass destruction that they expected to find. With success, the venture likely would eventually have achieved a considerable degree of (probably somewhat grudging) international legitimacy, and it might ultimately have been accepted as legal – rather in the manner of NATO's successful naked aggression against sovereign Serbia in 1999 or America's successful naked aggression against sovereign Panama in 1989 or against sovereign Afghanistan in 2001.[25] Neither convincing terrorist links nor WMD were found in Iraq, however, and efforts to establish quickly an effective, acceptable government there failed utterly.

As it happened, the foreign occupiers soon found that they were stretched thin in their efforts to rebuild a nation out of the rubble that remained after Saddam, American- and British-enforced international economic sanctions, and the war had taken their toll. It had been hoped that the Iraqis would greet the conquerors by dancing happily in the streets and somehow coordinate themselves into a coherent and appreciative government, rather as in the previous ventures in Panama and East Timor and maybe in Bosnia and Kosovo. But, although many were glad to see Saddam's tyranny ended, the invaders often found the population resentful and humiliated, rather than gleeful and grateful. Moreover, bringing order to the situation was vastly complicated by the fact that the government-toppling invasion had effectively created a failed state which permitted widespread criminality and looting. In addition some people – including some foreign terrorists drawn opportunistically to the area – were dedicated to sabotaging the victors' peace and to killing the policing forces. Shunned by the Bush administration and bemused (or relieved) by the debacle (the mission mostly inspired *schadenfreude*, without all that much in the way of *schaden*), the international community was not eager to join in the monumental reconstruction effort.

In September 2004, a year and a half after the invasion – after it had become abundantly clear that no WMD or terrorist links were likely to be found, and after the United States and the United Kingdom had become embedded in a military quagmire of occupation – United Nations Secretary General Kofi Annan labelled the invasion 'illegal' in a BBC interview.[26] It seems highly unlikely that he would have reached such a blunt, forceful conclusion if the invasion had been successful.

---

[25] For such anticipations as the war was launched, see Anne-Marie Slaughter, 'Good Reasons for Going Around the UN', *New York Times*, 18 March 2003, p. A33. Relatedly, America's naked aggression against Cuba at the Bay of Pigs in 1961 might eventually have inspired acceptance and even approval in the non-Communist world if the escapade had been able tidily to topple the Castro regime, even as American acts of war against Cuba and the Soviet Union during the Cuban Missile Crisis of 1962 become accepted, even lauded, after that venture proved successful.

[26] ⟨http://news.bbc.co.uk/2/hi/middle_east/3661134.stm⟩.

As in Somalia and particularly Vietnam, it is difficult to see how the insurgents in Iraq can be defeated at a tolerable cost in American and British lives: the insurgents are variously motivated, but they are likely, despite tactical setbacks, to be willing and able to continue their activities at least until the hated invaders leave. Accordingly, policy in Iraq seems to be evolving in a manner familiar from Vietnam and Somalia: a combination of cut, run, and hope. Responsibility for policing the resistance is increasingly being handed over to a shaky, patched-together government, army, and police force; American tactics seem to be in the process of being shifted to reduce its casualties and its troops will probably gradually begin to be removed; and support for the locals will increasingly be limited to economic aid and encouraging words. However, even an orderly retreat from Iraq will likely be taken by international terrorists as a great victory (even greater than the one against the Soviet Union in Afghanistan or the one against Israel in southern Lebanon) and therefore highly encouraging.[27]

The removal of Saddam Hussein's regime remains an achievement. However, military victory was achieved at the cost of creating enervating chaos in the country, killing tens of thousands of Iraqis, and alienating many of the rest.[28] Moreover, without an effective army or impressive weapons, the notion that Iraq ever posed much of a threat (particularly a 'grave and gathering' one) to anyone, even Israel, becomes highly questionable. In addition, oil supplies from the country are likely to remain uncertain for years, and international animosity to the United States generated by the venture remains high. Finally, any sort of democracy that emerges in Iraq may well lead to the certification of candidates who are hostile to the United States and to Israel.[29]

Force and legitimacy after the Iraq War

There are likely to be important international consequences of the Iraq experience. In particular, it will probably change American foreign policy and further deflate the already limited willingness of developed states to apply military force to police the world.

Among the casualties for American policy could be the Bush Doctrine, empire, unilateralism, pre-emption (or, actually, preventive war), last-remaining-superpowerdom, and indispensable-nationhood. Indeed, what seems to be emerging from this experience in the United States is something that will probably come to be called 'the Iraq Syndrome'. 'No more Vietnams' and 'No more Somalias' will be replaced, or updated, by 'No more Iraqs'.

---

[27] For discussion on this point, see John Mueller, 'The Politics of Cutting and Running', *History News Network*, 24 May 2004 (⟨http://hnn.us/articles/5324.html⟩). See also Daniel Byman, 'How to Fight Terror', *National Interest*, Spring 2005, pp. 125–7.

[28] For assessments of a study published in *Lancet* estimating that the war was responsible for the deaths of 100,000 Iraqis in its first 18 months alone, see the *Economist*, 6–12 November 2004, pp. 12, 81–2. That number would be vastly higher than the sum of all people who have been killed by international terrorists over the last hundred years.

[29] For a perspective on democracy that contrasts markedly with the democratic romanticism promulgated by many of the war's advocates, see John Mueller, *Capitalism, Democracy, and Ralph's Pretty Good Grocery* (Princeton, NJ: Princeton University Press, 1999).

Specifically, there will probably be notable decreases in the acceptance of a number of beliefs. Among these are the notions that the United States should take unilateral military action to correct situations or regimes it considers reprehensible but which present no very direct and very immediate threat to it, that it should and can forcibly bring democracy to nations not now so blessed, that it has the duty to bring order to the Middle East, that having by far the largest defence budget in the world is necessary and mostly brings benefits, that international cooperation is of only very limited value, and that Europeans and other well-meaning foreigners are naive and decadent wimps. There may also be new pressures to reduce the military budget, and the country is more likely to seek international cooperation, possibly even sometimes showing perceptible signs of humility.

The chief beneficiaries of the Iraq War are likely to be the rogue/axis-of-evil states of Iran and North Korea. In part because of the American military and financial overextension in Iraq (and Afghanistan), the likelihood of any coherent application of military action or even of focused military threat against these two unpleasant entities has substantially diminished,[30] as it has against what at one time seemed to be the next dominoes in the Middle East: Syria especially, as well as Libya, Saudi Arabia, Egypt, and Lebanon. The Iraq Syndrome suggests that any intelligence suggesting such states have become threatening will be deeply questioned, that any moves to apply military force to them will be met with widespread dismay and opposition unless there is severe provocation, and that any additional persecution by such regimes of their own people will be wistfully tolerated and ignored.

More broadly, developed states will probably become even more sensitive about intervening when their own national interests fail clearly to be engaged, and, moreover, they are likely to adopt more stringent standards for determining when such interests are engaged. They also may come to embrace even more the ancient ethnic hatreds dodge, concluding that any efforts they are likely to make will essentially prove futile in the long run. They are likely as well to become even more sensitive about suffering casualties, and to see even less political benefit in such ventures – although Bush was re-elected in 2004, virtually all observers think that his near-defeat was due primarily to the mess in Iraq and that, without that war, he would have done much better. Their ideological and emotional disinclinations against war, against the application of armed force, and against even well-meaning aggression are likely to be further reified. And, in particular, their wary aversion to long-term policing is surely going to be enhanced by the costly and bloody post-invasion experience in Iraq (and, to a lesser extent, in Afghanistan).

Some of this could be seen during the Iraq War itself. In 2003, crowds of desperate Liberian civilians unsuccessfully begged the international community, including especially the United States, forcefully to intervene to liberate them from their resident dictator, Charles Taylor, and from the armed thugs who were seeking to depose him. And, even worse, when depredations by government-inspired armed bands caused ethnic cleansing and tens of thousands of deaths in western Sudan ('genocide', some called it), the international community, after ten years of *mea culpa* breast-beating over its failure to intervene in Rwanda, responded with little more

---

[30] See, for example, Ronald Brownstein, 'Count Bush's Doctrine of Preemption as a Casualty of the Iraq War', *Los Angeles Times*, 17 May 2004. George Will, 'The Iran Dilemma', *Washington Post*, 23 September 2004, p. A29.

than huffing and puffing, pressure on the Sudan government, and the setting up of inadequate and underfunded refugee camps.[31]

It could also be seen in post-invasion policy toward North Korea. In 1994, the United States seems to have been just about ready to go to war on the peninsula spurred by a contested intelligence conclusion that there was 'a better than even' chance that North Korea had the makings of a small nuclear bomb.[32] By contrast, when that country abruptly declared in February 2005 that it now actually possessed nuclear weapons, the announcement was officially characterised as 'unfortunate' and as 'rhetoric we've heard before'.[33]

The solution: effective domestic government

It seems, then, that even though they are fully capable of doing it, developed states are likely to intervene with any sort of reliability, either by themselves or through international bodies, only when their interests seem importantly engaged or where they manage to become self-entrapped. And they are likely even then to do so with enormous concern about suffering too many casualties of their own and with a studied wariness about long-term policing commitments. Moreover, the British-American mess in Iraq is likely substantially to reinforce this reticence.

The attention of countries in the developed world may be arrested from time to time by international terrorism, the threatening dispersion of weapons of mass destruction to what are sometimes called 'rogue states', the flow of illegal drugs to their own populations, and refugee incursions that cause them trouble and cost them money. But for the most part, they are more likely to continue to see most civil conflicts and vicious regimes as essentially irrelevant to their interests and thus to remain aloof.

International bodies and consortiums of developed countries can often be useful to broker cease-fires and peace settlements, and they can sometimes assist with humanitarian aid and economic and political development once peace has been achieved. Thus, for example, violent conflict in Cyprus has probably been averted by the international community's very long-term intervention there, Bosnia and Kosovo may be settling down under international tutelage, Cambodia is better off thanks in considerable part to missions from the outside.

However, it seems clear that a truly effective solution to the problems presented by civil warfare and vicious regimes does not lie in the fabrication of effective and legitimate international policing forces, but rather in the establishment of competent domestic military and policing forces, tracing the state-building process Europe went through in the middle of the last millennium. And, remarkably, this process may be well underway.

To a very substantial degree, much of the civil warfare that persists in the world today is a function of the extent to which inadequate governments exist.[34] Civil wars

---

[31] Scott Straus, 'Darfur and the Genocide Debate', *Foreign Affairs*, January/February 2005, pp. 123–46.

[32] Don Oberdorfer, *The Two Koreas* (New York: Basic Books, 2001), pp. 307–8, 316.

[33] Sonni Efron and Bruce Wallace, 'North Korea Escalates Its Nuclear Threat', *Los Angeles Times*, 11 February 2005, p. A1.

[34] For an extended development of this point, see Mueller, *Remnants of War*, ch. 9.

are least likely to occur in stable democracies and in stable autocracies – that is, in countries with effective governments and policing forces.[35] Stable democracies, almost by definition, have effective policing forces, and they deal with grievance by bringing the aggrieved into the process (as long as it is expressed peacefully) and by listening to the grievance. Stable autocracies also have capable policing forces – in fact, they are often called 'police states'. They rule through the selective, but persistent, application of terror – through vigilant domestic spying and through effective, if often brutal, suppression. North Korea and Cuba provide contemporary examples. In fact, in an important sense many civil wars have effectively been *caused* by inept governments. Because of closed political systems and because of policing methods in which excessive and indiscriminate force is employed to try to deal with relatively small bands of troublemakers, inept governments can turn friendly or indifferent people into hostile ones and vastly increase the size of the problems they are trying to deal with. As David Keen has observed, 'the aggression of counter-insurgency forces has repeatedly alienated their potential civilian supporters, and this has often continued even when evidently counter-productive from a military point of view'.[36]

It appears that the trends in civil warfare as documented in Figure 1 track rather well with the existence of weak governments.[37] With the decolonisation of the late 1950s and 1960s, a group of poorly-governed societies came into being, and many found themselves having to deal with civil warfare. Moreover, as civil wars become criminal enterprises, they tended to become longer and to accumulate in number. This pattern may have been embellished by another phenomenon, democratisation, which often is accompanied by a period in which governments become weak.[38] Then, in the aftermath of the Cold War in the early 1990s, there was a further increase in the number of incompetent governments as weak, confused, ill-directed, and sometimes criminal governments emerged in many of the post-Communist countries replacing comparatively competent police states. In addition, with the end of the Cold War, the developed countries no longer had nearly as much interest in

---

[35] Håvard Hegre, Tanja Ellingsen, Scott Gates, and Nils Petter Gleditsch, 'Toward a Democratic Civil Peace? Democracy, Political Change, and Civil War, 1816–1992', *American Political Science Review*, 95 (March 2001), pp. 33–48. On this point, see also Bruce M. Russett and John R. Oneal, *Triangulating Peace: Democracy, Interdependence, and International Organizations* (New York: Norton, 2001), p. 70; Monty G. Marshall and Ted Robert Gurr, *Peace and Conflict, 2003: A Global Survey of Armed Conflicts, Self-Determination Movements, and Democracy* (College Park, MD: Center for International Development and Conflict Management, University of Maryland, 2003), pp. 19–20, 25; James D. Fearon and David D. Laitin, 'Ethnicity, Insurgency, and Civil War', *American Political Science Review*, 97 (February 2003), pp. 85, 88.

[36] *The Economic Functions of Violence in Civil Wars*, Adelphi Paper 320 (London: International Institute for Strategic Studies, 1998), p. 21. Developments in western Sudan are only the most recent case in point. See Straus, 'Darfur and the Genocide Debate', pp. 124–8.

[37] For similar trends using different definitions of war and of armed conflict, see Nils Petter Gleditsch, Peter Wallenstein, Mikael Eriksson, Margareta Stollenberg, and Håvard Strand, 'Armed Conflict 1946–2001: A New Dataset', *Journal of Peace Research*, 35 (September 2002), pp. 621; Marshall and Gurr, *Peace and Conflict*, pp. 12–14; Klaus Jürgen Gantzel and Torsten Schwinghammer, *Warfare Since the Second World War* (New Brunswick, NJ and London: Transaction, 2000), pp. 112, 170; Fearon and Laitin, 'Ethnicity, Insurgency, and Civil War,' pp. 77–8; 'The global menace of local strife', *Economist*, 22 May 2003.

[38] See also Paul Collier, 'Doing Well out of War: An Economic Perspective', in *Greed and Grievance: Economic Agendas in Civil Wars*, eds. Mats Berdal and David M. Malone (Boulder, CO: Lynne Rienner, 2000), pp. 98, 108; Jack Snyder, *From Voting to Violence: Democratization and Nationalist Conflict* (New York: Norton, 2000).

financially propping up some third world governments and in helping them police themselves – an effect particularly noticeable in Africa.[39] By the mid-1990s, however, a large number of countries had managed to get through the rough period and had achieved a considerable degree of democratic stability – especially in Latin America, post-Communist Europe, and east and southeast Asia – and relatively effective governments had emerged in most of them. As a result, the amount of civil warfare declined markedly.

The essential solution – and a longterm one – to the problems of civil warfare, then, seems to lie not in ministrations by the international community – so often half-hearted, half-vast, and half-coherent – but rather in the establishment of competent domestic governments in the many places that do not now have them. Sometimes international authorities, working out of or under the direction of the developed countries, have been able to aid or speed the process. And they can certainly be of assistance when a country sincerely desires to develop the kind of competent military and police forces that have helped bring peace and prosperity to the developed world.[40] Moreover, the example of the developed societies – civil, prosperous, flexible, productive, and free from organised violent conflict – can be most attractive, as indicated by the masses of people from the developing world who are trying to immigrate there, abandoning in fear and disgust the turmoil and violence of their home countries. However, it is likely that exercises in nation-building that are productive of peace and order will have to be accomplished – and, ultimately, with results that are most likely to be lasting – by forces that are domestic.

Over the course of the last few decades there seems to have been a decline of tyranny and an increase in the number of countries led by effective people who, instead of looting and dissipating their country's resources, seem to be dedicated to adopting policies that will further its orderly development. This has happened in almost all of Latin America as well as in many places in Asia – areas that, not coincidentally, have also experienced a considerable decline of warfare. Whether Africa will follow that pattern is yet to be determined, but there are at least some hopeful signs.[41]

Criminality and criminal predation will still exist, and so will terrorism which, like crime, can be carried out by individuals or very small groups. And there will certainly be plenty of other problems to worry about – famine, disease, malnutrition, pollution, corruption, poverty, politics, and economic travail. However, while far from certain, a further (or continuing) decline in civil warfare and in the number of countries with vicious governments does seem to be an entirely reasonable prospect. The international community is needed, and likely, to play only a supporting role – and international force, whether deemed legitimate or not, very little at all – in this highly-desirable development.

[39] Keen, *Economic Functions of Violence*, p. 23; Gray, International Law, pp. 215–17; Robert H. Bates, *Prosperity and Violence* (New York: Norton, 2001), ch. 5.
[40] See Human Security Centre, *Human Security Report 2005* (New York: Oxford University Press, 2005).
[41] Robert Rotberg, 'New Breed of African Leader', *Christian Science Monitor*, 9 January 2002, p. 9.

War and international relations: a military-historical perspective on force and legitimacy

Writing on international relations frequently makes reference to the use of force, but rarely integrates changes in its nature into a central role in the explanatory model. In particular, force, in the shape of military capability, is often seen as the 'servant' of ideas about its appropriate use, and thus of the norms of the international system, rather than as an independent element, let alone playing a central role in affecting the latter.[1] This article addresses the issue with particular reference to relations between the West and the 'non-West', arguing that the contested relationship between the different narratives of military history impinge directly on the character of international relations.

Differing narratives of military history

That this issue is directly pertinent today stems most apparently from the crisis in Iraq, but is in no way restricted to it, because differing views on the effectiveness and legitimacy of military capability play a major role in conflicts and confrontations around the world. Indeed, whether war is seen to stem from mistaken assessments of relative power or from bellicosity,[2] these differing views play a key role.

Nevertheless, the Iraq crisis indicates important aspects of the issue. First, a concern about the spread of 'weapons of mass destruction' played an important role, at least in the public explanation of American and British policy towards Iraq prior to the conflict; while it has certainly played a major part in the diplomacy focused on particular states, especially North Korea, Libya and Iran. Secondly, the military and political difficulties the US encountered in Iraq in 2003–05 once the government of Saddam Hussein was overthrown indicated the extent to which analyses of military potency based on American capability could be challenged.[3]

Linked to this is the issue of the legitimate use of particular types of force by the 'weak' against stronger powers. Examples of this encompass a continuum from

---

* I am most grateful to Theo Farrell and Stewart Lone for comments on earlier drafts.

[1] See, for example, P.W. Schroeder, *The Transformation of European Politics 1763–1848* (Oxford: Oxford University Press, 1994) and H. Duchhardt, *Balance of Power und Pentarchie 1700–1785* (Paderborn, 1997).

[2] J. M. Black, *Why Wars Happen* (London: Reaktion, 1998).

[3] See, for example, D. Frum and R. Perle, *An End to Evil: Strategies for Victory in the War on Terror* (New York: Random House, 2004).

127

(non-state) terrorism in its increasingly varied forms to the strategy apparently planned by Saddam Hussein in resisting American attack in 2003. This kind of force as a weapon of the 'weak' raises further questions of morality and feasibility, not least the question of entitlement to use otherwise unacceptable means in order to seek to counter the inbuilt military advantage of an opponent.

The contentiousness of this issue is further indicated by the question of whether the situation with Israel is analogous. There again, superior weaponry appears to dictate the outcome in overcoming resistance within the occupied territories, and indeed in Israel itself. In the event, however, Israeli capability has been challenged, certainly in so far as a sense of control is concerned, by other military practices. These include popular opposition (a military practice where there is no clear differentiation between a regular military and the rest of society) and terrorism.

The combination of these points with that about American capability ensures that the debate over force and legitimacy brings together two very different narratives of military history: the Western, largely technological, one, and a non-Western narrative that places less of an emphasis on technological proficiency, and does not rest on an expectation of technological superiority. This means that it is valuable to have a historical perspective on this issue. In theoretical terms, this bringing together can be presented with reference to the recent 'cultural turn' in strategic thought, and it can be argued that, in some respects, American practice represents the apogee of a Western model of warmaking.[4] By contrast, that of its opponents in Iraq is an example of non-Western systems.

This is a thesis that repays consideration, but there are major problems with it. For example, not only is Iraqi opposition an example but not a definition of non-Western systems, but the parallel is also the case with the US. In particular there are major contrasts between American doctrine and practice in warfare, with the American emphasis on overwhelming force and technology proving very resistant to the lessons of recent history, and the practice of other Western powers.[5] There is also a need to be wary of a geographical or cultural reification of what is a more widespread military practice *within* as well as *between* systems, namely the response of the weaker power. This classically focuses on developing an anti-strategy, anti-operational method, anti-tactics, and anti-weaponry, designed to counter and lessen, if not nullify, the advantages of the stronger, and sometimes to use the very nature of the latter in order to weaken it.[6] In other words, there may be a functional, rather than a cultural, explanation of the methods chosen, and this functional explanation can span West and non-West. The parallels in terms of diplomatic practice are instructive, as issues of legitimacy at once come into play, not least with the claim to the attributes of sovereignty by groups not recognised as such, but also by the rejection of the idea that sovereign governments have a monopoly of force.

In response in both cases, these anti-methods are presented by critics as unacceptable and illegal, and indeed unheroic, and thus the legitimacy of the cause with which

[4] V. D. Hanson, *Carnage and Culture: Landmark Battles in the Rise of Western Power* (New York: Anchor Books, 2002); J. Lynn, *Battle* (Boulder, CO: Westview, 2004). For a critique, see J. M. Black, 'Determinisms and Other Issues', *Journal of Military History*, 68 (2004), pp. 1217–32.

[5] J. Nagl, *Learning to Eat Soup with a Knife: Counter-insurgency Lessons from Malaya and Vietnam* (Westport, Ontario: Praeger, 2002); R. Cassidy, *Peacekeeping in the Abyss: British and American Doctrine and Practice after the Cold War* (Westport: Praeger, 2004).

[6] I. Arreguín-Toft, 'How the Weak Win Wars: A Theory of Asymmetric Conflict', *International Security*, 26 (2001), pp. 93–128.

they are linked is denied. This can be seen in the treatment of terrorism, but also, more generally, in practices, real or alleged, of eroding the distinctions between 'civilian' and 'military'. An instance of this was provided by allegations that military targets, such as missile-launchers, were located by Serbia in 1999 and Iraq in 2003 in civilian areas, and, in the latter case, by the employment of irregulars who did not wear uniform. As much of the legitimacy of the modern Western practice of force, and the legalisation of Western high-technology warfare,[7] is held to rest on drawing a distinction between military and civilian, these moves affected both the character of Western warmaking, especially in the case of the ease of target acquisition, and its apparent legitimacy. Attacks on 'civilian' targets indeed became a basic text in public debate concerned about the morality of Western interventions and the nature of Western warmaking.

This problem challenged pro-interventionist governments in their attempts to influence domestic and international opinion, as doing so in part rested on the argument that there was a distinction between the legitimate use of force directed against the military (and government targets), and usage that was illegitimate, whether by states, such as Iraq gassing Kurdish civilians, or by terrorist movements.[8] There was a parallel here with weapons of mass destruction, with conflicting views on which powers could legitimately possess them. Legitimacy in this case was a response to perceptions of governmental systems and strategic cultures; and the imprecision of the concept of the rogue state does not satisfactorily address the issue.[9] Instead, the ability of the world's strongest power to propose the concept and define its application was seen by many as a challenge both to the sovereignty of states and to international norms. This will become a more serious problem as the rise of China and India leads to a decline in America's relative strength.

The notion of the morality of military usage as depending in part on the uneasy relationship between the doctrine of target allocation and acquisition, and the technology permitting the successful practice of this doctrine, is an instance of the way in which theories of force and legitimacy move in a problematic relationship with shifts in military capability and also in the type of wars being undertaken. This was not the sole instance of this process. To return to the point made at the outset, the nature of the military power wielded by the US (as well as the assumptions underlying its use) is crucial to modern discussion of force and legitimacy across at least much of the world.

The historical perspective

In historical terms, there is a marked and unprecedented contrast today between the distribution of military force and the notion of sovereign equality in international relations. There have been major powers before, but only the Western European

[7] T. W. Smith, 'The New Law of War: Legitimizing Hi-Tech and Infrastructural Violence', *International Studies Quarterly*, 46 (2002), pp. 355–74.
[8] L. Freedman, 'Victims and Victors: Reflections on the Kosovo War', *Review of International Studies*, 26 (2000), pp. 335–58.
[9] R. Howard, *Iran in Crisis? Nuclear Ambitions and the American Response* (London: Zed Books, 2004).

maritime states – Portugal, Spain, The Netherlands, France and Britain – could even seek a global range, and, prior to that of Britain in the nineteenth century, the naval strength of these states was not matched by a land capability capable of competing with those of the leading military powers in the most populous part of the world: South and East Asia, nor, indeed, with an ability to expand into Africa beyond coastal enclaves. The success of the Western European powers in the Americas and at sea off India, did not mean that there was an equivalent success elsewhere, and this suggests that aggregate military capacity is a concept that has to be employed with care.[10]

East and South-East Asian powers, particularly China, were, in turn, not involved in an international system that directly encompassed the Western maritime states. In some respects, there was a curious coexistence as, from the 1630s, Spanish, Russian and Dutch military powers were all present in East Asian waters, but, in practice, this did not lead to the creation of a new system. The Europeans were insufficiently strong to challenge the East Asian powers seriously, and local advances were repelled by the most powerful, China: in the seventeenth century, the Dutch being driven from the Pescadore Islands and Taiwan, and the Russians from the Amur Valley,[11] while the English in Bombay were forced to propitiate the Mughal Emperor; and were also unable to sustain their position in Tangier.

The assumptions generally summarised as strategic culture also played a major role, as, despite their strength, none of the local powers sought to contest the European position in the Western Pacific: the Spaniards spread their control in the Philippines, and, from there, to the Mariana and Caroline Islands, and the Russians in north-east Asia and, across the North Pacific, to the Aleutians and Alaska. This was not challenged by China; nor Japan or Korea, both of which were weaker states.

The absence of any such conflict ensured that relations between East Asian and Western European powers did not develop and become important, let alone normative, in the context of warfare or international relations. Instead, although trade with China was important for the West, there was scant development in such norms. The same was true of relations between the Mughal empire in India and European coastal positions in the sixteenth and seventeenth centuries, and also in South-East Asia, where major, aggressive states, such as Burma and Thailand in the eighteenth century, were able to operate with little reference to Western power (and indeed are largely ignored in Western historiography).[12] This is a reminder of the late onset of modernity, understood in terms both of Western dominance, specifically of readily-evident superior Western military capability, and of Western international norms; although this definition of modernity is questionable, and increasingly so, as Asian states become more powerful.

This late onset of modernity clashes with the conventional interpretation of the international order that traces an early establishment of the acceptance of sovereignty in a multipolar system, an establishment usually dated to the Peace of Westphalia of

---

[10] The best introduction is J. M. Black, *War and the World: Military Power and the Fate of Continents 1450–2000* (New Haven, CT: Yale University Press, 1998).
[11] E. van Veen, 'How the Dutch Ran a Seventeenth-Century Colony: The Occupation and Loss of Formosa 1624–1662', *Itinerario*, 20 (1996), pp. 59–77.
[12] W. J. Koening, *The Burmese Polity, 1752–1819* (Ann Arbor, MI: University of Michigan Press, 1990).

1648.[13] However appropriate for Europe, and that can be debated, this approach has far less meaning on the global level. The idea of such a system and of the associated norms outlined in Europe were of little relevance elsewhere until Western power expanded, and then they were not on offer to much of the world, or only on terms dictated by Western interests. This was true not only of such norms but also of conventions about international practices such as the definition of frontiers, or rights to free trade, or responses to what was presented as piracy.[14]

The question of frontiers was an aspect of the employment of the Western matrix of knowledge in ordering the world on Western terms and in Western interests. Force and legitimacy were brought together, for example, in the drawing of straight frontier and administration lines on maps, without regard to ethnic, linguistic, religious, economic and political alignments and practices, let alone drainage patterns, landforms and biological provinces. This was a statement of political control, judged by the West as legitimate and necessary in Western terms,[15] and employed in order to deny all other existing indigenous practices, which were seen either as illegitimate, or, in light of a notion of rights that drew on social-Darwinianism, as less legitimate.

The global military situation, specifically the Western ability to defeat and dictate to land powers, had changed in the nineteenth century, especially with the British defeat of the Marathas in India in 1803–6 and 1817–18, and, subsequently, with the defeats inflicted on China in 1839–42 and 1860, and with the Western overawing of Japan in 1853–4. In terms of the age, the speed and articulation offered British power by technological developments (especially, from mid-century, the steamship and the telegraph), by knowledge systems (particularly the accurate charting and mapping of coastal waters),[16] and by organisational methods (notably the coaling stations on which the Royal Navy came to rely), all provided an hitherto unsurpassed global range and reach.[17] Within this now globalised world, force and force projection came to define both the dominant (yet still contested) definition of legitimacy, and its application. Indeed, the capacity to direct the latter proved crucial to the development of the practice of legitimacy as related to its impact on non-Western states.

The interwar years

British imperial power is generally discussed in terms of a nineteenth-century heyday. This refers mainly to naval power, and the options and ideas that stemmed from it. Yet this imperial power, which acted as the protection for free trade, and thus a major burst of globalisation, and brought what is presented as modernity to much of

[13] K. J. Holsti, *Peace and War: Armed Conflicts and International Order 1648–1989* (Cambridge: Cambridge University Press, 1991), p. 39. For an example of the widespread application of the term, F. H. Lawson, 'Westphalian Sovereignty and the Emergence of the Arab States System: The Case of Syria', *International History Review*, 22 (2000), pp. 529–56.

[14] T. Winichakul, *Siam Mapped: a History of the Geo-Body of a Nation* (Honolulu: University of Hawaii Press, 1994); S. Sen, *Empire of Free Trade: The East India Company and the Making of the Colonial Marketplace* (Philadelphia, PA: University of Pennsylvania Press, 1998).

[15] W. S. Miles, *Hausaland Divided: Capitalism and Independence in Nigeria and Niger* (Ithaca, NY: Cornell University Press, 1994).

[16] D. R. Headrick, *When Information Came of Age: Technologies of Knowledge in the Age of Reason and Revolution, 1700–1850* (Oxford: Oxford University Press, 2000), eg. p. 115.

[17] P. Burroughs, 'Defence and Imperial Disunity', in A. Porter (ed.), *The Nineteenth Century*, vol. 3 of *The Oxford History of the British Empire* (Oxford: Oxford University Press, 1999), p. 321.

the world, continued into the age of air warfare. Indeed British and French imperial power reached its territorial height after World War I, not only with the allocation of the German overseas empire, but also with the partition of the Ottoman empire. Britain increasingly acted as a land power (with air and sea support), in large part because of the commitments stemming from new and recent acquisitions, but also because there was no naval conflict in the interwar years. Instead, the 'low-level' struggles of that period, which did not entail war between major powers, were waged on land, albeit with the support of air or amphibious capability, prefiguring the situation since the end of the Cold War. In the Third Afghan War, in 1919, British planes bombed Afghanistan.[18] Equally, American operations in Central America and the West Indies in the 1920s and 1930s relied on amphibious capability and employed air support. Both were also at issue in the 1920s for the Spaniards in Morocco and the French in Syria.

Interwar military history serves to underline the general point that the uneasy equation of force and legitimacy is in part driven by the dynamic two-way relationship between capability and tasking, with the setting of goals arising from assumptions about relative capability, and in turn affecting measures to develop capability. In the interwar period, the capability gap between imperial and non-imperial forces was related to the tasking set for Western militaries by the need to maintain an hitherto unprecedented requirement for force projection. Western powers sought to dominate not only oceans and littorals, but also interiors. This geopolitical expansion was matched by a cultural expansiveness that saw Western power extended as never before into the Islamic world. As a result of World War I, Britain gained a protectorate over Egypt, as well as League of Nation mandates over Palestine, Transjordan and Iraq, while France gained mandates over Lebanon and Syria. Under Mussolini, Italy sought to enforce its claims to the interior of Libya.

Yet, as a reminder of the point about bringing different narratives into contact, the expansion of Western power encountered an opposition that combined both the usual action-reaction cycle of power and warfare (for example an ability to respond to air attack developing in response to air power) seen within a given military culture, with the particular issues that arise when contrasting military cultures come into contact, as when the Italians subdued Libya in 1928–32.[19] These issues overlapped with the willingness, in *some*, but not *all* cases, to take casualties and endure burdens greater than those of the Western powers. This, in turn, forced decisions on the latter, decisions about how best to respond to opposition in which issues of force and legitimacy, capability and tasking, were compounded. Indeed, it is striking to contrast the British response to opposition in Egypt, Iraq, and Afghanistan with that to the 1930s Arab rising in Palestine. The Third Afghan War (1919) was not used as an opportunity to try to subjugate the country, and revolts in Egypt (1919) and Iraq (1920–1) led to the British conceding authority (although a considerable amount of power was retained). A more forceful response, however, was taken in Palestine (1936–9).[20]

[18] D. E. Omissi, *Air Power and Colonial Control: The Royal Air Force 1919–1939* (Manchester: Manchester University Press, 1990).
[19] C. G. Segrè, *Fourth Shore: The Italian Colonization of Libya* (Chicago, IL: University of Chicago Press, 1974).
[20] E. Monroe, *Britain's Moment in the Middle East, 1914–1956* (Baltimore, MD: Johns Hopkins University Press, 1963).

Post-1945

Tasking and capability as factors in the military interaction of imperial powers and non-Western peoples remained an issue after 1945, first in attempting to sustain Western European empires, and, in the Far East, revive them after the Japanese conquests. The challenge to legitimacy (in the shape of colonial rule) however, came more strongly than hitherto because the ideology of national liberation was more centrally established in Western consciousness (especially that of the US and the Soviet Union); but, as with most notions of legitimacy, this was both controverted, and also rendered contingent in particular circumstances.

The definition of legitimacy came into greater play in a triple sense. First, it was necessary to consider the views of the colonial populations. Many of them were increasingly unwilling to accept the strategies of incorporation (alongside coercion) that had made empire work, and, indeed, in many cases had been instrumental in the successful process of conquest.

Secondly, it was more important than hitherto to note the views of international opinion, both those of other states and, albeit to a lesser extent, public opinion, which was given an edge by the role of international organisations, especially the United Nations. The hostility of the UN, the US, and the Communist bloc, both, in theory, to continued colonial rule, and, in practice, to such rule by Western European states, was very important in affecting the determination of the latter, for example the Dutch in Indonesia. This influenced the context within which force was employed by the colonial powers, for example the targeting of civilians and the acceptability of high casualties.

Thirdly, changing attitudes within Western publics was important, particularly in the case of France and Algeria: the despatch of conscripts to fight there made the war eventually more unpopular than the earlier French struggle in Vietnam. This political factor more than offset the enhanced military capability offered by the use of conscripts. More generally, shifts in the definition of the legitimacy of rule were more important than increases in military capability.

More rapid force-deployment, especially by air, became particularly important in the era of decolonisation, as the British sought to respond speedily to crises affecting colonies or recently-independent members of the Commonwealth. One example was the Indonesian confrontation of 1963–6, when Britain went to the aid of Malaysia against Indonesian aggression. Yet, the capability stemming from nuclear weapons and strategic bombers made little difference. The British were far more successful when they attacked Egypt in 1882 than when they did so jointly with France in 1956. In 1882, there had been an enormous capability gap at sea, but a far smaller one on land; in part because of the Egyptian acquisition of military technology. In 1956, in contrast, British forces, once landed, could draw on far superior air power and, indeed, the availability of parachutists greatly expanded the range of possible 'landings', and thus enhanced the risk posed to the defenders.

Nevertheless, the contrast between 1882 and 1956 indicated a major shift in Western attitudes towards force-projection. To be acceptable, they had to be able to conform, at least apparently, to ideological goals, rather than to aims more closely focused on power politics. Alternatively, power politics now had to be expressed in terms of the former, as with the cause of 'national liberation' supported by the Soviet Union and the anti-Communist crusade championed by the US.

American force-projection

Although post-1945 crises in the Third World involving outside powers brought up an instructive series of issues involving force and legitimacy, there was significant change between those in the immediate, colonial post-war years, and those that can be more clearly located in the Cold War. There was a chronological overlap, especially with the Korean War (1950–3), but American opposition to colonialism ensured that there was also a major contrast. The US increasingly deployed a completely new level of military capability, and also sought to direct a world order in which most peoples were independent. This military capability, however, is misunderstood if it is treated in aggregate terms. American superiority was particularly apparent in force-projection, but less so in combat, a contrast readily apparent during the Vietnam War, and repeated subsequently. The Americans could move large numbers of troops to Vietnam and support them there, but were unable to inflict lasting defeat on their opponents in the field.

Indeed, part of the conceptual problem affecting the modern discussion of military strength arises from the extent to which the capability gap in force-projection is not matched in the contact (fighting) stage of conflict on land, a problem that is enhanced in the case of guerrilla and terrorist opposition. This gap is a target of some of the changes generally summarised as the Revolution in Military Affairs (RMA). The use of guided airborne weaponry, which is particularly important to the RMA, seeks to overcome this divide by directing precise force-projection onto the battlefield.[21] Nevertheless, the gap remains, helping to ensure that discussion of capability and force has to be alert to what is being considered. As a result, as so often in considering both capability and military history, the use of aggregate measures is of limited value.

One particular sphere of importance in which there is only limited sign at present of a RMA is logistics, and this acts as a constraint on the rapid deployment of large forces, encouraging, instead, an emphasis on smaller expeditionary forces. This is an instance of the degree to which the largely 'silent' absences of, or limitations in, an RMA, have important consequences in doctrine, force structure, and operational method.

The American usage of force-projection has been strategic, operational and tactical. It is now possible to mount an individual operation, or fire an individual weapon, over a very long distance without apparently lessening the effectiveness of either. This has reordered the relationship between sea and land, the two basic components of international relations. In the age of Western sea power, or, phrased more selectively and accurately, the age not only when Western powers dominated the seas but also when the seas were the main axis of their power (an age incidentally that reached its culmination with the total American defeat of the Japanese navy off the Philippines in 1944), the capacity of sea-borne power to dictate outcomes on land was limited. Thus, the unbounded ability of Western powers (and Japan) to project power at sea was not matched by an ability to challenge (land) sovereignty.

Carrier-based planes threatened to alter this relationship, but their payload was limited, and post-World War II American and British plans to build super-carriers capable of carrying heavier bombers were abandoned. Thus, air power remained

[21] S. D. Wrage (ed.), *Immaculate Warfare: Participants Reflect on the Air Campaigns Over Kosovo, Afghanistan, and Iraq* (Westport: Praeger, 2003).

primarily land-based: the island-based American air assault on Japan in 1945, was followed after the war by the initial allocation of Western strategic power against the Soviet Union, in the shape of atomic weaponry, to heavy bomber units.[22] In contrast, naval air power was largely for anti-ship purposes, especially for anti-submarine warfare, and, as in the Korean and Vietnam Wars, its use against land targets was as an adjunct of land-based bomber capacity and of only limited effectiveness.[23]

Intercontinental missiles took air power further, challenging the sovereignty of all states, and prefiguring recent concerns about the potency and spread of weapons of mass destruction. The American (and British) deployment of submarine-missile systems added a dramatic new dimension to Western naval power projection, but, short of nuclear war or confrontation, they in fact had scant military effect. In particular, the deterrent capacity of such weaponry was of little value in asymmetrical warfare, or indeed in conventional conflict other than by affecting the possibility that such conflict might escalate.

Developments in military capability, however, are multi-track, and it is not only the maximisation of force that is at issue, a point that is of general applicability for military history and theory, but that tends to be greatly underrated. The practical ability of sea-based forces to challenge their land counterparts has been enhanced over the last two decades not by the development of sea-mounted weaponry for spreading mass destruction, but by less spectacular but more important developments, in particular enhanced mobility and shifts in sub-nuclear weaponry. The first has focused on the growth of helicopter lift capacity, and the second on the introduction and extensive use of cruise-missiles.

Indeed, the specifications of individual weapons, however improved, may make them inappropriate for the task at hand. Fitness for purpose is a crucial concept when judging the applicability of weaponry, but such fitness is frequently misunderstood by putting the stress on the capacity for employing force, rather than the ends that are sought. Although the term is frequently rather overly loosely employed, these ends, and thus the purpose, are culturally constructed, and in this process of construction notions of legitimacy, and thus appropriateness, play a major role in establishing both purpose and fitness. Furthermore, shifts in these can be seen as a motor of change in military history that deserves at least as much attention as the more habitual emphasis on weaponry.

The relationship between shifts in tasking and changes in technology is, as ever, complex, and not adequately addressed by the use of organic ('dynamic relationship') or mechanistic models, imagery and vocabulary. Furthermore, this relationship operates at different levels, and has a varied impact in particular contexts. In recent decades, for the US, one effect has been a shift in doctrine away from amphibious warfare and towards littoral projection, in other words the ability of sea-based forces to operate not only across the shore but also directly into the interior. Given that most of the world's population, especially, as in China, the economically most important percentage, lives within 500 miles of the sea, and much of it within 50 miles, this is of great significance for the relationship between force and sovereignty.

---

[22] W. S. Borgiasz, *The Strategic Air Command: Evolution and Consolidation of Nuclear Forces 1945–55* (New York, 1996).
[23] J. B. Nichols and B. Tillman, *On Yankee Station: The Naval Air War over Vietnam* (Annapolis, MD: Naval Institute Press, 1987); R. J. Francillon, *Tonkin Gulf Yacht Club: US Carrier Operations off Vietnam* (Annapolis, MD: Naval Institute Press, 1988).

It is in conventional capability that advances in American power, specifically force projection, have been most important. This has reflected both American doctrine during the Cold War, particularly the determination to be able to fight a non-nuclear war with the Soviet Union, and to maintain conventional capability even if the war became nuclear; as well as the changing nature of world politics after the end of the Cold War, specifically the American practice of interventionism. Looked at differently, this interventionism has been dependent on these very advances in capability, but such an approach must not see such advances as causing interventionism. To do so ignores the role of politics in setting and sustaining goals, as was readily apparent in the Iraq War in 2003. The same is true of Russia, whose Chief of the General Staff declared on 8 September 2004 that Russia could deliver preventive strikes on terrorist bases anywhere in the world. Russia may indeed be planning such action in the Caucasus.[24]

It is important not to exaggerate the end of the Cold War as a break, because many geopolitical issues spanned the divide, while, as suggested above, much of the American capability deployed in the 1990s and 2000s stemmed from Cold War procurement policies, tasking and doctrine. The ability to fight a conventional war in Europe had to be translated to other spheres, which created problems in adaptation, but much of the capability was already in place. The apparent legitimacy of such interventionism is a different matter, as much stemmed from the particular ideologies of the American administrations of the period. This indicated the central role of 'tasking', the goals set by political direction, and also the plasticity or changeability of what is referred to as strategic culture,[25] a term that can suggest a misleading degree of consistency. This was highlighted by discussion in 2004 as to how far the result of the highly-contested presidential election would affect at least the ethos and practice of American foreign policy.

The extent to which American developments in force-projection have not been matched by other powers is an important aspect of world politics, as the state that benefited most in economic terms from the 1990s, China, has instead concentrated, at present, on enhancing its short-range projection capability, thus matching the military consequences of Japan's economic growth in the 1970s and 1980s. Indeed, the contrast between, on the one hand, the force structures and doctrines of China and, on the other, those of Britain and France indicates the role of politics in shaping military capability and tasks, whether those politics are reified or not as strategic cultures.

More significantly, American developments have not been matched elsewhere by advances in anti-strategy/operational practice/tactics/weaponry.[26] The first, indeed, is one of the most important aspects of recent and current international relations, and

---

[24] P. K. Baev, 'Russia Insists Upon Preventive Strikes: The Possible Options', *RUSI Newsbrief*, 24:10 (October 2004), pp. 112–14.

[25] For a far from exhaustive list, R. Jervis, *Perception and Misperception in International Politics* (Princeton, NJ: Princeton University Press, 1976); K. Booth, *Strategy and Ethnocentrism* (London: Croom Helm, 1979); C. G. Reynolds, 'Reconsidering American Strategic History and Doctrines', in his *History of the Sea: Essays on Maritime Strategies* (Columbia, SC: University of South Carolina Press, 1989); A. L. Johnston, *Cultural Realism: Strategic Culture and Grand Strategy in Chinese History* (Princeton, NJ: Princeton University Press, 1995); C. S. Gray, 'Strategic Culture as Context: The First Generation of Theory Strikes Back', *Review of International Studies*, 25 (1999), pp. 49–70.

[26] Moreover, unusually for a state of its size, the US home base also remains strong, with no separatist or class-based violent opposition.

is one that would benefit from careful examination. Hitherto, the general pattern in military history *on land* has been to see such a matching of advances in capability and responses, although there has been no systematic study of the subject. In light of the Vietnam War, it was possible to anticipate at least elements of such a matching in response to the combination of the technological hubris central to the concept of the Revolution in Military Affairs and the greater intensity of American force projection that followed the end of the Cold War. In 2001, when conflict formally involving the US began in Afghanistan, there were frequent references to past British failure there, while, in 2003, it was widely argued that the conquest of Iraq would be much more challenging than its defeat in 1991. Indeed, Saddam Hussein appears to have anticipated that the problems of urban warfare would lessen American technological advantages and lead to casualties that obliged the American government to change policy,[27] an analysis that was certainly mistaken in the short term, and that anyway could not prevent conquest by a well-organised and high-tempo American-dominated invasion force.[28] Similarly, his hope that international pressure, particularly from France and Russia via the United Nations, would prevent the Americans from acting proved an inaccurate reading of the dynamics of contemporary international relations.

Attempted revolutions in military affairs

That American advances in capability were not matched, at least in the sense of being countered, does not establish a general rule that they cannot be, and it has indeed been suggested that the wide dissemination of technologies such as cruise missile design and production poses problems for the Americans.[29] The issue highlights the degree to which one of the real problems of both military history and military analysis is deciding how best to analyse and generalise from examples – but it is instructive. This is linked to an issue that divides analysts, namely how far recent and current changes in capability constitute a military revolution, or paradigm shift in military capability and warmaking, and, if so, with what results, and with what consequences, both in terms of analysing long-term trends in military capability, and in considering norms of behaviour within the international system.

The claims made for such a shift by military supporters, both in-post and retired,[30] civilian commentators,[31] and military-industrial companies, are bold, but yet also offer instructive clues about their limitations. For example, Northrop Grumman in

---

[27] T. Dodge, 'Cake Walk, Coup or Urban Warfare: the Battle for Iraq', in Dodge and S. Simon (eds.), *Iraq at the Crossroads: State and Society in the Shadow of Regime Change*, Adelphi Paper 354 (Oxford, 2003), pp. 59, 70–1.
[28] W. Murray and R. H. Scales, *The Iraq War: A Military History* (Cambridge, MA: Harvard University Press, 2003).
[29] L. Guy, 'Competing Visions for the US Military', *Orbis*, 48 (2004), p. 709.
[30] R. H. Scales Jr., *Yellow Smoke: The Future of Land Warfare for America's Military* (New York: Rowman and Littlefield, 2003); D. A. Macgregor, *Transformation under Fire: Revolutionizing How America Fights* (Westport: Praeger, 2003); W. K. Clark, *Winning Modern Wars: Iraq, Terrorism, and the American Empire* (New York: Public Affairs, 2003).
[31] For example, B. Berkowitz, *The New Face of War: How War Will Be Fought in the 21st Century* (New York: Free Press, 2003); N. Friedman, *Terrorism, Afghanistan, and America's New Way of War* (Annapolis, MD: Naval Institute Press, 2003).

its 2004 advertisements under the logo 'Share information. Share victory' for its ability to define the future ISTAR[32] battle space focused on the aerial vehicles and warships it linked in a blue world of sea and sky that left no room for the complexities of control on land.

If there is such a military revolution to match the greatly enhanced and partly redirected investment seen in American 'defence' (that is, military) budgets, then this indeed raises the question as to how far practices and theories of international relations will respond, or need to respond. At the same time, the very same issues are posed by other attempted revolutions in military affairs, in particular those sought by terrorist groups, and by so-called rogue states. In the first case, the attempt in 2001 by al-Qaeda to use terrorist methods for strategic ends, by crippling, or at least symbolically dethroning, American financial and political power, failed not least because it rested on a greatly-flawed assumption about the concentrated and top-down nature of American power; but it also indicated the extent to which the terrorist repertoire was far from fixed. Although it was true that al-Qaeda did not deploy weapons of mass destruction in 2001, its ability to make use of Western technology, in this case civilian aircraft, like its determination to ignore any boundaries between military and civilian, indicated the military as well as political challenge that is posed. Similarly, in 2004, a dependence on public transport was exploited in the terrorist attacks in Madrid. This terrorism is a more serious problem for international relations than those posed by particular states because the nature of a stateless entity is that it does not need to respond to the constraints that generally arise from claims to sovereign power, although such groups are also in a competition for legitimacy. The military equivalent is whether there is a territorial space that can be attacked or occupied.

As a result, however plausible it is to argue that there are terrorist states, nevertheless the challenge posed by terrorist movements is apparently greater, especially as they can seek to base themselves in 'failed states' where it is difficult to take action, short of full-scale military intervention, against them. Terrorism is part of a continuum described as criminal warfare and characterised as opportunistic warfare waged by pacts.[33] Although most terrorism is in fact aimed at states in the Third World, the challenge from terrorism is particularly notable for strong powers, especially the strongest, the US, as they have less practicable need to fear attack from other states, than weaker states do: even were the latter to be able to attack the US, the forces would very probably be defeated, and their territory could certainly be attacked.

This distinction between states, however, is challenged by the attempt by so-called rogue states to acquire weapons of mass destruction and, as seriously, related delivery systems. Although the regular forces of states such as North Korea and Iran probably lack the capability and ability in defence to defeat the conventional forces of stronger powers, which in this case means the US, and certainly could not stage an effective offensive war, such weapons would enable them to threaten these forces and, perhaps even eventually, home territory. The possession of such weapons by rogue states would also challenge the aspect of international aspirations and force projection represented by alliance systems.

[32] Intelligence, Surveillance, Target Acquisition and Reconnaissance.
[33] J. Mueller, *The Remnants of War* (Ithaca, NY: Cornell University Press, 2004).

If these are the key elements in the situation at present (with a number of developments the causative interaction of which is unclear), that situation does not in fact encompass the large majority of states in the world: most are neither leading military powers, nor 'rogue states'. Indeed, much of the conceptual problem with military analysis, as indeed with military history, stems from the extent to which it focuses on leading powers, with the corresponding assumption that other states seek to match, or at least copy, aspects of their warmaking capacity and methods: the notion of paradigm powers. This approach assumes a unitary tasking (and analytical methodology) that is in fact inaccurate.

For example, in many states, especially, but not only, in post-independence Latin America, sub-Saharan Africa and Oceania, the prime purpose of the military is internal control, with the army in particular as the arm of the state. In territorial terms, the challenge comes not so much from foreign powers as from domestic regional opposition to the state, some of it separatist in character, or from resistance that has a social dimension, such as peasant risings. The resulting warfare, most of which takes a guerrilla and/or terrorist character on the part of the rebels, is asymmetrical.[34] It can also overlap considerably with struggles against crime, specifically wars on drugs. Thus, in Mexico in the early 2000s, the army was used against the powerful drugs gangs, while a paramilitary Federal Investigations Agency was established to the same end. In functional terms, this might seem to have little to do with war as conventionally defined, but the firepower used by both sides was considerable. In Colombia, the left-wing FARC and the right-wing AUC paramilitaries are both involved in drugs.

The porous and contested definition of war suggested by its current usage, as in war on drugs or war on terror, let alone war on poverty, further complicates understandings of force and legitimacy, and makes it difficult to define the military.[35] If the 'war on terror' is crucial, then the Saudi security forces carrying out armed raids against al-Qaeda suspects in which people are killed are as much part of the military as conventional armed forces. Indeed paramilitaries play an important role in many states, not least in internal control. Similarly, troops are employed for policing duties, as in Quetta in Pakistan in March 2004 to restore order after a riot following a terrorist attack on a Shia procession.

The challenge to states from domestic opposition is 'internationalised', in so far as there may be foreign support for such opposition, or, with increasing effect from the 1990s, international humanitarian concern about the issue. On the whole, however, the nature of the conflict reflects an important aspect of international relations, namely the extent to which the use of force within sovereign areas is generally accepted within international legal constraints. This practice is seen as a challenge to humanitarian interventionist precepts, but the latter usually lack military capability unless they conform with the goals of great-power diplomacy.

The extent to which the conflation of humanitarianism with such goals sets a challenge to modern Western militaries has been apparent since the early 1990s. This challenge raises difficult issues of effectiveness, and ones in which the legitimacy of

[34] I. F. W. Beckett, *Modern Insurgencies and Counter-Insurgencies. Guerrillas and their Opponents since 1750* (London: Routledge, 2001); A. Clayton, *Frontiersmen: Warfare in Africa since 1950* (London: University College London Press, 1999), pp. 73–113, 155–208.

[35] For a critique, see G. Andreani, 'The "War on Terror": Good Cause, Wrong Concept', *Survival*, 46:2 (2004–05), pp. 31–50.

force plays a major role. The issue is also likely to become more of a topic in doctrine, though probably not to the same extent in weapons procurement.

If the state therefore emerges as a crucial intersection, between force and international relations, this is scarcely new, but serves as a reminder that the state and its military capability can be seen as acting in different ways and at several levels. The challenge for international relations theory is to address this variety. Current speculation about the relationship between force and international arrangements needs to address the future, not least because concepts of legitimacy and practices of legitimation in part depend on the likelihood of future consent. The pace of technological change is also a factor. New weapons systems create problems for judgment that reflect competing norms in international relations. To take the case of space-based anti-ballistic missile systems, its advocates stress its defensive character, but its critics include those who resist the idea of militarising space.[36]

Looking to the future

In the early 2000s, again reflecting normative dissonance, the key issues in international relations were variously presented as the response to unilateral American proactive interventionism, rogue states and terrorism, and it is likely that they will continue to be issues, but it is improbable that they will continue to so dominate the agenda as they did in the early 2000s. Even then, this agenda was in some respects misleading, as there were other conflicts and confrontations that were of great importance, not only for humanitarian reasons: the war in Congo, but also the serious rivalry between India and Pakistan. The apparently dominant agenda of the early 2000s reflected American interests, perceptions, and commitments, and the response of others to the US,[37] an important aspect of the extent to which the Western perception of developments (as of military history) can crowd out other changes worthy of attention.

It is unclear whether this perception will remain valid in future decades, not least as China becomes a more prominent, and probably more assertive, state, but also because the majority of conflicts in the world do not involve Western powers, and it is unclear how far they will feel it necessary to intervene in them. This, indeed, has always been the case, other than during the brief heyday of Western imperialism. China is often discussed by theorists in terms of a likely future confrontation with the US, not least on the basis of a 'neo-realist' assumption that states naturally expand and compete when they can, and that China's ambitions will lead it to clash with the US.[38] This, however, is less plausible than a regional ambition on the part of China that would involve India, Japan and Russia more closely than the US. Indeed, the US would have a choice over how far to intervene. This serves as a reminder that the world international system involves a number of complex regional situations, with

[36] M. E. O'Hanlon, *Neither Star Wars nor Sanctuary: Constraining the Military Uses of Space* (Washington, DC: Brookings Institution, 2004).

[37] C. S. Gray, *The Sheriff: America's Defense of the New World Order* (Lexington, KY: University Press of Kentucky, 2004); R. J. Pauly and T. Lansford, *Strategic Preemption: US Foreign Policy and the Second Iraq War* (Aldershot: Ashgate, 2004).

[38] J. J. Mearsheimer, *The Tragedy of Great Power Politics* (New York: W. W. Norton, 2001).

the US taking the leading role not because it is able to dominate the other powers (as might be implied by the word hegemony), but rather because, aside from its largely uncontested regional dominance of the Americas and the Pacific, it is the sole state able to play a part in these other regional situations.

At this point, history and the future combine to underline the problem of conceiving of the relationship between force and legitimacy in Western terms; allowing of course for the great variety in the latter. Such a conception can be seen as central to modern discussion, as the theories and analytical terms employed are those of Western intellectual culture and legal analysis. Indeed, one way to present the interventionist wars of the 1990s and 2000s was as conflict intended to preserve the normative structures that derive from Western assumptions. This was especially true of the language surrounding humanitarian interventions.[39]

The problem of definition

Reality, however, has a habit of defying ready classification, especially if in normative terms. This reaction by reality is generally conceptualised in terms of a non-Western reaction against Western norms, but, while correct up to a point, such an approach underrates the distinctions between Western powers and norms, and also between their non-Western counterparts. If the West, for example, is understood in terms of societies of European origin, that encompasses, over the last century, the leading capitalist state (the US), the leading imperial power (Britain), the centre of Communism (the USSR), the standard-bearer of National Socialism (Nazi Germany), and France, which played a major role in the language and customs of diplomacy and earlier in the ideals of liberty and justice, as well as a variety of other countries ranging from Argentina to Bulgaria.

To see these states as taking part in a system bounded by common norms is implausible, and therefore a challenge to the notion of the Western way of war. Indeed, serious differences in goals and attitudes helped vitiate international co-operation and understanding. These differences could also limit successful war-making. Thus, the racialist ethos of Nazi Germany led to harsh occupation policies that sapped consent and encouraged resistance, and therefore lessened the value of military success in so far as it was measured by the occupation of territory. Nazi practices also made war-exit a much harder goal, thus contributing to the situation already seen in World War I: German tactical and operational proficiency were undermined by strategic flaws that in large part rested on assumptions of legitimacy simply resting on force and in no way being dependent on consent.[40] These assumptions contrasted greatly with those in the US and Britain, and this was seen in the postwar reconstructions of West Germany and Japan, which differed considerably from those attempted (under wartime conditions) by the latter powers in states they had defeated and conquered.

---

[39] N. J. Wheeler, *Saving Strangers: Humanitarian Intervention in International Society* (Oxford: Oxford University Press, 2000).

[40] V. G. Liulevicius, *WarLand on the Eastern Front* (Cambridge: Cambridge University Press, 2000), pp. 247–77.

Conclusion

Over the last century, military strength and the intimidatory and coercive potency it offered, acted as the facilitator to differences between Western powers, but was not inherently responsible for a failure to make international institutions work, nor for an inability to keep the peace. In the case of the 'non-West', there was, particularly with the foundation of the United Nations in 1945, an apparent opening up of such institutions, and the related practices of international law and human rights, to encompass states across the world. This extension, however, did not transform pre-existing Western-derived norms about international and domestic conflict, but, irrespective of that, these norms were challenged by practice across much of the world. Thus, it would be mistaken today to look back to a golden age of apparently successful restraint, whether under the auspices of the competitive bipolarity of the Cold War or the normative policing of the UN, that has been allegedly challenged by the modern combination of new attitudes to international relations and particular practices in military power.

Instead, we should note that there has always been a degree of instability born of a combination of aggressive goals and contrasts in capability. This essay suggests that, in studying this relationship, it is important to treat the nature of force as an independent variable, and one that has played a major role, not only in the equations of international power, but also in the attitudes that help mould its purposes. As an independent variable, its development and interaction with international norms does not necessarily correspond in any clear-cut causative pattern to the development of the international system. To pretend otherwise would be to offer a facile systemic relationship that would be inappropriate. Instead, it is necessary to make this topic a subject for research while remembering, at every stage, to allow for the diversity of military and international environments around the world.

The judgment of war: on the idea of legitimate force in world politics

NICHOLAS RENGGER*

The twenty first century has opened, as so many centuries before it, with the drum roll of war depressingly audible. The optimism of the early 1990s that world politics was being remade, and that the threat of serious conflict was receding, vanished along with the twin towers that were so much a symbol of that world, one heart-breakingly beautiful September morning in 2001. And with the return of force and war to the forefront of international politics, so come the inevitable questions; when, under what circumstances, in what manner and with what restraint, may we (whoever the we might be) use force to secure our interests, protect our families, defend our communities or our values?

My aim in this article is to consider the idea of *morally* legitimate force in world politics. That will involve (how could it not?) saying something about the jurisprudential status of certain key contemporary ideas about legitimacy more generally, and especially with the idea of legality, but it is with moral legitimacy, rather than with legitimacy of other kinds, that I am centrally concerned here. This distinction is an important one to make in part (as we shall see in a moment) because a good deal of discussion about the 'legitimacy of the use of force' in the contemporary period elides the distinction or, worse, assumes that there is no distinction at all, but also because I need to stipulate from the beginning that I am concerned with one particular aspect of the understanding of the contemporary use of force (ways of morally justifying it, if one can) without denying that one can approach it from a number of other angles of vision.

I should also make plain that in this article I am going to concentrate on one particular way of thinking about the justification of force, without denying – or really even discussing – the obvious fact that there are other ways of thinking about it. My focus will be on the Just War tradition and aside from a few comments immediately below, and in the opening section, I am not planning to say anything about either claims that there are other, better ways of justifying force or claims that there is no possible way of (morally) justifying it. Both these sets of claims are, of course, important and to fully defend the position I adopt here I need, of course, to show that

* This essay forms part of a larger book, *Dealing in Darkness: The Anti-Pelagian Imagination in Political Theory and International Relations*, currently being completed. For discussions about that larger project, as well as this part of it, I would like to thank (but not implicate) Michael Bentley, David Boucher, Chris Brown, Christopher Coker, Grady Scott Davis, James Der Derian, Bob Dyson, Mervyn Frost, John Gray, Amy Laura Hall, Ian Hall, Stephen Halliwell, Stanley Hauerwas, Kim Hutchings, Renee Jeffery, Caroline Kennedy-Pipe, Tony Lang, James Mayall, Terry Nardin, Glen Newey, Onora O'Neill, Noel O'Sullivan, Mitchell Rologas, Joel Rosenthal, John Skorupski, and William Walker. For the invitation to contribute to this issue, and for help – and forbearance – throughout, I thank David Armstrong, Theo Farrell and Bice Maiguashe at the *Review of International Studies*.

both are mistaken[1]. My reasons for not doing so on this occasion are two-fold. First, simple practicality; I have neither the time nor the space to embark on that task here. Second, the principal aim of this article is to argue for a *different* way of conceptualising the just war tradition and its characteristic modes of argument than the ones that have tended to dominate the field in recent years. Of course, for this argument itself to be fully convincing I would have to show that thinking about the justification of the use of force in other ways is inferior to that offered by and through the just war tradition. But I need first of all to suggest why I think the tradition itself needs rethinking, and that is what I will attempt here.

These concerns shape the structure of what follows. The article is divided into four sections. The opening section takes the recent public discussion of the Bush and Blair government's decision to go to war in Iraq and the controversy surrounding it as a starting point for a discussion of the way in which just war rhetoric (and the language of the tradition in general) is being used by contemporary writers in the world. In particular it will look at the role played in such discussions of certain kinds of juristic reasoning and of the way in which the dominant modes of utterance within the tradition see the relationship between law and morality. The second section then traces these moves back to the revival of just war thinking after the Second World War, and examines in particular the most influential versions of the tradition in that revival. I will say something in brief about the revival of religious theorising but my main target in this section will be Michael Walzer's distinctively secular version,[2] far and away the most influential secular version of the tradition in the postwar period. The argument of this section will be that the way in which Walzer 'revives' or (in his own words) 'recaptures' the just war does violence to some of the central insights of earlier versions of the tradition, insights that might be able to help us to overcome the problems alluded in the opening section. The third section of the article then seeks to suggest what those other, earlier aspects of the tradition are that the dominant modes of thinking about the tradition today have marginalised, and what just war arguments might look like if the tradition was so reconceptualised. Essentially the argument here emphasises the necessity for *good judgment in the context of war*, rather than the language of justice in war per se and examining what this does to the traditional ways of understanding the just war (*jus ad bellum, jus in bello* and so on) and I also offer some thought about how such a reconceptualised just war tradition might offer us tools for understanding and reflection, in the context of the relationship between force and legitimacy today, returning to some of the concerns of the opening section. Finally, I say something about a central debate that needs to happen *within* such a reconceptualised just war tradition, and point to its significance both for the just war and for thinking about international politics more generally.

I

On 28 April 2005, one week before the date of the British general election scheduled for that year, the UK Prime Minster, Tony Blair, ordered the release of the full

---

[1] In *Dealing in Darkness*, chapters 1 and 2 will be largely taken up with evaluating these sorts of claims.

[2] See, of course, principally *Just and Unjust Wars: A Moral Argument with Historical Illustrations* (NewYork: Basic Books, 1977; 2nd edn. 1992; 3rd. 2000). But see also Walzer, *Arguing about War* (New Haven, CT: Yale University Press, 2004).

document prepared for him by the Attorney General on the legality of invading Iraq. The Prime Minister had been led to this point after a continuous and damaging dispute between himself and his critics (many of whom were in his own party) as to what advice had actually been received from the Attorney General prior to the British and American invasion of Iraq, and whether any undue pressure had been put on the Attorney General to come up with a view which favoured the legality of an invasion. The Iraq war had become easily the most controversial decision the Blair Government had taken in its second term and was threatening to dominate the last week of the general election campaign. Much, if not most, of the criticism focused on the justifications offered by both the Blair government and the Bush administration for the invasion. But the interesting point – from my point of view here – is the character of the debate both in Britain and – in a rather different way – in the United States.

The Attorney General himself, in an interview with Joshua Rozenberg, *The Daily Telegraph*'s legal editor, was unambiguous:

I stand by my conclusion that military action was lawful. That was a judgment I had to reach. I reached it and I stand by it. . . . And I want to reject the suggestions that I was leant on, or that this somehow was not my genuine opinion. These suggestions that this was not genuinely my view – these are fantasies and they need to be seen as such . . . I would not have hesitated to give negative advice if that had been my conclusion . . . I have been a practising lawyer for 30 years. I have been chairman of the Bar. I have chaired international legal organisations. I have been a deputy High Court judge. I was at the height of my profession when I was appointed Attorney General . . . I was not going to change that or throw that away – and I did not.[3]

Of course, in the case of the Attorney General himself, and indeed the British Government which had asked for his advice (in part at the urging, we are told, of senior military officers who were concerned about the possibility of prosecution by the recently created International Criminal Court), it is reasonable enough *at least to begin with* to focus on the question of whether or not a war would be legal. But, there are surely two questions that are prior to any answer that one might give to this question; the first, simply, consists in asking about the character of the 'law' in question – in this case the specific set of assumptions and agreements that make up 'international law' – in other words it is primarily a jurisprudential question. The second question, however, has to do with the relationship between a legal claim and a moral one.

In the case discussed above what was perhaps oddest, at least to my eye, was that the general discussion both amongst politicians and in the media, and independently of what particular position was taken (pro or con the war, pro or con the Government in general), was almost exclusively focused on whether or not the war was 'legal'. At no point that I am aware of, did anyone seriously discuss the surely related question that even if it was legal, was it morally justified? Or rather, in as much as they did, the assumption seemed to be that morality and legality were effectively, in this instance at least, one and the same. Yet a moment's reflection should serve to underline that this could not possibly be the case.

---

[3] *The Daily Telegraph*, 26 May 2005.

Of course, International Humanitarian law, in particular those parts of it that are known as 'The Laws of War' are inextricably bound up with the history and evolution of the just war tradition. But they are also bound up with the history and evolution of the idea of international law itself. The codification of 'the laws of war' was part of a much more general phenomenon to do with the gradual 'legalisation' of international relations, of international law being, in Martti Koskenniemi's words 'the gentle civiliser of nations'[4] and that, of course, is a political project. The laws of war in their current form are, therefore, bound up with the fate – and the debates over the fate – of that wider political project. This was one of things that the political disputes over Iraq partly demonstrated. In the United States, a very strong body of legal opinion had always been – to put it mildly – lukewarm about the idea of the 'binding' character of international law, regarding domestic law, rooted in the constitution, as binding but international law (as, obviously, not being so rooted) as being at best advisory. [5]

Such jurisprudential arguments, together with the necessarily interpretative character of legal argument in general, account in part for the variety of legal views on whether or not the invasion of Iraq (or any other possible instance of the use of force) is, or is not, legal. The point, of course, is to suggest that such arguments, far from determining with clarity the position vis-à-vis the rights and wrongs of this or that intervention are simply *part of* such arguments and cannot therefore be appealed to in order to settle them. Whether or not the invasion of Iraq was 'lawful', depends upon a particular understanding of law, of its application to the international realm and of what kind of binding force such rules might have, and these are all matters of considerable – and quite genuine – dispute.

But there is more. The question of the 'legality' of the Iraqi invasion is not only not separable from wider philosophical and jurisprudential questions to do with the status and character of international law (in particular) and law itself (in general) it is also centrally bound up with the question of the relationship between legal and moral argument. The two claims are normally, of course, seen as being related in that generally speaking in our domestic jurisprudence we think there is a moral requirement to obey the law, even in cases where we think the specific law in question may be wrong. This is in part simply what it is to have a legal *system* – there is a moral requirement to obey the law as such, independently of the moral worth of any individual part of that law.[6] But even in the domestic case, there are occasions when we would wish to set aside the claim that action A, while certainly illegal, is also immoral. It is perfectly easy to conceive of instances where actions we would regard as moral (perhaps even morally required) would also be illegal, and in such cases the general obligation to 'obey the law' would not normally be held to trump the obligation to act morally.

---

[4] See his wonderful book, *The Gentle Civiliser of Nations: The Rise and Fall of International Law 1880–1960* (Cambridge: Cambridge University Press, 2002).

[5] This dispute is manifest in the debates within the US Supreme Court over, for example, the banning of the execution of those under 18, partly on precedent drawn from existing international practice, Justice Antonin Scalia, for example, dissenting emphatically on the grounds that such precedents could not (and should not) count as binding precedents in US law.

[6] There is, of course a large body of philosophical and jurisprudential literature on this issue and those surrounding it. Classic modern statements, with special relevance to the international case, would be H. L. Hart, *The Concept of Law* (Oxford: The Clarendon Press, 1959), Hans Kelsen, *General Theory of Law and the State* (Cambridge, MA: Harvard University Press, 1945).

If this is true in the general realm of domestic jurisprudence, however, then it must be equally (if not more) true in the sphere of international law and this then raises the obvious question, if we cannot determine the specific sense of the legality of any instance of the use of force simply in terms of the internal specifics of international law, then we must surely look to a larger framework in which to embed such judgments. One of the starker messages, I think, of the recent debates over the Iraq invasion (and I have obviously only scratched the surface of them here) is the sense conveyed by many participants in the debate that no such larger framework is available. For many, as I have already suggested, there is a tendency to equate legality and morality. This is perhaps especially so in Europe. But for many others, the *dismissal* of the restrictions – as they are seen – of international law brings with it a belief in *state-led* morality, or perhaps a clear, if not very articulate or convincing attempt to substitute an ethos of 'pagan virtue' for the allegedly disabling views of Christian morality which is held to inform the just war tradition, also usually equated with international humanitarian law.[7] In other words, both for the critics of the Iraqi invasion as well as for many of its defenders, the idea that there was a framework of general moral argument one might refer to in order to discuss the moral legitimacy of the use of force was increasingly rejected.[8] And aside from any wider problems this might generate (of which more later) it made the debate over the invasion of Iraq itself increasingly ideological, in one way or another, and therefore also, increasingly strident and necessarily irresolvable.

II

The framework that most of the above rejects, of course, is usually referred to as the just war and in many respects this tradition is widely seen to be in very good health. In an article published in *International Affairs* in 2002,[9] I rehearsed the point – certainly not original to me – that the revival of the just war tradition in the second half of the twentieth century was one that had been in large part brought about by events in the world. Specifically (for example) the carpet-bombing of German cities (echoing, of course, the Germans' own practice earlier in the war) which led to the protests of Bishop George Bell, on traditional just war grounds – such bombing could only be the deliberate targeting of the innocent – and most importantly of all, of course, the Holocaust and its aftermath. Added to that were the Nuremberg and Tokyo tribunals and, in due course the creation (and, let us not forget, the use) of

---

[7] The specific reference to 'pagan virtue' is to Robert Kaplan's *Warrior Politics: Why Leadership Demands a Pagan Ethos* (New York: Random House, 2002) which combines a strong attempt to rubbish the just war, with a not especially nuanced approach to ancient thought. The wider tendencies, however, are visible in many places, from writers like Robert Kagan in *Paradise and Power* (New York: Atlantic Books, 2004) to the statements of many Bush administration officials.

[8] There were obviously a good many other aspects to this debate that I simply do not have time to go into here; that all such general moral arguments are necessarily cultural or religious and therefore bound by history and geography was one of the most common. I shall say something about this later on.

[9] See Nicholas Rengger, 'On the Just War Tradition in the Twenty First Century', *International Affairs*, 78:2 (2002), pp. 353–63.

nuclear weapons to end the war against Japan.[10] All of these events were forcing a rethink of the traditional view that states simply had a right to use force in defence of their interests, whatever they took them to be, which had been the standard view of international society at least from Vattel onwards.[11]

Initially, it was largely in the areas of religious thinking on questions of war and peace that the tradition was most obviously and most consciously rethought, perhaps unsurprisingly. Protestant theologians, most notably Paul Ramsey and then later James Turner Johnson, refined the traditional inherited categories and sought to deploy them in modern contexts. But in Catholic social thought too, the tradition was revived and discussed at length.[12] Perhaps the most interesting development, however, was the gradual secularisation of the concepts and categories of the just war tradition and the manner in which this was both attempted and achieved. In the academic world unquestionably the most influential contributor to this development has been Michael Walzer, and for a moment I want both to dwell on the significance of this in general terms and also say something about the specific arguments found in *Just and Unjust Wars*.

Walzer has been, of course, one of the most influential political theorists of the last forty years. He has written across a very wide range of topics in political theory[13] and has also been very active as a public intellectual, co-editing the leading magazine of the American centre left, *Dissent*, for many years. This combination of academic and

---

[10] This, in fact, led to one of the first sustained deployments of the just war tradition in post-Wittgensteinean Anglophone analytic philosophy, in that Elizabeth Anscombe – student, translator and heir of Wittgenstein – wrote two papers where she excoriated the decision to use atomic weaponry. Anscombe, a deeply devout Catholic, drew in fact on very traditional just war arguments (as had Bell in the controversy over strategic bombing) but her status in the philosophical world made her arguments stand out. It was also helpful that the first of the articles – 'Mr Truman's Degree' – was in fact a response to the proposal that Oxford (where Anscombe taught at the time) award Harry Truman, the President who authorised the dropping of the bombs on Hiroshima and Nagasaki, of course, an honorary degree. The essays are reprinted in vol. 3 of her *Philosophical Papers* (Cambridge: Cambridge University Press, 1981).

[11] For a discussion of the significance of this claim see, inter alia Richard Tuck, *The Rights of War and Peace: Political Thought and the International Order From Grotius to Kant* (Oxford: The Clarendon Press, 1999), Thomas Pangle and Peter Ahrensdorf, *Justice Among Nations: On the Moral Basis of Power and Peace* (Kansas: University of Kansas Press, 1999), and David Boucher, *Political Theories of International Relations* (Oxford: Oxford University Press, 2000).

[12] See especially Paul Ramsey, *The Just War: Force and Political Responsibility* (New York: Scribners, 1968) and also *War and the Christian Conscience: How Shall Modern War Be Conducted Justly?* (Durham, NC: Duke University Press, 1961). Ramsey's student, James Turner Johnson, is perhaps the person who has done most to explore the history of the tradition, especially in *Ideology Reason and the Limitation of War* (Princeton, NJ: Princeton University Press, 1975), and *Just War Tradition and the Restraint of War* (Princeton, NJ: Princeton University Press, 1981), but he has also illuminatingly discussed the content of the ideas; see *Can Modern War Be Just?* (New Haven, CT: Yale University Press, 1984) and *Morality and Contemporary Warfare* (New Haven, CT: Yale University Press, 1999).

[13] Aside from *Just and Unjust Wars*, his most influential academic studies have probably been *Spheres of Justice* (Oxford: Blackwell, 1983) and *Interpretation and Social Criticism* (Cambridge, MA: Harvard University Press, 1987), but earlier in his career he wrote on the political thought of the English Civil War [*Revolution of the Saints* (Cambridge, MA: Harvard University Press, 1965)], on the debates surrounding the French Revolution and the execution of Louis XVI [*Regicide and Revolution* (Cambridge: Cambridge University Press, 1974)] and many essays on various aspects of political thought and political thinking. Mostly these have been collected as volumes of essays, see especially, *Obligations: Essays on Disobedience, War and Citizenship* (Cambridge, MA: Harvard University Press, 1970) and *Thick and Thin: Moral Argument at Home and Abroad* (South Bend: Notre Dame University Press, 1994).

political influence is unusual and partly accounts for the influence of many of his writings, including – perhaps especially – his writings on war. In a symposium published to mark the twenty-fifth anniversary of the publication of *Just and Unjust Wars*, Michael Joseph Smith made the point that 'since its appearance the book has been a standard text at universities throughout the world – as well as at military academies including West Point' and adds that 'I would ... name it without hesitation as the indispensable modern classic in the field. Most of the people I know who teach in this area would agree.'[14]

Indeed. So we can agree, then, that Walzer's book is certainly amongst the most influential books to have revitalised the just war tradition in the postwar period. It is, as Smith suggests, and as a host of other writers have testified, a magnificent book and contains within it some of the best just war writing of recent decades. In this article, however, I want to concentrate on two aspects of the book that have been both crucial to its success but have also, I think, contributed considerably to the kind of problems when deploying the tradition that I highlighted in the first section above.

The first of these is the way in which Walzer sets up his account of the just war, and this has a good deal to do, both with the origins of the book and Walzer's more general philosophical assumptions. In the preface to the original edition of *Just and Unjust Wars*, Walzer disarmingly tells us that 'I did not begin by thinking about war in general, but about particular wars, above all about the American intervention in Vietnam' and added that ' in those years of angry controversy, I promised myself that one day I would try to set out the moral argument about war in a quiet and reflective way ... I want to defend the business of arguing, as we did and as most people do, in moral terms.' He goes on to say that 'my starting point is the fact that we do argue, often to different purposes to be sure, but in a mutually comprehensible fashion: else there would be no point in arguing. We justify our conduct; we judge the conduct of others ... these justifications and judgments ... are ... a legitimate subject of study. Upon examination they reveal, I believe, a comprehensive view of war as a human activity and a more or less systematic moral doctrine, which sometimes, but not always, overlaps with established legal doctrine.'[15]

This general argument seems to me to be exactly right. I think it does chime with the way most people think about moral decision-making in general and thinking about war in particular. Walzer is quite right to say that the framework for moral thinking about war overlaps with, but is not reducible to, legal thinking about war and he is also quite right to say, as he does a moment later, that 'the proper method of practical morality is casuistic in character'.[16] This claim flows from his concern with what he calls 'the present structure of the moral world'[17] rather than either possible ideal worlds (which are not ours and which, he suggests, are often the focus of philosophical attempts to understand morality) or with the *making* of the moral world, which would involve detailed historical reconstruction of the just war tradition. I also think (as I am sure Walzer does, though he nowhere explicitly makes this point) that this way of reasoning about practical morality is precisely the way in

---

[14] Michael Joseph Smith, 'Growing Up with *Just and Unjust Wars*: An Appreciation' in *Ethics and International Affairs*, 11 (1997), pp. 3–18, at 3–4.
[15] All the above quotations are from *Just and Unjust Wars*, 3rd edn., pp. xvii–xix.
[16] Ibid., p. xxii.
[17] Ibid., p. xix.

which the just war tradition itself reasoned, from Ambrose and Augustine to the neo-Scholastics of the sixteenth century.[18]

The problem is that as Walzer moves into his analysis *of* just and unjust wars, these claims recede and a rather more programmatic account of the tradition takes their place. Most especially, the way that he sets up the 'legalist paradigm' and the 'domestic analogy' in fact do the opposite of what his opening preface suggests. In the first place he adopts, almost causally, and from the beginning, the assumption that the principal agents of war are states and thus structures the legalist paradigm around his treatment of the rights of political communities. These rights, Walzer tells us, are merely the collective form of individual rights. 'The process of collectivisation is a complex one', he concedes, (but) it is best understood . . . as it has commonly been understood since the seventeenth century, in terms of social contract theory . . . contract is a metaphor for a process of association and mutuality, the ongoing character of which the state claims to protect against external encroachment . . . the moral standing of a particular state (therefore) depends upon the reality of the common life it protects and the extent to which the sacrifices required by that protection are willingly accepted and thought worthwhile.'[19] This way of thinking then generates, he argues, what he calls the 'legalist paradigm' which, however it might be slightly modified or reworked in practice (and he accepts that it would be) is the basic way we should ground and frame the just war tradition: 'It is', he tells us, 'our baseline, our model, the fundamental structure for the moral comprehension of war'.[20]

The problem with this claim is that, unavoidably, it sets up the just war as fundamentally state-based and connected with the language of rights as it has evolved and developed within liberal modernity. However one interprets these facts, they incline the tradition to a more juristic and less casuistic reading than Walzer's opening remarks indicated was his intention. They do so for the simple reason that to structure an account of the tradition on the basis of rights language inevitably slots it into the form of modern political vocabulary that engages in 'rights talk' and that, necessarily, in the modern world, pushes the tradition into the arms of legalistic reasoning. Of course, in Walzer's own treatment of the just war as a whole, casuistic elements remain in place (most especially in his discussion of the *jus in bello* in parts three and five of *Just and Unjust Wars*) but they are, I think, to a large extent vitiated by the overall setting of the *jus ad bellum*. And, inasmuch as Walzer's text has been the most influential academic and secular treatment of the tradition, this way of thinking about the tradition has become sedimented more generally in the wider political culture, as we saw above, and accounts in part for the rather strained aspects of a good deal of the discussion of the tradition in connection with contemporary conflict.

---

[18] This is, obviously, a large claim. And, of course, I am not suggesting that there are no differences between the original formulations of the tradition in Ambrose and Augustine and the 'School of Salamanca' version of it in the sixteenth and early seventeenth centuries. The point is merely to say that, to all intents and purposes, the general cast of the tradition for much of its existence into modern times was as a casuistic tradition of moral reflection not as a juristic one. I have made this point in more detail in 'On the Just War tradition in the Twenty-First Century'. Of course that does not solve – as we shall see – a different problem; which is how Aristotelian the casuistry in question has to be.

[19] Walzer, *Just and Unjust Wars*, pp. 52–4.

[20] Ibid., p. 61.

Of course, it is also true that this aspect of Walzer's book also fits very well with the manner in which war – and indeed politics more generally – has been discussed in the last hundred or so years; it foregrounds the state, it sees legal thought as the baseline, if not the be all and end all of moral thinking in politics, and without denying the powerful claims of morality on politics it also hints at the specific character of political ethics[21] and argues that in the context of war and violence, one should see this in the particular context that international society generates.[22]

There is one final point I want to make in connection with Walzer's 'recapture' of the just war. Whatever might have been the case initially (and it is clear that Walzer's intention had always been, quite rightly, to try and look at the phenomenon of war as a general part of the human moral realm) the events in the world since the publication of Walzer's book have tended to foreground certain issues over others. As Walzer himself notes[23] (and the comment is echoed in Michael Joseph Smith's reconsideration of *Just and Unjust Wars*[24]) the question of intervention – which had occupied only a small part of the original treatment – has become much more important, and in Walzer's treatment of intervention – quite consistently given the premises just mentioned – the state-centric and legalistic character of his account was dramatically obvious. In his recent writing, Walzer has given some ground to his critics on these issues and admitted a right of rescue rather more generous than his initial treatment allowed.[25] Nonetheless, he has retained a firm break on interventionary impulses as, given the initial development of his theory he must. The point I want to make here, however, is that by foregrounding intervention, Walzer's version of the just war has not only reinforced the state-centric and legalistic character of the dominant contemporary forms of the tradition, it has also tended to reinforce the view amongst both supporters and critics, that the purpose of 'just war theory' is to determine, by means of some kind of moral calculus, whether *this* or *that* war was 'just' or 'unjust'. And here, even the title of Walzer's book, unexceptional as it is in other contexts, encouraged this particular view.

These tendencies are, of course, not unique to Walzer. James Turner Johnson, another stalwart of the contemporary just war tradition, whose historical work is a masterpiece of reconstruction and sympathetic interpretation, gives support (perhaps unintentionally) to the same development when, as he does for example in the opening chapter of a recent book, he 'summarises' and lists the central points of the tradition in a set of lists.[26] It is not that Johnson's presentation of the tradition is inaccurate but rather that it encourages the tendency to think of it in terms of a juristically based calculus where certain boxes (just cause, right authority and so on) are ticked or not ticked and in the end one comes out with the view: yes, this was/was not a just war.

---

[21] A point that Walzer developed in detail in an earlier essay, one that strongly influenced *Just and Unjust Wars*. See Walzer 'Political Action: The Problem of Dirty Hands', in Marshall Cohen, Thomas Nagel and Thomas Scanlon (eds.), *War and Moral Responsibility* (Princeton, NJ: Princeton University Press, 1974).

[22] It is worth noting that, in this respect at least, Walzer's work is very close to the so-called 'English School' of IR scholarship and to certain older versions of realism, especially Hans Morgenthau and Rheinhold Niebuhr.

[23] See Walzer, *Just and Unjust Wars*, 3rd edn., new preface, p. xi.

[24] See Smith, 'Growing up with *Just and Unjust Wars*', cf. 'Perhaps no part of *Just and Unjust Wars* has inspired greater debate and controversy than its discussion of intervention', p. 15.

[25] See especially 'The Politics of Rescue', in *Arguing about War*.

[26] See James Turner Johnson, *Morality and Contemporary Warfare* ch. 1, pp. 22–40.

Let me summarise what I have tried to argue here. The dominant approaches in the revival of just war argumentation in the postwar period have all, to a greater or a lesser extent, continued and encouraged the broadly juristic reading of the tradition that, as we saw earlier, has led to the major problems with the tradition that have been exposed by recent controversies about the use of force. In many cases – as with Walzer – there is a recognition of the importance of the casuistical mode of moral argument but a failure to carry it through or to really consider what such a form of moral reasoning means for the tradition and, therefore, for the way in which we can use the resources of the tradition to properly consider instances of the use of force in contemporary world politics. And the failure to think this through properly has allowed many of the now standard criticisms of the tradition to flourish alongside its revival; that it encourages rather than restrains, war; that it is culture or time bound, bound to the 'West' or to Christianity; that it is in service to the 'powers that be' and allows them to find reasons to justify what they really wish to do for other reasons. And for all the above reasons, it is often said, the tradition – despite its great revival since the end of the Second World War – is now in deep philosophical trouble and in danger of effective collapse. Hence the criticisms that one hears, often from the lips of the powerful, that it is an unnecessary restraint, a relic of a bygone age, to which we no longer need, or should pay attention.[27]

III

This brings me to the crux of the matter. I strongly believe such views are incorrect, morally damaging and, in any event, unnecessary. I cannot put the matter better than to quote Oliver O'Donovan's recent statement that the just war tradition 'is in fact, neither a 'theory', nor about 'just wars', but '*a proposal for doing justice in the theatre of war*'[28] (emphasis in original). It is this claim that I now want to examine and contrast with the manner in which the dominant way of reinterpreting the tradition sees the issue. In doing so, I think, we can find resources to support and sustain the revival of the just war, without falling into any of the traps or temptations I have alluded to above and which helps us to ask important (albeit slightly different) questions than those asked by the dominant modes in the context of something like Iraq. However, such a reworking of the tradition *does* leave us with one profound question unanswered. The implications of that, I shall reflect upon in my final section.

Let me start by picking up the point I made a moment ago. The just war tradition cannot tell us – and is not designed to tell us – whether this or that particular instance of the use of force is 'just' or not in the generality. Again to quote O'Donovan;

it is very often supposed that just war theory undertakes *to validate or invalidate particular wars*. That would be an impossible undertaking. History knows of no just wars, as it knows of no just peoples . . . one may justify or criticise acts of statesmen, acts of generals, acts of common soldiers or of civilians, provided one does so from the point of view of those who performed them, i.e. without moralistic hindsight; but wars as such, like most large scale historical phenomena, present only a question mark, a continual invitation to reflect further'.[29]

---

[27] Consider, for example, the dismissal of the tradition by the likes of Robert Kaplan. See his *Warrior Politics*.

[28] Oliver O'Donovan, *The Just War Revisited* (Cambridge: Cambridge University Press, 2003), p. vii.

[29] O'Donovan, *The Just War Revisited*, p. 15.

What, then, *is* the tradition designed to do? We can grasp something of this, I think, if we reflect for a moment on one aspect of the tradition little considered by moderns: right intention. Johnson, in his account of the tradition cited above, accepts that this aspect of the tradition is 'not explicitly addressed' in the modern just war, being subsumed into questions of just cause and right authority.[30] Yet in classic just war writing from Augustine to the sixteenth century, right intention was most emphatically not so subsumed. Partly this was because it cut across the 'dividing line' of *jus ad bellum* and *jus in bello* that is in fact absent in Augustine and much less obviously present even in someone like Vitoria.[31] While part of the 'right intention' discussion is meant to apply to rulers – they must not have the intention of territorial or personal aggrandisement, intimidation or illegitimate coercion – part of it is also meant to apply to those who do the fighting; the enemy is not to be hated, there must be no desire to dominate or lust for vengeance, and soldiers must always be aware of the corruption that can flow from the *animus dominandi*.

The point here, of course, is that what the tradition – from Augustine onwards – insisted upon, and what right intention' was meant to gesture towards, was the extension into the realm of war of the normal practices of moral judgment. Of course, classic just war thinkers – Augustine above all – also recognised that war was an extreme realm and so such an extension represents (in O'Donovan's formulation) 'an *extraordinary extension* of ordinary acts of judgment'[32] but an extension of them all the same. This was why the two poles of the classic just war tradition were always authority on the one hand and judgment on the other, and why, when we come to think about judgment, the two central terms of reference were (as they are now known to us) discrimination and proportion. In the classic treatments of the tradition it is *these* distinctions that give rise to discussions about just cause, right authority and right intent (for example) not the later (and much more problematic) tendency to divide questions about war into the *jus ad bellum* and the *jus in bello*. O'Donovan refers to this distinction as a 'secondary . . . and not a load bearing'[33] distinction, which I think nicely captures how we should view it. It is a useful heuristic, no more. The problem is that the modern revival of the tradition has elevated it into an architectonic.

How does this change the way in which we should approach the tradition from the manner in which (say) Walzer approaches it? In the first place, it does not suppose, as Walzer effectively does, that the moral reality of war (as he puts it) is different from moral reality elsewhere. Although war is a realm of extremes, it is still the general human moral realm not some separate realm, and so the 'dirty hands argument' that Walzer develops elsewhere but then applies to much of his discussion of war (for example, and most notoriously, his discussion of 'supreme emergency'[34]) does not work. Secondly, it makes no assumption about the *moral* primacy of the state. The

---

[30] Johnson, *Morality and Contemporary Warfare*, p. 30.
[31] For an extremely powerful account of the views on war of the 'School of Salamanca' in general, and Vitoria in particular, see the introduction to Anthony Pagden and Jeremy Lawerence (eds.), *Francisco de Vitoria: Political Writings* (Cambridge: Cambridge University Press, 1991). An extremely good account of the background can also be found in Pagden, *Lords Of All the World: Ideologies of Empire in Sapins, Britian and France c. 1500–1800* (New Haven, CT: Yale University Press, 1995).
[32] O'Donovan, *The Just War Revisited*, p. 14., emphasis added.
[33] Ibid., p. 15.
[34] See, for example, ch. 16 of *Just and Unjust Wars*.

question of right authority is as much a source of debate and discussion as anything else in the tradition. It does not deny in principle that the state may be a right authority in any given context, but nor does it assume it. It will be a matter of judgment. States have certain competencies and not others, and other agents may have relevant competence depending on the circumstances. Authority, to be sure, normally flows from well-constituted government but not all such government has 'right authority' in all circumstances. This would need deliberation, and, in a democracy, the deliberation would involve the people, however constituted, not just the government. In other words, the whole framework on which Walzer (and indeed most other contemporary just war theorists) predicate their version of the tradition is thrown into question; not because anyone is denying either the power – either material or moral – of the state as such, but rather by saying that power (even moral power) does not necessarily translate into authority in the context of the use of force. It will depend.

The third difference between this approach and the more dominant one is the refusal to treat the *jus ad bellum* or *jus in bello* as a 'load bearing' distinction, which most contemporary writers do. This has a number of implications. In the first place, it would repudiate suggestions that one should add yet a third category, to be called (as Walzer does in *Arguing about War*) *jus post bellum*.[35] Of course, Walzer is quite correct to say that the issue he is getting at here – justice after war – is a very important one, but if one sees the tradition as I have suggested we see it here, it is already centrally implicit in it. Of course, one needs to deliberate about the problems, methods and issues that thinking about post-conflict situations raise, but these simply become part of the task of extending justice and judgment to the realm of war. And, of course, they should be thought about as part of the deliberation about the use of force in the first instance. This implies a second point, which is simply that many of the categories of the classical just war tradition flow from the twin poles of authority and judgment. In some contexts it will be unquestionably helpful to have a list of categories that we need to think about, but in others it will not and in any event, it is important not to give greater weight than is necessary to the excessively juristic aspects of the contemporary just war tradition. That these are a present and fairly permanent feature of the contemporary scene is true; that they have negative consequences I have tried to show. Nonetheless they are part of the way in which we think about the use of force and it would be foolish (and probably impossible) to ignore them. But we need to put them in context; they are tools, not masters.

So far, however, this has perhaps been a little bloodless. So how, then, might a just war tradition that was constructed on these assumptions make sense of the discussions we looked at earlier on, about Iraq and the decision to invade? What difference would it make? I want to briefly suggest – and, of course, this is the merest gesture towards what a much fuller account would offer – two areas where the way I have read the tradition would offer very different responses both from what governments have said and were saying and what some defenders of what I shall call the 'modern just war' have said as well.

The first such area is the various reasons (various and rapidly changing, one is tempted to say) offered by the Blair and Bush Governments for the invasion. Note, by the way, that in doing this I am not for one moment impugning anyone's sincerity.

[35] See Walzer, *Arguing About War*, p. xiii.

For the purposes of this essay, I will assume that the Bush and Blair governments were completely sincere in all their protestations, at all times. The defences that were offered for the attack on Iraq varied from concern over weapons of mass destruction, the failure of Iraq to comply with its obligations to the United Nations under the ceasefire agreements that ended the 1990–1991 Gulf War, the character and intentions of the regime of Saddam Hussein and the possibility of regime change in Iraq so as to increase the possibility of democratic change elsewhere in the Middle East.[36] Many, of course, have tried to link more than one of these together. The problem is that on no occasion was there an attempt to act in the manner that I have suggested the tradition would require. A discussion about what right authority might mean under these circumstances is not constituted either by constant appeals to the United Nations system nor by an assertion that State A will simply make up its own mind and act accordingly. It is not that in themselves these claims are wrong, it is simply that as such they are not *discussions* of anything, merely assertions. The point of the classical just war thinkers' constant emphasis on the twin poles of authority and judgment is that we need to *weigh* judgments about threat, proportion, and the like against one another.[37] This implies a deliberative posture and, of course, it is open to ask amongst whom the deliberation is supposed to take place. Yet that discussion did not happen either. Inasmuch as it was the governments of Britain and the United States that were *making* the claims – and who were, in slightly differing ways, claiming right authority and just cause (though of course not mentioning right intent) – it would seem to me that it was incumbent upon them both to initiate the dialogue and offer groundings for their judgments, and it is I think a legitimate criticism to say that they did not do so.

Legitimate, that is to say, in the context of the way I have suggested reading the tradition. It is a separate issue (for the moment) what side one takes on the substance. Walzer, in *Arguing about War*, is consistently hostile to the idea of an attack on Iraq in the circumstances of 2003. In his chapter on Iraq (actually five shorter pieces on Iraq put together) he offers an ingenious and subtle analysis that recalls the strongest sections of *Just and Unjust Wars*, and the nub of his argument is that the situation in Iraq in 2003 was no different from 2001, 1998 or at any time since the end of the Gulf war in 1991, but, if so, what had changed? If the threat had not (appreciably) changed then the response did not need to change either. In this context, as he puts it 'Saddam's war is unjust, even though he didn't start the fighting . . . he is defending his regime, which . . . has no moral legitimacy . . . (but also) America's war is unjust . . . at this time, the threat that Iraq posed could have been met with something less than the war we are now fighting. And a war fought before its time is not a just war.'[38] One can see the power in Walzer's arguments, but again, the sense of weighing the alternatives, of looking, not just at the givens – that there is a war here and now – but also at the larger questions of right authority and just cause, to say nothing of proportion and discrimation and how such questions reflect upon the war here and now, is missing.

[36] These are the best-known stated reasons; I do not deny there might have been others.
[37] For the importance of the fact of deliberation, see O'Donovan, *The Just War Revisited*, p. 131, and also Grady Scott Davis, *Warcraft and the Fragility of Virtue* (Idaho: University of Idaho Press, 1992), of which more in a moment.
[38] Walzer, *Arguing about War*, pp. 160–1.

A second area concerns what I will call the imperial temptation in some recent writing and thinking both about the just war and more widely. I should say at once that many just war thinkers have been profoundly opposed to this – Walzer, perhaps especially – so this part of the argument is most certainly not aimed at them. Rather it tends to be focused on those writers and thinkers who take the tradition's quite proper concern with justice and turn it into something other than the kind of concern that is appropriate for the realm of war. Here, I am perhaps especially thinking of writers like Jean Bethke Elshtain, whose support for, and development of, the just war tradition for many years was I think exemplary,[39] but also of some political statements, most interestingly perhaps Tony Blair's 'doctrine of the international community' outlined in the two key foreign policy speeches of his period in office.[40]

In his speech in Chicago in 1999, Blair outlined what he saw as a new approach to international relations as a whole but with very specific implications for the use of force. He predicated it on the operation in Kosovo, of which he had been one of the architects, but then went on to try and articulate a more general case based on that specific one:

The most pressing foreign policy problem we [in the West] face (he argued) is to identify the circumstances in which we should get actively involved in other people's conflicts. Non-interference has long been considered an important principle of international order. And it is not one we would want to jettison too readily . . . But the principle of non-interference must be qualified in important respects. Acts of genocide can never be a purely internal matter. When oppression produces massive flows of refugees which unsettle neighbouring countries then they can properly be described as 'threats to international peace and security'. When regimes are based on minority rule they lose legitimacy – look at South Africa.

Obviously this argument then needs to have a set of considerations of when to intervene. He lists five:

First, are we sure of our case? . . . Second, have we exhausted all diplomatic options? . . . Third, on the basis of a practical assessment of the situation, are there military operations we can sensibly and prudently undertake? Fourth, are we prepared for the long term? . . . And finally, do we have national interests involved? The mass expulsion of ethnic Albanians from Kosovo demanded the notice of the rest of the world. But it does make a difference that this is taking place in such a combustible part of Europe.[41]

There is much, of course, that is unobjectionable in this, but I merely want to point to two things. First, there is an *assumption* of 'international community' (for certain stated reasons) but no *discussion* of right authority. Not only how such a 'community' should be constituted but *what* kind of authority it would require and *how* it might acquire it. Yet for the morally legitimate exercise of force, such right authority must be in place. Secondly, while he is perfectly clear than one could not intervene in all cases of injustice, the prevailing assumption must be that we should seek to find reasons to do so, rather than to seek to find reasons to argue against the prohibition

---

[39] See perhaps most obviously, Elshtain *Women and War* (Brighton: Harvester, 1987) and Elshtain (ed.), *Just War Theory* (Oxford: Blackwell, 1992). But see, more recently, *Just War Against Terror: The Burden of American Power in A Violent World* (New York: Basic Books, 2003), that marks the change I am referring to here.

[40] See most significantly his speech in Chicago in 1999, which can be found at ⟨http://www.number-10.gov.uk/output/Page1297.asp⟩.

[41] Quotations from the above speech.

not to do so. And this, to my mind, is worrying if only because it tends to place the weight of the tradition on the attempt to secure justice rather than to prevent injustice.

This is even clearer if one looks at Jean Elshtain's recent book, *Just War Against Terror*.[42] Although, as always with Elshtain, it is very well written, the most significant part of the argument comes towards the end where she argues for a culture of strong 'rights protecting states' and argues that the only state that can truly perform that task globally is the United States. 'As the world's superpower', she argues, 'America bears the responsibility to help guarantee . . . International stability, whether much of the world wants it or not . . . we, the powerful, must respond to attacks against persons who cannot defend themselves, because they, like us are human beings . . . and because they, like us are members of states or would-be states.'[43]

For someone who has been so sympathetic to an Augustinian reading of politics and war for much of her career, I find this view astonishing, for the real danger of this version of the just war is the opposite of the tendencies of the dominant modes of thinking about it; far from juridicalising it, it runs the risk of turning it into an ideology, and more, a messianic one. Nothing could have been further from the thoughts or the intentions of the classic just war thinkers from Augustine onwards. The version I have briefly outlined here remains, however, true to what I take to be the express intent of the classical just war tradition; to extend into the realm of war, the judgments inherent in, and necessary for, our collective moral life *sui generis*. To do this is neither to 'legalise' it (important though legal and juristic concerns quite properly are) nor to messianise it (great and rightly demanding though the imperatives of justice in the common life must be). Rather, it is to do justice to ourselves and our common moral concerns even at the extremes of human life and conduct. If we wish to realise the proper – and realistic – way of regarding and considering the 'moral reality of war' it is to this that we must pay attention.

IV

And that, essentially, is the argument I wanted to make in this article. There is, however, one final point I also want to raise. I say raise, for I shall *merely* raise it and not – at least here – essay any kind of solution to it. Sharp-eyed readers will have noted that despite my criticism of Walzer's way of grounding the tradition, I have not offered an alternative. I have suggested, I hope plausibly, that more classical ways of reading the just war tradition will better serve our needs and are more appropriate for our concerns. And, of course – I hardly need add – the work that Walzer and many others have done on the *specifics* of the tradition – the discussions of the casuistry of the just war, as we might put it – will remain as essential to my reconstruction of the tradition as they are to anyone else's.

Yet the question of foundations remains. The just war tradition, like it or not, originated as a self-conscious tradition out of the Christian Church; its formulations, characteristic modes of discussion and some, at least, of its central concerns were

---

[42] I have examined this in much greater detail than I will here in 'Just A War Against Terror? Jean Elshtain's Burden and American Power', in *International Affairs*, 80:1 (January 2004).

[43] Elshtain, *Just War Against Terror*, pp. 169–70.

rooted in Christian, and indeed sometimes explicitly ecclesiological, concerns. This has given rise to what, in our own times, is one of the most damaging criticisms of the just war tradition as a whole, that it cannot speak to 'non-Western' traditions of thinking about war and peace. There is now a veritable avalanche of books, articles and so on that seek to speak to the allegedly very different ways that communities other than Christian ones have sought to think about war and its provenance and many of these are, indeed, adding a huge amount to what we know about the manner in which various different religious or normative groups see the problems of war and peace.[44] The problem, of course, is that this strategy suggests in general terms that the just war tradition itself is indeed a 'Western' (or at least a Christian) tradition and that therefore what we should do – indeed all we can do – is to engage in 'comparative international political theory' and see how all communities have understood the problems that the just war tradition understands *like this*. And this, of course, means that the just war tradition is not – and can never be – a universal tradition, which robs it, in a certain sense at least, of its principal *raison d'être*.

The modern just war writers – or at least those who are not themselves Christians[45] – have tried a variety of strategies to rebut this charge. Some, like Walzer, seek to erect the tradition on explicitly non-religious premises and argue that the legalist paradigm and the war convention work because it is manifest that this is how the world is. Others, for example Terry Nardin, suggest that the just war tradition be seen as merely one variant of a universal tradition of moral reasoning which he calls (following Alan Donegan) 'common morality' and which can be shared in principle by adherents of all faiths and none.[46] I have already suggested why I find these strategies implausible and so will not say more on this here. But in any case they are strategies chosen by those who already see the just war tradition in the ways that I have suggested are problematic, for all their attendant virtues.

So what about an alternative? The one that seems to be the most popular (outside, of course, of the explicitly religious) is to offer some form of Aristotelian grounding for the tradition. This is in keeping with a good deal of contemporary political theory that has taken Aristotle as a guide for rethinking certain aspects of our ethical and political lives.[47] The advantage, of course, is that Aristotle provides a template for an approach to human ethical and political life that is at once non-relativist and naturalist. Without appealing to the universalism of a Kant or a Bentham, with no overtly transcendentalist or theologically metaphysical presuppositions and yet insisting on our special character as human animals, an Aristotelian approach offers truth without God and universals without specific cultural baggage.[48]

[44] See, for the merest sample, Terry Nardin (ed.), *The Ethics of War and Peace* (Princeton, NJ: Princeton University Press, 1998), Perry Schmidt-Leukel (ed.), *War and Peace in the World Religions* (London: SCM Press, 2004).

[45] Or, at least, Theologians. The two communities are not always, of course, coterminous.

[46] For Nardin's work on the Just War see, especially, *Law, Morality and the Relations of States* (Princeton, NJ: Princeton University Press, 1983); and Nardin (ed.), *The Ethics of War and Peace*. He has also written many essays on the use of force and military intervention, which flesh out his defence of 'common morality', now far more pronounced than it was in the 1983 book.

[47] For three well known examples, see Alasdair MacIntyre, *After Virtue* (London: Duckworth, 1981), Martha Nussbaum, *The Fragility of Goodness* (Cambridge: Cambridge University Press, 1986) and Stephen Toulmin, *Cosmopolis* (Chicago, IL: University of Chicago Press, 1992).

[48] And, for those of a multicultural turn of mind, there are always the narratives of the Aristotelian School's meetings with other, non Greek, ways of thinking in Persia, India, even – according to some – China as well.

For defenders of the just war tradition, Aristotle offers the additional benefit of having already been hugely influential on the tradition. Not only on Aquinas, but also – and perhaps most importantly of all – on the neo-Scholastics of the sixteenth century, most especially Vitoria and Suarez. So the task for the Aristotelian-minded defender of the just war is to distil the common parts of the tradition, root them in Aristotelian concerns and language, thereby removing the problematic and more obviously 'Western', 'Christian' elements, and see how the tradition becomes reformulated in the process.

Perhaps the most impressive attempt to 'Aristoteleanise', the just war to date, Grady Scott Davis' *Warcraft and the Fragility of Virtue*,[49] does all of these things and comes up with a version of the just war tradition certainly close to the version I have defended here. And I would agree that an Aristotelian approach does indeed offer a good deal for those of us who have qualms about the way the tradition has evolved over the last few decades.

However, I would add, too, a note of caution. The greatest 'theorist' of the just war – if that is quite the word for him – remains, to my mind, Augustine, and this principally for two reasons. The first is simply his abhorrence – that is not too strong a word – of war. He recognises that the requirements of the common life may sometimes require it, but he still laments it; as he has it in the celebrated book XIX of *The City of God*, 'the wise man they say will wage just wars. Surely if he remembers that he is a human being, he will rather lament the fact that he is faced with the necessity of waging just wars; for if they were not just, he would not have to engage in them, and consequently there would be no wars for a wise man'. The second reason is Augustine's thoroughgoing scepticism about the claims we make for ourselves, and especially for the claims our rulers make for themselves. This scepticism is the root of Augustine's rejection of groups such as the Manichees (who had once claimed him) and even more, of course, the Pelagians (who never did). But it affects too his views of force and its legitimacy and also of the constant appeals to peace, while using force, that rulers – and soldiers – habitually make. 'Peace and war had a competition in cruelty', Augustine comments acidically during his denunciation of Roman imperial power in *The City of God*, 'and Peace won'.

In short, my fear about the Aristotelian turn in defending the just war is that it will forget the bracing scepticism and horror of war displayed by the tradition's first – and greatest – thinker. For all of the power and reach of his moral philosophy, and notwithstanding its ability to speak to many different ways of thinking about politics, Aristotle shares with the advocates of the modern just war a passion for classification and categorisation that was rightly emphasised by classical just war thinkers like Aquinas and the neo-Scholastics but which is very close to the juristic reading of the tradition I have sought to criticise in this article. I suspect that in part that is another reason why Aristotle appeals. If Augustine's just war is not always entirely clear, messier than its Thomistic or neo-Scholastic descendants and far less sure of itself that most contemporary variants, that does not mean, to my mind, that it is any the worse for all that.

---

[49] Though there are interesting signs that other scholars are beginning to plough this furrow as well. A Colloquium on *Natural Law and Humanitarian Intervention* held at Durham University in March 2005 at which I was present, contained a superb paper rooting the tradition in Aristotelian philosophy, from Bob Dyson. A harbinger, perhaps, of a (if not the) future.

An Augustinian approach[50] to the question of the legitimacy of force in world politics would preface any claim to justice in its use with the scepticism that is the hallmark of Augustine's thought in general. And Augustine, unlike Aristotle, was as sceptical of 'the powers that be', as he was of the claims of those that would oppose them (as critical of Rome as he was of the Donatists who would break with it). Having good judgment in the context of war is, as Augustine would have been the first to admit, a difficult, messy and always fragile condition which we should approach with great caution and because we should do so, we should put ourselves or others in that position as rarely as possible. In this context, the just war tradition becomes potentially a powerful critic of the tendency of political authority – all political authority, in all contexts[51] – to use force to achieve its aims and does not suppose (as an Aristotelian very well might, and as certain modern Kantians certainly do) that there are forms of political authority (liberal or democratic ones) that are somehow free of this tendency. Yet it allows also that there might be some circumstances where force is the morally appropriate response, notwithstanding all of its dangers and problems, and where this is the case, we need to see the realm of war as an extension of the moral realm more generally.

This view seems to me to recognise the truth in the fundamental realist claim that politics will always be about the use of force in some context or other and that force as such cannot be banished from human affairs (though any particular instance of it might, in the right circumstances, be mitigated or prevented) without claiming that as a result, force is beyond moral judgment. Augustine, and those of his successors who have written on such topics, have never supposed that moral judgment will prevent the use of force or denied that often, perhaps mostly, the force that is used will go beyond what moral judgment would, in fact, permit. Rather it is in the task of continually holding up the mirror of our considered moral judgments in the context of war that the tradition performs its most important role. It does not expect that human relations will 'progress' (or, indeed, regress) for in these respects, there is a certain permanence to them, but rather it offers a way of thinking about, understanding and dealing with the inevitable dissonances of human action and conduct in a particular sphere. In this respect, though I cannot develop this claim in detail here, the just war tradition, like political realism, is a species of modern anti-Pelagianism but one which I think recognises, in ways that most versions of realism do not, the complexity of the relations between the human moral and political realms.[52]

---

[50] Onora O'Neill, in a telling essay, has pointed out the distinction between Kant's ethics (that is the ethical thought of the historical figure Immanuel Kant), 'Kants ethics' (the usually erroneous ideas about Kant's ethics that have a good deal of contemporary currency) and Kantian ethics (ideas deriving in some form or other from Kant's ethics, but certainly not coterminous with them). Substituting Augustine for Kant, this essay – and the book of which it is a part – works from a broadly Augustinian position but does not suppose that this would necessarily be seen as in agreement with Augustine's thought.

[51] It is also worth pointing out here that Augustine believed this to be a tendency amongst all forms of political agents, not just 'properly constituted ones' – however we might interpret that condition. In other words, political agents other than the state would fall under Augustine's bracing scepticism as much as the state itself – in any of its forms – would.

[52] I am in the process of trying to think through the way in which what I call 'modern anti-Pelagianism' has manifested itself in general in political thought from the Renaissance onwards. A book on this theme will, I hope, eventually emerge and there I hope to discuss the relations between such ideas as the just war tradition and various versions of realism in more detail.

Of course that raises anew the question of grounding, the question that – I agree with the Aristotelians – is one that needs addressing. But even that, I think, might be possible in Augustinian terms. For now, I simply want to suggest that in questions as stark, and as far reaching, as judging the moral legitimacy of the use of force in contemporary world politics, Augustine's scepticism will serve us better even than Aristotle's naturalism. As Hedley Bull once wrote in a different though not unrelated context, 'it is better to recognize that we are in darkness, than to pretend that we can see the light'.[53]

---

[53] Bull, *The Anarchical Society* (London: Macmillan, 1977), p. 320.

Discourses of difference: civilians, combatants, and compliance with the laws of war

HELEN M. KINSELLA*

Introduction

Why have President Bush and his administration consistently, and publicly, stated their commitment to fully comply with the laws of war protecting civilians while, simultaneously, refusing to fully comply with the laws of war protecting prisoners of war? How do we understand President Bush and his administration's unquestioning acceptance of the protection of civilians, but the rejection of the same for prisoners of war? Are the strategic and normative costs of each so dissimilar as to justify this difference? Considering the recent exposé of abuses and torture of prisoners of war held in both Iraq and Cuba, the answers to these questions are not merely academic.

I contend that an understanding of this difference in compliance is to be found through a close analysis of the persistence and influence of discourses of civilisation and barbarism invoked by the administration. First, these discourses of barbarism and civilisation facilitate the construction of a barbarous enemy akin to 'fascism, and Nazism, and totalitarianism', against which 'civilization' must be protected, which, in turn, legitimates the suspension of the laws of war extending rights and protection to those detained.[1] Second, what marks President Bush and his administration as the right defenders of 'civilization' is their claim to protect 'civilians'. Indeed, insofar as the war on terror can claimed as war in defence of civilisation, it must be constituted as a war in defence of civilians. Thus, discourses of barbarism and civilisation enable the particular construction of categories of violence – detainee (combatant) or civilian – the treatment of which iterates the fundamental opposition of civilisation and barbarism by which the war on terror proceeds. Accordingly, this essay responds to the recent challenge by Christian Reus-Smit to 're-think long held assumptions about the nature of politics and law and their interrelation'.[2] Most significantly, it does so by introducing an analysis of the relations of international law and international relations as explicitly productive – to date, a neglected dimension of compliance.[3]

* I would like to acknowledge the assistance of Tarak Barkawi, Neta Crawford, Bud Duvall, Theo Farrell, Patrick T. Jackson, Colin Kahl, Richard Price, Tonya Putnam, participants in the 2004 CISAC social science seminar, and the two anonymous reviewers.

[1] President Bush, 20 September 2001, ⟨http://www.whitehouse.gov/news/releases/2001/09/20010920-8.html⟩, accessed October 2004.

[2] Christian Reus-Smit, 'Introduction', in Christian Reus-Smit (ed.), *The Politics of International Law* (Cambridge: Cambridge University Press, 2004), pp. 1–13, at 2.

[3] Martha Finnemore and Stephen J. Toope, 'Alternatives to "Legalization": Richer Views of Law and Politics', *International Organization*, 55:3 (2001), pp. 743–58; see also Reus-Smit, 'Introduction' 2004, Christian Reus-Smit, 'Politics and International Legal Obligation', *European Journal of International Relations*, 9:4 (2003), pp. 591–625, at 593.

As Martha Finnemore and Stephen Toope note, approaches to compliance primarily treat international law as a constraint.[4] Consequently, international law is simply regulative, and the role of international law in constituting international relations is obscured. Hence, the relationship of international law and international relations is conceived of as primarily strategic or instrumental, one in which the *techne* of international relations is regulated and evaluated according to the relationship of means to ends designed and instituted by sovereign actors. In fact, Kenneth Abbott writes 'designing institutions capable of affecting behavior in desirable ways' is not only at the centre of studies of compliance, but lies at the 'heart' of the interdisciplinary collaboration of international relations and international law.[5] As a result, studies of compliance focus on how to fabricate stable artifices of institutions and law, and how to regulate and evaluate compliance. But, notice how this determination of the relationship of international law and international relations is only enabled by a very specific conception of politics. Reus-Smit defines this conception of politics as one of 'strategic action', marked by 'rationalist assumptions'.[6] Compliance scholars agree. In their own words, Steven Ratner and Anne-Marie Slaughter call it an 'intermediate instrumentalist' conception of politics.[7] Such a conception emphasises a study of 'behavior as a reaction to norms in order to explain compliance'.[8] Law acts on international relations and upon political subjects through restraint and regulation. This, however, is an impoverished conception of international politics, reducing its flux and contingencies to questions of right design, consensual communication, and regulative institutions so as to manage and secure consistent behaviour. Overlooked, then, is the mutually constitutive relationship of international relations and international law, a relationship that is not simply or solely regulative but is also productive. As Michel Foucault specified, regulation has productive effects, in part because to be subject to regulation is also to become subjectivated through that regulation. In other words, the subject is not (contra conventional understandings of compliance) established prior to politics: there is no subject who participates in or presides over politics, that is not also produced by politics. Rather, it is precisely through regulation that the subject is incited and produced. Let me provide an example to demonstrate this point, and also to provide a historical detailing of the relationship among discourses of barbarism and civilisation, international law and international politics that, I argue, is still evident today.

The failure to observe the Geneva Convention of 1864 during the Franco-Prussian war of the 1870s deeply disturbed prominent lawyers of the nineteenth century. '(A) savagery unworthy of civilized nations' characterised these wars, betraying the hope that, at the least, 'undoubtedly civilized European nations' would conform *as a matter of course* with the laws of war.[9] With the memories of these wars lingering, the Russian Czar convened the 1899 Hague Conference, which codified the laws and

---

[4] Finnemore and Toope, 'Alternatives', 2001.
[5] Kenneth Abbott, 'International Relations Theory, International Law and the Regime Governing Atrocities in Internal Conflicts', in Steven Ratner and Anne-Marie Slaughter (eds.), *The Methods of International Law* (Washington, DC: ASIL, 2004), p. 130.
[6] Reus-Smit, 'Politics and International Legal Obligation'.
[7] Steven Ratner and Anne-Marie Slaughter, 'The Method is the Message', in Ratner and Slaughter (eds.), *Methods of International Law*, pp. 239–65, at 251.
[8] Antje Weiner, 'Contested Compliance: Interventions on the Normative Structure of World Politics', *European Journal of International Relations*, 10:2 (2004), pp. 189–234, at 190.
[9] Martti Koskenniemi, *The Gentle Civiliser of Nations: The Rise and Fall of International Law, 1870–1960* (Cambridge: Cambridge University Press, 2002), p. 84.

customs of land warfare. As was expressed by the delegates in attendance in 1899, a fighting *worthy* of civilised nations was a fighting governed and moderated by appropriate rules of engagement – rules which, by the late nineteenth century, included 'the distinction between members of armed forces and civilians'.[10] The conference was deemed a success and, at the close, one delegate announced assuredly that warfare would hitherto be restricted not only by the positive laws of war, but also 'by the laws of the universal conscience, and no general would dare violate them for he would thereby place himself under the ban of civilized nations'.[11] Notice here how the regulation of war, that is the positive codes of war and the laws of universal conscience, does not simply mark the difference of civilised and uncivilised nations, but also constitutes that difference which was otherwise obliterated in the conduct of past wars. I argue that by continuing to trace these reciprocal relations among discourses of barbarism and civilisation and the laws of war, we shall see how President Bush and his administration also come into existence as 'civilized' through compliance with the protection of civilians, a performance that is now threatened by the revelation of abuses at Abu Ghraib and elsewhere.

The structure of this essay is as follows. To provide the context for my argument I first introduce and discuss the 'war on terror' and the response of President Bush and his administration vis-à-vis the laws of war, specifically the protection of civilians as codified in the 1949 IV Geneva Convention (4th Convention) and the 1977 Protocol Additional I and the protection of prisoners of war as codified in the 1949 III Geneva Convention (3rd Convention) and the 1977 Protocol Additional I. Second, I explain the decisions made by President Bush and his administration regarding the detainment and treatment of the prisoners of war currently incarcerated in Guantánamo Bay or, as it is more prosaically known, Camp X-Ray. Third, I analyse possible alternative explanations for disparity in compliance with the laws of war. I focus on the two, strategic considerations and normative obligations, forwarded by President Bush and his administration, and central to the literature on compliance.[12] In reviewing these alternative explanations, I detail their inability, on their own terms, to explain the *disparity* in compliance. Finally, I show how tracing the discourses of barbarism and civilisation that inform the actions of President Bush and his administration elucidates the disparity in compliance.

Do the laws of war apply?

Although scholars may debate the degree to which the global war on terror is indeed 'new' and 'different', for President Bush and his administration, the war on terror is

---

[10] Gerrit Gong, *The Standard of Civilization in International Society* (Oxford: Oxford University Press, 1984), p. 75.

[11] Arthur Eyffinger, *The 1899 Hague Peace Conference: The Parliament of Man, The Federation of the World* (The Hague: Kluwer Law International, 2000), p. 313.

[12] For general discussions of compliance, see Abram Chayes and Antonia Handler Chayes, 'On Compliance', *International Organization*, 47:2 (Spring 1993), pp. 175–205; Jeffrey Legro, 'Which Norms Matter? Revisiting the "Failure" of Internationalism', *International Organization*, 51:1 (Winter 1997), pp. 31–63; Oona A. Hathaway, 'Do Human Rights Treaties Make a Difference?' *Yale Law Journal*, 111:8 (2002); Kal Raustiala and Anne-Marie Slaughter, 'International Law, International Relations and Compliance', in Walter Carlsnaes, Thomas Risse, and Beth A. Simmons (eds.), *Handbook of International Relations* (London: Sage, 2002), pp. 538–58; Christian Reus-Smit, 'Politics and International Legal Obligation' (2003), and Antje Wiener, 'Contested Compliance' (2004).

a war without precedent.[13] A simple review of comments made by President Bush and members of his administration captures the centrality of this presumption. In his address to the nation two months after September 11th, President Bush described the 'global war on terror' as a 'different war than any our nation has ever faced'. Approximately one year later, the National Security Strategy of the United States argued that war waged against global terrorism is 'different from any other war in our history'. In her daily briefings during this time, Pentagon spokeswoman Victoria Clark consistently referred to the global war on terror as a 'very unconventional war'.[14] In 2003, Secretary of Defense Donald Rumsfeld iterated that '(w)e have to deal with these new threats in different ways, for the world's changed and business as usual won't do it'.[15]

For President Bush and his administration the difference of this war goes so far as to potentially render the conventional understanding and use of the laws of war obsolete. As evidenced in his 7 February 2002 memo responding to the legal categorisation of those detained in Camp X-Ray, President Bush holds that the war on terrorism requires a 'new paradigm . . . new thinking in the laws of war.'[16] Clark had earlier suggested, 'every aspect of it, including the Geneva Convention and how it might be applied, should be looked at with new eyes and new thoughts as to what we're experiencing right now'.[17] They refer not simply to the *ius ad bello,* that is the laws of war governing the resort to force, but also to the *ius in bello,* that is the laws governing the use of force itself. Speaking of the rights and protections offered to prisoners of war, Alberto Gonzales, the legal counsel for the White House, argued 'as you (President Bush) have said, the war against terrorism is a new kind of war . . . this new paradigm renders obsolete Geneva's strict limitations . . . and renders quaint some of its provisions.'[18]

In the months following September 11th, the laws of war were subject to renewed scrutiny and analysis, with no satisfactory conclusions reached as to their applicability. Reflecting the widely held contemporary opinion, one legal scholar noted, 'attempting to apply existing international law to the novel circumstances . . . yields substantial controversy and reveals possible gaps in the law', while another confirmed that, most immediately, 'terrorism is disrupting some crucial legal categories of international law'.[19] After all, as the US ambassador for war crimes argued, "(t)he war on terror is a new type of war not envisaged when the Geneva Conventions were negotiated and signed."[20] Many have argued that the laws of war did not apply to the specific conflict of Afghanistan or to the larger war on terror because the Geneva

[13] 'Is This a New Kind of War?' ⟨http://www.crimesofwar.org/expert/paradigm-intro.html⟩, accessed October 2004.
[14] CNN News, 28 January 2002, ⟨http://www.cnn.com/2002/US/01/28/ret.wh.detainees⟩, accessed October 2004.
[15] Secretary of Defense Rumsfeld, 10 September 2003, ⟨http://www.defenselink.mil/transcripts/2003/tr20030910-secdef0661.html⟩, accessed October 2004.
[16] President Bush, memo signed 7 February 2002, ⟨http://news.findlaw.com/hdocs/docs/dod/62204index.html⟩, accessed October 2004; see also ⟨http://www.whitehouse.gov/news/releases/2002/02/20020207-13.html⟩, accessed October 2004.
[17] CNN News, 28 January 2002, ⟨http://www.cnn.com/2002/US/01/28/ret.wh.detainees⟩, accessed October 2004.
[18] John Barry et al. 'Torture and the Road to Abu Ghraib', *Newsweek*, 24 May 2004 pp. 26–32, at 30–1.
[19] Antonio Cassese, 'Terrorism is also Disrupting Some Crucial Legal Categories of International Law', *European Journal of International Law*, 12 (2001), pp. 993–1001.
[20] Quoted in Kim Sengupta, 'Geneva Conventions are Outdated', *The Independent*, 22 February 2002.

Conventions (the 1st–4th) are formally applicable only in wars among states and the war between Al- Qa'ida, which is a network of individuals and organisations, and the US is a war that does not fit easily into the state-centric categorisation of international humanitarian law. Others argue that the war on terror would be better fought as a police action, with criminal law becoming the applicable referent and not the laws of war.[21]

Yet, President Bush and his administration have not taken this position. From the start, however contested the description may be, President Bush and his administration have emphasised that the United States is engaged in a 'war' on terror and nothing less. At the same time, President Bush and his administration have never attempted to argue that the ground wars of Afghanistan and Iraq were beyond the reach of the Geneva Conventions altogether, nor did President Bush refuse to acknowledge that the parties involved were responsible to the dictates of the 1949 Geneva Conventions. More significantly, the potential ambiguity if the laws of war are applicable to the war on terror does not explain the *difference* in acceptance of the 3rd and 4th Conventions. Regardless of one's evaluation of the proper relationship between the laws of war and the global war on terror, the essential question remains: What makes compliance with the principle of distinction a certain element of military operations, while compliance with prisoner of war provisions remains uncertain?

Before I explain further, let me clarify two points. First, the argument in this article is concerned with compliance; that is, 'whether countries in fact adhere to the provisions of the accord and to the implementing measures that they have instituted.'[22] It does not evaluate the efficacy – 'the question of whether the goals . . . are achieved' – of either the 3rd or the 4th Geneva Convention in protecting civilians and prisoners of war.[23] This is an invaluable question, made all the more so in light of the abuses and torture of prisoners of war and efforts to determine numbers of civilian casualties in both ground wars. However, it is a distinct question for it evaluates the efficacy, or success, of the law once compliance is established. Second, this focus also means that compliance with the laws of war does not rest upon assessing the (greater or lesser) numbers of civilian deaths in the ground wars on terror. This essay focuses on *comparative* compliance with the laws of war, the 3rd and the 4th Convention, not with the efficacy of those laws. Moreover, it draws attention to the construction of the categories of 'combatant' and 'civilian' that, in turn, are then used to evaluate both compliance and efficacy.[24]

Disparity in compliance between the III and IV Geneva Conventions

President Bush and his administration accept the principle of distinction – that is the injunction to distinguish between combatants and civilians at all times during armed

[21] Mark Drumbl, 'Victimhood in our Neighborhood: Terrorist Crime, Taliban Guilt, and the Asymmetries of the International Legal Order', *North Carolina Law Review*, 81 (2002), pp. 1–114.

[22] Dinah Shelton, 'Introduction: Law, Non-Law and the Problem of "Soft Law" ', in Dinah Shelton (ed.), *Commitment and Compliance: The Role of Non-binding Norms in the International Legal System* (Cambridge: Oxford Press, 2002), p. 7.

[23] Dinah Shelton, 'Introduction: Law, Non-Law', p. 7.

[24] The controversy over the Lancet study captures the difficulties of identifying and counting civilian dead. Les Roberts et al., 'Morality Before and After the 2003 Invasion of Iraq: Cluster Sample Survey', *Lancet*, 5:364 (2004), pp. 1857–64.

conflicts and to direct military attacks only against the former. This principle was first codified in the 1949 IV Geneva Convention Relative to the Protection of Civilians in Times of War. It was supplemented in the 1977 Protocol Additional to the Geneva Conventions of 12 August 1949, Relating to the Protection of Victims in International Armed Conflicts. President Bush and his administration repeatedly emphasise the principle of distinction as central to their military operations although, as late as 2003, opinions were not unanimous. Voicing the concerns of some scholars and practitioners of the laws of war, one high ranking military officer argued that in a 'post 9/11' world what 'remains to be seen is whether it . . . provides an accurate, relevant, and ultimately credible basis upon which to regulate modern armed conflict.'[25]

Nonetheless, one month after the September 11th attack, the horror of which arises in part from the purposeful violation of the principle of distinction, the permanent representative of the United States to the United Nations stated that the 'United States is committed to minimizing civilian casualties'.[26] Referring to the ground war in Afghanistan, President Bush made clear that he would only intervene in targeting decisions if they would otherwise put civilian lives at risk and, likewise, operations in Iraq were designed to be 'laser precise' to avoid 'avoid endangering or humiliating Iraqi civilians'.[27] Most broadly, Charles Allen, Deputy General Counsel for the US Department of Defense, stated in an interview on 16 December 2002: 'With regard to the global war on terrorism, wherever it may reach, the law of armed conflict certainly does apply . . . in the sense of the principle of distinction.'[28]

Active military operations in both Afghanistan and Iraq conformed to the laws of war insofar as targeting decisions were evaluated with regard to the principle of distinction. In referring to the operations in Afghanistan, General Myers said, 'the last thing we want are any civilian casualties. So we plan every military target with great care.'[29] 'No nation in human history has done more', said Rumsfeld, speaking of the effort to avoid civilian casualties.[30] When assessing the ground war, legal historian and scholar Adam Roberts observed, 'there are strong reasons to believe US statements that civilian deaths were unintended'.[31]

Regardless of intention, the number of civilians killed – even when we isolate a reliable number – does not necessarily indicate a degree of US compliance because compliance does not necessarily lead to fewer civilian deaths. The principle of distinction does not outlaw the death of civilians; it outlines the responsibility of military commanders and their forces, as well as other civilians in positions of authority, to refrain from directly attacking civilians and civilian objects, to take reasonable precautions to avoid and to minimise civilian deaths, and to avoid and

---

[25] Colonel K.W. Watkin, 'Combatants, Unprivileged Belligerents and Conflicts in the 21st Century', Unpublished paper prepared for the Harvard Program on Humanitarian Policy and Conflict Research, 2003.

[26] *International Legal Materials*, 40 (2001), pp. 1281.

[27] Michael Gordon, 'Marines plan to use velvet glove more than iron fist in Iraq', *The New York Times*, 12 December 2003; Human Rights Watch, *Off Target: The Conduct of the War and Civilian Casualties in Iraq* (New York: Human Rights Watch, 2003), p. 5.

[28] Charles Allen, ⟨www.crimesofwar.org/onnews/news-pentagon-trans.html⟩, accessed October 2004.

[29] 21 October 2001 ⟨http://www.defenselink.mil/news/Oct2001/briefings.html⟩, accessed October 2004.

[30] Craig Nelson, 'Concern Grows over US Strategy, Tactics in Afghanistan', *Cox News Service*, 29 October 2001.

[31] Adam Roberts, 'Counter-Terrorism, Armed Force, and the Laws of War', *Survival*, 44:1 (2002), pp. 7–32.

minimise the destruction of civilian property and/or objects necessary to civilian survival. Indeed, high value military targets can be attacked, even if a large number of civilians are killed, insofar as the potential casualties are assessed as proportional and the target is classified as militarily necessary. As one military lawyer explained, 'I've approved targets that could have caused 3,000 civilian casualties and I've raised questions about targets predicted to risk fewer than 200 civilian lives. The issue is the importance of the target.'[32]

Yet, regardless of the prioritisation of military target/necessity allowed by the principle of distinction, President Bush and his administration did *not* unilaterally decide on targets. Rather, there was intra-governmental and non-governmental collaboration on target selection and prioritisation, and each target was subject to multi-level legal review during military operations and high collateral targets received extra review. Legal analysts reported that strikes were averted for fear of causing civilian deaths.[33] The controversial use of cluster bombs in Afghanistan by the Air Force was not repeated in Iraq – evidence of the importance placed on conforming to the principle of distinction. Moreover, the 2004 assault on Fallujah ended when President Bush and his administration ordered the Marines to withdraw, citing civilian casualties as too high.[34] This was a risky strategic and tactical decision that, in fact, facilitated a renewed Iraqi insurgency. Consequently, it underscores the central importance of compliance with the principle of distinction.

These statements and decisions attest to the acceptance of the principle of distinction as a legitimate, and undisputed, dimension of military operations – to the degree that criticisms of a particular strategy in Afghanistan led to alterations in military operations in Iraq. Additionally, it can be argued that United States exceeded its formal treaty obligations by implementing targeting criteria found in Additional Protocol I – a treaty that the United States has not ratified and for which the customary status of some of its provisions is still uncertain – or by taking extra precautions.[35] Thus, even if we wished to argue that President Bush and his administration complied with the principle of distinction *solely* because military necessity provides sufficient strategic flexibility in targeting decisions, this would not explain their relinquishing substantial control over the selection of targets, modification of specific strategies of war, and studied compliance with targeting criteria.

Nevertheless, it is only in the sense of the principle of distinction that the laws of war apply. President Bush and his administration have simultaneously concluded that the laws of war protecting prisoners of war are not fully applicable to US

[32] Carr Center, Harvard University, *Understanding Collateral Damage* (Cambridge, MA: Carr Center, Harvard University, 2002) ; see also Theo Farrell, *The Norms of War: Cultural Beliefs and Modern Conflict* (Boulder, CO: Lynne Rienner, 2005).
[33] William Arkin, 'Fear of Civilian Deaths May Have Undermined Effort', *Los Angeles Times*, 16 January 2002, A12, ⟨http://www.latimes.com/news/nationworld/world/la-011602milmemo.story⟩, accessed October 2004; Arkin writes 'avoidance of civilian casualties has become institutionalized even to the point of rejecting important targets if there is a high probability of civilian harm'. In 'Civilian Casualties and the Air War', *Washington Post*, Sunday 21 October 2001; personal interviews with Arkin, and with Col Lyle Cayce 2003–2004; see also T. E. Ricks, 'Target Approval Delays Cost Air Force Hits', *Journal of Military Ethics*, 1:2 (2002), pp. 109–12.
[34] 'Army will Shift Emphasis to Protecting the New Iraqi Government and the Economy', *New York Times*, 11 June 2004, A9; Edward Wong, 'Truce Extended in Falluja Siege, and Talks Go On', *New York Times*, 26 April 2004, A1.
[35] Filkins Dexter, 'Choosing Targets; Iraqi Fighters or Civilians? Hard Decision for Copters', *New York Times*, 31 March 2003.

operations in the current war on terror. Although the suspension of the rights and protections of prisoners of war was first publicised in regards to detainees at Camp X-Ray, the torture and abuse at Abu Ghraib provides further evidence.[36]

President Bush stated in early 2002 that those detained at Camp X-Ray are 'killers', unprotected by the laws of war; and further that 'Al Qaeda and Taliban detainees are not prisoners of war'.[37] President Bush and his administration since modified their initial claim, but have only agreed that those detained shall be treated in a manner 'consistent with' the principles of the 3rd Geneva Convention.[38] Those captured, detained, or deported (the practice is known as rendering) outside of Camp X-Ray are privy to less than 'consistent' treatment – the parameters of which are left to the discretion of the holding states, the practical interpretation of individual military commanders, or private contractors untrained and ungoverned by the laws of war. Although President Bush and his administration did not publicly argue that those captured in the ground war in Iraq were to be denied the legal rights and protections of the 3rd Geneva Convention, confidential memos from his legal counsel did.[39]

Battlefield detainees or prisoners of war?

The debates over the provision of Prisoner of War status to those captured by the United States in Afghanistan engage the extension of Prisoner of War status to the arbitrarily named 'battlefield detainees', approximately 600 of whom have now been held since 2002 in Guantánamo Bay, Cuba. The Bush administration maintains that these detainees or – returning to a phrase more in accordance with international humanitarian law (and current United States military manuals) – these 'unlawful combatants' are not entitled to the protection established by the 3rd Convention because their conduct and their chain of command did not meet the requirements outlined therein.[40] Rumsfeld pithily stated: 'they did not go around in uniforms, with their weapons in public display, with insignia and behave in a manner that an army behaves in, they went around like terrorists'.[41]

This position of the Bush administration is premised upon its interpretation of the requirements for the status of combatants set forth in the 3rd Convention. The Convention, like its 1929 predecessor, is primarily based upon the 1907 Hague

---

[36] See the 'torture memo' by Jay S. Bybee, 1 August 2002. ⟨http://www.washingtonpost.com/wp-dyn/articles/A38894-2004Jun13.html⟩, accessed October 2004.

[37] He uses the same description for the combatants in Iraq, see ⟨http://www.dod.gov/news/Oct2003/n10272003_200310272.html⟩, accessed October 2004. Alberto Gonzales, 25 January 2002. 'Memorandum for the President', ⟨http://pegc.no-ip.info/paust_the_plan.html⟩, accessed October 2004.

[38] CNN News, 28 January 2002, ⟨http://www.cnn.com/2002/US/01/28/ret.wh.detainees⟩, accessed October 2004.

[39] Department of the Army, Article 14-6, Investigation by Major Gen. Antonio Taguba at ⟨http://news.findlaw.com./hdocs/docs/iraq/tagubarpt.html⟩. See also ⟨http://news.findlaw.com/hdocs/docs/dod/62204index.html⟩, Seymour Hersh, 'Torture at Abu Ghraib', *New Yorker*, 30 April 2004, and Mark Danner,'Abu Ghraib: The Hidden Story', *New York Review of Books*, 7 October 2004.

[40] United States Army, Operational Law Handbook, JA 422 1997 (Virginia: JAG School, US Army), pp. 18, 19.

[41] Rumsfeld, 28 January 2002. ⟨http://www.defenselink.mil/transcripts/2002/t01282002_t0127sd3.html⟩, accessed October 2004.

Convention Respecting the Laws and Customs of War on Land, in which combatant status belongs to those who fulfil the following: (1) they are commanded by a person responsible for his subordinates; (2) have a fixed recognisable sign visible from a distance; (3) carry arms openly and; (4) conduct operations in accordance with the laws and customs of war. The 3rd Geneva Convention extended its purview to include combatants of regular armed forces who profess allegiance to a government or an authority not recognised by a Detaining Power (in this case, the United States) and to combatants of resistance movements (partisans) in occupied territories that belong to a specific Party to the conflict. Consequently, the 3rd Geneva Conventions broadened the definition of a lawful combatant. The significance of this status should not be underestimated for, as stated in the 3rd Convention, 'once one is accorded the status of a belligerent, one is bound by the obligations of the laws of war, and entitled to the rights which they confer. The most important of these is the right, following capture, to be recognized as a prisoner of war, and to be treated accordingly'.[42] Thus, the relationship between combatant and prisoner of war status can be understood as *reciprocal* and is made expressly so within the 1977 Protocols Additional.

In February of 2002, the Bush administration modified its initial stance. It agreed that the four 1949 Geneva Conventions were applicable to the conflict in Afghanistan and to these detainees.[43] Arguably this was a result of both pressure from Secretary of State Colin Powell and other military officers, for it occurred after Powell sent a memo to the President requesting he review his decision to withhold prisoner of war status from those detained. Powell voiced concern about potential repercussions for US soldiers who might be captured in the future and pointed out that such a move would overturn a 'century of US policy and practice'.[44] As US special operation forces in Afghanistan at that time would themselves have had difficulty qualifying under the criteria Rumsfeld set forth, this was no minor request.[45] Other influences included international pressure from Mary Robinson and other NATO allies who believed the 3rd Convention deserved absolute respect.

Nevertheless, the Bush administration decided that although all four of the Geneva Conventions were acknowledged to be generally applicable, only three would be so applied in their entirety and, in a notable feat of differentiation, those three would only be applied to the Taliban. As a senior US official explained, even the Taliban did not meet the basic regulations and would not be recognised as combatants and, thus, as prisoners of war. The Taliban 'did not have a responsible

---

[42] Jean De Preux, *Commentary on the III 1949 Geneva Convention Relative to the Treatment of Prisoners of War* (Geneva: International Committee of the Red Cross, 1960), Article 4, pp. 46–7.

[43] White House ⟨http://www.whitehouse.gov/news/releases/2002/02/20020207–13.html⟩, accessed October 2004; Rumsfeld, 8 February 2002. ⟨http://www.defenselink.mil/transcripts/2002/t02082002_t0208sd.html⟩, accessed October 2004.

[44] Memo from Colin L. Powell, 26 January 2002, in Michael Ratner and Ellen Ray, *Guantánamo: What the World Should Know* (Vermont: Chelsea Green, 2004).

[45] After photos were published of Special Operations forces in Afghanistan with full beards and turbans, and the debate over the detainees began, the Pentagon ordered that there be 'no more beards'. US soldiers were required to wear their arms openly and have a patch of the US flag on their clothing. James Brooke, 'Pentagon Tells Troops in Afghanistan: Shape Up and Dress Right', *New York Times*, 12 September 2002. The alteration in policy, which instructed both Special Operations Forces and Civil Affairs officers to don uniforms, overrode 'force protection' issues and may have placed SOF at a tactical disadvantage. Regardless, this policy was instituted because of concerns that non-uniform wearing SOF endangered the distinction of combatant and civilian – evidence that the distinction is institutionalised in military practice. Scott Holcomb, 'View from the Legal Frontlines', *Chicago Journal of International Law*, 4 (2003), pp. 561–9, at 563.

military command structure, turbans aren't a recognized uniform that distinguishes them, and, although they carry arms openly, everyone in Afghanistan carries their arms openly. They repeatedly failed to observe the customs and laws of war.'[46] As a result, the 3rd Geneva Convention, which determines a specific regime of rights and protections stemming from the designation of POW status, would only be implemented in regard to the *treatment* of the detainees at Camp X-Ray. In Rumsfeld's words, 'we plan, for the most part, to treat them in a manner reasonably consistent with the Geneva Conventions, to the extent that they are appropriate'.[47]

· This selective approach did not help when, as Powell feared, US soldiers were captured in March 2003. President Bush's injunction – 'we expect them to be treated humanely, just like we'll treat any prisoners of theirs that we capture humanely. If not, the people who mistreat the prisoners will be treated as war criminals' – was met with a certain scepticism by the international community; a scepticism now mixed with horror and disgust as the abuses at Abu Ghraib were publicised.[48] Likewise, the Bush administration's fury at the parading of the captured US soldiers was skewered by matching images of the detainees bound and blindfolded arriving at Camp X-Ray. More than a few commentators observed, 'there cannot be one rule for America and another for the rest of the world'.[49] Indeed James Rubin argues it was the Bush administration's position on Camp X-Ray that 'actually marked the beginning of the end of European sympathy for and solidarity with the United States after September 11'.[50] Out of the numerous condemnations of the Bush administration, it was Judge Steyn of Britain who inveighed against Camp X-Ray as a 'monstrous failure of justice', introducing the now famous description of the Camp as a 'black hole' into public conversation.[51]

To summarise, the Bush administration decreed that while the detainees at Camp X-Ray are not granted the protections of the 3rd Geneva Convention, it would treat them in accordance with the regulations found within. By parsing the rights of treatment and protection, the Bush administration creates for itself a unique position that at once extends and refuses the realm of rights and protection articulated within the 3rd Geneva Convention. These 'battlefield detainees' remain exactly within the reach of the laws of war, but decidedly outside the realm of its protection wherein protection is understood as the extension of particular rights of Prisoner of War status to the Taliban, the full application of the 1949 Conventions against all parties to the conflict including Al Qa'ida, and the extension of humane treatment to all

[46] Thomas Shanker and Katherine Q. Seelye, 'Who is a Prisoner of War? You Could Look it Up, Maybe', *New York Times*: Word For Word/The Geneva Conventions, 10 March 2002.
[47] Rusmfeld, 11 January, ⟨http://www.defenselink.mil/transcripts/2002/t01112002_t0111sd.html⟩, accessed October 2004; violation of the customs and laws of war is subject to legal sanction, but it does not automatically disqualify individuals from prisoner of war status – which must be judicially determined. The fact that all Afghanis carry arms openly is irrelevant to the question of whether the Taliban did. In addition, there are no strictures that limit exactly what is a 'fixed recognizable sign'. The Commentary on the 3rd Convention notes that no agreement was reached during the conferences, but that a 'coat, a shirt, an emblem or a coloured sign' suffices. Moreover, none of these arguments invalidate the extension of Prisoner of War status to the detainees until, and at such a time, their status may be determined by a 'competent tribunal'.
[48] 23 March 2003, ⟨http://www.whitehouse.gov/news/releases/2003/03/20030323-1.html⟩.
[49] *The Daily Mirror*, 25 March 2003; George Monbiot, 'One Rule for Them', *The Guardian*, 25 March 2003.
[50] James Rubin, 'Stumbling into War', *Foreign Affairs* (September/October, 2003), pp. 46–66, at 59.
[51] Lord of Appeal Johan Steyn, 'Guantanamo Bay: The Legal Black Hole', Address at the Twenty-Seventh F. A. Mann Lecture, 25 November 2003.

captured individuals. The 'battlefield detainees' are produced through the articulation of the laws of war with the particular war on terror in the service of President Bush and his administration.

Explanations for disparity in compliance

When confronted with this disparity in compliance with the laws of war, in an extant war that challenges the laws held to govern it, it is tempting to infer strategic or material considerations as 'trumping' all others, or to seek substantive differences in treaty obligation, formal or informal.[52] Certainly, the actions of the Bush administration suggest as much. After all, upon being asked why the US was not letting the 3rd Geneva Convention 'officially apply', Rumsfeld responded quite matter of factly 'well, first of all we don't have to'.[53] That is, due to its unique position in the world and the unique threat it faces, the US can decide not to comply with the Geneva Conventions, and its obligations to such treaties are minimal. The administration relied on similar arguments consistently to select out of international treaties, most notably the International Criminal Court. Likewise, scholars of international relations and international law focus on formal and informal obligation, as well as 'robustness', as a potential influence on compliance, and security or material concerns remain a central factor. Upon further reflection, however, neither element (security or obligation broadly defined) is sufficient to explain the disparity in compliance. For as significant as these elements are, and as surely as they are factors in understanding such a complicated series of events, they are not sufficient.

In assessing both formal and informal obligation for the protection of prisoners of war, note that it is the rights and protections of combatants in situations of vulnerability (sick, wounded, or prisoners of war) which have been the central subject of the laws of war since their inception.[54] It was this preoccupation, and not the protection of civilians, that prompted the founding of the International Committee of the Red Cross. It is not until 1949, under the 4th Convention, that the 'civilian' is formally made a subject of treaty law. And, it is not until 1977, in the Protocols Additional, that the civilian is given extensive protections within the laws of war. Certainly, the laws of war protecting prisoners of war and of civilians are both 'robust', but it is the protection of prisoners of war that is by far the older, more expansive law. The 4th Convention, for example, restricts the protection of civilians only to protection from 'arbitrary acts' on the part of the enemy. Thus generally, the protection of prisoners of war is certainly a 'robust' international norm, with a high degree of formal and informal obligation attached to it.

In terms of treaty law, or formal obligation, both the 3rd and the 4th Geneva Conventions are signed and ratified by the United States, as well as Afghanistan and Iraq. Both treaties have passed into customary law, binding on all states

---

[52] Stephen D. Krasner, *Sovereignty: Organized Hypocrisy* (Princeton, NJ: Princeton University Press, 1999), Richard K. Herrmann and Vaughn P. Shannon, 'Defending International Norms: The Role of Obligation, Material Interest, and Perception in Decision-Making', *International Organization*, 55:3 (2001), pp. 621–54.

[53] Rumsfeld, 11 January 2002, ⟨http://www.defenselink.mil/transcripts/2002/t01112002_t0111sd.html⟩, accessed October 2004.

[54] Jeffrey Legro, 'Which Norms Matter', 1997.

regardless of individual ratification. The US is a signatory to Protocol Additional I – which supplements and develops both the 3rd and 4th Geneva Conventions – but it has not ratified and neither has Iraq or Afghanistan. The US accepts Protocol I's relevant provisions on the protection of civilians as expressive of customary law and has acted in concert with these provisions in past conflicts, especially in recent conflicts when the US conducted its multilateral military operations in accordance with substantive principles of the laws of war, regardless of individual treaty ratification.[55] But, at the same time, the US has been a vocal critic of the broader definition of combatants and, thus, of prisoners of war found in the Protocol I. Nonetheless, President Bush and his administration do not explain their interpretations of US obligations in reference to Protocol I and, in fact, there is little public reference to Protocol I. Considering the failure to ratify could be a potential justification for the actions of President Bush and his administration, the absence of reference suggests an effort to minimise the status of Protocol I in the laws of war, or at least ignore its potential.[56]

Importantly, the customary status of the 3rd and the 4th Geneva Conventions is not affected by debate over particular provisions of Protocol Additional I. Thus, in terms of formal obligation and acceptance of the essential protections of prisoners of war, the US has already signalled its agreement. More specifically, it is the refusal of the President and of his administration to form competent tribunals to adjudicate the status of the detainees of Camp X-Ray and its abysmal treatment of those detained in Iraq that draws the most criticism. The US already conformed to these proscriptions by forming 'Article 5 tribunals' during the Vietnam war – when the status of those captured was no less complicated and no less uncertain – and quite recently by doing the same during the Gulf War, and in the current conflict in Iraq.[57] It has also included competent tribunals in the US manual on the laws of war, while its past record of humane treatment of suspect POWs is exemplary.[58] Moreover, the 1998 Department of Defense directive 5100.77 holds compliance 'with the law of war

[55] For example, the NATO bombings of Kosovo were governed by Protocol I.
[56] This is exemplified in Scott Horton's statement that Douglas Feith, the #3 civilian in the Pentagon, had a 'derisive attitude towards the Geneva Conventions', quoted in Chris Sullentrop, 'Douglas Feith: What Has the Pentagon's Third Man Done Wrong?', 20 May 2004, ⟨http://slate.msn.com/id/2100899/⟩, last accessed October 2004; Seymour Hersh, 'The Gray Zone', *The New Yorker*, 24 May 2004. Considering Feith wrote an article entitled 'Law in the Service of Terror: The Strange Case of Protocol I' in 1985, in which he dismissed Protocol I as illegitimate international law, it stands to reason he would be *both* derisive and dismissive.
[57] Briefly, the strategic 'benefits' of holding captured detainees without granting prisoner of war status to allow interrogation and to prevent repatriation are ambivalent at best. Not only may prisoners of war be questioned, thus overriding the need to deny such status, but also the intelligence 'benefits' from torture (facilitated by the extra-legal status of those detained) are deeply debated. Repatriation can occur at the discretion of the holding state when there is no longer a threat to security and, as this war on terror is one without seeming end, those detained need not be denied recognition of prisoner of war status to be detained for extensive periods of time. Those detained who have criminal charges pending may continue to be held. Therefore, there is no clear strategic need to deny prisoner of war status to prevent repatriation, nor is there necessarily an intelligence benefit from so doing. Finally, the relationship between the evaluation of prisoner of war status (in a military tribunal) and trial proceedings for violations of the laws of war (in military commissions) is unclear. Thus far, the two appear to be utterly unrelated, although certainly the general illegality of the US military commissions suggests that *regardless* of the status of the detainees – prisoner of war, civilian, illegal combatant – their trials will proceed according to the discretion of President Bush and his administration. On this subject see Human Rights First: ⟨http://www.humanrightsfirst.org/us_law/detainees/militarytribunals.html⟩.
[58] *Advocate General Operational Law Handbook*, 2004.

during all armed conflicts, however such conflicts are characterized', is a matter of United States policy, so both law and policy convene.[59]

In evaluating informal obligation, by tracing US socialisation and internalisation of the laws of war, the United States possesses a unique relationship with the laws of war personified by Francis Lieber.[60] Lieber was a Prussian immigrant and political science professor who drew up the first modern code of warfare, the 1863 General Orders 100, during the American Civil War. Importantly, the impetus for this code was the difficult question of how to discern the difference between combatants, civilians, citizens and seditionists, and thus decide the rights and obligations accorded to each. In other words, who was to be identified as a combatant? Referring to the disputed status of captured Confederate combatants and the contested character of their crimes, General Orders 100 declaimed that the laws of war 'admits of no rules or laws different from those of regular warfare, regarding the treatment of prisoners of war, although they may belong to the army of a government which the captor may consider wanton and unjust assailant'. Accordingly, the very founding of the United States involved questions not so dissimilar to those asked today.

General Orders 100 was the foundation for the Hague Conventions of 1899 and 1907 and not formally replaced in the United States until 1956.[61] Thus, it was the experience of the American Civil War, and the laws of war that developed from it, that informed the great surge of international codification of the law of war in the nineteenth century. Indeed, the US was at the forefront of codification of the 1949 treaties after World War II, and its delegates at both of the preparatory conferences for the 1949 and the 1977 treaties played pivotal roles in the development of the treaties.[62]

Finally, as I have earlier described, the training that US military forces receive in the laws of war reflects the importance attached to both formal obligation, but, even more tellingly, informal obligation as well. The laws of war are invoked as an example of the moral standards and ethical conduct expected and exemplified by the US military. For example, the immediate socialisation of Army recruits into the 'soldier's rules' that lay out the essential components of humane treatment and respect – such as that soldiers only fight enemy combatants – is justified for both legal

---

[59] ⟨www.dtic.mil/whs/directives/corres/pdf2/d510077p.pdf⟩, p. 4.
[60] See Kal Raustalia and Anne-Marie Slaughter, 'International Law, International Relations and Compliance', (2002); Thomas Risse, Stephen C. Ropp, and Kathryn Sikkink, *The Power of Human Rights: International Norms and Domestic Change* (Cambridge: Cambridge University Press, 1999); Martha Finnemore and Kathryn Sikkink, 'International Norm Dynamics and Political Change', *International Organization*, 52:4 (1998), pp. 887–917; Harold Hongju Koh, 'Address: The 1998 Frankel Lecture: Bringing International Law Home, Houston Law Review, 35:623 (1988), pp. 641–63; Harold Hongju Koh, 'Why Do Nations Obey International Law?', *Yale Law Journal*, 106 (1997), pp. 255–99.
[61] General Orders provided the basis for the Brussels Conference of 1874, which produced a (nonbinding) International Declaration Concerning the Laws and Customs of War and the 1880 Oxford Manual of the Institute of International Law. These documents were the principle sources of the 1899 and 1907 Hague regulations that codified protections of prisoners of war.
[62] George Aldrich and Richer Baxter negotiated the troublesome issue of combatant/prisoner of war status – informed by US experiences in Vietnam with US and enemy prisoners of war – achieving a compromise position and ensuring the success Protocol I. George Aldrich, 'The Laws of War on Land', *American Journal of International Law*, 94:1 (2000), pp. 42–63.

and normative reasons.[63] And, even when denying the full coverage of the 3rd Convention to those detained at Camp X-Ray, President Bush iterated that the US 'has been and will be a strong supporter of Geneva and its principles'.[64]

Consequently, it is difficult to attribute disparity in compliance to formal or informal obligation. As its history evinces, the protection of prisoners of war exceeds the scope of the formal treaty and is inextricably intertwined with the founding of the US The protection of prisoners of war has been deeply 'internalized' in US domestic political and military structures – no less so that that of protecting civilians.

Perhaps then it is pure strategic or material concerns, certainly an acceptable explanation in the context of the war on terror. But, again, upon reflection, the disparity in compliance is not accounted for by these factors. Take the most frequently forwarded strategic arguments for compliance with the laws of war – the presumption of reciprocity that founds the laws of war and the unique 'threat' posed by those detained.[65] Scholars of the laws of war and of international relations argue that compliance with the 3rd Geneva Convention is a strategic decision. Compliance increases the chances that, as in this case, captured US soldiers will be treated with due consideration. In fact, it was this logic that prompted Powell to petition President Bush, and it was this logic that contributed to the US decision to uniform its Special Operations Forces, clearly identifying them as combatants (and distinguishing them from civilians) in case of capture. The kidnapping and beheading of US and its allies' soldiers and civilians in explicit retaliation for the treatment of the detainees tragically confirms the accuracy of this argument. Yet, what has received less commentary is that the exact logic holds for the entirety of the laws of war – that is, the presumption of a reciprocal obligation as integral to compliance – and directly affects the protection of civilians. It is this presumption that the war on terror has so directly dispelled.

In both ground wars, and in the larger war on terror, Al-Qa'ida purposefully targets civilians; the Taliban purposefully hid military equipment in civilian quarters and sought refuge among civilians. For example, the Taliban placed 'a tank and two large antiaircraft guns under trees in front of the office of Care International', while the Iraqi forces purposefully placed civilians in direct danger as human shields.[66] Yet, the Bush administration complies with the 4th Geneva Convention, that is, with the principle of distinction, even as it is painfully clear that there will not be a reciprocal response from Al-Qa'ida or from Taliban and Iraqi forces. But, President Bush and his administration did not comply with the 3rd Geneva Convention, extending the

---

[63] Paragraph 14-3, Army Regulation 340-41, Training in Units, 19 March 1993. See the US Army 'The Considerations of Others'. 'KEY AREA #1: ETHICAL DEVELOPMENT – INDIVIDUAL AND ORGANIZATIONAL, *1. The Army is a values-based institution.* We reflect the values of American society and the values of the profession of arms. These values have both individual applications (for example, personal integrity) and organizational applications (such as selfless service or obedience to the Laws of War).' (http://chppm-www.apgea.army.mil/co2/CO2_book/ Intro.html).

[64] Memo from President Bush, 7 February 2002.

[65] Jeffrey Dunoff and Joel P. Trachtman, 'The Law and Economics of Humanitarian Law Violations in Internal Conflict', in Ratner and Slaughter (eds.), *Methods of International Law*, pp. 211–38; James Morrow, 'The Institutional Features of the Prisoners of War Treaties', *International Organization*, 55:4 (2001), pp. 971–91.

[66] Mark Mazzetti and Kevin Whitelaw, 'Into the Thick of Things', *U.S. News and World Report*, 5 November 2001; Bradley Graham and Vernon Loeb, 'Taliban Dispersal Slows US', *Washington Post*, 6 November 2001.

rights and recognition of prisoners of war even before there was evidence of a possible response from Al-Qa'ida or, in the case of Afghanistan, the Taliban. If reciprocity is a signal strategic element in compliance, why *pre-emptively deny* prisoner of war status while *maintaining* compliance with the principle of distinction? More pointedly, why bother with the principle of distinction at all? To return to Rumsfeld's remark, why would the US not 'have to' comply with the 3rd Convention, but 'have to' comply with the 4th?

In light of past actions and compliance of the United States vis-à-vis prisoners of war, President Bush and his administration repeatedly argue that the detainees are different from any others. Those detained at Camp X-Ray, and elsewhere, are a potential threat to international and domestic security. As Deputy Assistant Defense Secretary Paul Butler explained: 'We are holding enemy combatants in a global war on terrorism for security reasons, to prevent them from returning to the battlefield and injuring American soldiers and civilians, and civilians throughout the world'. 'They're dangerous'.[67] Compliance with the 3rd Geneva Convention is said to compromise security because it would facilitate the release of these combatants who, as Attorney General John Ashcroft explained, 'are terrorists . . . (and) are uniquely dangerous.'[68]

Yet, compliance with the principle of distinction is potentially no less dangerous, as any soldier can attest. Errors in judgment lead not simply to the deaths of civilians mistakenly killed, but also of US soldiers who mistake combatants for civilians – the 'Americans do not really know who they are aiming at'.[69] General Myers noted in discussing Iraq, 'some of the biggest losses we have taken are due to Iraqis . . . dressing as civilians and luring us into surrender situations and opening fire on our troops.'[70] Nevertheless, the principle of distinction, as codified within the Protocol I, requires combatants to do everything possible to avoid harming civilians, to take 'constant care' to distinguish between combatants and civilians and in 'case of doubt whether that person is a civilian, that person shall be considered to be a civilian'. Doubt extracts a high cost within armed conflicts where the 'dividing line between combatants and civilians is frequently blurred'.[71]

This is a consistent refrain voiced almost in unison by both witnesses and participants in war. The immediate reasons are many: the use of civilian infrastructure for military support confuses distinctions of legitimate targeting, while the merging of the 'home' and the 'front' into one makes any easy distinction between combatant and civilian difficult – especially as women and children, traditionally considered de facto civilians, are increasingly participating in war. The increased integration of civilians into contemporary militaries, in support operations and in the use of private security companies, does little to clarify the distinction. And, while there are legal repercussions for combatants who purposefully disguise themselves as

---

[67] Paul Butler, 13 February 2004, ⟨http://www.globalsecurity.org/security/library/news/2004/02/sec-00⟩, accessed October 2004, quoted in Bill Dedman 'US to hold detainees indefinitely', *Boston Globe*, 25 April 2004, ⟨http://www.boston.com/news/nation/washington/articles/2004/04/25/ us_to_hold_detainees_at_guantanamo_indefinitely/⟩, accessed October 2004.

[68] Quoted in Bob Franken, 'Ashcroft Defends Detainees' Treatment', ⟨http://edition.cnn.com/2002/US/ 01/21/ret.detainees/⟩, 22 January 2002.

[69] Doug Struck, 'Casualties of US Miscalculations', *Washington Post*, 11 February 2002, A1.

[70] Human Rights Watch Report, 2003.

[71] Kofi Annan, S/1999/957, 'Report of the Secretary General to the Security Council on the Protection of Civilians In Armed Conflict'.

civilians, a crime of war known as perfidy, it is still incumbent upon every combatant to essentially hold their fire in cases of doubt. As the wars of Afghanistan and Iraq illustrate, the consequences of such caution for the United States' military in the face of such confusion are deadly.

Strikingly, in the codification of the 4th Convention, it was exactly this problem that worried the delegates. In an exact inversion of the argument of President Bush and his administration, the International Committee of the Red Cross Commentary on the 4th Convention states, 'wounded and prisoners of war are human beings who have become harmless, and the State's obligation towards them are not a serious hindrance to its conduct of the hostilities; on the other hand, civilians have not in most cases been rendered harmless, and the steps taken on their behalf may be a serious hindrance to the conduct of war'.[72] It is not the prisoners of war that are uniquely dangerous, hidden killers in wait – it is the civilians.

There are other effects as a result of compliance with the principle of distinction. Increased combatant deaths can lead to potentially less national support for the war or, at the very least, create a volatile public environment in terms of support. Violation of the principle it is said to uphold exposes the US to international criticism and censure. And, consistent iteration of compliance with the principle of distinction may, conversely, create expectations of compliance that increase the bar for United States military operations that, when not met, results in resentment and anger from the 'enemy' population. Rumsfeld was aware of this effect, arguing that 'if you kill a lot of civilians, the people inside of Afghanistan will believe you are not discriminating and that you are against the people of Afghanistan'.[73] Now, interviews with Iraqis and returning military officers only confirm this point. 'At first they were filled with grief, but now they are angry. The Americans said no civilians were targeted . . . (w)hy did Americans tell the world they hit only places of the army. Why did they hit civilian homes?'[74] As one member of the Operation Iraqi Freedom team observed, 'President Bush had told civilians they would not be harmed, therefore many concluded that United States forces targeted the civilian population'.[75] Further, some have argued that complying with the principle of distinction hampers swift and decisive war fighting, protracting the war and ultimately making victory more difficult. To quote the author of the first modern code of war, Francis Lieber, the 'more vigorously wars are pursued, the better it is for humanity. Sharp wars are brief.'[76]

Irrespective of these strategic and normative considerations, President Bush and his administration have not engaged in such debates. Most significantly, US soldiers were told, even after it became clear that combatants and civilians were often indistinguishable, that they needed 'positive identification' before firing.[77] Thus the principle of distinction and its correlate injunction to protect and respect 'civilians'

---

[72] Oscar Uhler and Henri Coursier (eds.), *Commentary on the 1949 Geneva Convention Relative to the Protection of Civilian Persons in Time of War* (Geneva: International Committee of the Red Cross, 1960), p. 5.

[73] Rumsfeld, 7 November 2001, ⟨http://www.defenselink.mil/transcripts/2001/t11082001_t1107pbs.html⟩, accessed October 2004.

[74] Human Rights Watch, 2003.

[75] Sarah Sewall, *Targeting Humanity: Minimizing Civilian Suffering in War*. Unpublished manuscript.

[76] General Orders 100. para #6.

[77] Human Rights Watch, 2003, p. 101.

remains 'imperative and salutary'.[78] Indeed, it holds to the degree that Rumsfeld, in a sentiment shared by President Bush, *justifies* the disqualification of the Taliban from POW status on the basis of protecting 'innocent civilians'.[79]

But, why does uncertainty over who, precisely, are those detained at Camp X-Ray or elsewhere lead to the denial of the 3rd Convention, whereas uncertainty over who, precisely, are 'civilians' in Iraq and Afghanistan does not? The production of the detainees as the 'ultimate' threat does not necessarily correspond to the immediate situations in either Afghanistan or, now, Iraq. Rather, what *is* revealed is the continued construction of particular threats and obligations that differ according to the subject – combatant or civilian – of the action. This leads us to ask not only *why* does President Bush and his administration differentially comply with the laws of war, but *how* is this made possible? How is one subject produced as worthy of the rights and protections of the laws of war and the other not? By what means are the 'combatant' and the 'civilian' constructed? It is here that the analysis of discourses of barbarism and civilisation shows its worth, for such an analysis centres the production of *how* this difference in compliance is made possible, and in so doing highlights reasons *why* it was done.

Discourses of barbarism and civilisation

In the cognate scholarship on international law and international relations, discourse has a conventional use as 'verbal or written statements' or a form of Habermasian 'argumentation'.[80] While significant, by this definition discourse is understood as a mode of transparent exchange conducted for specific ends. Even those authors arguing for a more complex relationship of international law and international relations do not explicitly explore how an analysis of discourses, conceptualised differently than practical reasoning, give us purchase on the way the two are recursively constructed.[81] In this essay, drawing from Michel Foucault, discourses are open systems of meaning and authority, generative of specific subjects and specific practices. Discourses are not tools to be wielded by rational actors, nor is the influence of discourse measured by the belief or intention of said actors.[82] Instead, discourses are conditions of possibility that enable, or not, particular actions by particular individuals at particular times. Accordingly, subjects do not precede discourse (and thus cannot simply use, or be used by, discourses) but come into being through discourse. I contend that discourses of barbarism and civilisation condition

---

[78] Antonio Cassese, 2001, p. 998.

[79] Rumsfeld, 8 February 2002, ⟨http://www.defenselink.mil/transcripts/2002/t02082002_t0208sd.html⟩, accessed October 2004.

[80] Ellen Lutz and Kathryn Sikkink, 'International Human Rights Law and Practice in Latin America', *International Organization*, 54:3 (2000), pp. 633–60, at 634; Thomas Risse, 'Let's Argue! Communicative Action in World Politics', *International Organization*, 54:1 (2000), pp. 1–39; Michael Barnett and Raymond Duvall (eds.), *Power and Global Governance* (Cambridge: Cambridge University Press, 2005).

[81] Reus-Smit, *Politics of International Law* 2004, *Politics and Legal Obligation* 2003; Friedrich Kratochwil, 'How do Norms Matter?', in Michael Byers (ed.), *The Role of Law in International Politics* (Oxford: Oxford University Press, 2000); however, see Neta Crawford, *Argument and Change in World Politics* (Cambridge: Cambridge University Press, 2002), pp. 35–68.

[82] Richard K. Herrmann and Vaughn P. Shannon, 'Defending International Norms' (2001).

the extension of rights and protections to civilians and the denial of the rights and protections to prisoners of war, and, in turn, index a hierarchy of practices that distinguish the 'civilized' from the 'barbarians'.

At the origins of the laws of war lies a distinction of barbarism and civilisation that excluded 'barbarians' from the laws of war. This is captured most famously in the line of amity drawn during colonial endeavours of the sixteenth and seventeenth centuries, beyond which the laws of war no longer applied. But it is also conjured quite explicitly during the great surge of codification in the laws of war in the nineteenth century. Legal publicists held that 'public law, with slight exceptions, has always been and still is, limited to the civilised and Christian people of Europe or to those of European origin'.[83] The conviction that the laws of war were necessarily suspended in colonial wars had already been well expressed in the 1894 text of the international legal scholar John Westlake who held that 'savages of half-civilized tribes' should be treated quite differently in combat.[84] Furthermore, in the United States, the ardent supporters of the 1899 Hague regulations were among those who most fervently advocated the torture and extermination of Filipinos, accepting those practices as the reasonable counter to the innate barbarism of the Filipinos.[85] It was not until the twentieth century that laws of war applied to the 'barbarous' wars of decolonisation and liberation, and the previously 'barbarian' peoples of Africa and India participated in the formulation of the laws of war.[86]

But it was not solely that discourses of civilisation and barbarism limited the *scope* of the applicability of the laws of war, in which discourses of civilisation demarcate *static differences* between 'us' and 'them'. Discourses of civilisation also denote *processes of transformation* – from barbarism to civilisation – which immediately undermine the presumption of static or stable differences. Conformity with the laws of war distinguished individuals as restrained, moderate in their violence, and differentiated them from barbarians who are 'like children who allowed their passions to rule their behavior'.[87] At the 1899 Hague Conference, the prominent scholar Johann Bluntschli advocated the laws of war for this very reason. The laws of war would provide the progressive discipline necessary to excite self-control and moderation. He was convinced that the laws of war refined 'the fighting men's sensibilities so as to bring about those traits of character that were associated with civilized behavior'.[88] Bluntschli would applaud the fact that almost a full century later, this argument still compels: 'A world without armies – disciplined, obedient, and law – abiding armies would be uninhabitable. Armies of that quality are an instrument and also a mark of civilization.'[89]

What, then, does it mean to discipline? Michel Foucault uses the concept of discipline as a historical analytic to identify the elaboration, refined in the eighteenth

---

[83] Henry Wheaton (1866), *Elements of International Law*, ed. George Grafton Wilson (New York: Carnegie Institute, 1964), p. 15.
[84] Martti Koskenniemi, *The Gentle Civilizers*, p. 86.
[85] Roxanne Doty, *Imperial Encounters: The Politics of Representations in North/South Relations* (Minnesota: University of Minnesota, 1996), pp. 40–3.
[86] See my 'The Image Before the Weapon: A Critical History of the "Combatant" and "Civilian" in International Law and Politics', unpublished manuscript.
[87] Koskenniemi, *The Gentle Civilizers*, p. 76.
[88] Ibid., p. 85.
[89] John Keegan, *A History of Warfare* (London: Pimlico, 1994), p. 384.

century, of complex systems and tactics of power regimenting and producing selves and subjectivities. Specifically, he relies on military discipline as the paramount example of modern disciplining. It formed and informed subjects both in the rote sense of regulation and repetition and in the productive sense of constituting a specific character. The laws of war discipline in this sense; they do not simply act to prohibit and restrain violence, but also to *produce* and *identify* civilised entities – both states and men – and to differentiate the lawful violence of the civilised from the unlawful violence of barbarians. President Bush's own statements continue to link military conduct, military discipline, to civilisation, claiming that in 'every conflict, the character of our nation has been demonstrated in the conduct of the United States military'.[90]

And, yet, as the outcry over abuses at Abu Ghraib now illustrate, however crucial these distinctions are – of barbarism and civilisation – they are not stable. Indeed, it was the crises of the two World Wars that so brutally demonstrated to the 'civilised' world, that the distinctions of barbarism and civilisation were not so easily maintained. As the legal scholar Josef Kunz declared, the World Wars marked 'the total crisis of Western Christian culture, a crisis which threatens the very survival of our civilisation' for each demonstrated that the 'cultured man of the 20th century is *no more than* a barbarian under a very superficial veneer of civilisation'.[91] In a striking parallel to contemporary events, it was the practice of torture by the French during the Algerian war of liberation that exposed the savage artifice of the French claim to represent civilisation. Using France's claim against itself, one primary architect of the Algerian liberation, Franz Fanon wrote, '(I)n a war of liberation, the colonized people must win, but they must do so cleanly, without barbarity. The European nation that practices torture is a blighted nation, unfaithful to its history.'[92] The referent for the difference of barbarism and civilisation remains the capacity for self-control and moderation, a putative hallmark of civilised entities – that is of both states and men. We hear the echoes of this recognition in the cautionary words of a military officer, 'in the final analysis, the law of armed conflict keeps us from becoming the enemy we fight'.[93] Thus, we can see how subjectivation occurs through the regulation of war according to discourses of barbarism and civilisation that inform the relations of international law and politics.

Indeed, it is impossible to ignore the invocation of civilisation that suffused any and, seemingly all, statements from President Bush describing and defending the current parameters of the war on terror. In his address to the nation in September 2002, the actions of the US were portrayed not solely as defending national security, but the very security of civilisation itself. 'This is the world's fight. This is civilization's fight.'[94] A month later, in his speech to the United Nations, President Bush reiterated this broader theme stating that the conduct of the US was in

---

[90] 11 November 2002, ⟨http://www.whitehouse.gov/news/releases/2002/11/20021111–2.html⟩, accessed October 2004.

[91] Josef Kunz. 'The Chaotic Status of the Laws of War', in Judith Gardam (ed.), *Humanitarian Law* (Dartmouth: Ashgate, 1999), pp. 81–106, at 86.

[92] Franz Fanon, *A Dying Colonialism* (New York: Grove Press, 1965), p. 24.

[93] Carr Center, Harvard University, *Humanitarian Issues in Military Targeting* (Cambridge: Carr Center, Harvard University, 2002).

[94] 'President's Remarks to the Nation', ⟨http://www.whitehouse.gov/news/releases/2002/09/20020911–3.html⟩.

accordance with the 'most basic commitment of civilization'. That commitment, shared by all 'civilized nations', is to 'defend ourselves and our future against lawless violence'.[95] The 2002 United States National Security Strategy (NSS) identifies 'global terrorism' as the outstanding threat to national security and the security of all 'civilized nations'.

The NSS underscores that this threat stems from both its source – transnational 'shadowy networks' working in clandestine cooperation with rogue states – and its tactics. Specifically, these individuals, networks and states do not and will not seek to 'attack us using conventional means' or by selecting conventional targets. Instead, in an inversion of the modern laws of war, their target is 'innocents' with the specific objective of 'mass civilian casualties'. This killing of the 'innocent' is a primary measure, in the eyes of President Bush, of the existence of lawless violence, of evil itself. This lawless violence is painstakingly contrasted to measures taken by the US against 'these outlaws and killers of the innocent'. [96] For, as President Bush explains, the strikes undertaken by the United States 'seek to minimize, not maximize, the loss of innocent life'.[97]

President Bush and his administration underscore that it is this practice that demarcates 'civilized' from 'barbarian' actors and distinguishes the military actions of the US and its allies from its foes. As President Bush iterated in his memorial speech of 2002, the attack on 9/11 was not simply an attack on our nation. It was also an attack on the sanctity of innocent life. Crucially, he declared, what differentiates 'us' from the enemy we fight is our valuing of 'innocent life'.[98] This difference is presented as an example of the distinction to be made between lawful and lawless violence and, in turn, between lawful and unlawful combatants. One legal scholar 'held that the president appeared to have concluded that it was assaults on civilian targets like the World Trade Center that made the attackers unlawful combatants'.[99] For President Bush and his administration, compliance with the injunction to distinguish at all times between combatants and civilians is not only an explicit military consideration, but also a highly significant normative identification, and a fundamental means by which the conflict itself is defined. As the high-ranking Judge Advocate General explained, 'it is our heritage, it is our culture as the most civilized nation in the world' to obey the laws of war.[100]

It is here that observance of the distinction between combatants and civilians is invoked to order the difference between civilised and barbaric states. This observance equally cites a hierarchy of lawful, moral violence and an unlawful, immoral violence. Further, a categorical distinction between lawful and lawless violence, where the

---

[95] 'Remarks to the United Nations General Assembly', 10 November 2001. This construction has not disappeared. On 23 September 2003, President Bush was explicit: *All governments that support terror are complicit in a war against civilization.* ⟨http://www.whitehouse.gov/news/releases/2003/09/20030923–4.html⟩, 21 September 2004; ⟨http://www.whitehouse.gov/news/releases/2004/09/20040921–3.html⟩, accessed October 24.

[96] Remarks, 10 November 2001.

[97] Ibid.

[98] 11 September 2002, 'President's Remarks to the Nation'. ⟨http://www.whitehouse.gov/news/releases/2002/09/20020911–3.html⟩.

[99] William Glaberson, 'Critics Attack on Tribunals Turn to Law Among Nations'. *New York Times*, 26 December 2001. ⟨http://www.pcpafg.org/organizations/Human_rights/hrweb/Class2/Homepage/critics_Attack_on_Tribunals_Turns_to_Law_Among_Nations.html⟩.

[100] Author interview with Department of Defense Judge Advocate General, June 2004.

emphasis falls on the target (or object) of violence (that is combatant or civilian), becomes, in the words of President Bush and his administration, a characterological distinction, where the emphasis falls upon the agent (or subject) of violence – the violence of barbarians, the violence of evil-doers, murderers, and the violence of terrorists. This is not merely a rhetorical move, as is demonstrated in my reading of the debates on the extension of the rights and protections of POW status to those detained. Discourses of barbarism and civilisation legitimate what could otherwise be understood as an arbitrary *interpretation* of or straightforward *denial* of the laws of war – the refusal to contemplate the extension of POW protection to the detainees at Camp X-Ray and, now, in the denial of humane treatment for those imprisoned in Iraq. Specific rights of war are granted only to those so identified as already within the ambit of civilisation and, so it appears, humanity itself. By constructing a barbarous enemy, 'akin to fascism, Nazism, and totalitarianism' whose 'murderous ideology' may be different, but no less horrendous, as those of the early twentieth century, the rights and protections of war are rendered beyond their due. What is so significant about the Bush administration's suspension of specific rights of war to those imprisoned at Camp X-Ray and beyond is that it is *justified* in the name of humanity – underscoring the inherent ambiguity of the laws of war which are said to establish the rights of all of humanity, yet nevertheless allows the denial of those rights on the basis of barbarism.[101]

The second move, which I already touched upon, is that this exclusion and denial, premised upon the projection and assessment of barbarism, finds its referent in the figure of the 'innocent'. The immunity and defence of the innocent – which functions as synchedoche for civilian to the degree that 'guilty civilian' sounds oxymoronic – is presented as an unassailable ground of judgment for the actions of President Bush and his administration. Nonetheless, the sacredness of the innocent is sufficiently flexible as to also provide a rationale for war.[102] Thus, we must ask in a world where, according to President Bush, 'you are either with us or against us' what allows a determination of, much less a distinction between, combatants and civilians? Who possesses the right to judge innocence?

In a war in which the distinction of 'us' and 'them' is allied to the values of the civilised world, discourses of civilisation mark the authority of the 'civilized' to judge exactly who is worthy of protection, and who shall be considered innocent. In the ground wars against terror, especially in Afghanistan, discourses of gender and civilisation intersected in profound ways. As Gayatri Spivak demonstrated, 'the espousal of the woman as an object of protection from her own kind', and the concerted efforts of 'white men saving brown women from brown men', has long been a hallmark of civilisational efforts.[103] Moreover, discourses of gender invest 'women and children' with the innocence, an innocence seemingly derived from a pitiful corporeality of injury, necessary for rescue and, therefore, for the

---

[101] 'Remarks', 10 November 2001, in which the civilised world first comes to stand 'for humanity', but this continues throughout his speeches during 2003.

[102] Bush seeks to 'minimize' the loss of innocent life in the strikes against Afghanistan, a locution that underscores differences of value attributed to innocent life of 'civilization' and that of 'barbarism'.

[103] Gayatri Chakravorty Spivak,'Can the Subaltern Speak?', in Cary Nelson and Lawrence Grossberg (eds.), *Marxism and the Interpretation of Culture* (Urbana, IL: University of Illinois Press, 1998), pp. 271–313.

re-establishment of the purity of civilised and manly rescue.[104] But, as I argue elsewhere, the intersection is more profound than that. Discourses of gender also render *visible and stable* the very distinction of combatant and civilian that is most threatened by the conduct of this war on terror, yet absolutely necessary for its success.[105]

By waging war on behalf of civilians against those who would target civilians, the Bush Administration justifies and enforces the claim to represent and defend 'civilization'. Invoking discourses of barbarism and civilisation to denigrate those who target civilians as 'barbarian', the Bush administration places those individuals outside the 'realm of obligation', a zone of exclusion, whereby those detained are recognised, but only by the mercy of President Bush and his administration.[106]

Once again we see how the observance of the distinction between 'combatant' and 'civilian' that demarcates civilised nations from their barbarous brethren, but also distinguishes *men* from 'savage hordes', and *honourable men* from dishonourable.[107] In turn, this distinction remains the means by which such differences may be indexed and identified. Therefore, the laws of war form a pivotal and *productive* dimension of international politics, constituting the distinction of barbarism and civilisation upon which they rest. By complying with the principle of distinction President Bush and his administration legitimated their claims to defend civilisation.[108] Discourses of barbarism and civilisation conditioned the extension of the rights and protection of prisoners of war and of civilians and, in turn, articulated compliance with the principle of distinction to the constitution of civilised entities – men and states. The politics of identifying the 'combatant' and the 'civilian', and the rights and protections granted to each, are revealed in an analysis of the discourses of civilisation and barbarism – discourses that are not 'outside' the laws of war, but integral to its history and formulation.

Currently, the tensions and ambiguities of discourses of barbarism and civilisation, and their relationship to the 'combatant' and the 'civilian' are brought into relief by the cases before the Supreme Court and in the debacle over the abuse of prisoners of war. For no longer accepting a determination of what 'civilized nations' require, it is President Bush and his administration that are held to 'violate the values we share with a wider civilization'.[109] In the debate over *to whom the rights and protection of war refer*, our contemporary struggle to determine and distinguish the 'combatant' and the 'civilian' resonates with the conflicts and contests of the past.

---

[104] See the work of Liisa Malkki, 'Speechless Emissaries: Refugees, Humanitarianism, and Dehistoricization', *Cultural Anthropology*, 11:3 (1996), pp. 377–404; Anne Orford, *Reading Humanitarian Intervention* (Cambridge: Cambridge University Press, 2003) and 'Muscular Humanitarianism', *European Journal of International Law*, 10 (1999), pp. 679–712; R. Charli Carpenter, 'Women, Children and Other Vulnerable Groups: Gender, Strategic Frames and the Protection of Civilians as a Transnational Issue', *International Studies Quarterly*, 49:2 (2005), pp. 295–334.

[105] See Helen M. Kinsella, 'Sex and Gender in the Laws of War', in Barnett and Duvall (eds.), *Power and Global Governance*; Helen M. Kinsella, 'Gendering Grotius', in *Political Theory*, forthcoming.

[106] Helen Fein, *Genocide: A Sociological Perspective* (London: Sage, 1993).

[107] Josef Kunz, 'The Chaotic Status', p. 103.

[108] Although I do not have the space to adequately address it here, the very fact that President Bush and his administration comply with the principle of distinction in wars against barbarians points to a significant change in the laws of war and understandings of the requirements of civilisation. This can be dated, perhaps, from post-World War II. See my unpublished manuscript.

[109] Brief of Amici Curiae Bipartisan Coalition of National and International Non-Governmental Organizations in Support of Petitioners for 03-334 and 03-343.

For the question of what civilisation requires – of whom and in relation to whom – is one that lies at the nexus of the laws of war and politics. It is here that an analysis of discourses can facilitate our recognition of what is 'rich, complex, and intriguing' about international law and politics by surfacing their productive, recursive effects.[110] However, this requires an explicit engagement with the history and structure of international law and international politics – an engagement that the paradigmatic study of international law and international relations still only 'implicitly examines'.[111]

[110] Christian Reus-Smit, *Politics of International Law*, p. 44.
[111] Kal Raustiala and Anne-Marie Slaughter, *International Law and Compliance*, p. 548.

Fights about rules: the role of efficacy and power in changing multilateralism

MARTHA FINNEMORE*

Introduction

The American-led Iraq war that began in 2003 has generated intense discussion about when it is legitimate to use force and what force can accomplish. Often this debate is portrayed as a breakdown in consensus, with the US charting a new unilateralist course that undermines existing multilateral understandings of how force should be used. Often, too, the debate is portrayed as a transatlantic one in which Europeans (notably France, supported by Germany) are leading the multilateralist defence against growing US unilateralism.

Both portrayals are overblown and simplistic. While the US is resisting current multilateral rules in some spheres, it is actively promoting more and more intrusive rules in others (such as trade). Further, the US has usually opposed multilateral rules it does not like, not with unilateralism, but with alternative forms of multilateralism. This has been true even of an administration as suspicious of the existing multilateral rules as the current Bush administration. Thus, if the UN will not approve military action in Kosovo, the US goes through NATO (under Clinton). If the US thinks the Nonproliferation Treaty (NPT) is not working, it works through the Nuclear Suppliers Group or sets up a Proliferation Security Initiative (under Bush). Similarly, the perception of a large transatlantic gap in allies' attitudes toward use of force is overstated. There has been transatlantic agreement on many uses of force in recent years. Europeans were active participants in the 1991 Gulf War, with the French among those patrolling the no-fly zone in Iraq in the years after the war, and the Kosovo action was supported by all members of NATO. The gap in the Kosovo case was not a transatlantic one, but a gap between the transatlantic alliance and Russia.

Current debates over use of force look less like a fight between unilateralism and multilateralism than a fight over what exactly multilateralism means and what the shared rules that govern use of force are (or should be). Similarly, the gap in views on use of force is not only, or perhaps even primarily, a transatlantic one. There are many gaps in views on this question – gaps within Europe, gaps within the US, gaps across the international system. This is hardly an unusual state of affairs in world politics. Disagreements about when force should be used and can be used effectively are the norm, not the exception, historically. The more interesting questions for us as analysts are: what, exactly, do states think the rules governing force are; what do they think they should be; and how will these disagreements shape future action?

* I am grateful to Theo Farrell, Chiara de Franco, Rachel Epstein, Pascal Vennesson and participants at the European University Institute's workshop on 'Globalization and Transatlantic Security', 10 June 2005, for helpful comments on an earlier draft of this article.

187

To begin to answer these questions this article explores the contours of contemporary disagreements to identify some of the most prominent disagreements on use of force issues. Geographically, this brief survey identifies four important gaps and discusses some of the issues driving them. I then offer some conceptual tools for thinking about why these gaps exist and what is fuelling these arguments. Much of the disagreement about use of force can be understood as relating to two broad problems. One is the nature of multilateral rules and the ways they accommodate power. While action according to multilateral rules is broadly viewed as most legitimate, particularly among publics, actors disagree strongly about what the rules mean and what behaviour they require, particularly in the face of huge power asymmetries. Second, and related, actors often frame arguments about the legitimacy of force as if it were divorced from effectiveness and vice versa. Legitimacy and effectiveness are deeply intertwined. Understanding how this is so potentially offers some ways to reframe conversations in a more productive way.

Gaps, gaps, everywhere: disagreements about use of force

Harmony, much less unison, in world opinion about exactly when and how force should be used has been hard to come by over the centuries. Contemporary politics is not unusual in its discord on this topic. Episodes of widespread support for force, such as we saw in the 2001 invasion of Afghanistan, are as unusual as the 9/11 terrorist provocation for that action. Most uses of military force by most states are controversial among at least some parties. In contemporary politics I see at least four 'gaps' or ongoing disagreements about use of force issues that have the potential to shape global norms in significant ways. In addition to a transatlantic gap, there is an intra-Europe gap, and intra-US gap, and at least one large global gap between the world's biggest states (US, China, India, maybe Russia) and others.

Gap 1: the transatlantic gap

Disagreements between the US and its European allies over when force should be used are hardly new. They existed even during the Cold War. The Suez crisis, for example, rivals the recent Iraq crisis in the depth of anger and distrust it created within the alliance, particularly between the Americans and the French, but with some roles curiously reversed. In that case, ironically, it was the Europeans who used force against a sovereign state, bypassing the Security Council, and the US that took the matter to the UN. After the Cold War, serious disagreements began to surface in the mid-1990s, first over the Balkans and then over the issue of how to deal with threats from what Americans called 'rogue' states.[1] Failure of Europeans to manage crises in the Balkans effectively persuaded many in Washington, first, that diplomacy without force (or credible threats of it) could not solve these crises and, second, that the Europeans were unable or unwilling to use force. This view coloured other

---

[1] Anthony Lake, Clinton's National Security Council Advisor, initially termed these 'backlash states'. See his piece in *Foreign Affairs*, 'Confronting Backlash States' (March/April 1994), pp. 45–55.

transatlantic debates over Iran, Iraq, Libya, Cuba, and North Korea where Americans and Europeans consistently split in approach, with the US pushing for a tougher line than Europeans. Iraq, in particular, was a focal point because of the ongoing need to manage that sanctions regime. By the mid-1990s, both sides agreed that sanctions were unlikely to bring down the Saddam Hussein's regime or radically change his policies but could not agree on an alternative approach. Europeans were inclined toward policies of engagement; Americans, in this case supported by the British, were much more willing to use coercion and did so, for example in Operation Desert Fox, sparking protests from the French and others.[2] The initial result of the September 11th attacks was to paper over this split. NATO invoked Article V within hours and the biggest problem faced initially by the allies was that the Europeans wanted to send more troops to Afghanistan than Washington was prepared to accept.[3]

Differences arising from the US war against Iraq are obviously much more complex than I can deal with here, but in basic contour they boil down to some common types of disagreement. Americans perceived a much more serious threat from Iraq than did France or Germany; Americans are more able to use force to address problems and more willing to do so; Americans, and the Bush Administration in particular, were much less confident in the ability of non-forceful tools, such as UN weapons inspectors, to protect them from threats. These three issues – threat perception, power capabilities, and effectiveness of multilateral institutions – have shaped the transatlantic debate.

Differences among governments on these issues are well known and have been amply documented elsewhere.[4] However, government policies were often not supported by large swathes of the public, adding to the tension surrounding the conflict, and it is revealing to see where disagreements do (and do not) exist in public opinion on use of force.

- While Europeans and Americans generally agree in their assessments of major threats (terrorism, especially with weapons of mass destruction; military conflict between Israel and its neighbours; global disease such as AIDS), Americans are more likely to believe they will be the target of a terror attack.[5]
- American publics are more willing than Europeans to use military force for a variety of purposes: to prevent a terrorist attack, stop nuclear proliferation, defend a NATO ally.[6]

---

[2] For more on the UK role, why they sided with the US in this controversy, and what it might mean for evolving norms, see Christine Gray, 'From Unity to Polarization: International Law and the Use of Force Against Iraq', *European Journal of International Law*, 13:1 (2002), pp. 1–19. See also discussion in next section.

[3] Philip H. Gordon and Jeremy Shapiro, *Allies at War: American, Europe, and the Crisis over Iraq* New York: McGraw-Hill, 2004), p. 2.

[4] See, for example, Gordon and Shapiro, *Allies at War*; Joanna Spear, 'The Emergence of a European "Strategic Personality" ', *Arms Control Today* (November 2003); James Thomson, 'US Interests and the Fate of the Alliance' *Survival*, 45:4 (2003), pp. 207–30 at 216–17.

[5] German Marshall Fund of the United States and Compagnia di San Paolo, *Transatlantic Trends 2004*, ⟨http://www.transatlantictrends.org/⟩; www.gmfus.org at pp. 11–12 and topline data at ⟨http://www.transatlantictrends.org/apps/gmf/ttweb2004.nsf/0/ 461EA7D25CC77DA185256F020059C76D/$file/Topline+with+logo+final.pdf⟩. The *Transatlantic Trends* data were collected in June 2004.

[6] *Transatlantic Trends 2004*, p. 11.

- Fifty-four per cent of Americans agree with the proposition that the best way to ensure peace is through military strength; only 28 per cent of Europeans do.
- Seventy-two per cent of Europeans believe the war in Iraq has increased the threat of terrorism; only 49 per cent of Americans share this view.[7]
- Eight-two per cent of Americans believe that under some conditions, force is necessary to obtain justice; only half that proportion (41 per cent) of Europeans agree.[8]
- When asked about power capabilities, 71 per cent of Europeans believe the EU should become a superpower like the United States. However, 47 per cent withdraw that support if superpower status requires greater expenditure.[9]
- Fifty-nine per cent of Americans believe it is justified to bypass the United Nations when vital interests of their country are involved, although 44 per cent of Europeans also agreed with this statement about their countries.[10] However majorities in both the US and Europe believe international approval of some kind would be essential before using military force in a future Iraq-like situation.[11]

Overall, Americans seem more willing to use force than Europeans in part because they perceive greater threat but also because they believe force is effective. It is effective for dealing with threats but also for doing good in the world ('ensuring peace', 'securing justice').

Gap 2: the intra-European gap

While there are clear transatlantic differences on the use of force, there are also important differences within the European Union which have become clear, not only in the dispute over Iraq but in the efforts to negotiate a common security and defence policy. Governments differ, with Britain and many of the Eastern countries having different approaches than France, Germany, and the Nordics. They have differed both in their willingness (also ability) to project force, but also in their view of the appropriate relationship among multilateral institutions projecting force. Blair has had a much more globalist view of force projection than has France, for example, and Britain's policies toward CSDP and NATO, toward defence procurement, and general willingness to deploy, have reflected this view.[12]

Publics also differ, both across countries and from their own governments, in their views on appropriate use of force.

- When asked whether war is sometimes necessary to secure justice, support ranged from 69 per cent in the UK and 53 per cent in The Netherlands to 25 per cent in Spain.
- Only 24 per cent of Poles approve of their government's deployment of troops in Iraq; 28 per cent of Portuguese and 21 per cent of Slovenians similarly disapprove

---

[7] Ibid., p. 12.
[8] Ibid., p. 11.
[9] Ibid., p. 6.
[10] Ibid., p. 13.
[11] Ibid., p. 15.
[12] Jolyon Howorth, 'France, Britain, and the Euro-Atlantic Crisis', *Survival*, 45:4 (2003), pp. 173–92.

of their own deployments. By contrast, Dutch approval was 58 per cent in June 2004.[13]

- Europeans are divided over whether it is justified to bypass the UN when vital interests are at stake. While 44 per cent believe bypassing would be justified, 49 per cent disagree. Differences between European countries are significant, ranging from 58 per cent of Dutch supporting such a bypass to only 37 per cent of Italians.[14]

Thus, while European public opposition to the 2003 Iraq war was widespread and strong, attitudes toward use of force issues more generally are much more varied.

Gap 3: the intra-American gap

The 2004 US election revealed deep splits in the American public on many issues between what have colloquially become known as the 'red' and 'blue' factions of the country. 'Polarized', is the word often used in the press to describe US opinion, and use of force issues are among the most polarising. Public attitudes on national security issues have become more strongly associated with party affiliation than they were in the late 1990s when these issues barely registered as correlates of partisanship. Now, national security issues are twice as likely as economic or social issues to shape party identification.[15]

- Increasing numbers of Republicans believe that military strength, rather than good diplomacy, is the best way to ensure peace. The percentage endorsing diplomacy as the better strategy has dropped from 46 per cent in 1999 to 32 per cent in 2004. Views among Democrats are shifting in the opposite direction. In the 1990s roughly 60 per cent of Democrats endorsed diplomacy as the best way to ensure peace; that figure rose to 76 per cent in 2004.[16]
- Americans overall are cautiously supportive of at least the occasional use of force against countries that may seriously threaten but have not attacked the US (60 per cent) but views vary strongly with party affiliation. Conservatives support such pre-emptive force by margins ranging from 69–89 per cent. Democrats oppose it by margins of 54–67 per cent.[17]
- Americans continue to be split, largely on party lines, about whether the war in Iraq was the right decision. Republicans and conservatives support it by margins of 72–94 per cent; Democrats and liberals oppose it by 61–87 per cent. Overall, 49 per cent say it was the right decision; 44 per cent say it was the wrong choice.[18]

---

[13] *Transatlantic Trends 2004*, p. 14.
[14] Ibid.
[15] Pew Research Center for People and the Press, *Politics and Values in a 48%–51% Nation*, 24 January 2005, ⟨http://people-press.org/reports/display.php3?ReportID'236⟩.
[16] Pew Research Center, *Politics and Values*.
[17] Pew Research Center, *Beyond Red and Blue*, 10 May 2005, ⟨http://people-press.org/reports/display.php3?ReportID'242⟩. Note that Democrats show some splits on this with a group Pew terms 'Conservative Democrats' endorsing pre-emptive force by 58–32 per cent.
[18] Pew Research Center, *Beyond Red and Blue*.

- Republicans are much less likely than Democrats to believe that UN approval is required before using force (26 per cent versus 81 per cent.) However, 46 per cent of Republicans believe it is essential to secure approval from European allies before using force; 77 per cent of Democrats share this belief.[19]
- A strong majority of Americans supports a wider role for the UN and believes the United States should be more willing to take decisions to the UN even if that means the US will have to go along with a policy that is not its first choice.[20] However, partisanship colours these views. Democrats view strengthening the UN as a higher foreign policy priority than do Republicans (89–53 per cent). Party leaders are more split. Ninety per cent of Democratic leaders agreed that strengthening the UN should be an important policy goal: only 43 per cent of Republican leaders do and 55 per cent oppose it.[21]

Institutions of the US government are not split the way the public is. While the presidential election was decided on a 51–48 per cent vote, Republicans control both the executive and legislative branches. The recent election returned the Bush administration for another term and increased Republican majorities in both houses of Congress. Further, Republican leaders have stronger partisan views than the public generally.[22] Thus, unlike the EU, internal splits in the US have not influenced policy in marked ways in recent years, however they suggest caution when projecting current policies into the future.

Gap 4: global splits

The transatlantic community is hardly the sole arbiter of global norms on use of force. Other states have strong views on these questions and have been able to make those views felt on a variety of issues. Both China and Russia have been critical of transatlantic enthusiasm for use of force to accomplish various humanitarian missions. Both fear, with some reason, that making human rights violations a legitimate excuse for external military intervention will cause problems for them in places like Tibet, Taiwan, and Chechnya. The Chinese have been particularly vocal in their opposition to what they view as attempts to limit state sovereignty on humanitarian grounds.[23] This opposition has been widely shared by among developing countries and the G-7 Declaration at Havana declared: 'We reject the so-called 'right' of humanitarian intervention, which has no legal basis in the United Nations

---

[19] *Transatlantic Trends 2004*, p. 27.
[20] Chicago Council on Foreign Relations, *Global Views 2004*, ⟨http://www.ccfr.org/globalviews2004/sub/usa_summary.htm⟩.
[21] PIPA/Knowledge Networks Poll, *Opportunities for Bipartisan Consensus: What Both Republicans and Democrats want in US Foreign Policy*, 18 January 2005. ⟨http://www.pipa.org/OnlineReports/mandatepoll/Report01_18_05.pdf⟩.
[22] PIPA/Knowledge Networks Poll.
[23] See, for example, ⟨http://ee.china-embassy.org/eng/zggk/xzgwjjs/t110315.htm⟩; ⟨http://www.fmprc.gov.cn/eng/wjb/zzjg/gjs/gjzzyhy/2594/2602/t15218.htm⟩, for Chinese arguments about the Kosovo intervention.

Charter or in the general principles of international law'.[24] Developing countries like India and Pakistan argue strongly that the current nuclear regime, as embodied in the NPT, is an unfair attempt by the nuclear 'haves' to keep the 'have-nots' down. Failure of the 'haves' to reduce their nuclear arsenals as stipulated in the treaty have compounded resentment as became glaringly obvious during the recent negotiations over NPT renewal. Debates over the International Criminal Court also reveal global 'gaps'. While the US has been painted as the chief obstructionist in transatlantic debates over the ICC, it has important company in China, India, and Russia, none of which has ratified the treaty.[25] The fact that the ICC treaty negotiations bypassed the UN Security Council – the body held up by many ICC supporters in other fora as the necessary arbiter of legitimacy on force issues – raises some interesting questions about what, exactly, is implied when multilateral institutions legitimate action in use-of-force matters, questions that are discussed below.[26]

Global opinion surveys show very strong support for the United Nations generally but also strong support for UN reforms, particularly for adding new members to the Security Council. Germany, Japan, India, and Brazil receive the most support. Publics in most countries also support modifications to the UN veto. Among 23 countries surveyed in a recent BBC World poll, publics in all but two supported the idea of allowing the Security Council to override the veto of a permanent member. Publics in permanent member states were reminded that their own country would lose the absolute veto. They were asked if they would support a rules change such that 'if a decision were supported by all other members, no one member, not even (your country), could veto the decision'. Interestingly, 57 per cent of Americans polled favoured giving up the absolute veto; 56 per cent of Britons, and a plurality (48 per cent) of Chinese agreed (36 per cent opposed). Overall, citizens in 21 countries favoured such a rules change (16 by majorities, 5 by pluralities). Citizens in only two countries were not supportive: France and Russia. The French were evenly divided (44 per cent in favour, 43 per cent opposed); Russians were weakly opposed (25 per cent in favour, 29 per cent opposed with 46 per cent not answering).[27]

Disagreements about use of force issues are thus real and deep, but they are also far more complex than a simple transatlantic divide. Divisions are broad, indeed global, on many issues, with some of the world's largest states (and possessors of its largest militaries) having markedly different views from others. Disagreements also exist within states, including some of the most influential states on use of force matters. Further, people are arguing about some of the most basic issues concerning use of force. Divisions exist concerning the appropriate goals of force (for example, whether it can be used to secure justice or for humanitarian protection), whether multilateral authorisation is required and if so, by what body (the UN or NATO),

---

[24] Declaration of the Group of 77 South Summit, Havana, Cuba, 10–14 April 2000, ⟨http://www.g77.org/Declaration_G77Summit.htm⟩. However, note again that public attitudes diverge from government views. In a recent poll of 10,809 Africans in eight countries, 65 per cent believe the UN should have the right to authorise the use of military force to prevent severe human rights violations such as genocide. Program on International Policy Attitudes, 'The Darfur Crisis: African and American Public Opinion', 29 June 2005, ⟨http://www.pipa.org/OnlineReports/Africa/sudan/062905/Darfur_Report062905.pdf⟩.

[25] ⟨http://hrw.org/campaigns/icc/ratifications.htm⟩, as listed 31 May 2005.

[26] John van Oudenaren, 'What is "Multilateral"?', *Policy Review* (February/March 2003), pp. 33–47; David Davenport, 'The New Diplomacy', *Policy Review*, 116 (December 2002).

[27] BBC WorldPoll, 22 March 2005, ⟨http://www.pipa.org/OnlineReports/BBCworldpoll/032005/Report03_20_05.pdf⟩.

and whether it is effective (for example whether it will deter proliferators or reduce terrorism.)

One striking commonality, however, is the widespread public support for multilateralism in uses of force. A number of scholars have documented the rise and spread of multilateralism as a social form in world politics, and we should not be surprised that its effects have permeated use of force debates as well. Public support for multilateral action seems not to have translated into happy agreement on all issues, however, and the remainder of this article offers two arguments that might help us think about these differences conceptually. First, I examine debates over multilateralism and argue that controversy is best understood, not as a debate over unilateralism versus multilateralism, but as a debate over what the multilateral rules should be and how they should accommodate power disparities. Second and related, I explore debates over legitimacy in using force and how legitimacy might be related to effectiveness. Debates about the UN, for example, often turn on whether its procedures will actually work – whether they will bring about the results members say they want. Effectiveness is not irrelevant to legitimacy, and I explore how this interplay might operate.

Multilateralism

The rise of multilateralism as a policy preference is by no means unique to use of force issues. Indeed, many might say that use of force has been one of the last and most difficult spheres for multilateralism to penetrate. Countries can be particularly jealous in guarding their autonomy of action when it comes to matters of national security, yet we have seen a proliferation of multilateral security arrangements in the last sixty years that is unprecedented in world history. Multilateral laws of war have become more elaborate and more widely recognised. Multilateral treaties on arms control have mushroomed and now exist in many flavours: nuclear, biological, chemical, missiles, landmines. Deployments of force through and by multilateral organisations have increased in number and size.

Many of the reasons for multilateralism's spread are obvious and functional. States simply cannot get many of the things they want without engaging in multilateral action. Certainly they cannot build a robust economy without it, but they also cannot rebuild failed states, stop drug trafficking, or curb proliferating WMD without multilateral action. These clear functional reasons for multilateralism stemming from growing interdependence have long been understood and much of the neoliberal-institutionalist literature on regime creation and institutional design emphasises the way in which international institutions might be pareto-improving for members.[28] Functionality has not been the only spur to multilateralism, though, and, indeed, it is not clear that all multilateralism is functional. Much of it is driven by ideas, identities, norms, and values, often coupled with power. US foreign policy after 1945 prized multilateralism and institutionalised it in the architecture created after

[28] See *inter alia*, Robert O. Keohane, *After Hegemony: Cooperation and Discord in the World Economy* (Princeton, NJ: Princeton University Press, 1984); and more recently Barbara Koremenos, Charles Lipson, Duncan Snidal, 'The Rational Design of International Institutions', *International Organization*, 55:4 (2001), pp. 761–99.

the Second World War, in part as an alternative to empire.[29] Multilateral rules and institutions also draw support from their rational-legal character which, as Max Weber and others have argued, are culturally valued and uniquely powerful in modern life. The spread of bureaucracy and law at a global level, both of which serve to institutionalise multilateral action, are occurring for many of same cultural and ideational reasons that created bureaucratised institutions nationally a century ago.[30] These explanations for the rise of multilateralism are by no means mutually exclusive and, far from being surprised, we should probably view recent multilateralism's spread as overdetermined.

Despite its history as a proponent of multilateralism, much of the recent debate has been about whether the US is now turning its back on multilateral norms. The end of the Cold War and the unprecedented power disparities that now exist between the US and all other states have raised questions both inside the US and outside about whether and when the US needs multilateral cooperation to achieve its goals. Policy moves by American administrations in the last decade and strong rhetoric from some parts of the Bush administration have further fed fears abroad of US unilateralism: fears of a US that increasingly 'goes it alone' and does not play by the multilateral rules that have developed since 1945.

To assess these fears of declining multilateralism analytically we must ask: What, exactly, is multilateralism and how would we know it, or its opposite, unilateralism, when we see it? In the scholarly literature, multilateralism is generally understood to have two dimensions, one quantitative, the other qualitative.[31] Multilateralism entails acting in concert with two or more other states. This much is obvious just from the semantics. If unilateralism is acting alone then logically, multilateralism must be acting with others. By implication, too, the more others one acts with, the more multilateral the action and states often boast about the number of partners in their action as proof of its legitimacy and multilateral character. The Bush administration, for example, has been quick to mention the 30-odd countries involved in the 2003 Iraq action and takes pains to discuss its actions there as acts of 'a coalition'.[32]

However, multilateralism is more than a numbers game. If it were only that, 'coalitions of the willing' would be perfectly acceptable as would action by groups of countries most of whose participation is completely symbolic either because they are too small, too weak, or too unwilling to contribute significantly. Multilateralism is more than just concerted action with some number of partners. Those partners have to act in particular ways, specifically they have to act according to some set of generalised rules or principles. Contemporary multilateralism implies a relationship among partners that is based on rules rather than simple power. Those rules, norms,

---

[29] See, *inter alia*, G. John Ikenberry, *After Victory* (Princeton, NJ: Princeton University Press, 2001); Henry Nau, *At Home Abroad: Identity and Power in American Foreign Policy* (Ithaca, NY: Cornell University Press, 2002); Anne-Marie Burley [Slaughter], 'Regulating the World: Multilateralism, International Law, and the Projection of the New Deal Regulatory State', in John G. Ruggie (ed.), *Multilateralism Matters* (New York: Columbia University Press, 1993), pp. 125–56.

[30] See Michael N. Barnett and Martha Finnemore, *Rules for the World: International Organization in Global Politics* (Ithaca, NY: Cornell University Press, 2004).

[31] John G. Ruggie (ed.), *Multilateralism Matters*. Also Stewart Patrick, 'Multilateralism and its Discontents', in Stewart Patrick and Shepard Forman (eds.), *Multilateralism and US Foreign Policy* (Boulder, CO: Lynne Rienner, 2002), pp. 1–44.

[32] The number of contributors has varied over time and in type of contribution. See ⟨http://www.pwhce.org/willing.html⟩ and ⟨http://www.globalsecurity.org/military/ops/iraq_orbat_coalition.htm⟩.

principles apply regardless of power capabilities, individual country interests, or convenience of circumstances. It is this qualitative dimension of multilateralism that makes it a distinct form of political action.[33]

Multilateralism has a couple of notable features for current debates over US action. First, multilateralism entails some degree of Great Power restraint. Within a multilateral arrangement Great Powers cannot do just anything they want. They restrain themselves to conform with the generally accepted rules of the multilateral structure. Second, and related, multilateralism entails an odd form of equality. Multilateral action is governed by general, impersonal rules. These rules apply to everyone equally. Big states, little states: they all have to play by the same set of rules. These two features – Great Power restraint and equality under the rules – are an important part of what legitimates multilateral arrangements and make them broadly popular, particularly with publics and smaller states. However, it would be a mistake to think that Great Power acquiescence to multilateral rules is altruism of any kind. Strong states restrain themselves and play by multilateral rules out of self-interest. After all, Great Powers usually get to write the rules in these multilateral arrangements, and they write rules that on balance benefit themselves. The US, for example, has written many of the free trade rules and, as a strong economy, benefits disproportionately from that regime. Similarly, the US was an original author of the UN Charter and gave itself a veto in doing so. Despite this, weaker states often value the predictability in Great Power behaviour that comes with rule-governed behaviour, even if those rules favour the strong, and accept such rules as a consequence. This combination of utility and legitimacy has contributed to multilateralism's rapid spread in the past 50 years.

One common misunderstanding, often apparent in contemporary debates, is a notion that multilateralism demands the end of all independent action in foreign affairs and, conversely, that any independent action constitutes a unilateralist rejection of multilateral principles. This is a misreading of both multilateralism's history and the basic logic of the social form. Multilateralism involves acting according to a mutually agreed-upon set of principles and rules. It has never meant that all decisions get made by committee nor has it demanded that states abandon all independent action. Rather, multilateral rules specify what decisions are left to individual states (commonly self-defence, for example) thus delineating the range of agreed-upon unilateral action. The rules also lay out the procedures by which the multilateral 'committee' will operate in areas where it has been authorised. Thus, we have multilateral rules governing the production, use, and transfer of some types of weapons (missiles, nuclear material) but others are left largely to national authorities (for example small arms, which probably kill more people.) The UN's multilateral rules for peacekeeping only allow the organisation to demand financial contributions from members to support peacekeeping operations; it cannot require members to contribute troops. That matter is left to state discretion.

Another common misunderstanding is that the rise of multilateralism and the existence of common rules should somehow eliminate disagreement – far from it. Actors in any rules-based system, domestic or international, argue constantly about

---

[33] See, *inter alia*, Stewart Patrick, 'Multilateralism and its Discontents'; John G. Ruggie, 'Multilateralism: The Anatomy of an Institution', in Ruggie (ed.), *Multilateralism Matters*; Van Oudenaren, 'What is "Multilateral"?', pp. 33–47.

what the rules are, what they should be, and what they mean for behaviour in any particular situation. This is well understood in the area of trade, where states have set up a Dispute Settlement Body as part of the World Trade Organization precisely to arbitrate fights over what the rules demand of parties. In the security realm, we see similar fights albeit without such clearly organised modes of arbitration. For example, in the Iraq crisis, much turned on issues like what constituted 'material breach' of UN resolutions and what was meant by 'serious consequences'. The 9/11 terror attacks promoted the US administration to adopt a more expansive notion of what actions could and should be encompassed in legitimate 'self-defense' under UN rules and international law, notably arguing that 'preventive war' must be part of this realm in an age when technology and terrorism had made the previous standard of 'imminent danger' ineffective. Other heated disagreements in recent years have similarly turned on different interpretations of what the rules are, which rules apply, and what they require. The US use of alternative multilateral fora (NATO instead of the United Nations, Nuclear Suppliers Group or Proliferation Security Initiative instead of NPT or IAEA) is revealing. Yes, this is 'forum shopping' of a kind familiar to political scientists, but the fact that action is oriented to multilateral fora at all confirms the importance of multilateralism to legitimate action. An argument that says, 'I won't play by the rules' is a political loser. It is much more palatable and effective politically to fight rules with rules and argue, 'I am playing by the rules; they just aren't *your* rules, and your rules are wrong (or ineffective or inapplicable in this situation)'.

Most of the disagreements, particularly the transatlantic ones, we see over use-of-force issues are best understood as disagreements within a multilateral framework, not rejection of it. As in any rules system, actors have different interpretations of the rules and, not surprisingly, different agendas for changing them. Two issues in particular lie beneath much of the debate we see on use of force. The first concerns the ways in which multilateral rules do (or do not) accommodate power disparities. The second concerns the effectiveness of current rules.

Accommodating power disparities

One frequent source of friction in debates over use of force is the huge disparities in states' ability to project force. Everybody playing by the same rules concerning use of force sounds lovely, but if, as a practical matter, only a few states can wield force effectively, the rules need to come to some accommodation of those states, both as necessary enforcers of rules and as possible threats to others. Much of the debate in the 'gaps' described earlier hinges on this issue. The US has been explicit that its unique power projection abilities and worldwide military presence creates unique concerns evidenced, for example, in its elaborate system of bilateral agreements to protect its military personnel from foreign or ICC prosecution. Others, notably France, have been articulate about the need to use multilateral rules to constrain American 'hyperpower' and discretion in using its military capabilities. If rules and multilateralism become no more than tools for the weak to use to coerce and constrain the strong, they will be resisted and ultimately rejected. Conversely, if the rules are viewed as unfair and tyrannical by weaker states, they will be illegitimate and resisted. The challenge for multilateralism is, and has always been, to devise rules that both accommodate power (so the strong will 'buy in') but are accepted by others.

There is a notion, most commonly articulated in legal circles, that sovereign equality is incompatible with rules that recognise power asymmetries. Political scientists will quickly recognise the fallacy here. Equality of sovereigns is a legal phenomenon, and juridical equality is only one aspect of sovereignty.[34] Other aspects of sovereignty play a crucial role in any rules governing sovereign states. For example, empirical sovereignty – the ability to actually exercise control over people, territory and resources – plays a central role in the way rules are made, the way they are enforced, and what they actually say.

Recognition of the need to accommodate power in multilateral rules is hardly new. It was central, for example, in one of the earliest multilateral arrangements, the Concert of Europe. That was explicitly a Great Powers' club that operated, in part, according to a double-edged rule: first, that no Great Power would act alone but second, that no Great Power would be left behind or isolated. The latter was crucial since without it there was no reason for a Great Power to join the Concert.[35]

Most enduring multilateral arrangements show some accommodation to power asymmetries. The UN Charter does. Vetoes are one obvious mechanism by which power asymmetries are accommodated and interests of strong are protected. The international financial institutions do, and there is clear understanding within those institutions that multilateral rules that disregard power will be both ineffective and illegitimate.

There are a variety of ways to accommodate power within multilateral rules. One obvious way is by allowing the powerful a disproportionate say in writing the rules. Often this happens naturally in the security realm either because the powerful take an interest in some issue and draft rules or because rules are drafted within a body such as the Security Council where the strong have institutionalised power. If they get to write the rules (or at least have strong influence in their drafting), powerful states are more likely to embrace and respect those rules subsequently. Another means of accommodation is that mutually agreed-upon rules can specify special privileges for the powerful within the rules. Sometimes they might do this according to some general, seemingly objective criterion. For example, the international financial institutions distribute votes based on wealth and contributions to these organisations. The practical effect is obviously that strong states get much greater voting power than weak borrower states. Alternatively, rules might name the powerful as recipients of special status, for example the UN Charter specifies five members who get permanent seats and vetoes on the Security Council.

One problem with specification of unequal treatment is that distributions of power in the world often change faster than institutional rules. One might well ask, for example, whether the countries that have the UN veto are still the right powers to be accommodated. This is certainly one of the issues at stake in the 'global gap' in views on use of force, and much of UN reform debate is about whether vetoes have become out of line with the contemporary distribution of power and whether they adequately

[34] Stephen D. Krasner, *Sovereignty: Organized Hypocrisy* (Princeton, NJ: Princeton University Press, 1999).
[35] For more on multilateral norms operating in the Concert, see Martha Finnemore, *The Purpose of Intervention* (Ithaca, NY: Cornell University Press, 2003), ch. 4.

represent the world of the twenty-first century. The NPT similarly contains substantive recognition of power asymmetries, explicitly recognising nuclear haves and have-nots. It, too, has come under pressure as have-nots become more technologically sophisticated and capable of acquiring weapons technology. The international financial institutions have a system of quota review to help substantive power recognition (vote distribution) stay somewhat aligned with economic reality. Few security institutions have similar built-in review systems and this stickiness has been a source of conflict (or 'gaps').

Of course, there are times when states interested in devising new rules move their negotiations outside such formal institutions precisely because they know their aims are opposed by one or more powerful states who will use the rules to block their efforts. Agreements hammered out outside the UN on landmines, nuclear testing, global warming and the International Criminal Court all aimed to use the normative weight of numbers – numbers of signatories – against previously negotiated rules protecting the interests of great powers.[36] While the landmines treaty has the quantitative legitimacy that comes with numbers (it has 144 signatories), non-signatories (which include the world's largest states and militaries – the US, China, Russia, India) have objected to its failure to conform to shared principles of legitimate procedure at the UN, procedures which recognise the disproportionate power of these states. Similarly, the ICC has 139 signatories and 100 ratifications, but numbers alone have not guaranteed smooth multilateral sailing. It matters *which* states sign or do not, and the fact that the non-signatories include the world's largest states with its largest militaries detracts from the legitimacy and effectiveness of the treaty. Efforts to legitimise rule changes by force of numbers effort can work, at least partially, though. The US may not have signed the landmines treaty, but it has certainly changed its procurement planning with regard to these weapons.[37] Similarly, while the US has resisted joining the ICC, it has agreed to use it for trials of war criminals in Darfur for lack of a better alternative. As in any political system, people are creative in their efforts to change the rules, and even the strong can be brought around to grudging acceptance through a combination of shifting public opinion, peer pressure, and realisation of the utility of a policy tool.

One obvious reason to accommodate the powerful in a multilateral system is simply that the rules will not be effective without the support or at least acquiescence of powerful states. However multilateral rules can be ineffective, with or without the support of the strong. I turn next to this issue.

Effectiveness and legitimacy of force

One persistent source of tension on use-of-force issues involves the effectiveness of multilateral rules. When multilateral rules do not produce desired outcomes, people start asking hard questions which eventually take a toll on the legitimacy of those

[36] Van Oudenaren, 'What is "Multilateral"?', pp. 33–47; David Davenport, 'The New Diplomacy', *Policy Review*, 116 (December 2002).
[37] See, for example, Lincoln P. Bloomfield, Jr., Assistant Secretary for Political-Military Affairs, 'New Developments in the US Approach to Landmines', on-the-record briefing, 27 February 2004, at ⟨http://www.state.gov/t/pm/rls/rm/29976.htm⟩.

rules. This was a persistent problem with various UN Iraq policies. The sanctions programme produced humanitarian outcomes unacceptable to many, and the US, in particular, was not persuaded that the weapons inspection programmes were actually disarming the regime. It has also been a problem in many humanitarian crises. Failure of multilateral rules concerning genocide and human rights to produce effective responses to disasters in Rwanda and in Darfur (most would say the African Union response has been woefully inadequate) have made a sham of the proclaimed 'responsibility to protect' in the eyes of many, including UN staff.

Asking about the effectiveness of force only begs the question: 'Effective for what?' Effectiveness always must have a referent. One cannot assess the effectiveness of force without understanding its purpose or goals. States and other actors differ in their opinions about the purposes for which force can be effective and when they think it should be used. This is hardly surprising, nor is it new. Disagreements about whether and when to use force have always attended to its consequences as well as its appropriateness. Conceptually and logically, though, these disagreements can focus on different aspects of use of force, and unpacking these differences we can see a variety of dimensions of potential disagreement.

Different goals

Whether force is useful depends on what one wants to accomplish. Two actors might have very different perceptions about the utility of force that are easily explained by the fact that they have very different goals. If state A wants to maintain lucrative commercial ties to state B but state C is more concerned about B's stability in the face of civil unrest, A and C are likely to disagree about the role force should play in their respective policies. Force, or threats of force, might be useless or even counter-productive for accomplishing actor A's goals of preserving trade but essential for securing actor B's of stability.

States also often have private goals that differ from publicly-stated ones, and the fact that public goals are not achieved does not mean private goals were not met. For example, one common interpretation of the failure to intervene in Rwanda is that, far from failing, multilateral rules served states' goals perfectly. No state wanted to intervene in Rwanda and the rules allowed them to dither and obfuscate so they did not have to do so.[38] Any assessment of effectiveness would have to take these unstated goals into account.

Predicted consequences

Even if states agree on objectives, there is often uncertainty and disagreement about the consequences of force. Unintended consequences of force are common, and actors know this. Military actions often go awry. Even if one kills exactly the people one planned and destroys or captures exactly the machinery or infrastructure one

---

[38] 'Triumph of Evil', BBC/Frontline video.

planned, calculating the political effects of force is difficult. Death and destruction may create martyrs and resistance rather than submission. States had different views, for example, about the likely consequences of toppling Saddam Hussein's regime. The Bush Administration believed those using force would be greeted as liberators. Others, both inside and outside the US, were less sure. Believing the liberator prediction would logically incline one much more toward a belief in the utility of force in that case. Scepticism logically leads to a different conclusion. Worries about fickle public support for uses of force are another source of uncertainty that may be particularly consequential to decision-makers in democracies. Leaders may err in being overconfident of public support but also underconfident, as US leaders were in the wake of the Ranger killings in Mogadishu.[39]

Legitimacy

The effectiveness of force for any actor is not an objectively-dictated given; it depends heavily on the subjective perceptions and evaluations of others. These evaluations are much broader in scope than simple assessments of information and likely consequences, discussed above. These evaluations are also normative. Whether others view force as desirable, appropriate, or necessary determines whether they will support, oppose or acquiesce to its use and those reactions will shape the effects of force on the ground and the kinds of social outcomes force creates. These judgments might have several components. Actors often support (or oppose) force and regard it as 'good' if they gain in some self-regarding way – they gain territory, eliminate undesirable people, increase political control. However, the 'goodness' of force may also be judged in another sense. Most uses of force are accompanied by a great deal of debate, not just about what people want but about what is right. Goodness in the sense of rightness or oughtness is a crucial component of actors' judgments about force and reactions to its use by others. This oughtness or rightness is at the heart of force's legitimacy.

Legitimate action accords with recognised rules, standards, principles, or laws. Many scholars have focused on the effects of legitimacy on those using force: the 'compliance pull' it creates and the sense it engenders that rules 'ought to be obeyed'.[40] However, legitimacy affects action by shaping audience judgments, too. Because they are widely shared, such rules and principles become 'social facts' and shape audience notions about when force ought to be used. Legitimacy is rarely absolute or uncontested; very often it is a matter of degree. The degree of legitimacy of an action, in this case a use of force, depends on the degree of consensus about its 'oughtness' or 'rightness'. Such shared judgments are not naturally-occurring

---

[39] Steven Kull and I. M. Destler, *Misreading the Public: The Myth of a New Isolationism* (Washington DC: The Brookings Institution, 1999); James Burk, 'Public support for peacekeeping in Lebanon and Somalia: assessing the casualties hypothesis', *Political Science Quarterly*, 114 (Spring 1999), pp. 53–78; Theo Farrell, 'America's Misguided Mission', *International Affairs*, 76:3 (2000), pp. 583–92.

[40] Thomas Franck, *The Power of Legitimacy among Nations* (New York: Oxford University Press, 1990), esp. pp. 15–21; Ian Hurd, 'Legitimacy and Power in International Relations: The Theory and Practice of the UN Security Council', unpublished ms.; also Hurd, 'Legitimacy and Authority in International Politics', *International Organization*, 53:2 (1999), pp. 379–408, at 381.

phenomena and legitimacy is rarely obvious or unproblematic. It has to be consciously constructed. Actors spend a great deal of time attempting to shape the judgments of others about what actions are legitimate. Consequently, most uses of force leave a long trail of justification in their wake as forcers try to connect their actions with shared notions of justice – shared notions of oughtness or rightness in using force.

We know that the effectiveness of force is a function of its legitimacy. Of course, if one simply wants to destroy or kill, the legitimacy of bombs and bullets is not going to change their physical effects on buildings or bodies. However, simple killing and destruction are rarely the chief goal of political leaders using force. Force is usually the means to some other end in social life and attempts to use force alone for social control and social influence have not fared well over the long term. Force must be coupled with legitimacy for maximum effect. Legitimacy is important because it creates some degree of support for, or at least acquiescence to, those using force. Legitimate force attracts allies, contributions, and approval from outsiders and diminishes resistance in targets of force. We rarely like being the target of force (or threats of it), but if we see that force as legitimate we are less likely to resist. Illegitimate force has the opposite effect. It galvanises opposition, often forceful opposition. It damages the forcer's reputation among peers and creates resentment, if not rebellion, in the target.

However, the relationship between effectiveness and legitimacy runs in both directions. Yes, legitimacy makes force more effective but effectiveness also enhances legitimacy. The cynic's version of this is, 'nothing succeeds like success' but the aphorism reveals something important for our purposes. Very often states agree on goals but not about how to achieve them. If force is shown to be successful or effective at achieving goals, its use is more likely to be seen as legitimate. Conversely, if experience suggests that force does not produce desired results (or does so only at unacceptable costs), it loses legitimacy.[41] Economic sanctions, a form of coercion if not outright force, certainly have become more suspect in recent years for these reasons in large part on efficacy grounds: they often hurt people they are supposed to help and they often fail to produce the desired behaviour changes in their target. The 1990s sanctions against Iraq were only a particularly spectacular and well-publicised case of sanctions of dubious efficacy carried out at very high human cost.[42]

Of course, judgments of success can be contested. They often are. In the Iraq sanctions case, sanctioners disagreed about whether containing the regime's behaviour counted as success and over whether, in fact, the regime was being contained. Not only was there inadequate intelligence to judge either issue, but sanctioners had different goals vis-à-vis the regime, disagreeing about whether containment was sufficient or whether regime collapse was the real measure of success. Judgments about unacceptable costs also change. For example, civilian casualties weigh more heavily in the calculations of most democratic militaries than they did 50 or 100 years ago. They also weigh more heavily in the judgments of those observing or suffering

---

[41] Efficacy or 'reasonable hope of success' is also a criterion in the long-standing Just War tradition. See Ian Halliday, 'When is a cause just?', *Review of International Studies*, 28 (2002), pp. 557–75, at 569, for a discussion in the context of recent world events.

[42] For a related examination of some of these issues in the context of the 2002–3 Iraq debates, see Simon Duke, 'The Hyperpower and the Hype: Reassessing Transatlantic Relations in the Iraqi Context'. European Institute of Public Administration, Working Paper no. 2003/W/1.

force as the outcry over the high-altitude bombing in Kosovo suggests.[43] But to the degree there is agreement that force can help achieve some goal, it becomes more legitimate; agreement to the contrary tends to delegitimate.

Note, too, that assessments of legitimacy often change over time in part as a result of their effectiveness. Military action to remove Saddam Hussein from Iraq in 1991 was controversial at the time it was being contemplated, much more controversial than the 2002 action, and commanded only narrow approval by the US Congress. The perceived effectiveness of the 1991 military action in rolling back Iraqi forces from Kuwait, with relatively few of the dire consequences predicted by opponents, helped turn the 1991 action into a positive exemplar of 'good' use of force during the subsequent 2002 debates. Had the effects of the 1991 action been more obviously negative – had it prompted mass demonstrations that unseated regimes in the region, for example, or had it resulted in massive civilian casualties as the armies moved through Kuwait and Iraq – the 'goodness' and legitimacy of that action would have been less and the 2002 debates may have gone differently. Legitimacy (or lack thereof) is not an inherent or objective property of forceful action. Legitimacy is subjective and, indeed, intersubjective. Force is made legitimate (or not) by those of us observing, suffering, and ultimately judging it. Not surprisingly, people often do not agree on when force is legitimate. Forceful action to topple a regime or save a threatened population, for example, might be entirely legitimate in the view of the invader but draw mixed views from the local population, other governments, other publics, and international organisations. Some of these judges will be more conse- quential than others in influencing the ultimate effects of force, and states calculate carefully the likely acceptance (or not) of their actions.

As we analyse the various disagreements or 'gaps' in views on force, it is worth recognising what, exactly, is in dispute. Rarely is the debate about multilateralism versus unilateralism. Multilateralism is widely accepted as the most legitimate form of political action and most states most of the time go out of their way to conform to multilateral rules. Disagreements over use of force are largely happening within this multilateral framework and they are broadly of three types. Debates are often about what current multilateral rules mean and what they demand of states; they are about whether multilateral rules are effective; and they are about how multilateral rules can be changed.

Legitimation struggles: a marketplace of multilateral rules?

Multilateral rules about use of force are constantly changing. The debates we are now seeing, within and among the Atlantic allies as well as globally, are primarily about what these rules should be. As new threats arise and old ones linger, inadequately treated by existing rules, pressure for change mounts and people craft new visions of 'good' rules for use of force. Two issues, in particular, seem central to changes currently under discussion. The first is how rules can or should change in response to changes in the distribution of power. Much of this conversation in the transatlantic

---

[43] Nicholas Wheeler, *Saving Strangers: Humanitarian Intervention in International Society* (Oxford: Oxford University Press, 2000).

community has centred on dealing with US power and the power asymmetries it creates. However, within the US concerns are as strong, probably stronger, about how to deal with changing power in Asia particularly with the rise of China and India.[44] Both have been incompletely integrated into existing multilateral institutions governing use of force and both differ sharply from the transatlantic community on key issues. China has only recently and gingerly become involved in peacekeeping on a tiny scale. (It sent 40 peacekeepers to Timor.) It remains outside the ICC and only joined the Nuclear Suppliers Group last year. India has been an enthusiastic proponent of peacekeeping but its nuclear posture keeps it outside that regime structure. Both countries thus may have visions of desirable rules that differ from existing ones. For different reasons and in different realms, both may push for rules that are more protective of national decision-making (what some might call unilateralism.) It is not hard to imagine China pushing for limits on putative 'humanitarian' intervention and it is easy to see support for such limits among many governments outside the transatlantic alliance, especially in the developing world. Similarly, it is easy to imagine a role for India in rewriting parts of the nuclear regime and, again, this would most likely draw support from others. Devising multilateral rules to accommodate the interests of the newly-powerful will be a challenge.

Second, to remain legitimate, multilateral rules have to be at least moderately effective. Rules that do not produce at least modest progress toward desired results will be abandoned. In the security realm, the absence of rules to deal effectively with terrorism using WMD will be a persistent source of friction with the United States which perceives a real and pressing threat. Unimpressive results from humanitarian interventions or, perhaps worse, persistent failures to intervene at all, will continue to prompt calls for new rules, perhaps including broader powers for the UN and other international organisations to use force. Hypocrisy and ineffectiveness have made existing rules vulnerable to challenge and challenges backed by power (from the US, China or others) will be hard to ignore.

Underlying both issues are some very fundamental questions about how new multilateral rules are legitimated in world politics. Contemporary politics are marked by variety in the ways one can legitimate new rules, and actors strategise about how best to gain legitimacy for rules they like. Different legitimation options carry different political implications. For example, states can work through formal state organisations like the UN and NATO to legitimate new rules. These have the advantage of providing relatively well-organised and powerful mechanisms for dispensing legitimacy and promulgating new rules about when force is legitimate, but they can be hard to use since legitimation from these bodies requires unanimity among all (NATO) or a very diverse subset of members (the P5 in the UN). Consequently, those seeking to change rules (or, put differently, those seeking to legitimate new rules) that might be opposed in these forums have had to be creative.

US policymakers have intermittently attempted to set up alternative multilateral fora of 'like-minded' states. These obviously get around the opposition problem but do so at the price of producing less legitimacy. The problem with such groups is not like-mindedness per se. Action through groups of ideologically similar states is common in world politics and is still seen as multilateral, witness the European

---

[44] See, for example, the US National Intelligence Council's projections of the 'global landscape' in the year 2020, at ⟨http://www.cia.gov/nic/NIC_globaltrend2020.html⟩.

Union. Rather, the problem is convincing others that the group really is 'like-minded' in some principled way that will guide action across a variety of circumstances, even when abiding by principles may not be convenient for members. The problem is thus persuading others that the group is multilateral in a qualitative sense. Otherwise, the action looks like opportunism. To the extent that the US and its like-minded partners can articulate generalised principles of action and follow them even when it is costly, these fora may start to provide the kind of legitimation the US is seeking. Many long-lived multilateral endeavours started in exactly this way. Note, though, that such like-minded groups only provide legitimation for the actions of their own members. They have difficulty promulgating universal rules to govern those not so inclined. Thus, the Nuclear Suppliers' Group may promulgate rules that govern its own members but had difficulty claiming that non-members are bound. To the extent one's goals involve promulgating rules for all, this strategy may be of limited use.

Other legitimation mechanisms have relied on what David Davenport has call 'the new diplomacy'.[45] Efforts like those surrounding the landmines ban and the ICC have countered opposition from a few strong states by galvanising and organising support from (1) very large numbers of smaller states together with (2) prominent and credible NGOs and (3) cross-national public opinion.[46] The importance of NGOs and public opinion as arbiters of multilateral legitimacy is often underestimated, but should not surprise us analytically. Legitimation of international rules requires more than the formal obligation of treaties signed among states. Formal treaties, after all, have proved to be highly imperfect constraints on behaviour and generating compliance absent enforcement is a long-standing concern of international legal scholars. In such situations, compliance requires the generation of some felt sense of 'rightness' and of obligation in both policymakers and societies.[47] Governments can sometimes create this but they by no means have a monopoly on access to or control over public sentiments. With increasing democratisation and increasing organis-ational capacity of civil society actors, we should expect NGOs and public opinion to become more consequential players in generating acceptance or rejection of inter-national legitimacy claims, including multilateral ones. Note, however, that this 'new diplomacy' is hardly divorced from the old. The public opinion and NGOs that matter the most to the success in these efforts tend to be centred in strong states. These groups are just as likely to wield influence through domestic channels, by changing the positions of their governments, as they are to challenge and confront those governments in transnational fora such as those associated with the Ottawa Process (landmines) or the ICC negotiations.

This proliferation of mechanisms suggests that we may have something like a marketplace for multilateral legitimacy operating today. Policymakers from states of all sizes and activists of all stripes understand this better than scholars. There are many roads to multilateral legitimacy and actors are strategic about framing their preferred rules and choosing fora in which to propose them. If they do not like

---

[45] David Davenport, 'The New Diplomacy', *Policy Review*, 116 (December 2002), ⟨http://www.policyreview.org/dec02/davenport_print.html⟩.

[46] Note that NGOs should not be equated with public opinion since who, exactly, NGOs represent is often a matter of some dispute.

[47] For a discussion of this point and citations to relevant legal literature, see Martha Finnemore and Stephen Toope, 'Alternatives to "Legalization": Richer Views of Law and Politics', *International Organization*, 55:3 (2001), pp. 743–58.

existing choices, they create new ones. In so doing, they become 'legitimacy entrepreneurs'.[48] Other actors then 'buy' into or reject these rules.

As scholars we need to understand this process better. We need to understand what legitimacy claims are accepted, which ones fail, and why. Treating multilateralism as some static set of behaviours and standing outside to judge what is, or is not, multilateral, risks missing these crucial political processes. The ability to redefine what is multilateral and the huge effort people spend in doing so is part of what makes the concept so powerful and interesting. Being better attuned to the dynamics of multilateralism can help us redirect our inquiries in more productive ways.

---

[48] For an extended discussion of normative 'entrepreneurship', see Martha Finnemore and Kathryn Sikkink, 'International Norm Dynamics and Political Change', *International Organization*, 52:4 (1998), pp. 887–917.

Peacekeeping and enforcement action in Africa: the role of Europe and the obligations of multilateralism

CHRISTINE GRAY

Introduction

The duties, if any, of European states to participate in multilateral operations in Africa are currently a matter of some controversy. What are the obligations of European states with regard to the maintenance of international peace and security in Africa? How far is it legitimate for them to avoid the contribution of troops to UN peacekeeping operations in Africa? Does the reluctance of European and other developed states to participate in UN peacekeeping operations in Africa have significant legal consequences? This article will consider these issues in three main sections. The first provides an overview of UN peacekeeping in recent years at a time when there has been a substantial surge in demand for peacekeeping troops. It discusses the problems that the UN has faced in securing troops from developed member states, particularly for operations in Africa. The second section describes the pattern which has emerged in recent practice with regard to peacekeeping and enforcement action in Africa. Although developed states have generally been reluctant to provide troops for UN peacekeeping operations in Africa, they have undertaken Chapter VII operations in the Democratic Republic of Congo (DRC), Liberia and Côte d'Ivoire as 'coalitions of the willing'. They have also provided assistance to certain African governments threatened with violent overthrow, such as the governments of Sierra Leone and Côte d'Ivoire. They have turned to regional and sub-regional organisations to take the lead in certain conflicts: they have provided financial assistance, logistical support and military training for such organisations. The third section considers whether the reluctance of European and other developed states to participate in UN peacekeeping in Africa, and their preference that regional organisations should play the main role, leads to legal questions about the duties of member states and the nature of multilateralism. Could this recent practice even legitimate a reinterpretation of the UN Charter provisions in Chapter VII and VIII?

UN peacekeeping and the demands of multilateralism

Recently the UN Deputy-Secretary-General has warned of the danger that the war on global terror may cause states to lose sight of the needs of UN peacekeeping.[1] In

---

[1] Deputy Secretary-General Louise Fréchette, address to Foreign Affairs Committee of EU Parliament, March 2004; UN News Service, 27 January 2004.

the last two years there has been a massive increase in peacekeeping operations and a corresponding surge in demand for peacekeeping troops.[2] There are – as at the end of 2004 – sixteen UN peacekeeping operations, of which seven are multi-dimensional operations designed to secure the transition from war to peace; as well as security issues, multi-dimensional operations also deal with political aspects, human rights, humanitarian concerns, the rule of law and police activities. Seven of the sixteen peacekeeping operations are in Africa. The largest is MONUC, a force of up to 16,700 troops in DRC; next largest is UNMIL, a force of up to 15,000 troops in Liberia. The total number of UN peacekeeping troops at the end of 2003 was about 45,000, three-quarters of which were in Africa.[3] In 2004 the UN expanded its operation in Côte d'Ivoire;[4] it has created a new force in Haiti;[5] and has finally set up a long-awaited force in Burundi;[6] there are plans for possible new operations in Sudan[7] and also Iraq. The UN has spoken of a potential increase in the total number of troops to 80,000.[8] At one time it was feared that the 2004–5 peacekeeping budget might turn out to be \$4.5 billion, nearly double that originally estimated, and an amount unprecedented in UN history.[9] The current total of approximately 56,000 peacekeepers in December 2004 is already the highest since October 1995.[10]

This brief overview makes clear that there has been a 'surge in peacekeeping' comparable to that in the early 1990s. But, in contrast to the 1990s, this increase has taken place without the significant participation of developed states in the provision of UN peacekeeping troops that occurred in the UN operations in Yugoslavia and Somalia. Currently only about 10 per cent of UN peacekeeping troops come from the EU.[11] This figure on EU participation became a little more impressive after 1 May 2004 with the accession of new members to the EU and the addition of Poland, Hungary and Slovakia which are all significant troop-contributing countries (TCCs).[12] The top ten contributors of troops are all developing states; poorer countries are providing the greatest contribution to UN peacekeeping operations, but even this support is insufficient to meet rising demands.[13]

---

[2] UN Press Release DEV/2485, 7 September 2004; UN Press Release SG/SM/8311, 17 May 2004; UN Press Release SC/8095, 17 May 2004.

[3] ⟨www.un.org/Depts/dpko/dpko/contributors/⟩.

[4] SC 4918th meeting, UN Press Release SC/8012, 27 February 2004.

[5] SC Res 1542 (2004).

[6] SC Res 1545 (2004).

[7] UN Press Release SC/8120, 11 June 2004.

[8] UN Press Release DSG/SM/216, 30 April 2004; UN website, Department of Peacekeeping home page, 'Meeting new challenges' ⟨www.un.org/Depts/dpko/dpko/faq/q8.htm⟩, visited on 18 August 2004; UN Press Release DEV/2485, 7 September 2004.

[9] UN Press Release GA/AB/3613, 3 May 2004; UN Press Release GA/AB/3614, 4 May 2004.

[10] UN Press Release SC/8096, 17 May 2004; UN Press Release DEV/2485, 7 September 2004; ⟨www.un.org/Depts/dpko/dpko/contributors/⟩.

[11] UN website, Department of Peacekeeping home page, ⟨www.un.org/Depts/dpko/dpko/faq/q8.htm⟩, visited on 18 August 2004, 'Who contributes personnel?'. Earlier this figure of EU contribution was only 7 per cent, UN Press Release DSG/SM/216, 30 March 2004; UN Press Release GA/SPD/299, 27 October 2004.

[12] The US contributes 1 per cent of troops, but pays the largest financial contribution; in 2004 it paid \$790 m of the peacekeeping budget, UN Press Release GA/PK/180, 29 March 2004. The very restrictive US doctrine on participation in UN peacekeeping is set out in US Presidential Directive PDD 25 of 1994.

[13] UN News Release, 27 January 2004; UN website, Department of Peacekeeping home page, ⟨www.un.org/Depts/dpko/dpko/faq/q8.htm⟩, visited on 18 August 2004, 'Who contributes personnel?'

Immense challenges face UN peacekeeping.[14] There have been repeated warnings of a 'supply crunch'. The Under-Secretary-General for Peacekeeping Operations has acknowledged that 'Today's peacekeeping demands exceed what the UN or any other regional or sub-regional organisation by itself could meet'.[15] At the same time the armed forces of developed states are heavily committed in Afghanistan and Iraq. It is striking that the UN's concern to persuade more developed states to provide troops is openly set out even on the UN peacekeeping website, as a Frequently Asked Question (FAQ) on 'Meeting New Challenges'.[16] The Non-Aligned Movement (NAM) has also argued that countries from the developed north should participate with more troops; it opposed the establishment of any practice consisting of the participation of countries from the industrialised world in the more difficult operations only with equipment or senior officers and no troops.[17] Similarly, the Rio Group has said that it was high time the developed states took up a larger share of the troop demand for peacekeeping operations.[18] The High-level Panel on Threats, Challenges and Change set up by the UN Secretary-General also stressed in its Report, *A More Secure World: Our Shared Responsibility* (2004), that for peace-keeping and, in extreme cases, peace enforcement to continue to be an effective and accepted instrument of collective security, the availability of peacekeepers must grow. 'The developed states have particular responsibilities here, and should do more to transform their existing force capacities into suitable contingents for peace operations'.[19]

Japan, fearing that it would be faced with a peacekeeping bill of $900 million for 2005, has warned that although there has been a welcome revival of UN peace-keeping, the continuing creation and deployment of missions on an unprecedented scale was beginning to cast a 'grim shadow' over that revival. It went on to question the need for peacekeeping operations to engage in human rights and development activities.[20] But it is important to put the concern of Japan in context: as the Under-Secretary-General for Peacekeeping has said, 'Even with these new opera-tions, the cost of peacekeeping will still be less than one half of 1 per cent of the world's combined military spending. Another way of looking at it is that the cost of all UN peacekeeping combined is minimal when you consider that civil wars cost $120 billion annually'.[21]

The scope of UN peacekeeping and peace-building is currently under re-examination. The Under-Secretary-General for Peacekeeping Operations, briefing the Fourth Committee as it carried out its comprehensive review of the whole

[14] UN website, Department of Peacekeeping home page, ⟨www.un.org/Depts/dpko/dpko/faq/q4.htm⟩, visited on 18 August 2004, 'What are the current challenges to successful peacekeeping?'.

[15] UN Press Release GA/SPD/297, 25 October 2004.

[16] UN website, Department of Peacekeeping home page, ⟨www.un.org/Depts/dpko/dpko/faq/q4.htm⟩ visited on 18 August 2004, 'What are the current challenges to successful peacekeeping?'.

[17] UN Press Release GA/PK/180, 29 March 2004, Special Committee on Peacekeeping Operations, statement by Morocco on behalf of the NAM; see also UN Press Release GA/SPD/298, 26 October 2004, Fourth Committee, statement by Morocco on behalf of the NAM.

[18] UN Document GA/SPD/299, 27 October 2004.

[19] *A More Secure World: Our Shared Responsibility* (New York: UN, 2004), para. 216.

[20] UN Press Release GA/AB/3614, 4 May 2004.

[21] UN Press Release OBV/422, 24 May 2004. See also, UN Press Release DSG/SM/216, 30 March 2004, 'Deputy Secretary-General calls for increased support by EU for millennium goals, UN peacekeeping'; UN website, Department of Peacekeeping home page, ⟨www.un.org/Depts/dpko/dpko/faq/q6.htm⟩, visited on 18 August 2004; UN Press Release SG/SM/9311, 17 May 2004.

question of peacekeeping operations in all their aspects, said that five years after the *Brahimi Report*[22] peacekeeping was again at a crossroads. Should UN peace operations work on the scale that was currently demanded and if so were resources available? Or should they focus on a more limited number of niche tasks? The Special Committee on Peacekeeping in its 2004 session[23] and the Security Council in its day-long debate on peacekeeping operations in May 2004 engaged not only in consideration of practical issues such as rapid deployment of troops and rapid reimbursement of troop-contributing countries, but also in more general discussion of the nature of peacekeeping. Some states stressed the dangers of 'mission creep' and the essentially temporary nature of peacekeeping; others argued for the crucial importance of post-conflict peacebuilding for the prevention of the recurrence of conflicts.[24]

The Secretary-General in his contribution to the Security Council's day-long debate on peacekeeping operations said that there had been great advances in UN peacekeeping since the *Brahimi Report*: UN peacekeeping was definitely more efficient and better coordinated than it was five years ago. It was better equipped, both at Headquarters and at the Logistics base at Brindisi, to support its field operations and to respond more rapidly to sudden developments. But, notwithstanding these advances, 'the scale of the current surge might well outstrip our capacities to backstop the operations and we will have to look at augmenting those capacities'. UN missions remained hampered by a lack of specialised military capacities, generally available from the military forces of developed countries. Unfortunately those countries today make only limited contributions of troops to UN peacekeeping operations. At the same time many states that were willing suppliers of troops had great difficulty in deploying staff within the necessary time frames.[25]

It is notorious that the UN has in the past faced serious problems in securing enough and adequately trained and equipped troops, especially for operations in Africa.[26] These problems were also seen recently with relation to the UN operations in the DRC. In 2004 the Secretary-General sought an increase in the size of MONUC, the UN force in the DRC, to 24,000, but the Security Council was willing to authorise a total force of only 16,700.[27] The Secretary-General said 'I continue to believe that the total military and police strength recommended in my Third Special Report is the minimum required to effectively meet the current challenges in the DRC'.[28]

As another manifestation of the difficulties faced by the UN in securing contributions from member states in 2004, the UN Secretary-General warned of the problems that would be faced in securing troops for the transformation of the UN mission in Côte d'Ivoire into a peacekeeping operation (UNOCI).[29] He said that 'the Secretariat had recently encountered challenges in securing in a timely manner

---

[22] UN Document S/2000/809; 2000 United Nations Yearbook (UNYB), p. 83.
[23] Established by the General Assembly in 1965 to conduct a comprehensive review of all issues relating to peacekeeping. UN Press Release GA/PK/180, 29 March 2004; UN Press Release GA/PK/181, 30 March 2004.
[24] UN Press Release SC/8095, 17 May 2004.
[25] SC 4970th meeting, UN Press Release SC/8095, 17 May 2004.
[26] Christine Gray, *International Law and the Use of Force*, 2nd edn. (2004), at p. 239.
[27] UN Press Release SC/8203, 8 December 2004; SC Res 1565(2004).
[28] UN Press Release SC/8204, 1 October 2004.
[29] UN News Centre, 9 January 2004.

adequately equipped military contingents for UN peacekeeping operations. The proposed operation poses particular challenges with regard to force generation, especially because it comes at a time when recently established operations, as well as anticipated ones, are competing for limited resources.'[30]

Rwanda

This problem of securing adequate troops in a timely manner arose most dramatically in relation to Rwanda. It is now ten years since the genocide of 1994 and this anniversary has prompted many attempts at reappraisal and examination of the questions: 'could it happen again today?' and 'how to respond better in the future'.[31] As part of the response to the Rwandan genocide, there has been much discussion of how to change international law on humanitarian intervention: whether there is now a legal 'responsibility to protect' (as suggested by the Report of the International Commission on Intervention and State Sovereignty) – a duty to intervene in certain cases of humanitarian need. If so, should guidelines be drawn up as to when it would be legitimate to override an actual or a threatened veto by a permanent member which has the effect of obstructing humanitarian intervention for which there is majority support in the Security Council?

The UK in particular has pressed for the development of a strong doctrine of forcible humanitarian intervention, not only through the UN but also unilaterally. It was the first state expressly to put forward a legal right of humanitarian intervention by states in the absence of Security Council authorisation; it did so in 1991 with regard to Iraq. The UK used the doctrine of humanitarian intervention to justify the enforcement of no-fly zones over Iraq from 1991 to 2003 by the US and the UK in order to protect the Kurds and other civilians from repression by Saddam Hussein. But the use of this doctrine proved very controversial; the doctrine of humanitarian intervention was not expressly taken up by the USA and other states did not invoke this particular operation in Iraq as a precedent in support of the 1999 NATO operation in Kosovo.[32] There are some signs of support for the doctrine in NATO's justification for its actions in Kosovo, but few states (though many commentators) have expressly argued for the existence of such a legal right. Nevertheless, in recent years UK Prime Minister Tony Blair has consistently pressed the UN to adopt criteria for intervention in humanitarian crises. From his 1999 speech in Chicago calling for a doctrine of international community,[33] to the UK's submission of more detailed criteria to the Security Council as a framework for intervention,[34] he has sought international acceptance for this controversial legal doctrine. These efforts did not prosper at the time, but in 2004 the Prime Minister revisited the issue; his

---

[30] UN Document S/2004/3, 6 January 2004, Report of the Secretary-General on the UN Mission in Côte d'Ivoire. The ECOWAS contingents from Benin, Ghana, Niger, Senegal and Togo already present in the country were rehatted under UNOCI.

[31] See, for example, UN Panel Discussion on Rwanda Genocide, UN Press Release AFR/888, 7 April 2004; OAU Panel, *Rwanda: The Preventable Genocide.*

[32] Gray, *International Law and the Use of Force*, p. 47.

[33] 22 April 1999, ⟨www.number10.gov.uk/output/Page1297⟩.

[34] 71 *British Yearbook of International Law (BYIL)* (2000), p. 646.

Sedgefield speech of 2004 was another attempt to encourage other states to adopt the doctrine.[35]

However, the *High Level Panel on Threats, Challenges and Change* set up by the UN Secretary-General has taken a relatively careful approach in its Report, *A More Secure World: Our Shared Responsibility* (2004) of December 2004. The Panel reaffirms the need for Security Council authority for humanitarian intervention and sets out criteria for UN action, rather than for the unilateral use of force by states purporting to be acting on behalf of the international community. Its focus is on collective action.[36]

Moreover, it is clear that the main problem in Rwanda was not one of international law, but one of political will. Although there were some problems with the limited and ambiguous mandate of the UN peacekeeping force in Rwanda, it wasn't any inadequacy of international law which led to acquiescence in the massacres or to the choice by member states of the UN Security Council to reduce the authorised size of the UN force from 2,500 to 270 at the critical time and then, when the Security Council changed its mind in May 1994, to the delays in providing sufficient troops until it was too late.[37] The former Deputy Force Commander of UNAMIR, the UN peacekeeping force in Rwanda, blamed 'poor logistics support owing to lack of financial support for the mission; and, worst of all, lack of political will on the part of world leaders'.[38] The governments of Belgium, France and Italy had begun evacuating their own nationals while doing nothing to assist the Rwandans in their most critical hour of need.

Accordingly, the UN itself has focused mainly on practical measures in developing the *UN Action Plan to Prevent Genocide* launched on 7 April 2004.[39] This was offered as the 'only fitting memorial the UN can offer to those whom its inaction in 1994 condemned to die'. In outline it focuses on, first, preventing armed conflict; second, the protection of civilians in armed conflict; third, ending impunity; fourth, clear and early warning; and fifth, the need for swift and decisive action. The UN has already introduced significant reforms in peacekeeping following the recommendations of the *Brahimi Report*.[40] It has taken measures to establish more timely and more robust peacekeeping forces; to improve early warning; and to establish international criminal tribunals and the new International Criminal Court. The UN Secretary-General has been more willing openly and publicly to put pressure on the Security Council to act in the face of threatened disaster – with some belated success in the DRC, where the Secretary-General urged intervention in 2003 to stop the fighting between militias and end its devastating impact on civilian population in the mineral-rich Ituri province.[41] His call for member states to authorise action was rather less effective in Liberia – where the Security Council waited for the overthrow of Charles Taylor in 2003 before authorising a UN force.[42]

---

[35] 5 March 2004, ⟨www.number10.gov.uk/output/Page5461⟩.
[36] UN, *A More Secure World*, para. 199.
[37] *The UN and Rwanda 1993–1996*, the UN Blue Book Series Vol. X (1996); OAU Panel, *Rwanda: The Preventable Genocide*.
[38] UN Press Release AFR/888, 7 April 2004, UN Panel Discussion on Rwanda Genocide.
[39] UN Press Release SG/SM/9245, 7 April 2004, ⟨www.unog.ch/news2/documents/newsen/sg04003e.htm⟩.
[40] UN Document S/2000/809; 2000 *UNYB*, p. 83.
[41] Gray, *International Law and the Use of Force*, p. 258.
[42] Ibid., p. 259.

But there are still fundamental problems with peacekeeping as an instrument to prevent genocide or other humanitarian disaster: these make it unlikely that any great improvement can realistically be hoped for in the short term. The experience in Sudan since 2003 has not been encouraging to those who advocate military intervention, whether unilateral or through the UN, to prevent humanitarian catastrophe. First, the UN, although it has made major practical and administrative reforms in peacekeeping capability, has also had difficulties in meeting the targets of deployment within 30 days for a minor operation and within 90 days for a more complex operation. Second, the UN Security Council, following the *Brahimi Report* recommendations, is now more inclined to create robust mandates for peacekeeping operations. Moreover, when it authorises the use of force by UN troops under Chapter VII of the UN Charter it commonly adopts a formula which is a direct response to the experience of Rwanda: it authorises the UN troops to protect not only their own personnel and to secure their own freedom of movement, but also to protect 'civilians under imminent threat of physical violence' at least 'within its capabilities and areas of deployment'. But, on the other hand, following the *Brahimi Report* recommendations, the Security Council has also refused to authorise UN operations until adequate troops are guaranteed by member states to carry out the proposed mandate. The combination of these two factors – the need for a robust mandate and the competing need not to authorise a force until the resources are guaranteed – may have the (possibly unintended) effect of a recipe for inaction. However, the main problem for those who would like to see forcible humanitarian intervention on a principled basis remains one of 'indifference, narrowly defined national interest and lack of political will on the part of states'.[43]

Sudan

This is all too apparent with regard to Sudan; there has been much discussion as to whether the situation in the Darfur region of Sudan should be categorised as one of genocide and as to the possible consequences of such a categorisation. In early 2003, at the same time that the settlement of the long-running civil war between northern and southern Sudan was in sight, there was a rebel uprising in Darfur, in western Sudan. In its response to the uprising in Darfur, the government was accused of supporting armed groups – commonly referred to as Janjaweed militias – in brutal repression of the rebels, involving use of government aircraft against civilians and mass displacement of peoples. Many thousands have been killed and many hundreds of thousands have been internally displaced and displaced into Chad.[44]

Some UN officials began using the language of 'ethnic cleansing' in 2004.[45] But states generally avoided this, as they had in the case of Rwanda. The EU said that although there was widespread violence in the Darfur region it was not a situation of genocide.[46] The AU Assembly itself expressly held in July 2004 that 'even though the

---

[43] UN Press Release AFR/888, 7 April 2004.
[44] UN Press Release AFR/1005, 2 August 2004.
[45] *Keesing's Record of World Events* (2004), 45884.
[46] *The Guardian*, 10 August 2004.

humanitarian situation in Darfur is serious, it can not be defined as a genocide'.[47] The Security Council implicitly took the same line.[48] But the US Secretary of State, Colin Powell, in September 2004, after concurrent resolutions by the two Houses of Congress, indicated that the US was taking the position that there was genocide in Darfur.[49] The UN Secretary-General repeatedly stressed that, no matter how the crimes that are being committed against civilians are characterised or legally defined, it was urgent to take immediate action; there was a humanitarian crisis.[50] The Security Council was then, for the first time in its history, seized under Article 8 of the Genocide Convention. This provides 'Any Contracting Party may call upon the competent organs of the United Nations to take such action under the Charter of the United Nations as they consider appropriate for the prevention and suppression of acts of genocide'. The Security Council passed Resolution 1564(2004) under Chapter VII by $11 - 0 - 4$; this required the Secretary-General to appoint an international commission of inquiry to determine by the end of January 2005 whether acts of genocide had occurred, and to identify the perpetrators with a view to ensuring that those responsible are held accountable.[51]

The EU and the US were happy to see regional and sub-regional bodies play the leading role in Sudan: first the Intergovernmental Authority on Development (IGAD),[52] then the African Union (AU), have played the primary role.[53] The plans for a UN peacekeeping mission referred to in Security Council Resolution 1547(2004) have not materialised.[54] The AU initially created a relatively small – 300 strong – force to monitor the *Humanitarian Cease-fire Agreement* signed between the parties involved in the Darfur conflict on 8 April 2004.[55] It later agreed to expand the force to 3,000, still with the consent of the government of Sudan.[56] The Security Council has welcomed the role of AU monitors to protect the cease-fire commission and the protection force.[57] It has called on member states to provide generous support for the efforts of the AU.[58] The AU itself has repeatedly called for financial and logistical assistance to sustain the AU mission.[59]

But by December 2004 there were still only 800 troops and 100 military observers in the enhanced African Mission in Sudan (AMIS). The UN Under-Secretary-General commended AMIS for its proactive and positive role under increasingly

---

[47] Assembly of the AU, 3rd Ordinary session, 6–8 July 2004, ⟨www.africa-union.org/DARFUR/homedar.htm⟩.
[48] UN Press Release SC/8160, 30 July 2004.
[49] *Keesing's Record of World Events* (2004), 46105, 46188; *The Independent*, 10 September 2004.
[50] UN Press Release SG/SM/9484, 16 September 2004.
[51] SC 5040th meeting, UN Press Release SC/8191, 18 September 2004.
[52] UN Press Release SC/8120, 11 June 2004.
[53] *The Guardian*, 10 August 2004, 23 August 2004.
[54] UN Press Release SC/8120, 11 June 2004.
[55] *The Guardian*, 9 July 2004.
[56] UN Press Release SC/8206, 5 October 2004; *The Guardian*, 26 August 2004. The AU considered transformation of the Observer Mission into a full-fledged peacekeeping mission with the requisite mandate and size to ensure the effective implementation of the Ceasefire Agreement (AU Document, PSC/PR/Comm (XIII) para 9, 27 July 2004; UN Document S/2004/603, 27 July 2004). The request of the government of Sudan to the AU to increase its monitoring presence in Darfur was welcomed in SC Res 1564 (2004).
[57] UN Press Release SC/8160, 30 July 2004, SC Res 1556.
[58] UN Press Release SC/8104, 25 May 2004; UN Press Release SC/8120, 11 June 2004.
[59] AU Communique, PSC/PR/Comm.(XIII), UN Press Release SC/8195, 24 September 2004. Nigeria's President, the Chairman of the AU, stressed that the Darfur situation presented the Union with a huge undertaking of command and control, in a magnitude it had never undertaken before.

challenging circumstances with limited resources. But the security situation was deteriorating.[60] The AU had run into great difficulties in securing and deploying an adequate force. In December the Security Council reiterated their full support to the AU efforts and called for an expeditious and full deployment of the African force. In this regard they invited the Secretariat to consider 'further steps to galvanise and facilitate the rapid deployment of the force'.[61] At the same time that the AU was experiencing great difficulty and serious delay in providing an adequate force for Sudan, Somalia also called for a substantial AU force of 20,000 to be sent to help its government restore order throughout its territory.[62] The continuing problems involved in securing a military response to a humanitarian emergency in Africa are very apparent.

Europe and the use of force in Africa

The pattern which has emerged in practice over the years since the end of the Cold War with regard to peacekeeping and enforcement practice in Africa under the UN Charter is that most developed states, including European states, do not now provide substantial numbers of troops for UN peacekeeping operations in Africa.[63] However, European states contribute in other ways.

'Coalitions of the willing'

First, they undertake Chapter VII member state operations as 'coalitions of the willing' in Africa. These have been created (1) after a UN force has proved unable to act effectively because of limited resources. Thus in *Operation Artemis*, the EU's first military operation outside Europe, a 1,500 strong EU-led member state force was sent into the Ituri province of the DRC in 2003 when rival militias endangered the life of civilians. The conflict in the DRC had begun in 1998 after the overthrow of President Mobutu when several neighbouring states, including Uganda and Rwanda, intervened in the internal conflict in the DRC; the prolonged conflict was fuelled by the resources of the DRC as the warring parties exploited those resources to pay for their participation in the conflict. Although Uganda and Rwanda eventually withdrew their troops from the DRC in 2002 they left behind armed militias which continued the battle over resources. In particular, armed conflict continued in the mineral-rich Ituri province. The UN peacekeeping force established after the 1999 Lusaka peace agreement (MONUC) was too small to carry out the mandate assigned to it by the Security Council and proved unable to stop the fighting and protect the civilians in the Ituri province. The EU-led *Operation Artemis* was expressly created as a 'strictly temporary' operation; the Security Council in Resolution 1484 authorised

---

[60] SC 5094th meeting, UN Press Release SC/8262, 7 December 2004.
[61] UN Press Release SC/8247, 21 December 2004.
[62] UN Press Release SC/8148, 14 July 2004.
[63] UN Press Release DSG/SM/216, 30 March 2004 (with the limited exceptions of Ireland which has provided troops in Liberia, and Sweden for the DRC).

its deployment in May 2003 until 15 September 2003. It was then replaced by a reinforced MONUC.[64]

Also (2) 'coalitions of the willing' have been created to prepare for a UN operation, as with the French-led multinational force in Liberia in 2003. Charles Taylor had been elected President in 1997 after a lengthy civil war, but the election did not bring stability. Other states accused President Taylor of intervention in neighbouring states, including Sierra Leone, and the Security Council imposed sanctions on Liberia in 2001. Armed opposition to President Taylor built up in 2002 and he was indicted by the Sierra Leone Special Court for war crimes committed during the civil war in Liberia. There was a serious breakdown of law and order; opposition forces seized control of much of the country and the disintegration of Liberia seemed imminent. President Taylor, under pressure from the USA and France, agreed to stand down and a cease-fire was agreed. The Security Council, after the departure of President Taylor, finally passed Resolution 1497 authorising member states to establish a multinational force to support the implementation of the cease-fire agreement, to establish security and to prepare for the arrival of a longer term, 15,000 strong UN force.

Also in Côte d'Ivoire, after an attempted coup in September 2002, the UN authorised the French troops of *Operation Licorne* (together with a sub-regional ECOWAS force) to operate in Côte d'Ivoire until a UN force could be deployed. After the parties involved in the conflict had concluded the January 2003 *Linas-Marcoussis* peace agreement, the Security Council in Resolution 1464 (2003) welcomed the deployment of the ECOWAS forces and French troops with a view to contributing to a peaceful solution of the crisis and the implementation of the peace agreement. Acting under Chapter VII of the UN Charter, it authorised France and the member states of ECOWAS to take the necessary steps to guarantee the security and freedom of their personnel and to ensure the protection of civilians. This authorisation was continued until the establishment of a UN force, UNOCI, in April 2004.[65] After that date French troops were authorised to 'use all necessary means in order to support UNOCI' in accordance with an agreement to be reached between UNOCI and the French authorities.

It has been suggested that as the EU's first military mission outside Europe, *Operation Artemis* marked the start of a new military role for the EU. The EU had earlier undertaken a smaller, preventive operation in Macedonia where it took over from a NATO force, at the invitation of the government.[66] The EU has also taken over from SFOR, the NATO force in Bosnia and Herzegovina in 2004; the Security Council in Resolutions 1551 (2004) and 1575 (2004) welcomed this development.[67] But suggestions that there could be a similar EU force sent to Sudan in 2004 were not implemented.[68]

This possible new role for the EU – of providing a fast-response vanguard force, authorised by the UN under Chapter VII – was devised under a French, German, Italian and UK proposal of February 2004. The EU was to hold ready a permanent pool of troops to provide up to nine battle-groups of 1,500 available for deployment

---

[64] UN Press Release SC/7862, 3 September 2003.
[65] SC Res 1527, SC Res 1528.
[66] *Keesing's Record of World Events* (2003), 45312, 45759.
[67] UN Press Release SC/8144, 9 July 2004; *Keesing's Record of World Events* (2004), 46134.
[68] 'EU-led forces could intervene in Sudan conflict', *The Financial Times*, 12 April 2004.

at short notice to quell conflict beyond EU boundaries, in support of operations mandated by the UN.[69] This may well prove a more important contribution to international peace and security than more ambitious attempts at a common EU defence and security policy. The plan specifically refers to the need for units to deploy quickly to African hotspots. The UN has urged that NATO should also undertake such a role. The Secretary-General has said that NATO's increasing willingness to 'go global' presents important opportunities, in particular for Africa. NATO might be employed in a peace enforcement role, much as the EU deployed *Operation Artemis* in the DRC as a bridging force before the deployment of a UN operation.[70]

Assistance to governments

Second, European states also provide assistance to governments in Africa, often under the guise of protecting their nationals, but in reality sometimes going beyond this. It is interesting to note that there seems to have been a shift of attitude to European military intervention since the end of the Cold War, in that when a breakdown in order occurs in a former African colony there are now commonly calls to the former colonial power to intervene. This would seem to suggest that there is now rather less suspicion of their motives than existed formerly.[71]

The best known recent operations include those of the UK in Sierra Leone and of France in Côte d'Ivoire. The UN encountered difficulty in securing enough troops for UNAMSIL, its peacekeeping force in Sierra Leone, and the UN force ran into serious problems in May 2000 when hundreds of its troops were taken hostage by opposition forces. The UK was not willing to provide troops to UNAMSIL, but it did provide troops to assist the government of Sierra Leone and to provide logistical and intelligence assistance to the UN force. Thus the UK was willing to intervene but not to submit its troops to participation in the UN multilateral force.[72]

Similarly, France intervened in Côte d'Ivoire after the September 2002 coup attempt. French troops were already present in the country as they had remained there since its independence in 1960. France offered a mixed justification for its intervention; it claimed to be using its troops to protect its own nationals. But it also claimed that its mission included assistance to the government. It gradually moved in extra troops to expand *Operation Licorne* to a total force of 4,000.[73] This intervention aroused some suspicion as to the true motives of the French government in Côte d'Ivoire and anti-French riots broke out; some doubt was expressed as to whether France was really neutral in the conflict or whether it was actually providing assistance to the rebels in order to put pressure on the government.[74] But the UN Security Council consistently supported the French intervention. When government forces attacked opposition and French forces in apparent violation of the cease-fire

[69] UN Press Release DSG/SM/216, 30 March 2004; EU Presidency Statement – Special Committee on Peacekeeping, 17 March 2004.
[70] UN Press Releases SG/SM/9188, 8 March 2004; SC/8153, 20 July 2004; UN Press Release GA/PK/181, 30 March 2004.
[71] *International Herald Tribune*, 21 May 2003.
[72] Gray, *International Law and the Use of Force*, p. 245, n. 175.
[73] *Keesing's Record of World Events* (2002), 44968, 45131, 45126; (2003), 45231; (2004), 45775.
[74] *The Guardian*, 8 July 2004; *Keesing's Record of World Events* (2003), 45175, 45731.

in November 2004, France responded by destroying the small Côte d'Ivoire air force. The Security Council clearly took the side of France; it showed no concerns over French impartiality or doubts about its motives. It condemned the attack by the government of Côte d'Ivoire; it confirmed that the French forces and UNOCI were authorised to use all necessary means to fully carry out their mandate in accordance with Security Council Resolution 1528 and expressed full support for the action taken by the French forces.[75] It also imposed an arms embargo on Côte d'Ivoire in Resolution 1572 and threatened further sanctions.

Assistance to regional and sub-regional organisations

Third, the UN has turned to regional and sub-regional organisations to take the lead in certain conflicts, to provide peacekeeping forces and undertake Chapter VII actions, especially in Africa. European states have been happy that these regional and sub-regional organisations should take the lead. Instead of the provision of troops and direct involvement the European states have provided financial assistance to the regional organisations for particular operations, as well as military training and general financial assistance. The EU has undertaken many initiatives designed to assist African states to improve their peacekeeping capacity. It has adopted a policy on Enhancing African Peacekeeping capacity, and is helping in creating an African standby force.[76] In 2004 it created the EU Peace Facility for Africa at the request of the AU to strengthen the capacity of the AU to engage in peace support and peacekeeping operations; there is a new focus on capacity building and training of African troops.[77] The EU has adopted a superficially attractive rhetoric of a 'partnership of equals' between European and African states: this may be seen as reflecting a genuine desire to move away from neo-colonial intervention or alternatively as masking a desire to avoid direct involvement in UN operations in Africa.

Thus the sub-regional organisation ECOWAS, in particular, has played an important role in recent years. It took on a crucial role in Sierra Leone, Liberia and Côte d'Ivoire. But in all these operations it ran into financial difficulties. In Côte d'Ivoire the Secretary-General sought additional financial assistance from developed states.[78] In January 2004 he reported that ECOWAS did not have enough resources and therefore sought transformation into a UN force.[79] This took place and UNOCI was established under Resolution 1528 as from 4 April 2004. Similarly the AU has run into resource and financial problems as it has attempted to play the major role in African peacekeeping. It lacked the resources to support its first peacekeeping mission in Burundi. The AU and Burundi accordingly called for its replacement by a UN mission.[80] In May 2004 this was finally set up.[81] In Sudan the AU has taken

[75] UN Press Release SC/8239, 6 November 2004.
[76] EU Presidency Statement – Special Committee on Peacekeeping, 29 March 2004 (Ref: PRES04-035EN); see also UN Press Release GA/SPD/298, 26 October 2004, Netherlands on behalf of the EU.
[77] EU Presidency Declaration on Africa and the African Union, 6 July 2004 (Ref: CL04-135EN); UN Press Release GA/PK/182, 19 April 2004; UN Press Release SG/2092, 5 October 2004.
[78] UN Press Release SG/SM/8679, 30 April 2003; UN Press Release SC/7745, 30 April 2003.
[79] Secretary-General's Report, S/2004/3, 6 January 2004, paras 48, 50, 61. The UK committed £4 m to the West African peacekeeping effort in Côte d'Ivoire, FCO Press Release, 21 April 2004.
[80] UN Press Release SC/8001, 17 February 2004.

the lead in sending a force into Darfur, but it depends on financial assistance from developed states to carry out its role of protection for the cease-fire monitors in Darfur and oversight of the cease-fire agreement. The UK and the EU have provided substantial financial aid.[82] This was the first mission supported by the EU Peace Facility for Africa.[83]

In UN debates in 2004 the language often used in talking of conflicts in Africa is that of the need for African states to 'take ownership' of African conflicts and their settlement. But some are suspicious of this rhetoric and of any wholesale subcontracting of peacekeeping in Africa to regional bodies. In the 2004 debate of the Fourth Committee of the UN General Assembly a clear split was apparent between, on the one hand, those developed states stressing the increasing roles of regional organisations and using the language of 'partnership' between developed states and Africa and of 'ownership' and, on the other hand, certain developing states calling on developed states to provide troops for UN operations.[84] Thus, for example, Japan argued that it was essential that the governments and peoples of a region affected by conflict establish 'ownership in the area of peace and security'. Outside assistance would be designed to raise the level of ownership. The most appropriate approach was to utilise regional and sub-regional organisations. In contrast, Cameroon and Jordan argued that developed states should contribute their share not only of resources but also of troops.[85] An active role by regional organisations should not absolve the UN of its responsibility for peacekeeping.[86] The Secretary-General, while supporting the use of regional organisations in cases where they can be on the ground much faster than the UN,[87] and while giving examples of cooperation, has also said that not all regional organisations could sustain their deployments over a long period. And the legitimacy that flowed from UN operations was often needed for longer-term sustainability.[88]

To recap – the pattern that emerges is that developed European states do not generally themselves provide troops for UN peacekeeping operations in Africa, but they do offer financial assistance to regional organisations and take limited Chapter VII action when authorised by the UN. However, there are still calls from the UN and from many developing states for developed states – and in particular EU states – to play a more direct role in UN peacekeeping, to provide troops. The Deputy Secretary-General has said 'as EU member states you have a unique capacity to field the well-equipped, well-trained and proficient troops that form the glue of any successful peacekeeping operation ... It is clear that if rising demands for peacekeeping are to be met, EU member states will need to raise their commitment substantially.'[89]

---

[81] SC Res 1545 (2004).
[82] Communique of 13th meeting of AU Peace and Security Council, 27 July 2004, PSC/PR/Comm (XIII); UN Press Release SC/8153, 20 July 2004; *The Guardian*, 5 June 2004. Concern has been expressed at a move within the OECD to redefine spending on peacekeeping missions or training foreign armies as development aid (*The Guardian*, 15 December 2004).
[83] UN Press Release GA/SPD/298, 26 October 2004.
[84] Ibid.
[85] Ibid.
[86] See, for example, the arguments by South Africa, Côte d'Ivoire and Burundi, UN Press Release GA/SPD/181, 30 March 2004, and UN Press Release SC/8095, 17 May 2004.
[87] UN Press Release SC/8153, 20 July 2004.
[88] Ibid.
[89] UN Press Release DSG/SM/216, 30 March 2004.

The accusations of double standards – that developed states care more about other European states than about Africa – have become familiar ever since the comparison was drawn between the UN response to events in the former Yugoslavia and that to the conflict in Somalia. The UN Deputy-Secretary-General has subsequently contrasted the willingness of European states to create large Chapter VII forces in Bosnia and Kosovo with their reluctance to create any similarly large scale Chapter VII operation in Africa.[90] The three limited member state operations in Africa authorised under Chapter VII were clearly unlike the major and prolonged member state operations in Europe – in Bosnia and Kosovo – and that in East Timor.

But is this really an cause for concern? The UK Foreign and Commonwealth Office in considering 'why Africa should matter to us' set out the following case.[91] The first reason for concern is moral: the war, famine and disease that have haunted Africa for much of the twentieth century are simply unacceptable in today's world. Africa is the only continent to have grown poorer in the past 25 years; its share of world trade has halved; it received less than 1 per cent of direct foreign investment. But apart from any moral case, 'a more prosperous, stable and peaceful Africa would benefit not only Africa, but the whole world'. There are also reasons of strong self-interest why Africa matters; the UK Foreign Office Minister resorted to quoting Trotsky: 'You may not be interested in war, but war is interested in you'. That is, he warned that 'if we are not interested in Africa, the threats it poses – terrorism, illegal immigration and instability – are an even greater danger to us'. He said that there had been more Al Qai'da attacks in Africa than anywhere else. Also 'failed states' like Somalia were a breeding ground for terrorism.[92] Finally, the Minister also invoked reasons of 'energy security', (that is, oil and gas supplies) for being concerned over events in Africa. There is now increasing awareness of the growing importance of African oil supplies.[93]

Legal questions about multilateralism and legitimacy

The question arises from the pattern described in the previous section whether the desire of developed states not to get directly involved in UN peacekeeping in Africa has any *legal* consequences? The reluctance of European states to participate in UN peacekeeping in Africa, and their apparent preference that regional organisations should play the main role, leads on to questions about the duties of member states and the nature of multilateralism – a topical and important question at a time when a lot of critical attention is rightly being paid to the unilateralism of the US and the UK in the context of Iraq. This practice also leads to questions about the interpretation of Chapters VII and VIII of the UN Charter.

---

[90] UN Press Release DSG/SM/214, 20 February 2004; UN News Service, 27 January 2004, 'Rising Demand for Peacekeeping Stretches UN's Resources, Fréchette Says'.

[91] FCO News, PM launches Commission for Africa, 26 February 2004; FCO Minister's Address to the Centre for International Studies and Research, 24 February 2004.

[92] Somalia has now been accused of tolerating the operations of those responsible for the November 2003 bomb attack on the hotel in Mombasa, Kenya. *Keesing's Record of World Events* (2003), 45682.

[93] BBC News, How Important is African Oil?, 7 September 2003, ⟨news.bbc.co.uk/go/pr/fr/-/2/hi/business/3054948.stm⟩.

An increased role for troop-contributing countries

First – it seems that troop contributing countries (TCCs) from developing states which do provide troops for UN peacekeeping operations are increasingly arguing for a new, stronger role in Security Council decision-making on peacekeeping. This question of the proper role of TCCs was a significant feature of the *Brahimi Report*; there has subsequently been significant progress under Security Council Resolution, in increasing mechanisms for consultation between the Security Council and TCCs over the establishment of the mandate of a peacekeeping force and also in making any subsequent changes in that mandate, or the size of the force or the strategy to be followed. But major TCCs like India, South Africa and Egypt are pushing for a greater role; this may be seen as a challenge to the primary role of the Security Council in controlling peacekeeping operations.[94] While developed states members of the Security Council do not themselves participate in peacekeeping operations, claims will continue to be made by TCCs not just for consultation but for participation in decision-making. This also fuels calls for a change in the membership of the Security Council, to include more developing states. The High Level Panel set up by the UN Secretary-General could not agree on this issue which has proved intractable over many years of intense debate within the UN; the Panel could only agree to propose two alternative models for an increase in the membership of the Security Council in order to make it more representative.[95]

A reinterpretation of Chapter VIII of the UN Charter

Second, has the reliance by developed, including European, states on an increased role for regional and sub-regional organisations in peacekeeping and enforcement action brought with it a change in the interpretation of Chapter VIII of the UN Charter on regional action? The question has arisen whether, in their desire not to play a direct role in peacekeeping in Africa, developed states might be willing to rewrite the Charter, specifically to accept a more flexible interpretation of Article 53 on regional action to allow regional organisations greater autonomy and wider powers to use force. Article 53 expressly requires Security Council authorisation for enforcement action by regional agencies.

Some legal scholars make radical claims on the basis of the ECOWAS action in Sierra Leone and, even more controversially, on the basis of the NATO action in Kosovo.[96] It is argued that the use of force for the restoration of democracy/humanitarian aims does not need prior Security Council authorisation; implicit ex post facto approval by the Security Council is enough under Article 53, not just in exceptional cases but as a general rule. But there are legal problems with such arguments.[97] First, they seem to over-interpret state practice: they read too much into

---

[94] UN Press Releases GA/PK/180, GA/PK/181, 29 and 30 March 2004.

[95] Report of High-level Panel on Threats, Challenges and Change, *A More Secure World: Our Shared Responsibility* (2004), at para. 244.

[96] Franck, *Recourse to Force* (2002), at p. 155.

[97] De Wet, *The Changing Chapter VII Powers of the United Nations Security Council* (2004) ch. 7. On policy grounds it seems undesirable to pursue the imposition of democracy by force. It has to be doubted whether democracy can be successfully established by force in the light of the experience of Kosovo, Haiti, Iraq and Afghanistan.

these two episodes of Sierra Leone and Kosovo. In fact ECOWAS made only limited assertions of a right to use force – in self-defence and as authorised by the Security Council. And the Security Council response was articulated in general and ambiguous terms. In the face of this practice it seems to be going too far to argue for a change in the interpretation of the Charter – a change that was not acceptable during the Cold War when the US made similar arguments for a wide interpretation of the right of regional organisations to use force with regard to OAS action in regard to Cuba and the Dominican Republic.[98] There is a familiar division between commentators on this issue, between those who focus on what states actually say in legal justification and those who focus on what they might have said or should have said by way of legal justification.

Second, this approach of reinterpreting Article 53 distorts the Charter scheme for the relation between the UN and regional bodies, and is not acceptable to states such as China, Russia, Germany, Iran and South Africa which have gone out of their way recently to reassert the need for Security Council authority for regional enforcement action.[99] Also, ever since *Operation Desert Storm* provoked criticism that the Security Council had gone too far in abandoning control of the coalition operation against Iraq after its invasion of Kuwait, the Security Council has consistently manifested concern that it should exercise some control over Chapter VII operations by 'coalitions of the willing'. It imposes time limits for operations and requires reports to the Security Council. It is hard to reconcile this approach with a less strict approach to regional action. Why should the Security Council abandon control to regional organisations in a way it is not willing to do in the case of express Chapter VII authorisations to coalitions of the willing?

Third, this – the experience of Sierra Leone and Kosovo – seems to be a rather limited amount of practice on which to base such a radical change in the interpretation of the UN Charter. Subsequent practice does not provide any support for such an approach to Article 53. Thus the Security Council has not consistently concerned itself with democracy; it has allowed or connived in the overthrow of democratically elected governments in Haiti, Georgia, Liberia, the Central African Republic and elsewhere. Also it has in subsequent episodes followed what might be seen as the traditional approach to Article 53; in 2003 it expressly authorised Chapter VII action by regional organisations in Côte d'Ivoire and Liberia.

Multilateralism and legitimacy

Throughout this article contrasting notions of legitimacy are apparent. Developing states, international officials and the UN High Level Panel have all called on European and other developed states to contribute more troops to UN operations, especially to those in Africa. Underlying this call for resources is the view that member states on the UN have a duty to operate multilaterally. There is a clear challenge to the legitimacy of the developed states' preference to retain autonomy

[98] Akehurst, 'Enforcement Action by Regional Agencies, with Special Reference to the Organization of American States', 42 *BYIL* (1967), p. 175.
[99] UN Press Release SC/8153, 20 July 2004; UN Press Release GA/PK/181, 30 March 2004; UN Press Release SC/7724, 11 April 2003.

with regard to the nature of their participation in the maintenance of peace and security in Africa. And the reluctance of European and other developed states to supply troops for UN peacekeeping operations has lent strength to the arguments of those who seek a fundamental reinterpretation of the UN Charter to shift power away from the Security Council.

Thus we are left with the increasingly important question: how far is it legitimate for developed states to pay their peacekeeping contributions, to provide commanders and perhaps logistical support and transport, but not to provide significant numbers of actual troops for UN operations? For those who argue that there is an emerging 'responsibility to protect' in the context of *unilateral* humanitarian intervention in cases where the Security Council is unable to act because of the veto, the question arises: is there not an even stronger duty to contribute to UN operations when called on, especially where they are designed to prevent genocide or other humanitarian disaster? That is, for those who profess concern over humanitarian catastrophe is there not a duty not only to act unilaterally but also to enable the UN to act effectively?

For those states such as France and Germany which were (rightly) critical of the USA and the UK over the invasion of Iraq, and which strongly stressed the duty to act through the UN, the question is how far this commitment to multilateralism goes. In their opposition to *Operation Iraqi Freedom* they accused the US and the UK of violation of the UN Charter and of failure to respect the role of the Security Council under Chapter VII. However, they do not seem very willing themselves to take a multilateral approach: there are clear limits to their own commitments to UN rather than unilateral action, in that they make only very limited contributions of peacekeeping forces.

During the Cold War the UN deliberately chose not to use troops from permanent members in peacekeeping operations in order to maintain the appearance of impartiality and to avoid the danger that Cold War conflicts would affect peacekeeping. There was then a brief period during the first surge in peacekeeping in the 1990s when the troops of permanent members played a crucial role. But now these and other developed states clearly prefer to subcontract UN and regional peacekeeping to developing countries; they prefer not to provide troops for UN peacekeeping. Although in undertaking Chapter VII operations in Africa they may claim to be acting multilaterally, they retain greater autonomy in such operations then in UN peacekeeping. And again where they provide assistance to governments or to regional or sub-regional organisations they obviously retain greater autonomy.

For European states this is apparently seen as a legitimate division of functions, possibly reflecting the view that the lives of European soldiers are worth more than those of troops from developing states, as well as a mistrust of UN command. But in the short term the recent surge in peacekeeping has made it clear that the direct participation of developed states is necessary for effective UN peacekeeping. In practical terms the rhetoric of 'partnership' and 'ownership', however attractive, is no substitute for multilateralism. At a time when serious consideration is being given to a radical cutting back of UN peacekeeping operations, the competing notions of legitimacy of developed and developing states have significant practical consequences.

Identity, legitimacy, and the use of military force: Russia's Great Power identities and military intervention in Abkhazia

TED HOPF

An action is legitimate if the pertinent community deems it so. Most would agree that Russia's conduct in the 1990s in Georgia was illegitimate. Military intervention in another state, unless the other state is preparing an imminent attack on one's own territory, or is engaged in the systematic abuse of one's own citizens, is a violation of the international norm of sovereignty, at a minimum.[1] Some have argued that European politics has gone beyond this 'territorial integrity norm' to something more expansive, to a consensual renunciation of any and all territorial claims on other states. This was first codified in the Helsinki Final Act of 1975.[2]

The interesting question is whether Russia deemed its behaviour illegitimate. If it knew that it was violating international sovereignty norms, that would say a lot about Russia's lack of regard for normative constraints on its foreign policy conduct. It would also speak to the relative weakness of international norms to shape state behaviour. On the other hand, and perhaps more interesting, if Russia did not believe its behaviour illegitimate, but instead thought its use of military force in another country was within the bounds of international propriety, then the question is how is it possible for Russia to entertain such ideas?

The answer in this article is that different Russian identities yield different understandings of legitimacy. There is no one Russia. Instead, depending on which discursive construction of the Russian self is empowered by Russia's political system at a given time, a different Russia is acting in the world. It turns out that in the early 1990s, three different Russias were competing to control the Russian state. Which one ended up with the reins of power determined who Russia was, how it acted abroad, how it understood its interests there, and which actions it considered legitimate or illegitimate in pursuit of those interests. The prevailing discourse of Russian identity is simultaneously the product of both domestic identity construction, the interaction between the Russian state and society, and international identity construction, the interaction between the Russian state and international actors. What Russia considered to be legitimate actions by a 'great power' depended on the identity that was produced by both domestic and external interactions.

---

[1] These norms are stated most explicitly in the United Nations Charter Chapter 1, Article 2. ⟨http://www.un.org/aboutun/charter/⟩ (accessed June 2005).
[2] Mark Zacher, 'The Territorial Integrity Norm: International Boundaries and the Use of Force', *International Organization*, 55:2 (Spring 2001), pp. 215–50.

There were three main competitors for Russian identity in the early 1990s: Liberal, Conservative, and Centrist. Each of these was socially constructed in interaction with both domestic and international society. Each entailed the idea of Russia as a great power, but understood what a great power was differently. As will become clear below, each of the three discourses implied different policies in Russia's 'Near Abroad'. In short, had Liberals remained in control of the Russian state past the autumn of 1992, Russian military support for Abkhazian rebels might have been understood as illegitimate. Had Conservatives gained control of the Russian state, the 1990s might have been marked by frequent Russian military interventions in the Near Abroad, including in Estonia and Latvia, each one of which would have been regarded as legitimate by Moscow. The reality, however, was different from both of these hypothetical outcomes. Centrists won out, limiting Russian military intervention to just two cases: Abkhazia and Transdniester in Moldova, but understood as perfectly legitimate exercises of a great power's right to police its periphery.[3]

In what follows, I will try to explain how the Centrist discourse beat out its two competitors, although that is not the main focus of this article. Instead, the primary attention is on how these three different discourses of Russian identity imply different Russian interests, policies, and conceptions of legitimacy.

Strictly speaking, there was no Russian state for most of 1992. That is, there was no unitary actor in Moscow. The defence ministry and Russian armed forces were not even created until May 1992. The Russian Federation (RF) had been in existence for five months already. The foreign ministry found itself in control of foreign policy in the first months of the RF, but by the end of the year, had been eclipsed by the Supreme Soviet and the Presidential Administration.

Moreover, as most accounts concede, the initial use of military force abroad was not ordered by anyone in Moscow, but was instead carried out by local Russian military forces left stranded in foreign countries by the December 1991 dissolution of the Soviet Union. In this case, the Russian state was not even responsible for its own actions. In this sense 'its' use of force was not illegitimate, for no Russian state, per se, used force.

By late 1992, however, we can speak of a more unified Russian state. But that state, instead of reasserting command over the previously autonomous military forces, either encouraged them to continue violating international norms, remained silent, or issued conflicting orders. One action the Russian state never took was forceful action against its own soldiers who were violating the sovereignty of Georgia. Moreover, once the military actions were over, Russian forces continued to remain on Georgian territory, despite repeated requests from the Georgian government that they leave. Finally, to the extent these forces were peacekeeping forces, their authorisation to be there, their conduct while there, and their composition, violated most international norms on peacekeeping.[4]

---

[3] Military intervention occurred as well in the civil war in Tajikistan, but this is mostly understood as an invitation with regional authorisation.

[4] For six international norms of peacekeeping, see Dov Lynch, *Russian Peacekeeping Strategies in the CIS: The Cases of Moldova, Georgia, and Tajikistan* (London: Macmillan, 2000), pp. 19–20.

In this sense, then, if we even grant Russia the fact that it was not initially responsible for illegitimate actions, soon thereafter, and indeed for the next decade, it has persisted in illegitimate conduct in Georgia.[5]

The puzzle in this article is to understand how such conduct became possible. The answer is that Russian identity made it possible. In the conclusion, I will argue that this identity is not fixed, but rather is constructed in relationship to Russia's domestic society and external significant others. The latter are Europe and the United States. I suggest that Russia's interactions with these two great powers produces different Russian great power identities. European and US identities resonate differently with the discourses of identity in Russian society. They empower different understandings of the Russian self. Meanwhile, European and US identities also resonate differently with the Russian state, producing different understandings of what it means to be a great power. What is talked about and how it is talked about varies systematically according to whether Putin is meeting with US President Bush, or instead, with European leaders such as Gerhard Schroeder, Silvio Berlusconi, Jacques Chirac, or Javier Solana. Moreover, different Russian identities emerge at these meetings.

To put this in more general theoretical terms, a state's identity, and so interests, and understandings of legitimate international behaviour, is a social product. But it is a product that is the result of a state's interactions both with its own society and with other states. As such, it is a variable, subject to both domestic and international influence. This means significant international others can effect changes in a state's identity, working within the constraints of that state's domestic identity terrain. It is in this way that the US and Europe are in fact 'causing' Russian foreign policy, but only insofar as the identities that are reproduced also resonate with the discourse(s) of identity that predominate in Russia's domestic context.

For example, the broad public in Russia understands Russia as European. This day to day understanding manifests itself in popular novels, high school history textbooks, movie reviews, and other artifacts of popular culture. The Russian state has this identity when interacting with other states in world affairs, but it is most acutely evoked when interacting with European states. The conversations between Putin and Schroeder, therefore, tend to reproduce a European identity for Russia that is both being expressed at the very highest official state level, and reverberating throughout Russian society on a reciprocal basis. No such reverberation is possible when Putin meets with Bush, as there is a vanishingly small level of identification with the United States among the Russian public. The United States is not a significant Other for Russian identity construction at home; Europe is.

The article proceeds as follows. First, I present a short description of Russian conduct in Abkhazia. I rely on several sources which have corroborated each other on the key points. In particular I will point out the instances in which the Russian state is not fully responsible for its own foreign policy actions, as well as catalogue Russian violations of international norms. I then present the three different discourses of Russian identity that dominated the 1990s and relate each discourse to its implications for Russian interests and actions in the Near Abroad. I also hypothesise which actions might be considered legitimate within each discourse.

---

[5] Georgia and Russia have signed yet another agreement on Russian force withdrawals. This May 2005 agreement foresees Russian evacuation of its military bases by 2008.

Finally, I conclude with a discussion of how Russia's international interactions, in combination with its domestically constructed identity, help evoke particular Russian great power identities and different views of legitimate uses of force in other countries.

Russian (in)actions in Abkhazia

In this section I provide an abbreviated account of Russian conduct in Abkhazia in the early 1990s, and then describe its violations of international norms on the legitimate use of force it committed there.

A little history

Although the history of Abkhazia's relations with Georgia, the Russian Empire, and the Soviet Union is fascinating and important for a complete understanding of the conflict, my purpose here is more narrow. I will begin with events in Abkhazia as *perestroika* and *glasnost* were permitting the enunciation of national grievances all over the Soviet Union. In 1989 Abkhazia's population was just over 500,000. Of these, only 18 per cent, or 96,000, were Abkhazians. Georgians accounted for 45 per cent of Abkhazia's population, Russians 14 per cent. Abkhazia was only absorbed into Georgia in 1931, having spent the previous 10 years as a Union Republic itself, equal in legal status to Georgia. In 1978 and again in 1989, Abkhazia requested from Moscow restoration of its previous status.

On 25 August 1990 the Abkhazian Supreme Soviet declared sovereignty. This was in response to the Georgian Supreme Soviet's proclamation of Georgian as the official language to be used within the parliament five days earlier. Although the Georgian government refused to hold the 17 March 1991 referendum on the preservation of the Soviet Union in Georgia, Abkhazia held its own version of Gorbachev's referendum, and a reported 98 per cent of Abkhazians supported the maintenance of the USSR.

At the time of August 1991 coup and the December 1991 collapse of the USSR, Georgia was ruled by Zviad Gamsakhurdia, a leader whose aggressive campaign against autonomy for minorities in South Osetia and Abkhazia, in particular, had led both republics to look to Moscow for support against Tbilisi. Shevardnadze's replacement of Gamsakhurdia in March 1992 came too late. Three months later, the Abkhazian National Guard, by the orders of the Abkhazian Supreme Soviet Chairman, Vladislav Ardzinba, seized the Abkhazian Interior Ministry building from the Georgians protecting it. The next month the Abkhazian Supreme Soviet declared Abkhazia a sovereign and independent state. Three weeks later, on 14 August 1992, detachments of the Georgian National Guard, under Tengiz Kitovani, entered and occupied Sukhumi, the Abkhazian capital. The local Russian military, as well as fighters from the Confederation of the Mountain Peoples of the Caucasus (CMPC), fought on the side of Abkhazia. Meanwhile, the Russian military, following the agreement reached between Russia and the other Soviet republics in December 1991, continued transferring weapons to the Georgian government.[6]

On 27 August 1992, Russian President Boris Yeltsin enunciated official Russian policy. He affirmed Russian support for Georgia's territorial integrity, thereby rejecting Abkhazia's claims of sovereignty, and pledged Russia would prevent armed detachments from entering Georgia from Russia.[7] While Russia never did recognise Abkhazia as an independent country, it also did not stop the flow of men and materiel across its borders to the rebels.

In February and March 1993, local Russian fighter-bombers were used on the side of Abkhazian forces. On 16 March, Abkhazia launched an attack to retake its capital, Sukhumi, with the aid of 70 Russian tanks. Despite Russian Foreign Minister Andrei Kozyrev and Georgian President Eduard Shevardnadze reaching a ceasefire agreement in Sochi on 27 July 1993, Abkhazian forces regrouped to take Sukhumi just two months later. The rout of Georgian forces was spearheaded by volunteers from the northern Caucasus. As Dov Lynch concluded, 'More than anything else, the Abkhazian offensive highlighted Russia's inability to control the development of events on the ground'.[8]

As Sukhumi was falling, and Georgians were fleeing Abkhazia, pro-Gamsakhurdia forces, or Zviadists, were threatening Shevardnadze's regime. In October 1993, after meeting in Moscow shortly after Yeltsin had the Russian White House strafed with artillery and tank fire, Shevardnadze agreed to Russian requests for four military bases in exchange for Russian military help against Zviadist forces. In addition, Shevardnadze agreed to Georgia's membership in the Commonwealth of Independent States (CIS) and that body's Collective Security Treaty.

Shevardnadze's request for either a Conference on Security and Cooperation in Europe (OSCE after January 1995), or UN peacekeepers, having fallen on deaf ears, he further asked for Russian peacekeeping forces in Abkhazia. With the overthrow of the pro-Abkhazian Russian parliament, Shevardnadze was reassured of Russia's support for Georgian territorial integrity against the separatists.[9] In March 1994, Georgia and Russia signed a treaty with the eerily Soviet name: Treaty of Friendship, Neighbourliness, and Cooperation. In July 1994, Russia sent 3,000 peacekeepers to Abkhazia, but their nominal CIS approval did not occur until October. The next month Arzinba became the first president of the self-declared sovereign Republic of Abkhazia.

After Shevardnadze's trip to Moscow, the Russian government began to impose sanctions on Abkhazia and effectively closed Abkhazia's northern border, shutting down military and economic communication with local northern Caucasus sympathisers.[10] Throughout 1995 and 1996, Russia adopted a hard line against Abkhazia. Its electricity from Russia was regularly interrupted; the Sukhumi airport was

---

[6] Edward Ozhiganov, 'The Republic of Georgia: Conflict in Abkhazia and South Ossetia', in Alexei Arbatov, Abram Chayes, Antonia Handler Chayes, and Lara Olson (eds.), *Managing Conflict in the Former Soviet Union: Russian and American Perspectives* (Cambridge, MA: The MIT Press, 1997), p. 385.

[7] *Krasnaia Zvezda*, 28 August 1992.

[8] Dov Lynch, *Russian Peacekeeping Strategies in the CIS: The Cases of Moldova, Georgia, and Tajikistan* (London: Macmillan, 2000), p. 137. And this is saying something, as Lynch can hardly be accused of taking a sympathetic approach to Moscow's intentions in this volume.

[9] Ozhiganov, 'The Republic of Georgia', p. 389.

[10] Lynch, *Russian Peacekeeping Strategies*, p. 141.

repeatedly shut down; and railroad traffic was only sporadic. In January 1996, the port of Sukhumi was simply closed. At the CIS heads of state meeting in Moscow that month, only Belarus did not sign on to collective CIS sanctions against Abkhazia.[11]

Illegitimate Russian actions in Abkhazia

Russian violations of international norms of sovereignty, territorial integrity, and peacekeeping in Abkhazia should be divided into two categories. The first are outcomes which the Russian government could hardly be expected to control, although strictly speaking, was legally responsible to prevent. These might be called acts of illegitimate omission. The second category are acts of illegitimate commission, policies adopted by the Russian government that violate international norms of proper conduct by states. There are plenty of both to go around.

The category of uncontrollables, or illegitimate omissions, includes local Russian military forces acting for themselves in Abkhazia without being ordered from Moscow, the infiltration of arms and fighters across the Russian border into Abkhazia, and the actions by parts of the Russian state that were contrary to the expressed policy of the Russian government, especially by the Supreme Soviet and republic governments.

When discussing the Russian military left stranded in Abkhazia at the collapse of the Soviet Union, it must be borne in mind that a Russian defence ministry was not even created until May 1992, as there were still hopes for a CIS armed force. That said, much of the transgressive behaviour by Russian forces in Abkhazia occurred after May 1992. Russian forces not only transferred arms to the Georgian government, per agreement, but Georgian forces stole and plundered Russian matériel in Georgia, and Russian soldiers sold weaponry to eager local buyers.[12] Baranets further testifies that 'in the archives of the Rostov and Moscow military staffs are secret documents in which our tanks, planes, ammunition, and personnel supplied to Abkhazians are ingeniously camouflaged'. Moscow, in order to 'appease the attentive international public', asserted that Russian air support for Abkhazian forces around Guduat were 'training missions'. The fact that Russian forces 'bombed the positions of the Georgian army during the war . . ., delivered ammunition to Abkhazian forces during their approach on Gagra . . . and participated in battles on the side of Abkhazians are supported by photographs, documents, and testimony of many witnesses. It would be senseless to refute them.'[13]

Meanwhile, it should be pointed out that these local Russian soldiers had support at the highest levels of the Russian military back in Moscow. Baranets describes one meeting in the spring of 1992 at which the Chief of the General Staff, Colonel-General Vicktor Dubynin, argued against the MFA's policy of withdrawing the Russian military from the Near Abroad. Instead, 'we should insinuate ourselves, imposing military-political positions rewarding to Moscow on the Kremlin,

[11] Baranets, *Genshtab bez Tain* (Moscow: Politbiuro 1999), pp. 112–7.
[12] Ibid., pp. 250–4, 266–7. Baranets's testimony is particularly strong evidence as he supported a still more forceful Russian military response to events in the CIS in general.
[13] Ibid., pp. 106, 286–90.

government, and diplomats, if necessary'.[14] Events in Abkhazia looked very much like this strategy of presenting Yeltsin with faits accomplis that would be hard to overcome.

In November 1991 the CMPC held its third congress, significantly in Sukhumi.[15] In August 1992, the Confederation issued an ultimatum to Shevardnadze, demanding the withdrawal of Georgian forces from Abkhazia, threatening to take Georgians hostage on their own members' territory, and to send volunteers to fight for Abkhazia's independence.[16] The same month, volunteer detachments began crossing into Abkhazia from Chechnia, Daghestan, Cherkessia, Krasnodar, Stavropol, Adygei, and other Caucasian republics in the Russian Federation. In the autumn of 1992 alone, from four to seven thousand fighters from the Confederation crossed into Abkhazia to participate in the fight against Georgian forces.[17] Most (in)famously perhaps, Shamil Basaev's Abkhazia Brigade spearheaded the successful Abkhazian attack on Sukhumi in September 1993.[18] The Russian government officially condemned these infiltrations, but the extent of its action to prevent this illegitimate conduct was to open a criminal investigation which came to naught.[19]

The Yeltsin government was not in full control of all the institutions that conventionally constitute a state. Having already described the activity of Russian military forces in Abkhazia, and the actions of subjects of the Russian Federation in the northern Caucausus, we should add to the list actors further afield. For example, in September 1992, just as the military conflict was beginning, the Russian parliament, like the CMPC, passed a resolution demanding Georgian withdrawal from Abkhazia and an end to further Russian transfer of arms to the Shevardnadze government. Actions such as this one only encouraged Abkhazian forces to reject the cease-fire proposals being developed by Russian foreign minister Kozyrev at the time.

As the Abkhazians were retaking Sukhumi in September 1993, President Yeltsin publicly condemned Abkhazian fighters. But his defence minister, Pavel Grachev, demanded that all Georgian forces leave Abkhazia. It is not hard to imagine how encouraged local Abkhazians were by the support from the official in charge of the Russian military.[20]

As we recall, after Shevardnadze's October 1993 trip to Moscow, Russia imposed sanctions on Abkhazia. But the local neighbouring Russian republic of Krasnodar ignored the law, it being ruled by communists who sympathised not only with

[14] Ibid., p. 55.
[15] This interesting transnational group was formed in 1989 with representatives of most Soviet Caucasian republics: Chechnia, Daghestan, Adygei, Krasnodar, Stavropol, Cherkessia, Kabardino, North and South Osetia, Ingushetia, and significantly, Abkhazia. Originally the Confederation of Mountain Peoples of the Caucasus, the inclusion of Cossacks as observers deleted the Mountain. Its ultimate objective was to create a multinational state from the Black to Caspian Seas. For a most extraordinary analysis of this most extraordinary project, see Georgi Derluguian, *Bourdieu's Secret Admirer in the Caucasus* (Chicago, IL: University of Chicago Press, 2005).
[16] Lynch 2000, p. 133.
[17] V. A. Zolotarev, *Rossiia (SSSR) v Lokalnykh Voinakh I Vooruzhennykh Konfliktakh Vtoroi Poloviny XX Veka* (Moscow: Kuchkovo Pole, 2000), 390 and Lynch 2000, 131.
[18] Ozhiganov, 'The Republic of Georgia', p. 381. Basaev would go on to become one of the most notorious Chechen rebels/terrorists/field commanders. He remains at large.
[19] Lynch, *Russian Peacekeeping Strategies*, p. 133.
[20] Some might attribute Yeltsin's failure to fire Grachev immediately to the fact that Yeltsin already felt that he needed Grachev and the military in the showdown with Khasbulatov and Rutskoi in the next few weeks.

Abkhazia, but with those who had just been routed in the White House strafing in Moscow.

In August 1994, that is, long after the Yeltsin government had begun to restrain Abkhazian forces, the governments in Tatarstan and Bashkortotstan signed Treaties of Friendship and Cooperation with the self-declared Republic of Abkhazia.[21] Actions such as this only encouraged Abkhazia in the belief that Russia's official nonrecognition was only de jure, not de facto.

As noted above, Russia sent CIS peacekeepers to Abkhazia in July 1994, before the CIS had even met to approve the deployment some three months later. Lynch enumerates six international norms of peacekeeping:

1. They should be established by the UN under the command and control of the Secretary General, with the costs met collectively.
2. They should be established with the consent and cooperation of the parties involved.
3. The forces should be impartial.
4. The forces should be volunteers.
5. The forces should limit themselves to self-defence.
6. The forces should be deployed only after a ceasefire is in place.[22]

The Russian record here is mixed. The Russian government repeatedly requested UN authorisation for its deployment of a peacekeeping force to Abkhazia and tried to convince the UN to accept the CIS as a regional organisation identified as a legitimate authoriser of such missions, but failed in both cases. Of course, Russia would have been delighted had UN members picked up the cost of the Russian mission in Abkhazia, and made requests to that effect.

It is hard to say that there was 'free' consent given by Georgia to the deployment. Georgian forces had already been driven out of Abkhazia by a collection of forces at least indulged by the Russian military, and the Georgian government accepted the Russian offer of peacekeepers only after all was mostly lost, and their preference for UN or OSCE forces had been unmet. At the most, Georgia agreed in exchange for Russian control over its Abkhazian allies.

The force has been arguably impartial since its deployment, and largely acting in self-defence, but this ignores the two years of activity prior to its official arrival. The forces are mostly all-volunteer, and any conscripts would doubtless be delighted to serve in the Russian Riviera over duty in Sakhalin. A ceasefire had been reached prior to the deployment of Russian forces.

Three discourses of Russian identity: Liberal, Conservative, Centrist

At the birth of the Russian Federation in 1992, a Liberal discourse of Russian identity predominated, one which understood all Russian actions and inactions enumerated above as illegitimate. But this discourse was increasingly opposed by a Conservative discourse, which not only understood all these actions as legitimate, but demanded far more aggressive violations of international standards of conduct. By

---

[21] For the text, see: ⟨http://www.tatar.ru/english/00000078.html⟩ (accessed April 2005).
[22] Lynch, *Russian Peacekeeping Strategies*, pp. 19–20.

late 1992, neither Liberal nor Conservative discourses of Russian identity were predominant; instead, a Centrist discourse had arisen that understood what Russia had done as legitimate, but which rejected any more forceful Russian actions.

To make sense of this pivotal year, I will describe the three discourses very briefly. I should make one critical methodological point. Finding Russian identity in Russian foreign policy toward Abkhazia, Georgia, the Near Abroad, or even in foreign policy more generally, risks a circular specification of the relationship, and so vitiates any claims about the societal dimension of Russian identity. The content of the Liberal, Conservative, and Centrist discourses was derived from texts – novels, film reviews, history textbooks, and newspaper and journal articles – that were not about either Russian foreign policy or Russian identity. In this way, the contending discourses of the Russian self were recovered and analysed separately from the dependent variable, and so guarded against tautology.

In what follows, then, I present the three contending discourses and their implications for Russian foreign policy. I then offer an interpretation of Russian policy in Abkhazia from the perspective of these different discourses. Each discourse has a particular relationship to its significant Others: the Historical Other of the Soviet past; the External Others of Europe and the United States; and the Internal Other of the Russian periphery.

Within Liberal discourse, Russia was identified with the United States, against the Soviet Union, and as part of a universal civilisation of modern Liberal market democracy.[23] Domestically, Liberal discourse identified its Conservative competitor with a discredited and dangerous Soviet past. While Liberal discourse rejects Soviet economic achievements, the Orthodox Church, and ethnonationalism as desirable parts of contemporary Russian identity, Conservatives value all three. More directly, Liberal discourse admires US individualism and its economic model, while Conservatives declaim both. Within Conservative discourse, Russia was identified with a Soviet Union shorn of its Stalinist brutality, and with a Russia defined ethnonationally. Russia was a unique Eurasian great power. Domestically,

---

[23] While I derive these discourses from popular novels, history textbooks, film reviews, and newspaper articles in Hopf, *Social Construction of International Politics: Identities and Foreign Policies, Moscow, 1955 and 1999* (Ithaca, NY: Cornell University Press), pp. 153–210, it is encouraging that other scholars, relying on vastly different sources, have developed taxonomies of Russian foreign policy thought itself in the 1990s that track quite well with my interpretation. See, for example, James Richter, *Khrushchev's Double Bind: International Pressures and Domestic Coalition Politics* (Baltimore, MD: Johns Hopkins University Press, 1994), pp. 207–10; James Richter, 'Russian Foreign Policy and the Politics of Russian Identity', in Celeste Wallander (ed.), *The Sources of Russian Foreign Policy after the Cold War* (Boulder, CO: Westview Press, 1996), pp. 69–94; Andrew Bennett, *Condemned to Repetition? The Rise, Fall, and Reprise of Soviet-Russian Military Interventionism, 1973–1996* (Cambridge, MA: MIT Press, 1999), pp. 306–9; Johan Matz, *Constructing a Post-Soviet International Political Reality: Russian Foreign Policy Toward the Newly Independent States* (Uppsala: Acta Universitatis Upsaliensis, 2001); Robert English, *Russia and the Idea of the West: Gorbachev, Intellectuals, and the End of the Cold War* (New York: Columbia University Press); Ilya Prizel, *National Identity and Foreign Policy: Nationalism and Leadership in Poland, Russia and Ukraine* (Cambridge: Cambridge University Press, 1998), pp. 220–68; Margot Light, 'Post-Soviet Russian Foreign Policy: The First Decade', in Archie Brown (ed.), *Contemporary Russian Politics: A Reader* (New York: Oxford, 2001), pp. 419–28; Neil Malcolm, 'Russian Foreign Policy Decision-Making', in Peter Shearman (ed.), *Russian Foreign Policy since 1990* (Boulder, CO: Westview, 1997), pp. 3–27; Andrei Tsygankov, *Pathways after Empire: National Identity and Foreign Economic Policy in the Post-Soviet World* (Lanham, MD: Rowman and Littlefield, 2001); and William Zimmerman, *The Russian People and Foreign Policy: Russian Elite and Mass Perspectives* (Princeton, NJ: Princeton University Press, 2002).

Table 1. *Discourses and their paths to Russia's Great Power identity.*

	Liberal	Conservative	Centrist
Military Power	No	Yes	Yes
Economic Recovery	Yes	No	Yes
International Institutionalisation	Yes	No	Yes
Recovery of the Union	No	Yes	Yes

Conservative discourse understood its Liberal alternative as a disloyal unpatriotic fifth column of the United States.

Within Centrist discourse, Russia identified with a genuine and unique Russia, although associated with European social democracy. It also identified with an idealised Soviet past, but explicitly rejected an ethnonational conceptualisation of Russia. Centrist discourse instead adopted a civic national 'Rossian' identity designed to capture the multinational character of the Russian Federation.[24] While Russia was unique, it was situated within a universal civilisation of modern social democracy.[25]

As Table 1 shows, each discourse contained different ideas about how Russia could maintain or regain its great power identity.

As might be expected, Liberal and Conservative discourses are exact opposites. The Centrist discourse, meanwhile, accepts all roads to greatness. Their foreign policy implications were similarly differentiated.

Liberal Russian identity entailed a Russian alliance with the United States and the West, and stressed the centrality of economic power as Russia's only route to restoration of great power status in the world. Great hope was placed on working through multilateral institutions, such as the UN, OSCE, Council of Europe (CE), and European Union (EU). Russia's interests in the Near Abroad were negligible, because post-Soviet republics should be permitted to go their own way, and any conflicts could be handled through multilateral institutions holding all states to universal standards of human rights.

Conservative identity implied a Russian alliance with anybody in the world who would balance against the United States and the West. While not ignoring the importance of economic recovery, far more emphasis was placed on Russian military power as a counterweight to the United States. Multilateral institutions were scorned, in good realist fashion. Russian interests in the Near Abroad were absolutely vital, as the Soviet Union should be restored. These post-Soviet republics were 'unnaturally' separated from Russia, the centre of the Soviet Union and Eurasia. Moreover, the 25 million ethnic Russians living abroad were of vital importance to Moscow, as they were ethnic kinfolk.

Centrist discourse alone suggested no alliance with any particular state, but rather a Russia as one among several Great Powers in a multilateral management of global

---

[24] Kolsto, *Political Construction Sites: Nation-building in Russia and the Post-Soviet States* (Boulder, CO: Westview, 2000), pp. 203–27 and Tadashi Anno, 'Nihonjiron and Russkaia Ideia: Transformation of Japanese and Russian Nationalism in the Postwar Era and Beyond', in Gilbert Rozman (ed.), *Japan and Russia: The Tortuous Path to Normalization, 1949–1999* (New York: St. Martin's Press, 2000), pp. 344–7.

[25] Matz, *Constructing Post-Soviet Reality*, p. 169 and English, *Russia and the Idea of the West*, p. 237.

affairs. Restoration of Russia's great power status was to be through economic development and maintenance of military power at home, and the empowerment of multilateral international institutions abroad. Russian interests in the Near Abroad are important, but they should be vindicated through multilateral institutions first, and by Russian use of military force or economic coercion, second. A civic understanding of Russian identity makes Russian interests in the ethnic disapora less crucial.

In 1992, Russia was polarised between Liberal and Conservative identities, with Liberals implementing their economic and political plans to make Russia into a liberal market democracy. The collapse of the Russian economy, the failure of the US to provide any significant aid, the rampant and rising crime, corruption, and violence associated with privatisation and democratisation, and the new issue of 25 million Russians living in the Former Soviet Union (FSU), rapidly and irreparably discredited the Liberal discourse.[26] But Conservative discourse did not take its place, largely because of three dangerous identifications: with the failed Soviet economic project; with an ethnonational Russia within a multinational state, and against the United States and the West. Instead, a Centrist discourse emerged, which, by the end of 1992, had already replaced Liberal discourse as the prime competitor of the Conservative one.

Russia's Liberal identity was institutionally privileged in early 1992.[27] In many respects, it was the heir to Gorbachev's new thinking, and the Ministry of Foreign Affairs (MFA) was its primary institutional home. The MFA under Andrei Kozyrev was initially the only coherent foreign policy institution in Russia, and Kozyrev had purged it of any remaining Soviet holdovers. But the MFA's monopoly did not go unchallenged. The Russian Ministry of Defence (MOD) and presidential Security Council (SC) were created in the spring. The defence and international relations committees in parliament became sites of Conservative and Centrist attacks on the Liberal MFA. The 'power ministries', the different intelligence and security branches of the federal government, and General Staff of the armed forces, also institutionalised Centrist-Conservative discursive renderings of Russian identity.[28]

The Communist Party of the Russian Federation (KPRF) was the only organised mass national political party, and it, along with what came to be known as national-patriotic forces such as the Liberal Democratic Party of Russia under Vladimir Zhirinovskii, formed a brown-red coalition, propagating the Conservative discourse. By early 1993, the MFA had become a policymaking arm of the increasingly Centrist Yeltsin government, and so Liberal identity was to be found mostly in national daily newspapers such as *Kommersant* and *Izvestiia*, as well as in the research institutions revived under Gorbachev.[29] In October 1993, Yeltsin crushed a primary institutional carrier of Conservative identity, the parliament, replacing it in December 1993 with a no less Conservative collection of legislators in the Duma, but in a constitutionally subordinate position to the Centrist president.

---

[26] Prizel, *National Identity and Foreign Policy*, pp. 222–47.
[27] My discussion of institutions relies on Bennett, *Condemned to Repetition*, pp. 306–10; Matz, *Constructing Post-Soviet Reality*, pp. 40–143; and Hopf, *Social Construction*, pp. 153–210.
[28] Bennett, *Condemned to Repetition*, pp. 313–23, and Emil A. Pain, 'Contiguous Ethnic Conflicts and border Disputes Along Russia's Southern Flank', in Renata Dwan and Oleksandr Pavliuk (eds.), *Building Security in the New States of Eurasia* (Armonk, NY: M. E. Sharpe, 2000), p. 185.
[29] Prizel, *National Identity and Foreign Policy*, p. 241.

The three discourses and Russia's conduct in Georgia

These three very different Russian identities implied different Russian policy toward the events unfolding in Abkhazia. We would hypothesise that if Liberal discourse were in control of the Russian state, no Russian support would have been given to the Abkhazian rebels, efforts would have been made to rein in local military forces, the parliament, and local governments, and a diligent search for UN, OSCE, and EU intervention would have been made. Had Conservative discourse been in control of the levers of the Russian state, we might hypothesise direct Russian military intervention on behalf of the Abkhazians, rather than the muddled and indirect Russian actions that occurred there. Moreover, Russia would have rejected any European or international institutional participation in the resolution of the conflict. Had Centrist discourse prevailed, we might expect initial interests in an international or European approach to the problem, followed by unilateral Russian action, if necessary.

Discourses of identity do not float freely. Which one ends up being reflected in the state is a function of institutional empowerment. Given the fact that the Russian state was only forming in 1992–3, no single discourse dominates a single unitary state, but instead different parts of the state – the Ministry of Foreign Affairs, Ministry of Defence, armed forces, Supreme Soviet, Presidential Administration, and Security Council – reflect different Russian identities. As the Russian state solidifies, first against its own Liberal Foreign Ministry, and then violently, against its Conservative parliament, the Centrist discourse of Russian identity is institutionally empowered in the Presidential Administration, its Security Council, increasingly in the Duma, and in the foreign, security, and military institutions of state.

It turns out, therefore, that all three Russian identities were in action with regard to Abkhazia in 1992–4. Liberal discourse prevails at first. Institutionally empowered by the military and parliament, Conservative discourse prevails through the local military and in parliamentary resolutions. Centrist discourse, once it occupies the presidential administration, and then the foreign ministry, determines Russian policy by late 1992.

Andrei Kozyrev, in one of his very first interviews as Russia's foreign minister, intimated that the Soviet Union was the significant hostile other of the new Liberal Russia: 'Unlike Bolshevik Russia, our country will not have to wait many years to become a full-fledged member of international society. We are welcomed as a democratic, free, peaceloving state which threatens neither its own citizens nor other states.'[30] While identifying against the disappeared Soviet Union, Kozyrev identifies with the 'Western democratic countries ... our true friends.'[31]

Kozyrev, in defending the Liberal preference for relying on international institutions to defend the human rights of Russians abroad, painted the alternative as Soviet. 'We of course are in favour of defending Russians outside Russian borders, but with methods acceptable to a contemporary sense of justice ... Of course it is possible to defend human rights on the CPSU (Communist Party of the Soviet Union) platform using tanks . . ., but one may also use legal methods . . . To cross the

[30] *Izvestia*, 2 January 1992.
[31] Kozyrev, 'Andrei Kozyrev: "Rossiia obrechean byt velikoi derzhavoi ..."', *Novoe Vremia* 14 January 1992, p. 24. On 'Western states as natural partners and allies', see Kozyrev's interview in *Le Monde*, 19 June 1992, quoted in Matz, p. 15.

border of a sovereign state . . . is absolutely unacceptable.'[32] There could be no clearer statement of the Liberal position on the illegitimacy of using military force, and its association of such violations of international practice with the Communist Soviet past . . . and present. The Soviet way of 'occupying the territory of republics' must be rejected in favour of 'international law. There is simply no third way to defend Russian-speakers . . .'[33] Kozyrev later identified Russian military interference in Georgia not only with Bolshevism, but with Nazi Germany. 'The party of war and of neo-Bolshevism is rearing its head in our country . . . Massive transfers of arms are occurring in the Caucasus and Moldova . . . What is happening here resembles 1933 in Germany . . .'[34]

By 1993, the Liberal discourse was empowered neither in the MFA nor in Yeltsin's Presidential Administration, but neither was its Conservative opposite. Instead, a Centrist discourse had emerged, which was explicitly situated between the two extreme alternatives. Indeed, one could argue that its very emergence was predictable, given the ongoing discreditation of Liberal identity, and the recent disappearance of the Conservative, embodied, as it were, in the dissolved Soviet Union.

Kozyrev navigated this middle ground in stipulating that Russians abroad sometimes had to be defended. 'Russia intends to do this primarily through political-diplomatic methods, with the use of international organisations. But in case these means of persuasion do not stop infringements on the life and security of people, I will not rule out the use of economic and military force, . . . but within legal and peacemaking frameworks.'[35] Here we see the Centrist first resort to non-military, multilateral institutional means of advancing Russian interests in the protection of Russians living abroad, while reserving the right to adopt more Conservative methods if the preferred choice is not effective. The Russian government consistently appealed to international institutions to legitimise its peace-keeping activities in places like Abkhazia. Yeltsin, in a speech often quoted to summarise his clear rejection of a Liberal identity for Russia, said that 'I believe it is time for distinguished international organisations, including the UN, to grant Russia special powers as a guarantor of peace and stability in the region of the FSU'.[36]

Here we see the crystallisation of the idea of Russia as a great power with some kind of 'special' responsibilities, obligations, and rights to police its neighbourhood. Again, this Centrist understanding of Russian great power identity was distinct from the Liberal idea of integrating into the American-West European world of multi-lateral institutional membership, or the Conservative idea of Russia as carrying on the fight against American hegemony. In his address before the UN General Assembly in September 1993, Kozyrev asked not only that the UN 'recognize Russia as the only power that can manage conflict within the FSU', but suggested that the UN finance Russia's role as a regional peacekeeper.

---

[32] Interview in *Nezavisimaia Gazeta*, 1 April 1992.
[33] *Izvestiia*, 30 June 1992. See also Andrei Kozyrev, 'Russia and Human Rights', *Slavic Review*, 51:2 (Summer 1992), p. 291.
[34] *Izvestiia*, 30 June 1992.
[35] *Diplomaticheskii Vestnik*, January 1993, p. 4.
[36] 28 February 1993, quoted in Lynch, *Russian Peacekeeping Strategies*, p. 52. See also Yeltsin's speech reported in *Nezavisimaia Gazeta*, 18 March 1993.

The Centrist discourse on the Near Abroad was explicitly situated between its two alternatives. Kozyrev argued that there 'are two extremes: to hold on the USSR (Conservative) – this is hopeless, or, pull out completely from this traditional zone of influence ... (Liberal) this would be an unwarranted loss ... (While) it would be wrong to ignore the role of the UN and CSCE, it would be extreme to completely hand over this sphere to these organizations.'[37] As Yeltsin concluded, 'both the neoimperial and isolationist approaches for Russia are inadmissible'.[38]

To summarise, different discourses of Russian identity imply different interests, foreign policy choices, and views of legitimate conduct in world affairs. In the final section, I discuss how Russian use of force might have been brought into more legitimate bounds.

Russia's Great Power identities: opportunities for legitimate action

Could Russian behaviour have been more constrained in Abkhazia? What kind of Russia would ever withdraw its troops from Georgia today? In this final section, I wish to speculate on how Russian behaviour could have been different in the early 1990s, and how it might evolve today. Building on what I have already argued, Russian views of legitimate action in the Near Abroad would have been radically different had Liberal discourse remained in power in the newly aborning Russian state. I argue that the West missed an enormous opportunity to prolong the Liberal honeymoon. Second, even with the Centrist discourse in place, the West, especially Europe, missed another opportunity to institutionalise a more legitimate use of Russian military force in the Near Abroad.

Finally, while Russian identity has deep daily roots, its great power identity is in a daily construction project with the external world, especially with the US and Europe. Interaction with the US and Europe produces, reinforces, and counteracts the discourses of Russian identity at home. Perhaps proper European and American cultivation of a Russian great power identity that adheres to norms of legitimate use of force is still possible.

Liberal discourse lost its place of predominance largely because of its complete failure domestically. The collapse of the economy, skyrocketing violence, crime and corruption, loss of basic public health services, and all around state impotence was directly and closely associated with Liberal identification of Russia with the West, in particular, with the United States. As Soviet President, Mikhail Gorbachev had begged Western leaders to invest in the new Soviet Union, a social democratic project. As Russian President, Yeltsin, perhaps less credibly, did the same. There was precious little response. One could imagine that some large and sustained commitment of financial support from the West could have, just perhaps, legitimised the Liberal experiment in Russian identity. Had this worked, the Conservative alternative would not have arisen, or the Centrist co-optation of both, become possible. In this event, Russian actions in the Near Abroad would have doubtlessly been far more pacific, and subject to multinational institutional control.

---

[37] *Nezavisimaia Gazeta*, 24 November 1993.
[38] *Rossisskie Vesti*, 9 February 1994.

But even given Centrist predominance, the West repeatedly missed opportunities to shape Russian conduct through precisely these institutional mechanisms. As was noted above, Kozyrev and Yeltsin repeatedly asked for OSCE and UN authorisation for its actions in Georgia, and elsewhere in the Near Abroad. The West could and should have taken these requests far more seriously. They could have, at a cynical minimum, called Russia's bluff. But far more importantly, they could have traded Western authorisation of Russian actions and Western delegation of authority to Russia in the Near Abroad for strict adherence to a consensual set of standards of legitimate conduct in these places. The intense European involvement in the Baltic region should have been replicated in the Caucasus, Moldova, and Central Asia. In the former case, we should recall, many expected Russian use of military force in Estonia and Latvia in defence of Russians living there. Instead, the credible work of the CE and OSCE in these two countries convinced Russia that universal European standards of conduct were being applied to both the Baltic states and to Russia. The same attention, had it been given to Abkhazia, for example, might have institution-alised legitimate great power conduct by Russia in the Near Abroad.

For the most part, however, this concerns what might have changed the discursive balance, and so levels of legitimate Russian conduct, in the past. Let me close with the contemporary construction of Russia's great power identity.

'The practice of foreign policy . . . helps Russia to become Russia. Interaction with the surrounding world helps her to formulate a Russian stateness and helps in gaining knowledge of Russia's interests.'[39] One might think this is a quote from a construc-tivist IR theory textbook, but in fact it is from a speech given by a former adviser to Yeltsin.

In order to assess this hypothesis I have collected the transcripts of 38 meetings President Putin has had with US President Bush and European leaders from May 2000 to May 2005.[40] I analysed them in terms of what topics were discussed, how these topics were discussed, and which identities were present in the conversations. The findings are presented in Table 2.

In Table 2, the major differences between conversations with Bush and conversa-tions with European leaders are highlighted in bold.

What kind of great power emerges from Putin's conversations? When interacting with the US, Russia is a partner with the US in a global war on terror and against the proliferation of weapons of mass destruction, period. When interacting with Europe, on the other hand, Russia is a European great power, who, along with other European powers like Germany, Italy, and France, fights terrorism under the authority of the United Nations and international law.

While not surprising that interacting with Europe evokes Russia's European identity, it is critically significant. Unlike identity relations with the United States, which do not have broader and deeper resonance in mass Russian society, European identity is a natural part of the daily identity terrain of Russian society.[41] A fair amount of recent research in international relations has shown that an international

---

[39] Sergei Stankevich, 'Vystuplenie S. B. Stankevicha', *Diplomaticheskii Vestnik*, 6:1992 (31 March 1992), p. 39.

[40] All these documents may be downloaded at ⟨http://kremlin.ru⟩. Last accessed 1 June 2005.

[41] This is evident from the high school textbooks, crime novels, and other mass texts sampled to arrive at the domestic discourses on Russian identity. See Hopf, *Social Construction*, pp. 153–210.

Table 2. *Constructing Russia in conversation.*

	Terrorism 9	Economics 7	Proliferation 6	Partners 4	Democracy 4
	Civilisation 3	Terrorism & Human Rights 2	Allies v. Terrorism 2	Roots of Terrorism 1	Chechnia & Terrorism 1
US N=15	UN Central 1	Friends 1			
	Partners 11	**European Identity** 11	Terrorism 10	**UN Central** 10	Democracy 7
	International Law 6	Civilisation 6	Proliferation 6	**Multilateralism Multipolarity** 4	Racism/ Xenophobia 4
Europe N=23	Chechnia & Terrorism 2	Terrorism & Human Rights 2	Roots of Terrorism 2	CTBT 2	

One each space weapons ban, BCW ban, light weapons ban, world order

norm is more likely to be adopted by a state if its society already has a dominant discourse within which that norm resonates.[42]

The average Russian understands herself as European, as part of European culture and civilisation, and as engaging in European daily practices. This implies Europe has a greater capacity to more profoundly affect how Russia understands itself than the United States. In fact, the latter, to the extent its identity relations are restricted to that of great power partners in terrorism and nonproliferation, evokes a Soviet identity for Russians, reminding them of the time when the USSR and the US bilaterally negotiated the level of (in)security in the world for everyone else. Europeans should therefore be a more effective conduit for socialising Russia into legitimate great power conduct than the United States, since Russia's European identity is more deeply embedded in the daily practices of Russian life.

To bring the point home I will contrast the presence of Russia's identity relations with Europe to the absence of any such relations with the United States. Putin, for example, refers to Russia's 'European calling', or *prizvanie*.[43] An 'American calling' is simply unthinkable in Russia, except for a narrow slice of the already small Liberal discourse. Similarly Russia's place in the 'common European home' is never matched to any common space with America.[44] Putin also refers to the deep roots of leftist

[42] Jeff Checkel, 'Norms, Institutions and National Identity in Contemporary Europe', *International Studies Quarterly*, 43:1 (March 1999), pp. 83–114; Andrew P. Cortell and James W. Davis, Jr., 'Understanding the Domestic Impact of International Norms: A Research Agenda', *International Studies Review*, 2:1 (2000), pp. 73–6; and Theo Farrell, 'Transnational Norms and Military Development: Constructing Ireland's Professional Army', *European Journal of International Relations*, 7:1 (2001), pp. 63–102.

[43] Meeting in Moscow 29 May 2000 with EU representatives Guterresh, Solana and Prodi.

[44] Interview 2 April 2002 with German and Russian media in Moscow. The idea of the Soviet Union in the 'common European home' was, significantly, Gorbachev's formulation.

ideas ... communism and social democracy', in Europe and Russia.[45] It is incon-
ceivable for Russia and the United States to share deep Lockean or republican roots,
let alone roots farther to the left.

Putin repeatedly refers to the great contributions Russia and other countries, such
as Germany and Italy, have made to the 'enrichment of European civilization'.[46] In
a joint statement with Berlusconi, Solana, and Prodi in Rome, they speak of 'our
common intellectual heritage and possessions'.[47] Putin once tells Berlusconi that 'the
unique national traditions of our countries have absorbed the best features of
European civilization'.[48] Putin observes that 'the value of the spiritual legacy of
Russia and Germany has global significance, and for many centuries has been a kind
of cultural beacon ... for the entire world, for all of Europe'.[49]

Contrast this to the following excerpt from the 'Joint Statement on Russian-
American Contacts between People', in which the development of future US-Russian
relations at the societal level are elaborated. 'For centuries, the great poets, writers,
artists, composers, and scholars of Russia have made outstanding contributions to
world civilisation. The study of this cultural legacy spiritually enriches the lives of
Americans'. Consistent with a conversation with Europeans, the statement might
have gone on to speak of the similar contributions and shared achievements of the
French, or Dutch, or Italians. Instead, 'For their part, Rossians (not ethnic Russians,
or *narod*, about which more below), show genuine interest in getting to know the
American contribution to art and science'.[50] Russians need not 'get to know'
European contributions; they live them, and live with them every day. But they have
to familiarise themselves with the heretofore unremarked Americans.

In a very real sense, Russia's partnership with the United States is based almost
exclusively on tactical interests in fighting terrorism. There is no deeper identity
relationship between the two states. There is no social foundation that could create
a stable intersubjective reality that could go beyond mere policy preferences. There
are no discursive hooks on which normative legitimising claims could be connected
in advancing arguments about Russian use of force. In the 'Moscow Declaration on
New Strategic Relations between the Russian Federation and the United States', a
document borne out of the closer relationship developed between Washington and
Moscow after 9/11, there is not a single reference to any shared identity between
Russia and the United States.[51] Instead, it is a long list of common threats and
interests. Even in the section on 'contact between peoples', there is a set of
instrumental goals in education, health care, tourism, combating AIDS, and so on,
but not a word about common values, traditions, norms, identities. As Putin put it
at his press conference with Bush in Bratislava, 'What unites the US and Russia are
longterm interests and strategic goals ...'[52]

It is also very significant that Putin, referring to the peoples of Russia and Europe,
uses the word *narody*, while using *liudi* when referring to the peoples of Russia and

[45] 2 April 2002.
[46] Meeting 11 April 2003 in St. Petersburg with Schroeder. See also 29 August 2003 meeting with
Berlusconi in Sardinia.
[47] 6 November 2003.
[48] 3 November 2004.
[49] Speech 14 January 2005 in St. Petersburg with German President Horst Kohler.
[50] 24 May 2002.
[51] 24 May 2002.
[52] 24 February 2005.

the United States.[53] This is not a trivial semantic issue, but one of profound significance for identity relations. *Narod* in Russian refers to kinship or blood ties, ethnicity, loosely speaking, while *liudi* are simply a collection of unrelated people.[54] In other words, Russians and Europeans are relatives in the same family, while Russians and Americans are just part of the human race with no particular closeness or similarity.

During Bush's summit visit to Moscow in May 2002, for example, a joint statement on Russian-American contacts between people is issued. The word for people, is *liudi*, not *narod*. In the 'Moscow Declaration', issued at the same summit, Russians become Rossians, that is, *rossisskie*, citizens of the Russian Federation. Often in conversations with European leaders, Putin uses the ethnonational word, *russkie*, to refer to the Russian *narod*, and their ties to other Europeans. In other words, relations with America are official and instrumental, not rooted in history, culture, family even.

It is obvious in Table 2 that terrorism is an important topic in Putin's meetings with both Bush and European leaders. But how the topic is discussed differs in important ways. In conversations with Bush, the war on terrorism is fought by the United States and Russia according to their common vision of the threat.[55] In conversations with Europeans, the very same war is fought in accordance with the appropriate UN Security Council resolutions, with international law more generally, and multilaterally.[56] In fact, a multilateral approach according the central role to the UN in the fight against terrorism and proliferation of weapons of mass destruction (WMD) is fixed in the Road Map on the Common Space of External Security between the EU and Russia. In this way, Russia's interactions with Europeans explicitly ground the use of military force in legitimating and authorising international law and institutions. Interaction with the US provides no such opportunities.

Moreover, collaboration with the US in the global war on terrorism, absent any reference to norms, legitimacy, or authority, provides opportunity for Putin to link his own war on terrorism in Chechnia to American (mis)conduct. Responding to a German reporter's question on violations of human rights in Chechnia, Putin reminds his audience of American actions in Iraq.[57]

This is not to say that Russian adherence to international norms on the legitimate use of force depends on interaction with Europe. After all, Russian behaviour is consistent with such adherence most of the time most everywhere. Putin's conversations merely suggest that the probability of such adherence increases when Russia understands itself as a European great power, rather than as a partner of the United States.

---

[53] 6 November 2003 joint statement with Berlusconi in Rome and 9 May 2005 meeting with Schroeder in Moscow.
[54] *Narod* is formed around the root *rod*, which by itself means family, kin, clan, birth, origin, stock, and in science, genus. It gives rise to words, such as, *roditeli*/parents, *rodina*/Homeland or Motherland, *rodit*/to give birth, and so on.
[55] For example, Joint Statement of Putin and Bush on New Relations Between Russia and the United States, 13 November 2001 in Crawford, Texas.
[56] See, for example, Putin's joint statement with Schroeder in Moscow on 9 September 2004. See also Putin's joint statement with Berlusconi in Moscow on 3 November 2004.
[57] 5 May 2005.

Conclusions: identity and legitimacy

Exploring Russian conduct in Abkhazia showed that different Russian identities implied different Russian behaviour there. Had the Liberal discourse on Russian identity remained predominant, it is very likely that Russian foreign policy toward Georgia would have been far more consonant with international normative desiderata. Moreover, it is even possible that had European and international institutions made a concerted effort to normatively guide Russia in its Near Abroad, even Russian conduct guided by Centrist discourse would have been responsive to multilateral institutional demands, as it demonstrated in the Baltic. Finally, and fortunately, we have seen how Conservative understanding of Russia, read as it was through the Soviet past, found less and less resonance in Russia, and so its neo-imperial restorationist strategy in the FSU was never implemented.

In going forward, however, it is evident that Russia's great power identity is partly the product of interaction with other great powers. The survey of Putin's conversations with Western leaders appears to show that a Russian foreign policy that respects international norms of legitimacy is more likely to develop in interaction with European, rather than American, leaders. Not only is the substance of the two broad conversations different, but interactions with Europeans easily evoke a common European identity that resonates deeply in daily Russian life. In this sense, talk is hardly cheap, but rather an unusually important power resource in the construction of a more European Russia which more commonly adheres to the rules of great power conduct in international affairs.

Dead or alive: American vengeance goes global

MICHAEL SHERRY

After 11 September 2001, the Administration of George W. Bush dismissed any criminal-justice model, put forth by various voices at home and abroad, for understanding and combating terrorism. This was 'war', the President insisted on 17 September, as he did repeatedly – directly, implicitly, and by analogy – in his 20 September address to Congress and on many later occasions, with American war in Afghanistan and later Iraq making that claim true. The criminal-justice model persisted, however, not least in Bush's more colourful rhetoric. As he commented on the 17th regarding Osama bin Laden, 'There's an old poster out west, as I recall, that said, "Wanted: Dead or Alive" '. On the 20th came his odd analogy, 'Al Qaeda is to terror what the mafia is to crime'. On 11 October, drawing on crime-fighters' lingo, he announced a 'Most Wanted Terrorist list' as part of his effort to 'round up' – both cowboy and cop words – 'the evildoers'.[1] In word and action, he kept blurring the neat line between war and crime he asserted.

To be sure, war and crime have long overlapped in deed, law, and rhetoric. Hence the term 'war crimes' and the recognition in international law that starting a war may be a crime (as some foes accused Bush of committing by invading Iraq). American leaders on occasion had figured the fascist and communist threats as criminal enterprises, and Al Qaeda had abundant attributes of such an enterprise and few of conventional war-making. But Bush's fondness for the crime-fighting mode was more persistent and ingrained. It owed to his faux-cowboy style, Texas adulthood, political conservatism, and religious beliefs, but also to a swelling punitive system at home that shaped American responses to 9/11. Just as terrorism crossed the smudgy line between war and crime, America's responses straddled waging war and fighting crime, for all the rhetorical bluster and real-life action privileging war.

This essay traces the growth of that punitive system and its connections to American, primarily Bush Administration, words and actions after 9/11. Those connections hardly alone explain post-9/11 policy, but they have been neglected by most pundits and scholars.[2] In turn, this essay revisits an old claim: that American foreign relations (like those of most nations) are shaped as much by the nation's character – its defining attributes and ethos – as by its interactions with the world.

---

[1] President's Remarks, 'Guard and Reserves "Define the Spirit of America" ', 17 September 2001; Address to a Joint Session of Congress and the American People, 20 September 2001; 'President Unveils "Most Wanted" Terrorists', 10 October 2001, all as recorded at ⟨www.whitehouse.gov/news/releases/2001⟩.

[2] See, for example, the otherwise excellent collection, *The New American Empire: A 21st Century Teach-in on US Foreign Policy*, eds. by Lloyd C. Gardner and Marilyn B. Young (New York: The New Press, 2005).

The nation acts abroad much as it does at home, albeit with different results. Historians have found that claim, seemingly self-evident, hard to sustain – agreement on 'defining attributes' is nearly impossible, and connecting them to the actions of the state and other players difficult.[3] Moreover, recent scholarly emphasis on multi-national perspectives and transnational patterns can make the American-values approach seem old-fashioned, even reeking of 'American exceptionalism'. But it is still useful. Given how a Progressive mentality shaped American occupations of the Philippines, Panama, and the Caribbean early in the century, and how a New Deal ethos filtered into the occupations of Germany and Japan after World War II, we might ask what ethos shaped the American occupation in Iraq and other post-9/11 policy. More suggestive than conclusive, this article will, I hope, provoke further inquiry along those lines.

Punitive America

In a far-reaching change, the United States became a strikingly more punitive nation late in the twentieth century, above all by imprisoning far more people. Almost no one predicted or sought that development at its start, at least on the scale that emerged.[4] Indeed, it ran counter to the de-institutionalisation and deregulation otherwise fashionable and to the proclaimed distaste for 'social engineering' among conservative elites.[5] This indeed was social engineering – 'a utopian experiment: a social cleansing by penal means', although, 'like many utopia, it has become dystopia'.[6] In two decades the imprisoned population quadrupled its 1980 size, reaching over 2 million, and the federal inmate population doubled between 1990 and 2000. Those increases resulted from more arrests and convictions, but also from longer and fixed sentences, especially for drug-related crimes, and more vigilant enforcement of probation and parole. Incarceration rates in Western Europe and America had been roughly comparable thirty years earlier, but in another way that the two parted company over these years, by 2002 the US rate was six to twelve times

---

[3] Notable examples include: Robert Dallek, *The American Style of Foreign Policy: Cultural Politics and Foreign Affairs* (New York: New American Library, 1983); Loren Baritz, *Backfire: A History of How American Culture Led Us into Vietnam and Made Us Fight the Way We Did* (New York: Ballantine, 1985); and Michael Hunt, *Ideology and US Foreign Policy* (New Haven, CT: Yale University Press, 1987).

[4] On the surprising nature of this development, see Marc Mauer, 'The Causes and Consequences of Prison Growth in the United States', in David Garland (ed.), *Mass Imprisonment: Social Causes and Consequences* (London: Sage, 2001), p. 4.

[5] Historical scholarship on the broad changes sketched here is thin. I have instead relied on journalists' reporting, and especially on historically-informed sociology. Katherine Beckett, *Making Crime Pay: Law and Order in Contemporary American Politics* (New York: Oxford University Press, 1997), is a concise, careful, critical summary of these changes and the scholarship about them. Norwegian sociologist Nils Christie's *Crime Control as Industry: Towards GULAGS Western Style?* (London and New York: Routledge, 1993) is chilling and angry – he contends 'that the prison system in the USA is rapidly moving in the same direction' as that of Hitler's effort to obtain 'the purified product' (p. 163) – but also offers complexity, international perspective, and much information, and his predictions about the growth of incarceration in the US were largely borne out in the subsequent decade. Valuable essays generally critical of surging imprisonment rates can be found in Garland, *Mass Imprisonment*.

[6] David Downes, 'The *Macho* Penal Economy: Mass Incarceration in the United States – a European Perspective', in Garland, *Mass Imprisonment*, p. 54.

higher than in Western Europe and Canada.[7] Western Europe was hardly immune to direct US influence and to the forces shaping US patterns: its own drug wars pushed up incarceration rates, and especially after 2001, imprisonment of Muslims moved nations like France closer to the American model of mass minority incarceration, with the attendant characteristics and problems as well.[8]

Still, American distinctiveness was glaring. By 2002, the US had surpassed Russia and even China in not only incarceration rates but the gross size of its imprisoned population, and California's correctional system had become 'the largest in the western hemisphere' – trends that kept US unemployment low, allowing champions of a deregulated American economy to claim its superiority over statist Europe.[9] The larger 'correctional population' – those on probation and parole as well as those under lock-and-key – reached a new high in 2003 of 6.9 million, about 3.2 per cent of the adult population.[10] Millions more had once done time. As of 2002, 13 million Americans either had been or were jailed – nearly 7 per cent of the adult population.[11] Among them, African Americans constituted about half of those 'admitted to prison' in 1992, compared to only 22 per cent in 1930 under the coercive rule of Jim Crow, and black men were imprisoned in the 1980s at a far higher rate than in South Africa under apartheid.[12] Beyond them were thousands of foreigners, some children, in detention centres awaiting deportation or status rulings or simply lost in a complex, secretive system, and new fences and other barriers (not altogether effective) to illegal immigrants, especially from Mexico.

Just when American leaders were pulling at the walls of their enemies – the Berlin Wall, the Iron Curtain, the walls of communist prisons and Baathist jails – they were erecting more walls at home. Nor did these developments draw much notice from scholars outside the criminal-justice field, except when politicians and journalists cheered them on, suggesting 'how nearly hegemonic the law and order perspective has become', wrote Katherine Beckett in 1997.[13] Also muting attention was the incremental nature of the changes. They were scattered over hundreds of jurisdictions and several decades, enacted in countless administrative and court rulings as well as formal legislation, and never the product of a grand national debate. Among those with the greatest stake in resistance – poor and minority Americans – a few championed the new punitive order and most lacked political power, especially ex-felons disenfranchised in some states, although civil rights leaders offered vigorous criticism. Since some states counted non-voting inmates in determining apportionment and districts for elections, opposing the system was even harder.[14] The new century saw more opposition, as when Illinois Governor George Ryan set aside capital punishment for those on death row and imposed a moratorium on new death

[7] See, among many sources, the table given under the heading 'Gentle Finland, Lenient Europe. Number of Prisoners per 100,000 inhabitants in 2002', *New York Times*, 2 January 2003.
[8] See Craig Smith, 'In Europe's Jails, Neglect of Islam Breeds Trouble', *New York Times*, 8 December 2004.
[9] On this use of unemployment figures, see Downes, 'The *macho* penal economy', p. 62. Joan Didion, *Where I Was From* (New York: Knopf, 2003), p. 185, on California.
[10] Fox Butterfield, 'US "Correctional Population" Hits New High', *New York Times*, 26 July 2004.
[11] Estimated by University of Minnesota sociologist Christopher Uggen, as reported in Fox Butterfield, 'Freed From Prison, but Still Paying a Penalty', *New York Times*, 29 December 2002.
[12] Beckett, *Making Crime Pay*, pp. 89, 119.
[13] Ibid., p. 106.
[14] On New York state in this regard, see Brent Staples, 'Why Some Politicians Need Their Prisons to Stay Full', *New York Times*, 27 December 2005.

penalties, but the opposition was as piecemeal and incremental as the changes it challenged.

Incarceration rates were only a crude measure of changes that made the US a far more policed and punitive nation. Some states spent more on prison systems – not counting their other criminal-justice apparatus – than on higher education, even as growth in spending and employment by private security firms far outpaced that of public agencies.[15] The death penalty was reintroduced in many jurisdictions, mandatory minimum sentences instituted, and judicial discretion restricted, with sentencing effectively automated under point systems. 'Three strikes and you're out' laws were passed in California (1994) and elsewhere, and the autonomous juvenile system was partially dismantled, with more teenagers tried and housed in the adult system. Jails and prisons themselves changed. Private companies operated more of them (or services like health care within them), placing them further beyond public accountability. Many became more Spartan, or inhumane as critics saw it: configured to deprive inmates of natural light and recreation, to increase isolation, and to minimise costs, as if incarceration alone was insufficient punishment, which had to be maximised in inmates' daily lives. Many facilities tried to bill inmates for those costs, even though the effort was legally dubious, more expensive than the revenues secured from mostly poor inmates, and damaging to the rehabilitation of released convicts.[16] The federal system, facing charges (akin to lore about women on welfare driving Cadillacs) that it operated 'Club Feds', reduced the privileges and services it provided. Nor did severe incarceration compensate for leniency elsewhere. Systems to monitor probation and parole advanced mightily – a major reason many were re-jailed without further trial. The 'electronically governed home prison' tracked individuals' movements and use of drugs, alcohol, telephones, and television. These developments contributed to the formation of what critics called American 'gulags' and 'mass imprisonment'. 'Land of the free is now home to 25 per cent [of] world's prison population', ran a complaint from England in 2000.[17]

Punishment was the point of the system, which thrived by swelling the numbers who entered or re-entered it. Regarding crime (and other social problems like mental illness), management replaced explanation, control replaced redemption, and retribution replaced rehabilitation (though its place was never secure). Speaking of 'the war on crime' in 1981, President Ronald Reagan asserted that 'some men are prone to evil' and 'retribution should be swift and sure for those who prey on the innocent'. 'Nothing in nature is more cruel or more dangerous' than the criminal, he maintained, hinting that even for conservatives the criminal was supplanting the communist as enemy. Politicians like Reagan excoriated social explanations for crime as the dangerous plaything of weak-kneed liberals. Crime was a choice evil people made, they insisted, although with no hint of irony they advanced one environmental explanation: liberal 'permissiveness' and welfare fostered the irresponsibility and dependency that nourished crime. Often, no goal beyond punishment seemed in

---

[15] Didion, *Where*, p. 187, on California. Christie, *Crime Control*, p. 105, on spending by private firms.

[16] See 'Many Local Officials Now Make Inmates Pay Their Own Way', *New York Times*, 13 October 2004.

[17] 'Gulags' is the term of choice in Nils Christie's *Crime Control*, and for other critics; 'mass imprisonment' is the title of the Garland volume cited above. On the electronic 'home prison', see Christie, *Crime Control*, p. 114. The quotation comprises the title of an article by Duncan Campbell, *Guardian Limited UK*, 15 February 2000, ⟨www.commondreams.org/headlines/021500–01⟩, accessed 6 January 2005.

mind. After careful study showed that the death penalty had little deterrent effect, 'Vengeance and retribution – the misunderstanding of the Biblical limitation of "an eye for an eye" – . . . emerged as the primary rationale' for the death penalty.[18]

The punitive turn in criminal justice highlighted a larger shift toward surveillance and punishment. That shift was manifest in workplace and school drug testing, private security forces, gated communities, missing child posters, Amber alerts, a metastasis of surveillance cameras in public and private spaces, a massive if messy corporate and governmental apparatus of electronic surveillance, tougher requirements for welfare recipients, more demanding academic tests for public school students, and, under legislation pushed by the Bush Administration, a system for flunking entire schools. For the most part, that shift bore down on the less powerful and coincided with growing disparities in wealth and income between the richest Americans and the rest. 'Historically, the watchtowers of the American penal system stood at the fringes', three experts note, 'separating the most violent and incorrigible offenders from the rest of society'. Now they are deeply 'disruptive of the social networks of kin and friendship' in poor and minority communities, determining their fundamentals.[19]

What caused this punitive turn? The obvious explanation was that growing crime did, but it was deeply flawed.[20] 'Crime' was a slippery benchmark, since its statistical bases shifted over time, behaviours were newly or more harshly criminalised (though some, like abortion, were largely decriminalised), and crime became more vigilantly analysed and prosecuted. To some extent, there was more crime because authorities defined and found more. Moreover, while crime rose in the 1970s and 1980s, incarceration still soared in the 1990s even as crime levelled off or fell – proof, some argued, that incarceration worked, but proof also that the urge to incarcerate floated free of crime rates. Imprisonment became 'an experiment that cannot fail – if crime goes down, prisons gain the credit; but if it goes up, we clearly need more of the same medicine whatever the cost'.[21] Nor did popular agitation force the punitive turn. At least as measured by polls, that agitation usually followed, rather than instigated, politicians' efforts to highlight crime and punish it more severely.[22] Moreover, changes in sentencing policy increased the prison populace far more than changes in crime rates. The drug war, declared by every president from Richard Nixon through to Bill Clinton – the subject of President George H. W. Bush's first prime-time address – accounted for much of the growth. A 1978 Michigan law, for example, required a first offender to be sentenced to life without parole – 'the same penalty as for first degree murder' – for the sale of 650 grams of heroin or cocaine.[23]

In one perspective, the punitive turn involved little novelty. Slavery, convict labour, indentured service, extermination of Indians, lynching, Jim Crow, and similar

[18] Beckett, *Making Crime Pay*, p. 47, (Reagan), p. 28 ('permissiveness'); Mauer, 'Causes and Consequences', p. 10 ('vengeance').

[19] Mary Pattillo, David Weiman, and Bruce Western, in the Introduction to their edited volume, *Imprisoning America: The Social Effects of Mass Incarceration* (New York: Russell Sage Foundation, 2004), pp. 2, 5.

[20] Among many who see that explanation as flawed, Beckett, *Making Crime Pay*, offers a lengthy critique; see also Christie, *Crime Control*, especially pp. 90–2.

[21] Downes, 'The *Macho* Penal Economy', p. 57.

[22] Beckett, *Making Crime Pay*, in particular develops this point.

[23] Mauer, 'Causes and Consequences', p. 6.

practices had a large place in American history.[24] Perhaps coercion, rather than increasing, merely changed form late in the twentieth century. When other coercive systems diminished, the prison system swelled as an inadvertent consequence, not just the intended result of a lock-'em-up mentality. As hospitalisation of the mentally ill met disfavour and underfunded alternatives failed, patients often drifted onto the streets and into crime, mostly petty, and then into prisons. Downsized mental hospitals also sometimes shifted gears – the state hospital in Rochester, Minnesota was reborn as a Federal Medical Center in the Bureau of Prisons, housing prisoners for many reasons besides medical ones. If California is now the archetypal penal state, a century earlier it was the archetypal asylum state. 'The idea of how to deal with insanity in California began and ended with detention', Joan Didion notes, even though many of the detained fit no definition of insanity.[25]

Downsizing of the armed forces played a similar role. When conscription ended in 1973 and active personnel shrank from over 3 million in 1970 to 1.41 million in 2002, many who once would have seen military service entered the prison system as either inmates or workers. By one limited measure – inmates sentenced to maximum terms of more than one year – growth in the prison population, from 200,000 in 1970 to 1.345 million in 2001, closely matched declines in the armed forces. Meanwhile, employment in criminal justice leaped from 600,000 in 1965 to over 2 million in 1993 and 'crime control expenditures' from 0.6 per cent to 1.57 per cent of gross domestic product, while defence expenditures declined from 7.4 per cent to 4.4 per cent of GDP.[26]

Correlation does not prove causation – and this was hardly the only correlation – but the penal and military systems did draw on similar populations, fears, pressures, and interests. The Cold War military-industrial complex hardly disappeared, but as it attenuated, parts of it found new life in the criminal-industrial complex. Private companies provided guards and armaments and built and ran prisons in the US and abroad, further eroding tenuous distinctions between 'private' and 'public', 'civilian' and 'military', and 'foreign' and 'domestic'. Industry lobbies and unions of construction and prison workers demanded new prisons and measures like 'three strikes' laws that would fill them, as Joan Didion reported.[27] Small towns that once laboured to gain or hold military bases now bid for prisons as a reliable industry amid deindustrialisation, although the jobs often went to outside unions or contractors. The United States became not so much more coercive as differently coercive.

Yet this was no simple trade-off. However coercive and degrading, mental

---

[24] Christie, *Crime Control*, pp. 116–22, stresses this point.
[25] Didion, *Where*, p. 195, drawing on Richard Wrightman Fox, *So Far Disordered in Mind: Insanity in California 1870–1930* (1978).
[26] Figures on military personnel, defence spending, and inmate population drawn from Census Bureau, *Statistical Abstract of the United States: 2003*, Tables HS-51 and HS-024, as found in the Census Bureau website under 'Mini-Historical Statistics', accessed 1 June 2005. The numbers of those incarcerated were much larger in any given year than the figures provided by the Census Bureau on inmates 'under jurisdiction of federal and state authorities rather than those in the custody of such authorities'. Figures on criminal justice employment and criminal justice as percentage of GDP are drawn from Beckett, *Making Crime Pay*, pp. 99, 3. Beckett may underestimate crime control spending as percentage of GDP: although 'defense spending' was scattered among many agencies and measured in different ways, it was still largely a federal and well-monitored activity; crime control spending was scattered among far more numerous, and often obscure, federal, state, and local jurisdictions, making complete figures far harder to assemble.
[27] See Didion, *Where*, esp., pp. 184–5.

hospitals still had offered a greater prospect for treatment than prisons, especially since mounting prison costs prompted cuts in 'frills' like counselling and education, and ex-patients bore fewer legal restrictions and less stigma than ex-inmates. Military service, though deadlier than jail and sometimes equally degrading, still carried no blatant stigma. It drew soldiers into service to the nation and survivors enjoyed many benefits; imprisonment signified betrayal of the nation and abundant penalties afterwards for its survivors. Those who traded military service for prison jobs – many did both as members of the National Guard or Reserves – still got low pay, few of the benefits of military service, and many of its dangers. In such ways, the US became more coercive, not just differently so.

The ascendant criminal-industrial state also meshed well with resurgent suspicions of centralised authority flowing out of the Vietnam era. The militarised state of World War II and the high Cold War dispersed resources and patronage widely but concentrated power in Washington. Despite new federal crimes and mandates, crime-fighting remained largely a state and local operation, with power and resources widely scattered. Each state and good-sized city could have its own little Pentagon. The role of private companies in surveillance, crime-fighting, and prison operation also reflected suspicion of centralised authority.

Yet institutional forces do not fully explain these shifts. The resources freed by shrinkage in mental health and defence systems might have gone elsewhere had education lobbies, parks agencies, road-builders, or environmentalists prevailed. That the criminal-industrial complex was the winner suggests not only its power but the appeal of the fears it played to, especially among conservatives determined to diminish social welfare and increase social control. When leaders like Reagan called for 'retribution' against criminals, they invited players in the criminal-industrial complex to expand their roles and demands.

The punitive trend also responded to the upheavals of the 1960s and 1970s, including the defiance of authority, urban riots, drug use, and anti-war agitation they featured. The response was conservative in a loose rather than ideological sense. It included liberals like President Lyndon Johnson, and moderates like Governor Nelson Rockefeller, who championed New York's draconian anti-drug laws, and Bill Clinton, who as Arkansas governor supported the death penalty and as president pushed harsh anti-drug and anti-terrorism measures. Diverse forces converged on the same result for different reasons: some liberals complained that indeterminate sentencing allowed judges to discriminate against minorities, while many conservatives asserted that it let criminals off too lightly. Some feminists sought harsh treatment of anti-abortion radicals and sex offenders or joined the Reagan Administration crusade against pornography. Other voices pursued hate crimes laws. The politics in notorious crime panics, like that over the alleged sexual abuse of children in day care, were too murky to fit on any liberal-conservative grid.

But the core of the urge to imprison was fear of 'a newly jobless marauding underclass', a fear that conservatives more often raised and exploited.[28] A reaction against the black quest for equality was also evident in how incarceration surged for African Americans while social welfare for poorer Americans diminished – two trends linked by politicians who charged that civil rights agitation had been 'criminal' and associated welfare with 'underclass' blacks. The Reagan Administration

---

[28] Downes, 'The *Macho* Penal Economy', p. 57.

strengthened that class and race focus by neglecting white-collar crime in favour of addressing 'street violence', which often became synonymous with all crime. Seen this way, as Katherine Beckett does, the punitive turn indicated an 'effort to replace social welfare with social control as the principle of state policy'.[29] While US-European differences in welfare spending were less than often assumed, Western Europe did deal with the 'underclass' more through the soft power of welfare and the US more through the hard power of prison bars. That over half of prisoners were by 1991 serving drug-related sentences indicated how much social control was at issue, especially of an 'underclass' (drugs favoured by affluent whites were less criminalised and policed).[30]

The punitive impulse also surged when many Americans, from Nixon on down, decided during the Vietnam era that their greatest enemies were stateside, rather than in Moscow, Hanoi, or Peking.[31] Although the Cold War continued, much energy once devoted to it turned inward. As both candidate and president, Nixon was a master practitioner of law-and-order politics. Reagan's Attorney General, William French Smith, viewed the Justice Department as 'not a domestic agency' but 'the internal arm of the nation's defense' and the 'Internal Defense Department', language placing criminals on a par with foreign enemies.[32] The resonance and durability of the term 'drug war' hinted at how much it displaced the Cold War. That the aftermath of 9/11, when a newly recognised external enemy coincided with sharper questioning of criminal-justice policies at home, further underlines this hydraulic model of change – passions, energies, and resources remain fairly constant but shift in outlets and targets. Fiscal trends also suggest that model: many states tightened prison budgets and reduced prison populations after 9/11 as national resources shifted from domestic crime to enemies abroad.

Finally, incarceration may have surged because other threats to security diminished after the Vietnam War, when, it is claimed, 'Expectations about safety and security . . . increased hugely.' Fewer Americans entered the armed forces and faced war's violence, and other forms of security – medical and economic – prospered, if unevenly. In that environment, violent crime stood out in sharp relief against a more pacific and secure background, with 'victimization by crime' remaining the 'principal source of risk that could not be personally controlled or ameliorated'. That explanation ignores new sources of insecurity in this era such as deregulation of the economy, oil shocks, and AIDS. But it does draw on the fungibility of war and crime in the fears, interests, media coverage, and political manoeuvring of American life.

The urge to control and punish was not solely American. Major efforts went forward against war criminals in Africa, South Asia, and the Balkans. International agencies like the World Trade Organization delivered penalties in the economic realm. Although Amnesty International and Human Rights Watch opposed many punitive practices – including in US prisons – they unavoidably sanctioned penalties for individuals, groups, or states that violated international norms. Systems of crime and punishment – or put more positively, the rule of law – flourished widely. To some extent, the United States participated in a broader change.

[29] Beckett, *Making Crime Pay*, p. 47, ('street'), p. 106.
[30] Christie, *Crime Control*, p. 114, offers the 1991 figure.
[31] On that shift, see Michael S. Sherry, *In the Shadow of War: The United States Since the 1930s* (New Haven, CT: Yale University Press, 1995), chs. 6–9.
[32] Beckett, *Making Crime Pay*, p. 53, quoting David Stockman's account.

But it offered a distinctly harsh, unilateral, global, and militarised version of that change. Especially under George W. Bush, the US rejected many international legal arrangements, even as American leaders fought crime by reaching abroad. Bush's father presented his 1990 invasion of Panama as an exercise in crime-fighting, and the US brought captured Panamanian ruler Manuel Noriega into federal court for trial (and conviction) on drug-dealing and other charges. The drug war dispatched US agents, soldiers, and policies to much of the globe, while retired general Bernard McCaffrey oversaw it under Clinton. Influence went beyond formal state efforts. As a Norwegian expert claimed in 1993, 'American criminology rules much of the world, their theories on crime and crime control exert an enormous influence'.[33] Criticised by groups like Amnesty, American crime control also became an issue in international relations.

Promoting those policies was a surge in punitive strains long present in American culture. Leaders of the religious right – Catholic and Jewish as well as Protestant – denounced a lengthening list of sins and sharpened the line between the saved and the damned (to commit or condone abortion was akin to the Holocaust). Many American colonists had regarded criminal punishment as an occasion to underline the sinfulness common to all, but that sense of common frailty diminished in the nineteenth century. In a more self-righteous climate, crime often seemed to mark its perpetrators as beyond humanity. Many Americans learned that at the end times God would make non-believers vanish in the twinkle of an eye – vaporised, in some treatments, as in science fiction – while the rapture lifted up the saved. Starting with low-budget church-basement films like *A Thief in the Night* (1972), that prediction reached millions in best-selling books and costly films by the 1990s. It marked 'a shift in American portrayals of Jesus', Nicholas D. Kristof claims, 'from a gentle Mister Rogers figure to a martial messiah presiding over a sea of blood', though the martial version certainly had antecedents.[34] If the sinful deserved total eradication by God, surely mortals were entitled to deal harshly with them through the law. Secular voices echoed this religious outlook: some forensic psychiatrists began regarding predatory murderers 'as not merely disturbed but evil', doing so 'long before President Bush began using the word to describe terrorists or hostile regimes', the *New York Times* noted.[35]

Vengefulness mounted in popular culture as well. Crime had long been a staple of fiction, film, and television, but the ubiquity of TV crime shows by the 1990s was striking – *Law & Order* alone became a giant franchise of spinoffs and re-runs. And the tone was far darker than in shows like *Dragnet* and *Gunsmoke*, indeed literally darker – sunlight and full-wattage bulbs rarely penetrated the dark offices and courtrooms of *Law & Order*. Earlier shows treated criminals in matter-of-fact fashion, expending little effort to condemn them – they were simply plot mechanisms. *Law & Order* explored and condemned criminality at length and subjected criminals to the moral outrage of victims, police, and prosecutors, as figures beyond civilisation and comprehension. They were 'mean little bitches', a prosecutor dubbed the teenage killers in one episode – a far cry from earnest treatments like *Rebel Without a Cause*

---

[33] Christie, *Crime Control*, p. 79.
[34] Nicholas D. Kristof, 'Jesus and Jihad', *New York Times*, 17 July 2004, paraphrasing his colleague David Kirkpatrick.
[35] Benedict Carey, 'For the Words of Us, the Diagnosis May Be "Evil" ', *New York Times*, 8 February 2005.

(1955), which offered sympathy and understanding of the teen criminal. Likewise, 'courtroom television shows had become increasingly prosecutor friendly', one expert noted. 'On *Perry Mason*, the lawyers were always working to save defendants who were wrongly accused', Stanley A. Goldman observed. 'On *Law & Order* everybody's guilty once they take them to trial'.[36] Not since *film noir* in the 1940s had American culture presented so many twisted, evil characters, but with a difference: in film noir the line between sinners and saved usually was blurry.

Crime dramas were part of a broader media culture of law, justice, and punishment. 'Judge shows', *America's Most Wanted*, and reality cop shows became the rage. Talk shows showcased lower-class violence, infidelity, and treachery. HBO's *Oz* was set in prison. The gladiatorial spectacles of 'reality' shows – from Donald Trump's *The Apprentice* to more obviously vulgar and brutal versions – offered humiliation, expulsion, and other punishment in enormous volume. Local TV news had been obsessed with crime since the 1970s, as critics complained, and cable news carried that obsession further onto the national stage, as shown by the all-Monica-all-the-time coverage of the Clinton scandal and the air time given the Washington sniper and Laci Peterson stories. After 9/11, some observers hoped that weightier issues would make TV get serious and downplay crime stories. But with any lull in war news, crime stories surged back – and sometimes with no lull. Indeed, given the equal billing and similar language employed by TV news for both war and crime – for the death of thousands and the loss of one – and the quicksilver way they switched from one to the other, the two played almost interchangeable roles in the media.

In this stew of media and politics, almost everyone, it seems, was out to get someone: the cop killers, or the cops who killed; fat-cat corporate chiefs, or those who challenged them; illegal immigrants, or those who abused them; those under-going abortions, or those who impeded them. Not that everyone got his way: despite waves of business-related convictions in the 1980s and after 9/11, wealth and power still substantially determined who fell afoul of the law. But media politics recurrently stoked these punitive strains. The acquittal of ex-football star O. J. Simpson on murder charges unleashed a chorus of string-him-up chants. The Terry Schiavo case over the winter of 2005 yielded demands among conservatives like Congressman Tom DeLay that the judges who ruled against them be punished. Earlier sensations, from the Salem witch trials to the Lindbergh baby kidnapping case of the 1930s, indicate how old the punitive strains were, but the frequency and ugliness of their eruption in contemporary America remain striking.

A politics and culture of victims rights emerged as well, asserting that victims had a right, increasingly enshrined in law, to help set the punishment of criminals. In particular, the Oklahoma City Bombing prompted new laws to protect victims' rights, an intensified campaign for a victims' rights amendment to the Constitution, and the Effective Death Penalty Act of 1996 signed by President Clinton to speed executions.[37] News media often asserted that victims were not heard, even as they were heard once again. The 'perpetrator in this situation ... was being treated more like a victim than I was', a victim of priestly abuse complained to the

[36] Goldman as paraphrased and quoted in 'Even for an Expert, Blurred TV Images Became a False Reality', *New York Times*, 8 January 2005.
[37] See Edward T. Linenthal, *The Unfinished Bombing: Oklahoma City in American Memory* (New York: Oxford University Press, 2001), pp. 103–6.

New York Times. 'I feel my story hasn't been told at all'.[38] Victims gained a major presence – interviewed on TV, mobilised in neighbourhood marches, networked with each other, courted by criminal-justice lobbies. They spoke the idiom of an expressive culture, articulating their rage rather than squelching it. Usually, they claimed that criminals were insufficiently punished.

Victimisation and vengeance were dominant themes in the new politics and culture of crime. A nation so changed in how it regarded crime at home would not likely be unchanged in how it responded to threats from abroad, especially ones that took on more characteristics of criminality and fewer of war than had America's mid-century enemies. Here was a double shift whose parts had unfolded in parallel to each other – as crime more and more defined American life, it more and more defined threats from elsewhere.

Vengeance abroad

How did punitive culture legitimate American responses to 9/11? The oscillation between war and crime in rhetoric, images, and actions offered clues. At first the war category flourished, as in analogies between 9/11 and Pearl Harbor and in treatment of uniformed personnel at the World Trade Center as war heroes, with the flag-raising there compared to the flag-raising by Americans at Iwo Jima in 1945. But responses to 9/11 also established those killed and injured as victims of a giant crime as much as casualties of war. Congress established a Victim Compensation Fund for the deceased's survivors, many of whom organised into groups such as the 9-11 Widows' and Victims' Families Association. The fact that survivors had roles and rights as victims was telling. World War II involved the sacrifice of civilians' rights to a common cause – the nation itself was the imagined victim, and survivors of the dead at Pearl Harbor had little special status. Responses to 9/11 echoed the language of victim rights in punitive culture. The resonance for many of the 9/11 attacks with the 1993 World Trade Center bombing and the 1995 Oklahoma City bombing – events rendered as crimes more than acts of war – strengthened crime as a category. The methods of attack – no major armaments involved, civilian airliners as the weapons – also fell outside a familiar war category. All this was understandable because thousands were indeed victims, but also congruent with decades of discourse about victimisation by crime. In turn, responses by national leaders took on the punitive character of earlier responses to crime, including a tougher regime of internal surveillance and policing. Unsurprisingly, the punitive impulse scattered in many directions, aimed sometimes at American Muslims, or, in the celebrated post-9/11 comments of Reverend Jerry Falwell, at 'the pagans and the abortionists, and the feminists, and the gays and the lesbians', who presumably had triggered God's wrath on America.[39]

For other reasons, too, 'war' proved an awkward fit for America's post-9/11 actions, and the language of war underwent recurrent slippage. Americans had so

---

[38] 'Positive Publicity for an Abusive Priest Adds Insult to Injury for a Teenage Victim', *New York Times*, 3 March 2003.

[39] Quoted in Patrick Allitt, *Religion in America Since 1945* (New York: Columbia University Press, 2003), p. 253. Allitt surveys a range of such responses.

promiscuously declared war on so many things for so many years – to name only a few: drugs, abortion, trade deficits, illiteracy, AIDS, cancer, smoking, and often those blamed for those things – as to rob the word of its power to define. Presidents had declared war on terrorism since Reagan did in 1981, muddling even the onset of the war Bush now declared. And while most Americans agreed that they were at war, few were sure what they were at war *on* or *against*. The preferred official terms, terror or terrorism, referred, critics complained, to a method of war, not an enemy – as if the Allies had declared war on the *blitzkrieg* or the *kamikaze*, not on Germany and Japan. Al Qaeda was the obvious enemy, but also an indistinct one composed of loosely aggregated elements, while Islamic fundamentalism seemed too broad or politically risky to be identified formally as the enemy. Bush's impulsive favourite – 'evil' – certainly added no precision. The wars to overthrow the Taliban regime in 2001 and Saddam Hussein's regime in 2003 momentarily provided specificity – bombers dropped bombs, tanks lumbered forward, troops seized objectives. Yet these state regimes were distantly related to the stateless terrorist enemy, and official assertions of links between Hussein and Al Qaeda convinced few critical observers. Familiar drum-and-trumpets warfare in Iraq quickly yielded to war against shadowy enemies (increasingly, and tellingly, called 'insurgents' rather than 'terrorists'). Other features of American action robbed it of powerful associations with war. There was no enemy body count – the US was unable or unwilling to count, or loathe to disclose numbers; no successor to the defeated regimes had an interest in such numbers; and Al Qaeda hardly wanted to announce its losses. US losses were publicised, but official practices – the Administration barred photographs of the coffins of service personnel returning to the US, for example – muted death, the most obvious measure of war. The Administration's insistence that the US was at war was dogged but denuded of much precision or colour.

Instead, leaders devoted rhetorical richness to other language. Bush's famous evocation of outlaw-hunting in the old West conjured up images of 'Sheriff Bush leading a posse after a varmint', complained Senator Robert Byrd, who saw Bush as voicing 'a kind of retribution-soaked anger'.[40] The deck of fifty-two cards showing leaders of Hussein's regime that the US government circulated in 2003 employed a similar 'wanted' vocabulary. Fittingly, when Hussein was captured late in 2003, he was ordered to put his hands up like a captured criminal; video footage resembled a scene from television's reality crime shows more than the capture of an enemy ruler. Critics saw in these moments a peculiarly puerile style of Bush and those around him, but they missed how much that style was congruent with broader punitive culture and with precedents that his presumably patrician father set with the capture of Noriega. Bush offended some critics when on 2 July 2003, referring to insurgents in Iraq who think 'they can attack us there', he observed: 'My answer is, bring 'em on'.[41] But with its echo of cinematic crime-fighters like Dirty Harry, Bush's rhetoric seemed natural rather than idiosyncratic. Critics also missed how these moments cut against the Administration's stated preference for 'war' as the category governing its actions.

Bush's pronouncements on 'evil' flowed from that punitive culture. He intended,

[40] Quoted in Russell Baker, 'Troublemaker', a review of Byrd's *Losing America* (2004), *New York Review of Books*, 12 August 2004, p. 7.
[41] Or 'bring them on', as the official account recorded it: ⟨www.whitehouse.gov/news/releases/2003/07⟩. For what reporters heard, see ⟨www.cbsnews.com/stories/2003/07/03/iraq⟩. Both accessed 6 January 2005.

he said grandiosely after 9/11, 'to rid the world of evil',[42] and he repeatedly depicted American, Western, or 'free world' forces as pitted against 'evil'. Those words echoed Reagan's talk of the Soviet 'evil empire' two decades earlier, but that empire was a fading memory for many Americans and unknown by younger ones. More effectively, those words reflected the nation's punitive culture and religious conservatism, and Bush's particular Protestant outlook. 'Evil' rendered the enemy, like the criminal, beyond the pale – beyond rational and moral understanding, beyond humanity rather than sharing its sinfulness, beyond redemption.

Bush's emphasis on the enemy's 'evil' was distinctive. While national leaders had dubbed earlier enemies evil, politicians, pundits, and scholars had also tried to explain the mind, motivation, and purpose of the Axis foes and the communist enemies. With Bush, 'evil' seemed its own explanation, not the starting point for inquiry. It placed the enemy beyond explanation – beyond politics itself. The question that first arose among Americans, 'why do they hate us so much?', faded away soon after 9/11, given no answer by the Bush Administration beyond the claim that terrorists hated America for its freedom and liberty. Explanation also implied possible rehabilitation – by understanding an enemy, the victor could correct what had gone wrong, as the US tried to do in postwar Europe and Japan. 'Evil' placed the terrorist enemy, and by implication the larger environments that nourished or tolerated it, beyond rehabilitation, except, improbably, through religious conversion. Only death or other punishment would stop the enemy and deter others from succouring him. 'Evil' provided Bush with an effective vocabulary for expressing national shock, grief, and anger, as it had when Franklin Roosevelt condemned Japan's 'infamy' at Pearl Harbor. But his persistent use of it muffled other lines of explanation and circled back to how many Americans regarded criminals among their own kind – cast out of humanity.

To be sure, Bush did promise rehabilitation, especially through the Iraq war: the US and its allies would liberate oppressed Iraqis, usher in democracy there, and in turn insinuate it into all the Middle East and the Islamic world. Yet many critics, including some sympathetic to Bush's objectives, found his Administration wanting in the practical efforts to implement rehabilitation. After victory against the Taliban, efforts to rehabilitate Afghanistan and crush Al Qaeda faltered. Planning for the security and rehabilitation of postwar Iraq was notoriously inept, and the occupation regime was amateurish, crowded with party and religious cronies of the Administration rather than the sophisticated, experienced experts who had flooded into Europe and Japan after World War II, the Balkans in the 1990s, and other war-torn areas.[43] Rehabilitation, the Administration apparently assumed, would come about through the sheer redemptive fervour unleashed by the overthrow of evil regimes. Those who resisted or backslid would get the same treatment their kind did in the United States: prison, or death.

Al Qaeda abetted this slippage from war to crime. It made (so far as I know) no demand that its captured members be regarded as prisoners-of-war under the Geneva Convention. Its modus operandi, however sophisticated the planning, eschewed the accoutrements of warfare, including the all-important uniform of the soldier. Men

---

[42] 'President's Remarks at National Day of Prayer and Remembrance', 14 September 2001, ⟨www.whitehouse.gov/news/releases/2001/09⟩.

[43] See the extensive piece, Andrew Zajac, 'Insiders Shape Postwar Iraq', *Chicago Tribune*, 21 June 2004.

seizing airplanes and ramming them into buildings were at most reminiscent of fringe aspects of past wars, like Japanese suicide pilots. Al Qaeda operatives bombed buildings (and trains), but so too had Timothy McVeigh in the 1995 Oklahoma City bombing, an act prosecuted through criminal-justice means. Lacking status as a state, Al Qaeda in turn lacked the legal protections of a state at war. Nor did it appeal to international institutions – the United Nations, the Red Cross, the World Court – which tried to avert war, minimise the crimes it involved, or punish those who broke its laws. While Al Qaeda had its own rhetoric of war, its methods and aspirations spilled far beyond that category.

The crime-fighting ethos was also evident in how leaders told Americans to meet the threat of further terrorism. They were asked to be wary and vigilant, to report suspicious activity, and otherwise to pursue normal activities – fly airliners and shop at malls, as they were urged in the fall of 2001 – all steps they might take in dealing with crime. As for the sacrifices associated with protracted war – ones that make war 'war' for non-combatants – those were few, borne mainly by military personnel and their families. Other sacrifices simply expanded on what Americans had already experienced: security checks at airports and other public places, and the legal restrictions imposed under the 2001 USA Patriot Act and other measures, had ample pre-9/11 precedents, many set in the wake of the Oklahoma City bombing. The economic sacrifices of war seemed to disappear altogether in a wave of income tax cuts pushed by the Bush Administration, and even the implicit tax of inflation seen in many wars was held in abeyance. With war so little in evidence, and further terrorism feared but not unleashed, crime-fighting filled the vacuum.

Wars are usually finite, but post-9/11 conflict was too open-ended and normalised to have that quality. It was more like the Cold War, itself punctuated by hot wars, than the World War II often invoked. Crime-fighting for any society is a normal, never-concluded enterprise – pursued while normal activities persist, except in extreme circumstances. The point is not that there was some correct nomenclature the Administration should have used. The point instead is that the friction between its avowed term – 'war' – and its frequent resort to the language of crime went largely unnoticed by defenders and critics alike, reflecting how powerful the punitive turn in American life had been.

One expression of the punitive impulse was the war against Hussein's regime. It probably had personal dimensions: Bush had complained about an earlier Hussein effort to kill his father and had reasons to both upstage his father and complete his work by overthrowing Hussein. Publicly the Bush Administration insinuated that Hussein was linked to Al Qaeda, and hence to the 9/11 attacks. It thereby implicitly presented the war as punishment for those attacks and tapped an unsurprising desire for revenge among many Americans. Meanwhile, it explicitly avowed other reasons – eradication of Iraq's presumed weapons of mass destruction, the nourishment of democracy in the Islamic world, the evil of Hussein's regime – with the first later revealed to be a fiction and the second a fragile hope. Revenge is an inescapable element of war, and especially when an avowed enemy proves elusive, it can be directed at loosely-related substitutes. The incarceration of Japanese-Americans in 1942 came amid Japan's humiliating defeats of American forces, just as the attack on Iraq came when Al Qaeda and its leader, Osama bin Laden, proved maddeningly elusive. In that sense, the punitive dimension of the American war in 2003 was nothing new.

But the politics and circumstances differed. Unlike Japan's successes, Al Qaeda's attacks came against the American homeland, took the lives primarily of civilians (not all Americans), elicited a coarser presidential rhetoric about 'evil', and erupted in a culture far more attuned to victimisation and its redress. Those attacks also came when American military supremacy was uncontested – a far cry from the situation in 1941 – so that American leaders were far less constrained from using it as an instrument of retribution. No war springs from a single factor, and punitive war-making had a venerable American past, as with the grandly named (and not very successful) Punitive Expedition into Mexico by American forces in 1916 in response to Pancho Villa's depredations against Americans in Mexico and New Mexico. But the American war of 2003 had an unusually wilful character. It was the grandest punitive expedition of all.

To be sure, Bush presented his efforts to punish 'evildoers' as means to further ends: the promulgation of democracy, the pacification of the world, and the protection of the United States. These were all familiar goals of American foreign policy, from whose contours Bush hardly broke loose. Yet he so often and effortlessly issued his proclamations about 'evil' that its eradication seemed like a goal in itself, to be pursued even at the cost of other declared ends. Moreover, in the religious background of Bush and many of his supporters was a vision of the destruction of evil-doers in the end times, as well as his reported comment that he had been 'chosen by God' to run for President. As with other presidents, it was impossible with Bush to separate deep belief from political calculation. But certainly he presented himself and his nation – between which he made little distinction – as instruments of God's wrath against sinners, with no patience for others, like Jimmy Carter, who preached (perhaps no less self-righteously) humility before the common sinfulness of all people. Moreover, his views were echoed by other figures near him, John Ashcroft most of all. In the 1990s their impulse to purge evil was directed mainly at homeland sins such as abortion, gay rights, and Clinton's infidelities, and in stout defence of tough-on-crime measures like the death penalty. Post-9/11, that urge flowed abroad, although even without that day's attacks, the Administration most likely would have taken on Hussein.

In other ways, too, Administration postures and policies exuded crime-fighting as much as war-fighting. Even for appointments distantly related to national security (or crime), Bush's fondness for cops and other crime-fighting types showed. Gale Norton, his Interior Secretary, had been Colorado's Attorney-General. His 2002 choice of Surgeon General was Richard H. Carmona, 'who has a swashbuckling past', touted by Bush, 'as a soldier and crime-fighter'.[44] While Secretary of Defense Donald Rumsfeld was the leading face of military operations, the leading face of the broader war on terror was Attorney General Ashcroft, the nation's top crime-fighter. Justice's role went well beyond appearances, as it worked hard and successfully to limit the role and resources of the new Department of Homeland Security. The Administration expended enormous capital maintaining that combatants it seized in Afghanistan and elsewhere were not prisoners-of-war, undercutting its own claim that the US was at war. By insisting that incarceration and interrogation, not rehabilitation and repatriation, were its priorities for prisoners, it moved further toward a penal, rather than martial, model, especially since it foresaw a 'war' without

---

[44] 'Bush Taps Carmona as Surgeon General', *Washington Post*, 27 March 2002.

end and thus no foreseeable opportunity for postwar repatriation of those captured. Other than execution, lock-'em-up, perhaps for their lifetimes, was the only option. Most of the American media followed its lead, referring to Guantanamo and Abu Ghraib less often as prisoner-of-war camps than as prisons.

The scandal in 2004 over American personnel's abuse of prisoners at Abu Ghraib and elsewhere exposed associations in reality and perception between America's punitive system at home and its actions abroad. That prisons gained so much political and media attention, for a while eclipsing other aspects of the strife in Iraq, alone suggested the connection. Torture was also outsourced by American officials, despite Bush's flat denial of the practice, with some captives undergoing 'rendition' to other countries (Egypt, for example), trusted to carry out the worst. While Bush and others insisted that torture was un-American, a few critics complained that such abuse resembled what went on in American jails and prisons, using the similarity as another argument against the punitive course of American criminal justice.[45] Some apologists for and defendants in the torture, on the other hand, pointed to American prison practice for justification – a telling claim even if it poorly justified the behaviour. Lawyers for accused torturer, Specialist Charles A. Graner Jr., 'insisted that he was simply following orders and using lessons from his civilian life as a prison guard'.[46]

But for all the momentary sensation, the scandal waned quickly. Official efforts to quell it and confusion created by multiple investigations muted the scandal, but so also did the similarity many Americans sensed between practice abroad and practice at home. Some evinced a ho-hum reaction – what happened in Iraq seemed little different from what occurred in the US – and some assumed that prisoners there, like those in the US, had to be guilty of something and got pretty much what they deserved. Few journalists explored that apparent similarity, however. Most saw torture as a problem that began abroad, or when Washington decided what to do abroad, albeit with precedents in the past practices of the US abroad and other governments quelling insurgencies – the French in Algeria, for example, and Latin and Central American dictatorships (or Israel in Palestine, a precedent rarely mentioned).[47]

That view of American practice was hardly wrong, but it was incomplete. Where Administration officials maintained that torture was the work only of a 'few bad apples' (a phrase widely attributed to Rumsfeld) over there, critics saw only a few – or many – bad apples in the Administration. It was a curious metaphor, especially in Administration hands, since in its common meaning, a few bad apples spoil the whole barrel. But both sides shared the 'bad apples' perspective. That something more rooted and American was operating rarely drew comment. The connection between practice at home and abroad was, to be sure, indirect and therefore hard to make. It involved values, policies, and personnel which moved from one setting to the other, not a direct chain of causation or command. But it was also

---

[45] Among the few, see Joyce Braithwaite-Brickley (identified as a syndicated columnist and campaign manager for former Republican Governor William G. Milliken), 'Torture of inmates not limited to foreign prisons', *Traverse City Record-Eagle*, 8 August 2004, and distributed by MinutemanMedia.org.

[46] 'Portraits Differ as Trial Opens in Prison Abuse', *New York Times*, 11 January 2005.

[47] Two examples, rightly well regarded, of this approach are: Mark Danner, *Torture and Truth: America, Abu Ghraib, and the War on Terror* (New York: NYRB, 2004), based on his reporting for the *New York Review of Books*; Jane Mayer, 'Outsourcing Torture', *The New Yorker*, 14/21 February 2005, pp. 106–23.

hard to see because of 'how nearly hegemonic the law and order perspective ha[d] become', as Katherine Beckett wrote in 1997.[48]

Torture, a panel headed by former Defense Secretary James Schlesinger maintained in 2004, had 'migrated' from Guantanamo to Abu Ghraib.[49] But how had it 'migrated' to Guantanamo in the first place? Most directly, through legal reasoning by government officials in memos that, as Anthony Lewis put it, 'read like the advice of a mob lawyer to a mafia don on how to skirt the law and stay out of prison'.[50] But few observers asked where they in turn got the idea, attributing it only to the exigencies or conveniences of the post-9/11 moment. Torture had been an aspect of the American penal system and many others, and massive growth in the penal population probably had made torture more frequent, in sheer numbers if not in per-inmate terms, especially since it met little resistance until scandals about coerced confessions, fabricated evidence, and other practices bubbled up in many jurisdictions during the 1990s. Even then, the focus was largely on wrongful convictions, not on the treatment of prisoners. 'Rendition' also had stateside precedent in the growing practice of shipping convicted felons out of state, even across the continent.

In turn, thousands of people cognisant of, complicit in, or culpable of torture at home found their way into the systems that fashioned or carried out American policy abroad. These included military guards and interrogators who handled prisoners and soldiers who patrolled streets, many of whom had held jobs – or as Guard or Reserve personnel, still did – in the criminal-justice system at home. These included prosecutors and politicians who worked their way from local, state, and federal wings of that system into positions in the armed forces, federal agencies, or the Bush White House in growing numbers after 9/11. These included thousands of private security employees newly dispatched from stateside duties to service abroad. Of course, many in the federal apparatus were career personnel; some resisted, protested, or reported abuses against captured personnel; and some guards and interrogators abroad may have been more disciplined by virtue of their experience in crime-control work at home. But the system was weighted toward those who had become used to a good deal at home. Occupation forces in postwar Japan and Germany had a different profile: at the lower ranks they were heavily war veterans or young draftees, and among civilians, New Deal bureaucrats, academic experts, humanitarians, and managers of wartime mobilisation bulked large. Few came out of America's criminal justice system, which was tiny in comparison to the vast force of 16 million mobilised for uniformed service during World War II. They brought other prejudices and impulses, borne of the ferocity and racial intensity of the war, to occupation duties, but not ones steeped in a punitive culture.

The weight of punitive culture was also evident in the US turn to incarceration as an instrument of social control, not just a means to manage POWs or military threats. In Iraq, US and Iraqi forces rounded up – Bush's operative phrase – thousands of locals, many or most, by numerous accounts, guilty only of routine criminal activity or simply caught in various dragnets. Others faced de facto imprisonment, such as the thousands forced out of Fallujah into resettlement camps by US forces seeking to reclaim that city in 2004. The process of screening and

[48] Beckett, *Making Crime Pay*, p. 106.
[49] See 'Top Pentagon Leaders Faulted in Prison Abuse', *Washington Post*, 25 August 2004. See also Mark Danner, 'A Doctrine Left Behind', *New York Times*, 6 January 2005.
[50] Anthony Lewis, 'Making Torture Legal', *New York Review of Books*, 15 July 2004, p. 4.

judging captives at Guantanamo moved so slowly as to leave hundreds of them long-term prisoners, and by late 2004, US authorities were weighing a permanent prison facility for those who might never be tried. Although these policies involved indeterminate incarceration, not the fixed sentences increasingly imposed by law within the US, a more general impulse – imprisonment as social control – was shared.

Of course, the conflation of war with crime, and the overlap (and conflict) between civil and military institutions in dealing with both, were hardly new. The armed forces had repeatedly seen action against labour strife, urban riots, and internal dissent, for example. Yet if the line had always been blurry, it had not been blurry in a static way. The nation's militarisation in the twentieth century had vastly compounded and complicated traffic across that line.[51] After 9/11, the traffic intensified anew and took on distinctive forms. That it did so was not in itself surprising. More striking was how the Bush Administration insisted that the nation was at 'war' while acting more like a cop on a beat or a warden in charge of the world's inmates. Confusion seemed more at work in that process than calculation. Conservative self-righteousness about crime and disorder and decades of gathering punitiveness in American life undercut the Administration's instincts to proclaim 'war' and operate in its mode.

The Administration, its defenders, and even some critics tried to account for this confusion: this was a war 'unlike any other we have ever known', Bush told Congress on 20 September 2001. Well before 9/11, pundits had anticipated 'fourth generation warfare' featuring 'no definable battlefields or fronts' in which '[t]he distinction between "civilian" and "military" may disappear'. At the start of 2005, one critic seemed to embrace those claims, noting how 'peace wears the face of war, and war dissimulates as peace'.[52] But the Cold War had not gained its name for nothing – its uneasy mixture of war and peace had made the name work – and during it the 'distinction between "civilian" and "military"' had often disappeared. Frequently offered to and by people with no lived experience of the early Cold War, the insistence after 9/11 that the US faced a new kind of war oddly mimicked Cold War rhetoric while being oblivious to it. Ultimately, it offered a cliche: what major war is not, in some substantial way, unlike any 'ever known' before it? For explaining the rhetoric and practice of the Bush Administration, it was too empty and ahistorical to offer much.

The rise of punitive culture also helps explain the oddly pessimistic, non-triumphal manner in which the Administration often presented the 'war on terror' as open-ended, stretching into some indefinable future. Of course, seeing the war as endless served multiple purposes – it was a writ for the endless assertion of power by the Administration and the United States and a way to guard against expectations of victory that might backfire. It also, presumably, was a response to the nature of terrorism. But it made sense in another way too. Wars are to be won and concluded. But no one thinks that policing crime ever ends – crime is like death and taxes, and policing it is the permanent obligation of governments. Conceived as a giant policing action for Globalcop, the 'war on terror' need not, and could not, have any end.

Nothing in this analysis suggests that American responses to 9/11 would have been altogether different had not punitive culture gained force. Some American military

[51] See Sherry, *In the Shadow of War*.
[52] Jonathan Raban, 'The Truth About Terrorism', *New York Review of Books*, 13 January 2005, p. 22, which also offers the Bush quotation and passages from a *Marine Corps Gazette* article, 'The Changing Face of War: Into the Fourth Generation' (October 1989), pp. 22–6.

response to 9/11 was inevitable. Large-scale incarceration, resettlement, and other policing practices evident in Iraq have been endemic in neo-imperial wars, as in America's Vietnam War, as has been the torture of captives (British soldiers too were charged with mistreating Iraqi prisoners). And leaders in most wars have sent mixed messages about their nation's values and purposes as they catered to different constituencies and groped through their own confusion. The particular content, not the fact, of the mixture is always at issue. But punitive culture did further sanction the America's role as Globalcop, inform the rhetoric of the Bush Administration, underwrite the invasion of Iraq, and legitimate – make seem unremarkable – dubious practices of incarceration and torture: that is, the whole punitive character of official policy after 9/11. Once again, American values were projected outward, but these were not the values of Progressive uplift, New Deal liberalism, or Cold War management. They were the values of religious vengeance and punitive treatment of those whom Bush called 'evildoers'.

At least through 2004, the Bush Administration continued, in rhetoric as well as policy, its unsteady oscillation between the categories of 'war' and 'crime'. On the campaign trail, John Kerry suggested that the right policies might reduce terrorism until it would become more akin to the problem of crime. Vice President Richard Cheney, warning that with Kerry's election 'the danger is that we'll get hit again', condemned a 'pre-9/11 mindset, if you will, that in fact these terrorists attacks are just criminal acts and that we're not really at war'.[53] With Bush's re-election, the punitive strains seemed likely to moderate: second-term presidents are usually more cautious, the costs of the Iraq war constrained further action, and courts questioned some US treatment of prisoners. Yet in November Bush made the dubious choice of Bernard Kerik, New York City's Police Commissioner on 9/11, to be secretary of the Department of Homeland Security. 'The President loves cops', one Republican insider insisted after the Kerik's nomination unravelled. Cops are 'not pretentious, they do a hard job, they don't get paid a lot of money, they're real people and they live in a world that is fairly black and white, with good guys and bad guys. And that's the way President Bush looks at the world.'[54] Indeed it was. After Kerik's demise, he nominated in his place Michael Chertoff, a federal judge, former prosecutor, head of the Justice Department's criminal division, and author of the Patriot Act.

---

[53] Andrew Welsh-Huggins, 'Cheney suggests nuclear threats', 20 October 2004, at ⟨www.boston.com/news/nation/articles/2004/10/20/cheney⟩, accessed 3 January 2005.

[54] Elisabeth Bumiller, 'In Kerik, Bush Saw Values Crucial to Post-9/11 World', *New York Times*, 19 December 2004.

Index

www.ingramcontent.com/pod-product-compliance
Ingram Content Group UK Ltd.
Pitfield, Milton Keynes, MK11 3LW, UK
UKHW030900150625
459647UK00021B/2709